HIJAB AND THE REPUBLIC

Gender and Globalization
Susan S. Wadley, *Series Editor*

Other titles in Gender and Globalization

Hijab & The Republic

UNCOVERING THE FRENCH
HEADSCARF DEBATE

Bronwyn Winter

SYRACUSE UNIVERSITY PRESS

11824581

Copyright © 2008 by Syracuse University Press
Syracuse, New York 13244-5160

All Rights Reserved

First Edition 2008
08 09 10 11 12 13   6 5 4 3 2 1

The paper used in this publication meets the minimum requirements
of American National Standard for Information Sciences—Permanence
of Paper for Printed Library Materials, ANSI Z39.48–1984.∞™

For a listing of books published and distributed by Syracuse University Press,
visit our Web site at SyracuseUniversityPress.syr.edu.

ISBN-13 (cloth): 978-0-8156-3174-3   ISBN-10 (cloth): 0-8156-3174-X
ISBN-13 (pbk.): 978-0-8156-3199-6   ISBN-10 (pbk.): 0-8156-3199-5

Library of Congress Cataloging-in-Publication Data

Winter, Bronwyn, 1955–
Hijab and the republic : uncovering the French headscarf debate / Bronwyn Winter.—1st ed.
    p. cm. — (Gender and globalization)
  Includes bibliographical references and index.
    ISBN 978-0-8156-3174-3 (cloth : alk. paper)— ISBN 978-0-8156-3199-6 (pbk. : alk. paper)
    1. Hijab (Islamic clothing)—France.   2. Veils—Social aspects—France.   3. Muslim
women—France—Clothing.   4. Clothing and dress—Religious aspects—Islam.   5. Clothing
and dress—Political aspects—France.   6. Islam and secularism—France.   7. France—Race
relations.   I. Title.
    GT2112.W56 2008
    391.4'30944—dc22
    2008038003

Manufactured in the United States of America

C'est une arme politique extraordinaire.
(It is an extraordinary political weapon.)
　　　　—Mernissi on the hijab, *La peur-modernité* (1992)

A notre époque de décolonisation généralisée, l'immense monde
féminin reste en effet à bien des égards une colonie.
(In our times of generalized decolonization, the immense world
of women remains, in fact, a colony in many respects.)
　　　　—Tillion (1907–2008), *Le harem et les cousins,* 1966

BRONWYN WINTER teaches in the Department of French Studies at the University of Sydney, where she is also program director of International and Comparative Literary Studies in the School of Languages and Cultures. Her transnational feminist research covers feminist and lesbian politics and theory; women in international and national politics; human rights; women and the politics of race, nation, religion, and culture; and globalization and militarism. She is contributing co-editor, with Susan Hawthorne, of *September 11, 2001: Feminist Perspectives* (Melbourne: Spinifex Press, 2002).

Contents

Acknowledgments

NONE OF US WORK in isolation or unaided so of course there are a number of people who deserve thanks for this book. First, I would like to thank the many women in France, too numerous to name, who, over more than two decades, spoke with me, campaigned with me, sent me documents, invited me to meetings, communicated insights, and encouraged me in my work. Some of these women stand out, and may perhaps be surprised to see their names here. Colette Guillaumin is one: her enthusiasm for some of my early work, and our many conversations since, have given me incentive to continue, and I am honored that someone of such fine intellect holds my own work in such esteem. Nadia Châabane, Monique Dental, Judith Ezekiel, Françoise Gaspard, Fatema Mezyane, and Juliette Minces, all wonderful women whom I first met in a context of activism or research around issues related to those discussed in the book, and who subsequently became pals or even close friends, are others. More recently, Cynthia Enloe, Liliane Kandel, Judith Lorber, Claire Moses, and Val Moghadam have been enthusiastic about this book; in particular, I thank Val for her suggestions during its planning stages, and Claire for her suggestions after reading a first draft of the manuscript. Closer to home, Véronique Delaunay has been one of my most generous and perspicacious critics during the grueling process of writing. I also owe thanks to the former and current heads of the School of Languages and Cultures at the University of Sydney, Tim Fitzpatrick and Jeff Riegel. Tim arranged some teaching release in 2006 to allow me to finish the first draft of the manuscript, and Jeff has provided support for indexing assistance in the final stages of manuscript preparation in 2008. At Syracuse University Press, I owe, first of all, great thanks to executive editor Mary

Selden Evans, for her unreserved enthusiasm for this book and her careful and gracious management of the process from proposal to publication. In this process she has been ably assisted by a number of people, some of whose names I do not know, but to whom I am nonetheless indebted. Others, with whom I have had more direct contact, have guided me through the editorial process and promptly, efficiently, and good-humoredly addressed my queries and handled problems. These are Mary's assistant Marcia Hough, managing editor John Fruehwirth, Kay Steinmetz from the editorial department, and Lisa Kuerbis, marketing coordinator. Finally, I owe thanks to copyeditor Julie DuSablon, whose skill, good humor—and humor *tout court*!—have greatly eased the passage through copyediting stage; I will miss our email conversations!

A note about sources: All Web site URLs were valid at the time consulted, and every effort has been made to provide the most up-to-date URLs at the time of final copyediting.

Abbreviations

ASFAD	Association de Solidarité avec les Femmes Algériennes Démocrates
ATTAC	Association pour une Taxation des Transactions Financières pour l'Aide aux Citoyens (Association for Taxation on Financial Transactions for Aid to Citizens)
CADAC	Coordination des Associations pour le Droit à l'Avortement et à la Contraception (Coordination of Associations for the Right to Abortion and Contraception)
CCTR	Collectif Contre Tous les Racismes
CFCM	Conseil Français du Culte Musulman
CNDF	Collectif National des Droits des Femmes (National Collective of Women's Rights)
Cojep	Conseil de la jeunesse pluriculturelle de France (Council of Multicultural Youth in France)
CRIF	Representative Council of Jewish Institutions of France
DOM-TOM	Départements d'Outre-Mer et Territoires d'Outre-Mer (overseas departments and territories)
ECFR	European Council for Fatwa and Research
EMAF	Expressions Maghrébines au Féminin
EMF	Etudiants Musulmans de France
ENVEFF	Enquête nationale sur les violences envers les femmes en France (National Study of Violence against Women in France)
FEN	Fédération de l'Education Nationale
FIS	Front Islamique du Salut (Islamic Salvation Front)
FLN	Front de Libération Nationale
FN	Front National
FNMF	Fédération Nationale des Musulmans de France
GIA	Groupe Islamique Armé

IDLR	Indigènes de la République
IESH	Institut Européen des Sciences Humaines (European Social Sciences Institute)
LDH	Ligue des Droits de l'Homme (League of Human Rights)
LIDF	Ligue Internationale du Droit des Femmes (International League of Women's Rights)
MRAP	Mouvement contre le Racisme et pour l'Amitié entre les Peuples (Movement Against Racism and for Friendship among Peoples), formerly Mouvement contre le Racisme et l'Antisémitisme et pour la Paix
MTI	Mouvement pour la Tendance Islamique
NPNS	Ni Putes Ni Soumises
PaCS	Pacte Civil de Solidarité (Civil Solidarity Pact)
PMF	Parti Musulman de France
RG	(Service des) Renseignements Généraux (French police intelligence service)
RISFA	Réseau International de Solidarité avec les Femmes Algériennes
RMF	Rassemblement des Musulmans de France (Rally for French Muslims)
RPR	Rassemblement Pour la République (Rally for the Republic)
UDF	Union pour la Démocratie Française
UEPT	Une Ecole Pour Tous-tes
UFAL	Union des Familles Laïques (Union of Secular Families)
UJM	Union des Jeunes Musulmans
UMP	Union pour un Mouvement Populaire (formerly Union pour la Majorité Présidentielle)
UOIE	Union des Organisations Islamiques d'Europe
UOIF	Union des Organisations Islamiques de France
WIL	World Islamic League
ZEP	Zone d'éducation prioritaire

HIJAB AND THE REPUBLIC

Introduction

Why France?

ONE AUTUMN DAY in May 2006, as I crossed a parking lot at the elite university where I work in Sydney, a young hijab-clad woman crossed my path. The fact that she was wearing a modern Islamic headscarf was in itself unremarkable. What caught my eye was the combination of the hijab with the rest of her clothing, which was not only Western but also as body-hugging as possible. Certainly, the sleeves of her top were long, but the top was short in comparison to the hip- or thigh-length tops usually worn by headscarved girls. It barely covered the waistband of her jeans. The top and the jeans were tight and of a stretch material that enabled all the contours of this young woman's body to appear clearly. The headgear symbolized ethnoreligious identification, modesty, piety. The bodywear symbolized the fashions of what deeply religious Muslims generally describe as a decadent Western disregard for women.

This image is a quintessential statement of cultural hybridity: ethnic belonging within both a local and worldwide community of Muslims—a kind of twenty-first-century *umma* ("community of believers," also "nation")—as much as religious conviction, combined with a social belonging, both to a national Australian culture and to a particular subculture: young fashionable university student. It reinforces the idea of the hijab as a modern and polysemic garment; it is also indicative of the fact that the hijab, especially as worn in the West, may be many things but it is never neutral. It pulls focus, it makes a statement. Paradoxically, in covering women according to religious values, it makes them highly visible, attracting reactions from non-Muslims that range

1

from the physically abusive (usually from men) to the walking-on-eggs careful, much as those of us from Christian culture, regardless of our own beliefs, might react to a nun. It is the hostile reactions, however, that are the most evident and the most discussed. One of the first reactions in Australia following 9/11 was the stoning of a bus in a suburb in Brisbane, in which hijab-clad girls were traveling to school. During the so-called race riots in late 2005 in my childhood suburb of Cronulla, notorious both for its macho urban beach culture and its macho whiteness, one of the incidents that was reported was the forced removal of a hijab from a young woman's head.

The hijab also, however, attracts reactions from other Muslims. It sends particular messages concerning the beliefs and identifications of its wearers. For many Muslims, it sends further messages concerning the social and political presence of certain conceptions of Islam to which they may well be hostile. Two Muslim countries—would-be European Turkey and the former French Maghrebian (North African) colony of Tunisia—even have legislation similar to that of France, banning the hijab in public institutions. This legislation has sparked highly vocal public protests in Turkey in particular. Others, such as Egypt, the birthplace of both Arabo-Muslim modernism and Arabo-Islamic revivalism, do not have national bans but are nonetheless grappling with hijabization and, more recently, niqabization (the *niqab* is a face veil), notably in women's dormitories on university campuses (Winter 2006d). Yet others, such as Algeria, have faced serious internal conflict, that in Algeria's case became a so-called "undeclared civil war," between oppositional Islamist movements and the state. Women who did not veil or who were otherwise deemed anti-Islamic—feminists, single mothers, journalists—were particularly targeted by the Front Islamique du Salut (Islamic Salvation Front, FIS), and many sought refuge, paradoxically, in France, Algeria's former colonizer. In Palestine, women who did not veil twenty or even ten years ago are now doing so, or their daughters are. Following the 2006 Palestinian elections, the secular resistance to the Israeli occupation was put in the position of attempting to form a government of national unity with Islamist party Hamas, which now holds the parliamentary majority.

In fact, the hijab is arguably the most discussed, and fought over, item of women's clothing (or any clothing) ever. It has come to be the primary globalized symbol, for Muslims and non-Muslims alike, of a feminized and often fetishized Muslim identity, and is brandished as a political weapon in the supposed confrontation between Islam and the West.

The hijab as identity politics is also, however, about Islam *in* the West, and Islam transnationally. It is part of what Paul Silverstein has referred to as "transpolitics" (Silverstein 2004). Although Silverstein was writing specifically of "Algeria in France," the term has wider applications. Muslim "transpolitics" would describe the situation of ethnic and often "postcolonized" Muslims whose political and cultural points of reference are *both* the West and the Muslim country of family origin, to the point that the politics of the country of origin are played out on another level in the country of residence, citizenship, and probably birth.

Transnational Islamic revivalism and what has been described by Chahdortt Djavann as "Muslimism" are also, however, part of a wider transnational and culturally hybridized phenomenon of religious revival (Djavann 2004). The religious right everywhere is finding itself a new youth market, a new translation into ethnic identity politics. Mormons have churches in Tahiti and indeed throughout the Pacific, Hispanic Jehovah's witnesses meet in Sydney and San Francisco as well as throughout South America. In my home state of New South Wales, the 2005–7 leader of the right-wing opposition, Peter Debnam, was reputed to be close to Opus Dei, and the Hillsong Church, complete with African American ambassadors to promote its pseudo-egalitarian, democratic, and generally hip image, is doing a brisk trade on university campuses in Australian cities. "Muslimism" is not an exception to this transnational religious marketing trend, but part of it (Sahgal and Yuval-Davis 2000; Fourest and Venner 2003; Sallenave 2004).

The specific example of the culturally hybridized hijab that I used in the opening paragraph was Australian. I could find similar examples in France. Even if the hijab-plus-body-hugging-clothing remains relatively uncommon, hijab-plus-Western-clothing more generally does not. Some hijabis may well wear dull colors and long tunics, with sensible shoes and no makeup, but most wear some combination of Western feminine clothing such as fashionable long skirts or jeans and loose tops in bright colors, high heels or sneakers, makeup, jewelry.

At the same time, Australia is not France. In fact, no other Western country is France, *l'exception française* being a byword there as elsewhere, and the source of many jokes (there as elsewhere). What is different about the French hijab? *Is* it different? If so, what makes it so? Why has it pulled focus in such particular ways, for so much longer than it has elsewhere in the Western world? Why did the hijab become such a subject of national debate (many both inside and outside France would say national hysteria), of school expulsions, court cases, and legislation? Even if many other countries in Europe, including the United Kingdom, the Netherlands, Belgium, and Germany, are now having similar debates, nowhere have they been so acute and complex, and nowhere have they gone on as long, as in France. It is in France that the debate over bans started and has been the most volatile and polarized, involving, over the close to two decades it has now gone on, strikes by teachers, at least one hunger strike by a student, multiple expulsions, tribunal decisions, demonstrations for, demonstrations against, and enough public and media debate to fill several volumes—indeed, it already has, in France at least, particularly in recent years. It has also attracted attention in the English-speaking world, with an almost obligatory reference to it in any work on either the hijab, Muslim women, or contemporary France, although few have gone into the topic in great detail. Recent exceptions, apart from my own work, include Ardizzoni (2004), Scott (2005), Ezekiel (2006), Najmabadi (2006), Wing and Smith (2006), and the first two (and only two to date, and to my knowledge) entire books in English on the subject, both published in September 2007. The first of these is John Bowen's *Why the French Don't Like Headscarves* (2007). This book, however, written by a specialist on Indonesia who has recently turned his attention to France, is not written from a feminist perspective. In this, it differs significantly from the second book: *The Politics of the Veil,* by well-known feminist scholar Joan Wallach Scott (2007). Scott develops the line of argument pursued in her 2005 article, that French universalism confuses sameness with equality and that the 2004 law is yet another example of the assimilationist French state's inability to accept difference.

It is good that the French case is starting to attract more sustained attention in the English-speaking academic world, although as I will argue in this book, much of the literature published in English to date provides insufficient background to help us understand why the French case, and related feminist debate, are so involved, what is involved about them, and why they have the potential to be illuminating for other Western countries. Or, if the literature does provide such background, it gives vastly different perspectives from those I will offer in this book.

The peculiarity of the French hijab debate is necessarily entwined, first with the peculiarity of French secularism and its links with the ideas of nation, state, and citizenship; second, with the history of France's pre-colonial, colonial, postcolonial, and noncolonial relationship with the Arab and Muslim worlds, particularly the Maghrib (North Africa); and third, with the rise of Islamism and its implantation in Europe. It is also necessarily, from a feminist point of view, tied up with the peculiarities of French feminist and antiracist activism and their relationship both with each other and with the state.

All Western countries are more or less secularized, although the influence of the Christian church remains strong and has even increased in recent years in countries such as the United States and Australia. In none of them, however, is secularism so closely imbricated with nation-formation and national values as it is in France. In no other Western country does secularism have a national birthday.

On December 9, 2005, French secularism had a very special birthday: the centenary of the 1905 law of separation of church and state, or, in other words, the 100th birthday of *la laïcité*, or French secularism, and by extension, *l'école laïque*: secular schooling. The subject was evoked, debated, celebrated, criticized by practically all players from politicians to journalists to academics to activists representing a variety of associations, including those specifically founded in the context of the contemporary debate over secularism, the hijab and Islam, such as Islam et Laïcité (Islam and Secularism), Mouvement des Maghrébins Laïques de France (Mouvement of Secular Maghrebians of France), and Coordination Féministe Laïque (Feminist Secular Coordination), to name but a few of many. Considered the cornerstone of the Republic by politicians, historians, political scientists, and many activists across the political spectrum within France, and a peculiarly French form of intransigent anticlerical nationalism by many outside France, secularism, and the appropriate interpretation and application thereof, are at the heart of the now close to twenty-year-old debate over the Islamic headscarf in French schools.

In his book published on the occasion of the 100th anniversary of the 1905 law, Jean Baubérot, France's "chair of secularism" noted:

> The situation of religion in society is never established once and for all. Today those who criticize it find that it takes considerably more space than thirty or forty years ago, yet the number of people who practice a religion is lower. Those who are religious are more numerous than a few decades ago in thinking that they are being got at because of their faith. (Baubérot 2004, 225)[1]

Baubérot suggests a little more distance and intellectual exercise on both sides would be advisable (226). No doubt. If nothing else, the hijab debate, along with other issues such as gay and lesbian civil unions or the 1984 and 1994 proposals to modify the Falloux law regulating state funding of private schools (most of which are Catholic in France), has drawn attention to, and repolarized, French fracture lines over religion, secularism, and state.

What has now become known internationally as the first headscarves affair (*affaire du foulard*) began some forty kilometers north of central Paris, on September 14, 1989. On that day, Ernest Chenière, principal of junior high school Gabriel-Havez in Creil, expelled Leïla, Samira, and Fatima, aged thirteen and fourteen, two of them sisters, of Moroccan and Tunisian background, for refusing to remove their hijab in class. This expulsion came after talks and proposed compromises had failed to resolve the matter, and some reports tell of agitation by Islamists that resulted in the girls hardening their stance.

These expulsions gave rise to a prolonged political and media debate that lasted well into the following year.[2] It was from the outset intense and polarized, leading Jean-Pierre Chevènement, at the time Socialist minister for defense, to quip, in an evident play on words, that it was a *fichu fichu* (darned headscarf) (cited in Langlois 1989). The term *fichu*, when used to refer to a headscarf that traditionally covers the head, throat, and shoulders, calls up

---

1. Unless otherwise specified, all translations from French are my own.

2. For example, the weekly newsmagazine *L'Evénement du Jeudi* contained a supplement devoted to the affair (issue 297, July 12, 1990), and Elisabeth Badinter, one of the main players in the media debate in late 1989, referred to it in an interview with the same magazine in December that year (Badinter 1990).

images of traditional rural France rather than anything to do with Islam, and thus serves as an oblique reminder that some form of female head covering is common to the monotheistic cultures.

The headscarf debate was, in fact, so apparently all-consuming that five years later, at the time of the so-called second affair in 1994, it was to be characterized by the national daily *Le Monde* as both a "national psychodrama" and a "saga" (*Le Monde,* October 20, 1994). (The second affair was centered around a ministerial circular issued by François Bayrou, education minister with the then right-wing government, in which he recommended prohibition of "ostentatious" religious insignia in schools.)

From the beginning, the hijab debate encompassed a range of issues: the interpretation and application of secularism, the place of Islam in France, racism and the "integration" of "immigrants" (the latter term having become synonymous with postcolonial and especially Maghrebian immigrants and their descendants), and the identity of the French Republic at the beginning of the 1990s. The old divisions between church and state reappeared in another guise, with the debate over "intransigent" versus "flexible" interpretations of secularism being waged in tandem with that over immigration and racism. The issue divided left and right alike, it divided the antiracist movement, it divided the feminist movement—some groups even split over the issue. Some interesting moments of monotheistic religious "solidarity" also emerged, however, as did new alliances between sections of the previously secular left and Islamist organizations (these were to become more pronounced over the years of the saga), or between certain left-wing intellectuals and some more conservative elements within the right. The meaning of at least two elements of the Republic's motto—*liberté* and *égalité* (equality)—came under scrutiny as possibly never before, along with its implicit "fourth element": *laïcité* (secularism). Only *fraternité* seemed to remain well and truly intact, at least in the mainstream media debate, particularly in the early years.

Yet, according to Michel Pezet, of the Executive of the Socialist Party, France had not known a public debate of such magnitude since the debate over abortion in the early 1970s.[3] This is an interesting comparison: in both cases women and girls were at the center of a debate waged largely by men,

3. Quoted in *Le Nouvel Observateur* 1304 (Nov. 2): 1989.

and in both cases religion appeared as a pivotal and highly emotive factor. Notwithstanding the obvious differences, including the fact that the abortion debate concerned all women while the hijab debate primarily concerned teenage girls from an ethnic and largely (although not exclusively) postcolonial minority, the magnitude and polarizing, emotion-charged nature of these two debates highlighted the centrality of women's behavior to men's concerns with social cohesion.

The concerns over social cohesion sparked by the 1989 Creil incident were nonetheless very different to those around abortion. In 1989, secular France was facing not its own contradictions with relation to Catholicism but difficulties with another religion, which was not only every bit as hostile to secularism as Catholicism had been in the past—and, indeed, remained to a great extent in the present—but was also both "foreign" and associated with a racialized and problematized postcolonial minority. This time, France was facing the undermining not of the "family" but of the "nation." It was facing its old fears of the Arab invader combined with more modern concerns about social unrest that favored the rise of both the European extreme-right and Islamic fundamentalism. It was facing, in short, the present disturbing legacy of its colonial past, at the end of a decade during which that legacy had been much in the forefront of social movements and public debate.

Added to all of this is the fact that the affair happened at school, which has always constituted a privileged space for constructing and safeguarding Republican identity. In fact, the affair would not have been "the affair" if it had happened elsewhere. More than in many other countries, the education system in France is the place where national identity and the individual's sense of herself or himself as a citizen is forged. It is the place where the battle for the Republic has always been waged, on several fronts. First, it is the site of the double struggle against particularist identities (historically regional, now both regional and non-Western) and against the power of the Church. Second, it is the place where one learns the laws of the Republic and the rights and duties of a citizen: civic education is an obligatory part of the French school curriculum, from primary school. This function of French secular schooling represents, for historian Claude Nicolet, the "essential aspect of Republican asceticism," in that the Republic "creates itself through education": if it does not educate, it does not exist (Nicolet 1992, 63).

Throughout the 1990s, the hijab saga had its high and low points, its new plot developments, new actors and new generations, but never completely went away. Its resurgence in 2002–3, however, came after a relatively quiet period on the hijab front—and if the 1989 debate had been lively, it paled into insignificance beside that waged between 2003 and 2005. The obvious explanation for this rekindling of the hijab debate would be the fallout from 9/11, although crucial factors also include a combination of the Israeli-Palestinian conflict and internal French politics, marked in particular by the 2002 presidential election runoff between mainstream-right President Jacques Chirac and extreme-right leader Jean-Marie Le Pen. Other internal factors include a Maghrebian-background feminist mobilization around violence against women in the immigrant ghettos coupled with a campaign for strict application of secularism, which was the object of considerable polemic in 2003 and 2004. In July 2003, President Chirac set up a Commission to Reflect on the Application of Secularism (known as the Stasi Commission), which, in December of that year, handed down its lengthy report containing twenty-three recommendations. In between came the high-profile case of Alma and Lila Lévy, expelled from their school in an inner suburb of Paris for refusing to remove their hijabs.

The culmination of this latest headscarves affair was the March 15, 2004, law banning "conspicuous" religious insignia in schools: the only Stasi Commission recommendation that the government immediately and wholeheartedly actioned. Despite some very vocal protest and some expulsions, the law was fairly well observed and the feared widespread unrest at the start of the 2004–5 school year in September 2004 did not occur. The unrest occurred a year later, in the form of riots that lasted three weeks from October 27 to November 17, 2005. Although these were not directly connected to the hijab polemic, they, and the brutal response of then interior minister and now President Nicolas Sarkozy, fell within the nest of issues that had been connected to the hijab debate since 1989. Also, earlier that year, in April, the same right-wing government that had in 2004 championed secularism and the law against "conspicuous" religious insignia fell all over itself to "conspicuously" mourn the passing of the Pope.

This flagrant contradiction in official government positions in relation to religion is indicative not only of the complex history of secularism in the country still known as the "eldest daughter of the Catholic Church," but also of contradictions of French egalitarianism. It is indeed ironic that a country that prides itself on having invented human rights in 1789 did not abolish slavery until 1848, did not give women the vote until 1944, and has been extraordinarily slow in recognizing and condemning all sorts of crimes of violence against and harassment of women, unless it suited its colonial interests to do so. It is this complex history that makes the hijab affair such a specifically "French" story.

The hijab affair is, however, far from being solely "about" the hijab. To put it somewhat ironically perhaps, focusing on the hijab to some extent covers more than it reveals. In this, the French debate probably has a great deal in common with the debate elsewhere in the West, as the number of sensationalizing books with "veil" in the title seems to indicate. The hijab is merely the tip of a rather larger iceberg that both the French state, in adopting the 2004 law and doing little else, and international commentators, in condemning the actions of the French state as simply another example of French racist universalism, have largely ignored. The central question to be asked in seeking to render that iceberg visible is: why this fuss about religion—and women and religion—when in fact the number of people practicing a religion in France is diminishing, including among Muslims and particularly among Muslim women? In particular, the number of hijab wearers is an infinitesimal minority of French Muslim girls and women: at the very most, two percent, and probably less than one.

In exploring the above question, one discovers the "iceberg" is multifaceted, and many of those facets are part of a wider, and in many respects quite different, global and national debate on race, sex, and socioeconomic exclusion:

• the ongoing complicated relationship between religion and state, exacerbated both by the development of French Islamism and the sharp rightward turns of the French state

• the development of "Muslimist" identity politics surrounding the hijab, accompanied by a high level of manipulation by, and of, the media

• the internationalization of the debate through the more recent imbrication of the hijab issue with the Palestinian issue, and, in connection with this, a complicated French polemic around both anti-Semitism and the concept of "Islamophobia"

- the battle to claim ownership of "feminism" (or "women's emancipation")

The common thread running through these different elements, however, is the importance of women's behavior, and particularly of appropriation of the "rights" of racialized Muslim women, to men for whom women's interests are not exactly at the top of the priority list. Even the extreme-right National Front party has gotten into the act. Its poster advertizing its leader Jean-Marie Le Pen's 2007 presidential campaign, released on December 11, 2006, showed a young "integrated" Maghrebian women (unheadscarved and wearing hipster jeans), giving the thumbs down to both the mainstream right and the mainstream left, who have "broken everything": "nationality, assimilation, upward social mobility, secularism."[4] It is a particularly perverse image, from a party that has consistently demonized Arabs, Muslims, and Jews, and instead of celebrating the traditional workers' holiday on May Day, celebrates its own nationalist and very Catholic Joan of Arc day. But the poster played on the imagery of the moment.

It would be simplistic, however, to line up the players in these debates along class, sex, and race lines. It would be particularly simplistic to assume that these lines mark an opposition between a white male French state and a Muslim female minority voice. Those who identify—whether culturally, ethnically, or religiously—as Muslim in France have as many different views on the role of religion in public life, in the state apparatus and legislature and in regulation of so-called "moral issues" such as abortion and homosexuality, as do French citizens and residents of Catholic background. Though for most of France's approximately six million Muslims these questions are framed within the added complexities of race, ethnicity, collective experience as diasporic populations, and, for many, collective memory of colonization, they have necessarily inscribed their own experience, and their own collective memory, within the French context. (Moreover, not all involved in the hijab debate are postcolonial, and postcolonial sub-Saharan French Muslims

---

4. Antenne 2 for French television news, Dec. 11; *Le Nouvel Observateur*, Dec. 13.

are not involved in it at all, even if there are some slight indications in recent years that just as Maghrebian-background girls are tiring of the hijab, sub-Saharan-background girls may be starting to don it.[5])

In the political debate over the hijab and related issues, it has been necessary for feminists—and indeed, for the broader left—to take strong stands and to articulate as simply as possible a clear position. It has been necessary to aim for some solid ground amid the shifting sands of dodgy allegiances, odd compromises, and ideological maneuverings that range from the naïve to the manipulative. As a sometime participant in that political debate, as someone with a deep and decades-old personal connection to France, and indeed as author of this book, I also, necessarily, take a stand. More importantly, as a feminist thinker and researcher committed to better understanding the multiple complexities of a given geopolitical, historical, and (multi)cultural context so that we may progress in our transnational feminist analyses, I had to come to a decision that a more detailed discussion of the French hijab debate than those currently available in English would be necessary, if it were to be illuminating for those increasingly caught up in similar debates elsewhere.

In embarking upon this book now, I am tempted to paraphrase Simone de Beauvoir's opening sentences to *The Second Sex: I have long hesitated to write a book about feminism and the French hijab debate. The subject is irritating, especially for the French feminist movement* (with apologies and homage to Beauvoir 1949, 11). I have been writing and talking about this subject since the first headscarf affair in France in 1989, as, indeed, have French feminists. I would have liked to have left the topic behind years ago (as, indeed, would French feminists), but have had to resign myself not only to the fact that this subject continues for many to be perplexing, fascinating, and polarizing, but also to the fact that the French saga does not seem to be anywhere near an end.

---

5. Anecdotal evidence based on personal observation and on personal communications by friends living in high-immigrant inner suburbs to the north of Paris. A recent book in English on Muslim girls in one of these suburbs tends to give further credence to the idea that sub-Saharan African girls may be starting to adopt "Muslimist" identity politics (Keaton 2006). It is, however, possible that this is due as much to the assumptions of the author as it is to actual self-identification by the girls.

Indeed, it appears to be developing new forms: even if the hijab issue appears to have quieted down, at least for the moment, as far as France's classrooms are concerned, it has become anew a hot topic in other areas. On June 27, 2008, the Council of State, in yet another of its many landmark rulings in matters hijab (see chapters 4 and 5), refused French nationality to a Moroccan woman who wears a "burqa" on the grounds that her clothing represented a "behavior in society that is incompatible with the essential values of the French community, in particular the principle of equality between the sexes" (cited in *Le Monde,* June 27, 2008). This ruling confirmed a 2005 refusal of nationality on the grounds of "lack of assimilation," the main grounds for refusal of naturalization (once other legal requirements are complied with) under the terms of the 1973 nationality law. The woman, Fawzia M., who had been living in France since 2000 and whose children are born in France, claimed that her "burqa" is imposed on her by her husband, a French citizen. The decision has been met with public outcry both in France and internationally. As law professor Danièle Lochak argues, Fawzia M. is reproached with being oppressed and as such not adhering to French values. "If we were to pursue this logic to its end, then battered women, for example, would not be worthy of being French" (Lochak 2008).[6]

So, the French hijab saga seems set to continue for a while yet, with, it seems, ever new and surprising chapters unfolding.

Hence this book. It does not set out to be an ethnographic or anthropological study focusing on "ordinary" hijab-wearers and their personal motivations. Not only is there already a strong focus on this in the literature in both French and English, but the concept of "the ordinary Muslim woman" is itself in need of interrogation. Setting aside the intense media attention

---

6. This affair is breaking news at the time I am completing final edits to this book. I discuss it in an article in progress, along with the annulled marriage affair that occurred earlier in 2008 (in which a husband, also Muslim, obtained an annulment because his wife had lied about being a virgin). The annulment has been stayed and goes to appeal in September; the legal arguments hinge on whether, under French law, virginity can be seen as an "essential quality" of persons. (Deception on such "essential qualities" constitutes legal grounds for annulment under paragraph 2 of article 180 of the civil code. This article is usually invoked in cases of bigamy and other matters of deception concerning identity.)

paid to hijab-wearing schoolgirls, who are mostly albeit not exclusively from poorer suburban ghettos, most hijab-wearers who write at length about their personal experience, or who are interviewed by the media and researchers, are as "ordinary" as any tertiary-educated professional or intellectual in France. My focus in this book is thus not on individual motivations of the small minority of women of Muslim culture who wear the hijab in France or of the overwhelming majority who do *not*. Nor am I particularly concerned with their "ordinariness" or otherwise. My aim is rather to provide more detailed feminist analysis of the many complexities and contradictions of the current political debate and its history than is, at the time of this writing, available in English.

This book is divided into three sections, each further divided into three chapters and a brief section introduction, presenting the individual chapters. Part I, titled "Contextualizing the Debate," provides the historical background to the emergence of the debate in the Muslim world and in France, dealing in turn with the contemporary history of reveiling in the Arabo-Muslim world, the history and politics of secularism in France, and the history and politics of Muslimness and race in France. Part II, titled "A Fifteen-Year Saga," is a history of the hijab debate from the first affair in 1989 to the adoption of the 2004 law. Part III, titled "Feminists Caught in the Contradictions," will look at the politics surrounding the hijab debate since 2003 and the particular issues these create for feminists.

There is an expression in French: *dialogue de sourds*. It means "dialogue of the deaf" and refers to situations in which people talk past each other because they are remaining within two separate logics, two frames of meaning, and so are "deaf" to the arguments of their interlocutor. If the Franco-French debate on the hijab has in many ways resembled such a dialogue, as we will see, its effects are multiplied when one steps outside France. Many of my feminist friends and colleagues from the English-speaking world write France off as monoculturally "assimilationist" and imperialistically "universalist," and the drawn-out fuss over the hijab appears to them to have been simply another example of this. For many of my French feminist friends and colleagues, however—including some of the Muslim secularist women centrally involved in the hijab debate—the Western English-speaking world is monolithically "cultural relativist," and reactions from feminists located therein to the French debate are similarly so, and thus, to their mind, suspect. National stereotyping? No doubt. But most especially, *dialogues de sourdes.*

Metaphorically speaking, then, this book is, among other things, offered as a "hearing aid."

Part One | Contextualizing the Debate

॰ॐ

THESE FIRST THREE CHAPTERS paint the historical and contemporary backdrop against which the French hijab debate has been waged. They will focus respectively on the "new veiling" in the Muslim world and diaspora in the last few decades of the last century and the beginning of this one, as well as the rise of Islamism, its relationship to modernity and its hostility to the West and to feminism; the history, philosophy, politics, and contradictions of secularism in a France that still carries its Catholic baggage; and the history, demographics, and politics of French Muslims and their relationship both to the French state and to Islam, in a country that has one of Western Europe's largest and oldest Muslim populations and arguably its most diverse.

These histories are long and vast, and exploring them has already filled several volumes, written by scholars far more learned and specialized in these areas than I. If I retrace them here, linking them as I do so, it is because I am firmly persuaded that if generalizations from the French experience are possible and useful, they can only have resonance if one also has some appreciation of the ways in which that experience has been shaped historically.

Chapter 1 traces the history of reveiling to the emergence of modernist versus revivalist debates in Egypt in particular, in the late nineteenth and early twentieth centuries, and the more recent reveiling trend from the 1970s. It was in the 1920s, however, that both modernist Arabo-Muslim feminism and modern Islamism took shape in Egypt; their influence throughout the Middle East and North Africa (and indeed beyond) and Muslim diaspora was to be profound. In chapter 1, I also discuss debates over the nature of the differences between revivalism, traditionalism, fundamentalism, and Islamism as well as the rationale of veiling, exploring to what extent it is a practice particular to Islam or even required within Islam. I close the chapter with a brief overview of Islamist networks in France, the role of which in the hijab debate has been more significant than the available literature in English to date would lead one to suppose.

Chapter 2 briefly traces the history of the battle for religious pluralism and then secularism in France that led to the 1905 law separating church and state. It will provide insights into the key pieces of legislation as well as into the meanings of secularism in France and its imbrication with nationalism. It will also look at the continuing tensions, contradictions, and, indeed, battles within a nation that is both the birthplace and bastion of modern secularism and the "eldest daughter of the Catholic Church." Finally, I provide a brief overview of the steps taken by the French state to institutionalize and regulate Islam.

Chapter 3 traces the history of France's interaction with the Muslim world, which predates its colonial history but is most deeply marked by it, as well as the impact of the Algerian war and of postcolonial immigration. It explores the 1980s debates over immigration, "integration" and racism, and the emergence of a Maghrebian youth culture in which women were attributed a particular role. This culture, and women's role within it, seemed to be light years from the Islamic revivalist culture associated with the appearance of the hijab in French schools by the end of the decade. It also provides information on the ethnic background and degree of religious practice of French Muslims (as well as the degree of religious practice of Catholics).

1

A Very Modern Tradition

Background to the "New Veiling"

MANY SCHOLARS HAVE NOTED that women are the guardians of culture and honor, and women's appearance and body language have been the primary visible marker of this.[1] Clothing symbolizes women's submission, rebellion, or emancipation, and through these, society's progress, security, or moral degradation, as debates in the West over the last century concerning the length of women's skirts, the wearing or not of trousers, bras, or high heels, length and style and color of hair, and so on, have demonstrated. Outside the West, during colonial, postcolonial, and now "globalized" times, women's appearance and changes thereto—in particular, a greater or lesser degree of Westernization—have been the litmus test of cultural and moral values, of their preservation or loss. Although women are at the center of these debates, the latter are instigated and generally waged primarily by men. As Cynthia Enloe noted in 1989 with relation to the hijab, "One is hard pressed to think of an equally heated debate in any national community about men's attire . . . in which women have had so prominent a role to play" (Enloe 1990, 53).

But why the hijab? More than the sari, the kimono, the salwar kameez? Or indeed, more than bras, skirts, or high heels? Why has this headscarf become such an emotionally and politically charged garment? What stakes are riding on its donning or removal?

1. For example, Yuval-Davis and Anthias 1989; Enloe 1990; Hélie-Lucas 1990; Moghadam 1993, 1994; Yuval-Davis 1994, 1997; Howard 1995; Moghissi 1999; Winter 2002c.

21

In this first chapter, I attempt to address these questions through a brief examination of the issue of the "new veiling" within Muslim countries and the Muslim diaspora in late twentieth- and early twenty-first-century society.

The Hijab and Muslim "Authenticity"

Among the many remarkable and arguably unique aspects of the contemporary debate over the hijab is the confusing array of positions taken about the exact nature of the relationship between hijab-wearing and Islam. For some, it is a religious prescription—no good Muslim woman would be seen in public without one—whereas for others, the hijab has far less to do with Islam than with sexual politics in Muslim societies and diasporic communities.

In modern usage, the term "hijab" denotes, in the West and in many Muslim countries, a headscarf that fully covers the hair and the neck of Muslim women. It is supposedly to be worn once women reach puberty, although prepubescent girls may be dressed in some form of headscarf in more deeply conservative communities in both Muslim and Western countries. The term originally meant "curtain," or "separation," derived from *hajaba,* meaning "to hide from view," the word for headscarf used in the Qur'an being *khimar.* In Egypt, the supposed birthplace and heartland of 1970s Islamic revivalism, hijabization was accompanied, as it has been elsewhere, by a new sex segregationism: "Interaction was marked by reserve and austerity, almost ritualized" (El Guindi 1999, 133). The widespread use of the term "hijab" to refer to the modern Islamic headscarf thus highlights its deployment as the physical expression of the symbolic and ideological curtain separating women from men.

In French as in English, the two terms *foulard islamique* (Islamic headscarf), or simply *foulard* (headscarf) and *voile* (veil) tend to be used interchangeably to refer to the hijab phenomenon, although "veil" would more accurately translate *niqab.* Many, including me, thus prefer the term *foulard*/headscarf to *voile*/veil to refer to the actual garment, in the interest of accuracy. That said, I will, in accordance with the terminology used in scholarship on hijabization in the Muslim world and diaspora, use the terms "veiling" and "reveiling" here.

More religious or conservative women may also wear the *jilbab,* which means "mantle" or "outergarment." Nowadays this is a long loose tunic-like or coat-like garment that covers the whole body except for the face and hands (although the Qur'an remains vague on the precise form of the garment to be worn). The term *chador,* more well-known in the West, originated in Iran and describes the particular version of the jilbab worn there, but it has been generalized in much of the West as a synonym for any type of jilbab. The term has frequently been used erroneously, in the Western and particularly French press (the daily *Le Figaro* being a primary offender at one time), as indiscriminately synonymous with both hijab and jilbab.

A further note is warranted concerning French vocabulary more specifically, to clear up a misunderstanding that may be created by a recent popular book on the French debate. Contrary to what is asserted by Bowen (2007, 69), French people have not taken to substituting the word *écharpe* for foulard when they wish to designate a headscarf that is *not* Islamic. It would not occur to them, because these are two quite different garments. A foulard is a roughly square-shaped piece of lightweight material that is usually folded in two to form a triangle and can be worn either around the neck and shoulders or on the head. An écharpe is a long strip of material, often knitted but not necessarily so, worn around the neck to keep it warm in winter: nothing to do with a foulard. The French are even less likely to start talking about *carrés,* the luxury small square-shaped neckerchiefs made (and so named) by Hermès, also mentioned by Bowen, as these are quite specifically connotated in class and fashion terms.

As for the extent to which the hijab is central to Muslim practice, this is a hotly debated topic. High-profile French Islamist Tariq Ramadan, who has presented himself as the face of "moderate Islam" in France, claims that hijab-wearing is an obligation under Islam (Ramadan 2001, 70). This is false. There is no directive within the Qur'an for all Muslim women to wear the khimar, jilbab, or niqab, and even less to wear a "curtain" (hijab). This has been pointed out by many, from Egyptian modernist Qasim Amin, who will be discussed briefly below, to participants in the French debate, including those who do not support the 2004 ban in schools, such as Fawzia Zouari (2004).

The hijab is mentioned eight times in the Qur'an, most not in relation to Muslim women at all but in relation to God (Sura 42, v. 51), the separation between heaven and hell (Sura 7, v. 46), the "veiled" sun at dusk (Sura 38,

v. 32), the separation between infidels and the Prophet (mentioned in three different suras), and Mary's confinement when she gave birth to Jesus (Sura 19, v. 17). The only reference to women concerns protocols when believers address the wives of the Prophet: they should do this from behind a curtain so neither the wives nor, especially, the Prophet, are importuned (Sura 33, v. 53). This same verse also directs believers not to marry the Prophet's widows, as this would be a monstrous act in front of God. This verse is thus less about women than about the Prophet and pertains only to his wives in any case. Moreover, according to lawyer Abderrahmane Fraikech, this verse was written within the context of the Prophet's marriage to his seventh of twelve wives, Zaynab, daughter of Jahsh. Zaynab was apparently renowned for her voluptuousness, and according to Fraikech, the Prophet needed a way of keeping his disciples, who frequented him often in the evening, at bay so that he could enjoy himself in peace with his beautiful new wife (Fraikech 2004).

The khimar and jilbab are mentioned a couple of times, specifically in relation to women. In Sura 33, v. 59, the Prophet and believers are directed to tell their wives and daughters to draw their mantle around them (literally: "as far as the bottom/ground"), for this is a sure way for them to be recognized and not to be "given offense" or be harassed by men in the streets (*Le Coran* 1967, 912).[2] Scholars have noted that that this "recognition" is of them as free women, of some social standing, as distinct from servants or slaves, who were forbidden to veil (Ahmed 1992, 14) and who were fair game for harassment and assault by local rival gangs during a time of social unrest (Kacem 2004, 53; Geadah 1996, 64). The wearing of "outergarments" thus blends a sign of religious adherence with a sign of social standing, as shall be discussed presently. Finally, Sura 24, v. 31 advises women "not to show their charms, except what emerges" but to draw their headscarf across their bosom. The term used in Arabic for "bosom" denotes the upper chest,

---

2. I am using Denise Masson's French translation as my source. Masson is one of the rare female translators of the Qur'an. A devout Catholic and student of Muslim theology, she lived in Marrakesh for 56 years until her death, at the age of ninety-three, in 1994. Her translation is considered one of the most authoritative in France, but some conservative Muslim male scholars have objected to the Qur'an being translated by a woman.

closer to the collar bones—what in French was once also called, somewhat euphemistically, *la gorge* (throat), a word often used in French translations of this verse. The implication would thus be that décolletage is not favored in the Prophet's world (Kacem 2004, 52), although the proviso "except what emerges" is sufficiently vague and suggestive to be open to a fascinating range of interpretations, from the most restrictive to the most liberal.

A total of three sura thus refer to protective clothing or curtaining off of women. They use three different terms and all of them are relatively vague as to the precise nature of the covering or curtaining. Moreover, none of them is a strict directive; there is no "hijab law" in Islam. The other references to head or body covering of women are in the hadiths, that is, the sayings attributed to the Prophet and reported by third parties. Collectively, the hadiths make up the sunna, or "tradition" from which Sunni Islam gets its name. One hadith records the Prophet as stipulating that all women should cover all but their face and hands as soon as they reach puberty: this, clearly, is the source of the most fundamentalist interpretations of Islamic law. Kacem (2004, 56) has argued, however, that the collection of hadiths in which this appears is one of the least creditable. Another hadith, apparently more soundly based, recommends that women should cover their heads during prayer, which presumably means that they do not need to outside prayer times.

It is largely through reference to hadiths, and through differing interpretations of the two Qur'anic references to the jilbab and the khimar, that political assertions of the necessity for women to cover up find tenuous theological justification.

It is all the more tenuous when one considers that in many traditional societies, such as rural areas in the countries of the Mediterranean and the Adriatic, most of which are not Muslim, women wear, or have in the past worn, some sort of head covering that has more to do with prescriptions concerning women's dress and behavior than with religious piety. Such practices invariably continue among the first immigrant generation in diaspora, even when they have changed in the home country. These clothing choices may follow fairly prescriptive customs and may be ethnically coded, but they are not necessarily elements of a practice of piety and are even less likely to be an overt statement of religious adherence. This has also been observed, at least historically, with relation to Muslim women's headgear: the wearing of a scarf or shawl, however named and however styled, is an ante-Islamic practice in the Middle East and North Africa (El Guindi 1999, 149ff). For Noria Allami, "The first veiling of women is represented by the congregation formed by their fathers, uncles, brothers and cousins," and evidence of it in practically all societies can be traced to the beginning of recorded history (Allami 1988, 35–36). Leila Ahmed has suggested that veiling and confinement of women represented "a coalescence of similar attitudes and practices originating within the various patriarchal cultures of the region" that had become widespread under Christianity before Islamicization (Ahmed 1992, 18).

Whether secular or linked to pre-Islamic religious traditions, such traditional clothing practices are closely linked to patriarchal culture and in particular to control of women's sexuality. Many scholars, among them Fatima Mernissi (1975), have noted the symbolic relationship between women's hair and sexuality, which is most apparent in religious contexts. Muslim girls supposedly don the hijab at puberty; Hasidic Jewish women wear head coverings or wigs after marriage; Christian women used to—and in many places, still do—wear head coverings in church.[3] But it is also apparent in other contexts, such as the public shaming, through shaving their heads, of women collaborators by male French resistants at the end of World War II, a practice described by Claire Duchen (2000) as symbolic rape. One could also find a wealth of anecdotal evidence within Western fashion, advertising, entertainment, and sex industries, where models, dancers, singers, strippers, "escorts," "hostesses," and street sex workers alike display and toss, with practiced nonchalance, often elaborately coiffed locks in a carefully coded performance of titillation. From this point of view, the hijab is a hypersexualizing marker par

---

3. I note in passing the peculiarity of wigs worn by Hasidic women, which have come to replace more traditional scarves. The hair of the wigs is often straight and can on occasion be red or light brown or even blonde. The wigs are thus very Western-looking: "Jewish" hair is (stereo)typically (although by no means always) dark and curly. More peculiar again is the use of hair to cover hair, which, if hair symbolizes sexuality, is analogous to wearing a merkin. These comments arise from a conversation on this subject between me and an Israeli feminist friend, in Yafo (Jaffa) in June 2005.

excellence. Not only does it indicate that under it is a woman, it indicates, as Imam of Sydney's Lakemba Mosque, Sheikh Al-Hilali put it in late 2006, in admittedly extreme terms, that without it, woman are "uncovered meat" that men, who become "cats" in Al-Hilali's analogy, cannot then be blamed for assaulting.[4]

If hair and sexuality are linked, so are the ways in which one hides or displays hair and social status. Married women in traditional societies cover their hair, not only as a symbolic covering of their sexuality, but also to denote their "arrival" as fully fledged social actors through their role as spouse and, presumably, mother or mother-to-be. Beyond this, the fact and form of covering are also a marker of social class. I mentioned above, in discussion of 33:59 of the Qur'an, the connection between covering, however interpreted, and social-status marking of women associated with the Prophet and his class. Scholars have also pointed to the class dynamics inherent in ante-Islamic veiling and to the link between veiling and seclusion within the private sphere. In ancient Mesopotamia, head covering distinguished "decent" women from prostitutes; there was even an enforceable Assyrian dress code to this effect (Nashat 1999, 33). More recently, as we shall see presently, reveiling has become a marker of upward mobility or aspiration thereto for women of lower middle class or petit-bourgeois backgrounds.

If the link between female head covering and Islamic tradition or prescriptions is tenuous, so is the claim that the hijab has greater "traditional authenticity" where it is worn than, for example, Western forms of dress. In most places where the hijab (and jilbab) are worn today, they are introduced garments. That is, they are no more "traditional" or "authentic" than the Western high heels that are often worn under the long skirts, coats, or tunics. In fact, the hijab is a "novel contemporary ensemble, deployed as a uniform" (Moghadam 1993, 138).

Pointing out that the hijab is both exotic and contemporary may for some appear to be a hair-splitting argument, as the indigeneity status of a

4. The Lakemba Mosque is the largest in Australia and affiliated with Lebanese groups. While Hilali's remarks produced an outcry among Muslim women, including conservative hijabis, others, such as the Lakemba-based United Muslim Women Association, leapt to his defense.

garment may have little to do with the ideological and personal reasons for which it is donned, but it is nonetheless one that needs to be made. For, within the context of "new veiling" or "reveiling," the hijab has become the symbol of a return to the "traditional values" of a somehow purified Islam and as such, a banner of religious and cultural "authenticity." This claim to "authenticity" can be traced historically and politically to a backlash against deployment, by colonialists, of pseudo-feminist arguments to harness colonized women to a colonialist project. Women's dress and behavior have typically been the battleground upon which colonizing and colonized men have fought their culture wars; in the face of a colonizing discourse of "progress" and "feminism," the colonized needed to (re-)invent their own "authentic" traditions. The hijab has become the quintessential "invented tradition," to use Hobsbawm's term (Hobsbawm and Ranger 1983), in the neo-Islamicized world.

Islam, Modernity, Revivalism, and Feminism

The beginnings of hijab-waving as an anticolonial banner are generally traced to the debate over women and modernity in colonized and early postcolonial Egypt, for four main reasons.

First, it is in Egypt that the roots of Arab Islamic modernism can be found, as exemplified in the work of thinkers such as Rafi' al-Tahtawi, Sayyid Jamal al-Din al-Afghani, and in particular Mohammed Abdu, all of whom were influenced to varying degrees by French Enlightenment thinking, as was Ali Abd al-Raziq, one of the first Muslim intellectuals to argue for a secular state, in the 1920s (Hourani 1962). Abdu advocated abandonment of *taqlid* (adherence to traditional formulations by established schools of Islamic law) in favor of a new *ijtihad,* that is, use of the faculty of reason to develop a new interpretation of the Qur'an and the Shari'a that would be more applicable to the context of modern Egyptian society.[5]

Second, it was in Egypt that the manipulation of "feminism" as an instrument of colonial or pro-Western modernity was brought to the forefront with the publication of Qasim Amin's *The Liberation of Woman* in 1899.

---

5. For more on Islamic modernism in Egypt, see Hourani 1962, 1991; Moaddel and Talattof 2002.

Third, Egypt is seen to be the birthplace or at least the early intellectual hub of the Arabo-Muslim world's feminist movement: that is, a local movement made up of local women, and not men nor colonizing women. A number of proto-feminist organizations, representing a diversity of positions in relation to religion, tradition, modernity, and colonialism, were formed in the last years of the nineteenth century and particularly the early years of the twentieth (Ahmed 1992; Badran 1995).

Finally, and on the face of it somewhat paradoxically, Egypt is the birthplace of modern Islamism, with the founding of the highly influential Muslim Brotherhood in 1928, five years after equally influential modernist feminist Huda Sha'rawi founded the Egyptian Feminist Union, focusing initially on campaigning for women's suffrage.

These four aspects—sometimes linked, sometimes diametrically opposed to each other—have continued to be key elements informing debates over Islam, authenticity, ethnicity, and the West ever since.

The Egyptian debates also contained from the outset the particular mix of oppositions, manipulations, and contradictions that have informed the contemporary French one. The beginnings of the Egyptian tradition-versus-modernity debate featured, apart from the British colonizers and in particular the figure of Lord Cromer, pro-Enlightenment or pro-British figures including Qasim Amin, and more traditionalist anticolonialists such as nationalist businessman Tal'at Harb, founder of Egypt's first bank, Bank Misr (Bank of Egypt). Amin advocated a basic level of education for women, not for their own sakes, but to make them better wives—thus echoing the words of fellow Egyptian modernist Tahtawi, pronounced some twenty-five years earlier (Hourani 1962, 78; Haddad 1982, 54). He was also trenchantly opposed to veiling, although he did not advocate the uncovering of women's heads, merely their faces and hands (Amin 2002). His views nonetheless "brought the issue of the status of women into the forefront of controversy and provoked Egypt's first major journalistic debate" (Hoffman-Ladd 1987, 25). Harb and his supporters, on the other hand, took an anti-British stance and advocated a return to traditional Islamic practices, which included veiling. This opposition, and other similar oppositions that have occurred throughout the colonized world, have typically been characterized as a pro-Western, pro-imperialist and "Western feminist" stance versus a pro-indigenous, anti-imperialist and pro-"authentic traditional values" stance. As Ahmed has noted, however, while Harb and Amin sat on opposite sides of the fence with relation to the embracing of "Western values," their argument "centered not on feminism versus antifeminism but on Western versus indigenous ways. For neither side was male dominance ever in question" (Ahmed 1992, 163).

In fact, the (post)colonial "culture wars" that men have fought over women's appropriate behavior and attire have never been about feminism versus antifeminism, but about who gets to control women and to what nationalist or imperialist agenda they are to be harnessed. Deniz Kandiyoti has noted that, throughout the Muslim world, women's "emancipation," whether along secularist or Islamic modernist lines, or alternatively, their reinscription within religious traditions, has historically been a major component of nation-building (Kandiyoti 1995, 21ff). As Amin put it:

> The status of women is inseparably tied to the status of a nation. When the status of a nation is low, reflecting an uncivilized condition for that nation, the status of women is also low, and when the status of a nation is elevated, reflecting the progress and civilization of that nation, the status of women in that country is also elevated. (Amin 2002)

This nation-building strategy is common to both Muslim and non-Muslim worlds, and its supposed origins in Western Enlightenment philosophy have been used to discredit it within traditionalist and Islamist movements. Two oft-compared secularist nationalist pseudo-feminist projects are those of Jules Ferry in France and Kemal Atatürk in Turkey. Although more than half a century apart, they are startlingly similar in their intent and expression. Both understood, to cite Ferry himself, that "he who has the women has everything: first because he has the children, and second because he has the husbands."[6] This argument, made during the crucial formative years of what was to become the Third Republic, in the context of advocating free secular public schooling for girls, is similar to that used almost thirty years later in Egypt by Amin: "The family is the foundation of the nation. And since woman is the foundation of the family, her progress or backwardness

6. Speech at the Salle Molière, Apr. 10, 1870

in intellectual level is the first influence on the progress or backwardness of the nation" (cited in Hoffman-Ladd 1987, 25). Over thirty years later again, Atatürk told a meeting of the International Women's Congress in Istanbul: "I am convinced that the exercise of social and political rights by women is necessary for mankind's happiness and pride."[7]

All of these men who wished to marry women to science and reason rather than to the church and tradition nonetheless still wished to marry them off. Their anti-Western opponents rightly saw the way in which colonial and postcolonial governments deployed this "women's equality" discourse as a tool of colonialism at worst and double-edged at best, but wrongly saw it as feminism. Even if there were demonstrable benefits to women in the educational reforms brought in by Ferry and the social reforms brought in by Atatürk, the central objective for these politicians was never women's well-being in and of itself. Women mattered, perhaps, but not anywhere near as much as bringing the nation into modernity, which involved wresting power from religious institutions.[8]

Unfortunately, "Western feminism" has continued to carry the stigma ever since. In recent years, for example, there have been robust discussions among feminists and women's studies scholars concerning the "feminist" justification for George W. Bush's 2001 war on Afghanistan, in which "Western feminism," and thus all white Western feminists, were blamed for Bush's dishonest appropriation of "feminist" arguments in the service of his military and economic aggression.[9] Other feminists have exposed this pseudo-"feminism" as, in fact, antifeminist (Delphy 2002).

7. Address to International Women's Congress, Apr. 22, 1935.

8. It should be noted, however, that the case of Turkey is a little different. State secularism there has involved direct state intervention in the practice of Islam rather than state withdrawal from religion; at the same time, paradoxically, the Turkish state is much more intransigent than France concerning hijab-wearing by *adult* women in public institutions. The Turkish ban on hijab-wearing by adult women is widely denounced by all but the most hardline Kemalist Turkish feminists as sexist, because adult Islamist *men* can go where they please, no matter how conservative their politics, as is plainly evidenced since the passage to power of the Islamic party Justice and Development.

9. I have had some difficulty in finding evidence to back up these claims of "feminist" support for Bush's "war on terror," yet they are given credence in some serious academic writing,

Not that Western feminists, or other "progressive women," have always and necessarily sat outside the Western colonial project. Sadly, they have frequently not done so, even when very well intentioned. As concerns France, critiques of the orientalist prejudices of writers such as Isabelle Eberhardt abound (see, for example, Brahimi 1984; Zayzafoon 2005). (Eberhardt [1877–1904] was a French convert to Wahhabi Islam who dressed as a man and traveled extensively in North Africa and was thus a rather more complex and contradictory figure than some critiques of her "orientalism" may have one believe.) Even those who were explicitly feminist and overtly critical of the French regime, such as Hubertine Auclert, have nonetheless on occasion approached the issue of women's oppression in colonized countries with a "maternalistic" missionary zeal (Brahimi 1984; See also Knibiehler and Goutalier 1985).

If saying "I am a feminist" had the performative power of transforming us, our thoughts, our emotions, our internalized phobias and prejudices and well-learned behaviors, then our world, or at least some small parts of it, would already look very different. We grapple on a daily basis with the complex networks of domination in which we are tangled up. Sometimes, even often, we collude, whether through self-interested choice, strategic necessity, or survival imperative. How the issue of feminist accountability is addressed within such complexity is a fraught question indeed and has been the source of endless divisions among feminists, the French hijab debate being no exception, as we shall see in part III. But none of this is the same issue as that of co-opting of "feminism" by political actors who have little more than a tokenistic concern for the interests of the women in whose name they claim to be acting. Conflating the two problems thus only serves to obfuscate and confuse.

Moreover, the first to be targeted by the co-opting of "feminism" by Western governments and other institutions are Western women. Today,

---

such as Young (2003). It is possible that such claims are made in relation to Phyllis Chesler's support for the "war on terrorism" and anti-Muslim statements (where she cites such extreme-right luminaries as Oriana Fallaci) (Chesler 2005, 2006). Chesler, however, is quite isolated and has become notorious for her statements directed against both the feminist movement and individuals. It is thus difficult to consider her representative of any sort of "feminism."

this co-opting operates through, among other things, industries of cultural production such as advertising, fashion, and the sex industry, a notorious example being the proclamation in 1968 by Philip Morris, manufacturers of Virginia Slims "cigarettes for women," that "You've come a long way, baby." The Virginia Slims ads featured falsely sepia toned photographs of how it was for women back at the turn of the twentieth century, contrasted with supposedly "liberated" (and thin) fashion models dressed in ultra-feminine garb.[10] Western culture industries have become expert in redefining women's "liberation" as access to the means to better do what men want women to do, whether this be consuming goods or becoming themselves a consumable commodity.

While the agents of such messages as the arrival of "baby" into consumer heaven rarely call what they are doing "feminism," their rhetoric of pseudo-liberation for women is easily manipulated in turn by the agents of Islamic revivalism and particularly of Islamism. Islamists have adroitly harnessed the dishonest pseudo-embracing of pseudo-feminism by Western colonial and neocolonial powers on one hand and the capitalist commodification of Western women on the other, in their moves to discredit indigenous secular women's rights movements. Women criticizing religious conservatism are discredited as "tainted" by Western values or even as agents of Western imperialism. It is a discourse that has been readily—often enthusiastically—picked up in the West by women and men of both Western and Muslim backgrounds, many of whom are demonstrably not Islamist, as we will see in the case of opponents of the 2004 law in France (part III).

Interestingly, religious traditionalists such as Harb in Egypt and even more hard-line conservatives who followed him did not express the slightest opposition to other aspects of "Western" modernity such as capitalism. Not only did Egypt have a trading relationship with Britain prior to British occupation, but as one of the world's first supposedly "modern" post-colonial nations, its political and economic ruling classes, whether pro- or

---

10. The ads can be seen on the Web site http://www.wclynx.com/burntofferings/ads-virginiaslims_ads.html. Wikipedia provides a fairly comprehensive treatment of the Virginia Slims story, including reference to a denunciation of this marketing strategy at the time by the U.S. Surgeon General. http://en.wikipedia.org/wiki/Virginia_Slims.

anti-Western on other levels, thoroughly embraced the single most powerful expression of that modernity: the economic one. This hybridity between
traditionalism on one hand and modernity on the other is played out again
and again in the Muslim world, as many scholars have observed (Moghadam 1993; Béji 1997; Winter 2001a). Rejection of "Western values" does
not necessarily mean rejection of Western political and particularly economic processes.

Islamist Agendas

The terms "Islamic revivalist," "traditionalist," "fundamentalist," "integrist," and "Islamist" are deployed in a range of ways, often synonymously,
and the last is often used, erroneously to my mind, as synonymous with
"Islamic," which simply means "pertaining to or belonging to Islam." The
terms "fundamentalism," "Islamism," and "integrism" in particular have
been subject to debate as to their precise meanings and degree of overlap.
Often, what one person calls "Islamist" another, particularly in French, will
call "integrist," and yet another will call "fundamentalist." I will use the
term Islamism, which I consider to be broadly synonymous with "Islamic
fundamentalism," to describe a religion-based right-wing Islamic political
movement that seeks to intervene in politics and society in order to assert
conservative religion–based social control over specific populations. As I
noted in 2001, Islamism is the only term that is specific to Islamic fundamentalism, as the three terms revivalism, fundamentalism, or integrism
were originally coined in relation to Christianity, even if integrism is now
used fairly exclusively, particularly in French, in relation to Islamism (Winter
2001a, 12–13; See also Sfeir 2002, 265).

The 2002 *Dictionnaire mondial de l'islamisme* makes a tenuous distinction between Islamism and traditionalism in its entry on *islamisme*:

> Not all fundamentalist movements are militant, many are far from ortho-
> doxy and some should be distinguished from traditionalist movements
> because of their radicalism or their manipulation of modern technology.
>
> Globally, Islamism—or rather, Muslim fundamentalism—is a polit-
> ico-religious ideology that aims to set up an Islamic state ruled by the
> shari'a and to reunify the *umma* (Islamic nation [also translated as "the

community of believers" in this context]). This relatively simple definition, however, covers a complex situation, realities that change according
to the country or the ideological faction. Moreover, Islamist factions oscil-
late between literal faithfulness to tradition and aspiration to renewal via
reforms or revolutionary situations. (Sfeir 2002, 265)

The dictionary thus appears to make a distinction between Islamism or
Islamic fundamentalism, which has a modernist aspect, and traditionalism,
which may be synonymous with revivalism, although Islamism is also characterized as sometimes traditionalist, which makes the distinction unclear
to say the least. The editors of the journal *Maghreb-Machrek* (literally: the
West and East of the Arabo-Muslim world), make a distinction, in their
discussion of women activists with the Islamist political party FIS in Algeria, between "political Islamism" and "religious fundamentalism" (press
review, September–October 1994, cited in WLUML/FSLM 1995, 235).
The distinction here would appear to be between movements that are political parties (Islamist) and those that are not (fundamentalist). Olivier Roy
similarly argues that "neo-fundamentalism" is based on re-Islamicization via
"personal piety" (which would thus be synonymous with revivalism), while
Islamism is based on re-Islamicization via the state (which would thus be
synonymous with integrism), and accuses Caroline Fourest, harsh critic of
French Islamist Tariq Ramadan, of conflating the two terms (Fourest 2004;
Roy 2005, 101). In that case, however, Sfeir (2002), editor of the above-
cited *Dictionnaire mondial de l'islamisme,* is guilty of the same conflation.

Even if one accepts this distinction between "fundamentalism" and
"Islamism," the former being more or less synonymous with revivalism and
the latter with integrism, and even if one accepts the added and implied
Maghreb-Machrek distinction that Islamist movements are political parties,
there are still significant overlaps. Some, even many, revivalist movements
have integrist tendencies or may have links with integrist movements, that
is, movements for the integration of religion and state (a term first used in
France against Catholic antirevolutionaries, and now more commonly used
against Islamist movements). There are also, however, divergences: many
Islamist movements are not political parties and those that are active in
diaspora may not be seeking to Islamicize the state in the country in which

they are based, even if they are in their country of origin. They nonetheless have a clear political agenda in relation to the state and seek certain things from it.

In fact, the case of Islamist movements in the West does not fit at all comfortably with Roy's definition nor with his distinction between fundamentalists, perceived as some sort of neotraditionalists, and Islamists, who are modern and politically active. As we will see below, Islamism invariably blends modernist and traditionalist arguments. As we will also see in the case of France, hybridized, nonintegrist forms of Islamism have emerged in diaspora, although many of them have ties to integrist groups or individuals in exile from Muslim countries. In Western diasporic contexts, many groups and individuals that may bear all the other hallmarks of Islamist political agendas espouse a public discourse of coexistence of Islam with secularism. Behind such discourse invariably sits a type of mentality that in French is often called *communautariste*—"communitarianist"—that is, in favor of a particular group status on specific matters (usually related to education, family, and women), which is different to that enjoyed or adhered to by the rest of French citizens.

In other cases, the movement in question is clearly revivalist, or simply traditionalist, and not particularly concerned with politics—even in a broad sense—although it can provide a training ground and springboard for future radical Islamists. The case of Talblighi Jama'at or Jama'at al Tabligh (literally, groups for delivering the message), founded in the 1920s in what would later become Pakistan, immediately comes to mind. The organization, originally founded to divest Indian Hindu converts to Islam of "folkloric" or hybrid practices, is essentially a pietist—some would say archaist—missionary-style movement that seeks not to convert but to bring Muslims away from worldly pursuits and back to a "true," pure faith. It is apolitical; its association with Islamism is more through the fact that some who later become Islamist activists or even cadres may have at some time been members. Its French branch, centered initially on the Omar Mosque in the 11th arrondissement of Paris, was set up in 1979. It would fit the generally accepted understanding of "Islamic revivalism" as summarized by John L. Esposito: reemergence of Islam as "a potent global force in Muslim politics during the 1970s and 1980s," characterized by an appeal to Islam for legitimacy on the political and institutional stage, personal reengagement with religious observances and development of new sociocultural norms, even prescriptions, through dress and behavior codes and cultural production (Esposito 1995, 11–12).

The seeds of late twentieth- and early twenty-first-century Islamism were sown well before the period identified under the label "Islamic revivalism," said to be born out of post–Six Days' War (1967) blues on the one hand and Khomeinist anti-Westernism on the other. Both "moderate" and "fundamentalist" revival movements were influential during the process of decolonization, whatever the progressive character of the state formed, as we saw in the case of Egypt, and discourse on women's "emancipation" through education or workforce participation was often accompanied by restrictive Shari'a-based personal status laws. In Egypt, notwithstanding the modernist discourse and the eventual establishment of an "Islamic Socialist" state, legislation with regard to women's rights was significantly less progressive than in Tunisia at the time (Ahmed 1992, 175). In Algeria, that other great hope for Islamic socialism, the Association of Ulamas actively agitated for a religion-based state, and the first article of the Algerian Constitution inscribes Islam as the national religion. The much-criticized Family Code, which became law in 1984 under the one-party state of the Front de Libération Nationale (FLN), was first mooted as early as the mid-1960s, at the time of the ousting of Ben Bella, and first presented to Parliament in 1972 (Claire 1985; Lazreg 1994, 150ff).

Islamist movements can use a variety of tactics from nongovernmental organizing to political-party formation to use of organized violence. Many have been outlawed in the past or are now, and either operate illegally in the "home" country, such as the Muslim Brotherhood in Egypt, or in exile, such as Tunisian political party *Ennahda*—"Renaissance"—and its leader, Rachid Ghannouchi, who is now operating from London. They are invariably transnationally networked although they may compete with other more extreme or more moderate Islamist groups in their own countries. In Muslim countries, Islamist movements are also invariably integrist; in diaspora they are rarely so in the way in which "integrism" has to date been understood. Some Islamist political parties such as the FIS in Algeria and Hamas in Palestine have a military wing or have had one at some stage in their history. Most have explicit clauses in their charters concerning women's role and some, such as Hamas in Palestine, are also explicitly and often violently anti-Semitic. Other Islamist groups do not have political party structures and within the spectrum of Islamism, many are perceived as more moderate, or may have warring extreme and moderate factions within them. This was the case, for example, of Ennahda in Tunisia, which was outlawed because of its more violent wing. It continues to function clandestinely from Europe and while its objective remains the establishment of an Islamic state in Tunisia, it is considered by some to be more moderate than other Maghrebian Islamist parties such as the Algerian FIS.

The ideological and activist roots of modern Sunni Arab Islamism are varied but Salafism looms large. Ironically, this was originally an intellectual movement combining modernism and revivalism, and following the *as-Salaf as-Salihin* (righteous or pious predecessors or ancestors; originally the followers of the Prophet's Companions). The movement began grouped around above-mentioned modernists Mohammed Abdu and Jamal al-Din al-Afghani, along with Rashid Rida, at Cairo's al-Azhar university. The basic idea was to use a combination of Enlightenment thought, *jihad* as personal struggle (see below) and *ijtihad,* refocusing on *tawhid* (unity, also understood as monotheism) and original texts (Qur'an and Sunna) to operate Islamic renewal along the lines of the so-called "Golden Age" of Islam following the Prophet's death. Today, Salafism, like "Islamism" more generally, has many confusing meanings. It is associated for some with ultratraditionalist Saudi Wahhabism, although it seems the reality is that Saudis embraced Salafism (and Salafi scholars and activists), becoming more "modern," and more influential internationally, in doing so. Notably, members and followers of the Muslim Brotherhood were influential in setting up the transnational and supposedly nongovernmental Saudi organization World Islamic League (WIL, also known as the Muslim World League) in 1962. The WIL is today one of the world's largest, if not the largest, Islamic charitable and educational organizations and has branches in eighty countries. Others associate Salafism with Saudi worldly political and economic power: what Kepel (2003) calls "Sheikhist Salafism." For others again, notably the intellectual (as distinct from militant or jihadist) inheritors of the Muslim Brotherhood, it remains a broad intellectual current of modern Islamic thought looking to the *as-Salaf as-Salihin* for Islamic renewal. For others, it is a jihadist movement of which Al Qaeda is part (Roy 2001; Moaddel and Talattof 2002; Kepel 2003; Stanley 2005).

The main Salafist-inspired activist organization in the Arabo-Muslim world is the Muslim Brotherhood. Founded in 1928 by Hassan al-Banna and six workers of the Suez Canal Company, the Muslim Brotherhood is the most influential and long-lived Islamist movement in the Muslim and particularly Arab world, notably in the Middle East. It provided a prototype for many revivalist and particularly Islamist movements that were to form in the 1970s and 1980s, including in the West. Its credo is "God is our objective; the Qur'an is our constitution, the Prophet is our leader; struggle (jihad) is our way; and death for the sake of God is the highest of our aspirations."

It is worth pausing on the Islamic idea of "struggle." Jihad, from *jahada,* to struggle or make an effort to achieve a goal, means, within Islam, a struggle to repel the enemies of Islam and support those who struggle for the ways of Islam to prevail. It is not synonymous with war but has become so for armed Islamist organizations. A *mujahid* (m) or *mujahida* (f) is simply a struggler for Islam. In anticolonial wars this term became synonymous with "freedom fighter," most famously during the Algerian war, where the *mujahidin* and *mujahidate* were the men and women of the FLN who resisted the colonial oppressor. More notoriously, in Afghanistan, the mujahidin, known in Dari (Afghan Farsi) as the *jehadi,* were the U.S.-supported Islamic, and Islamist, fighters against the Soviet occupier, from whose ranks came the Taliban (Moghadam 2002). Former non-Taliban jehadi members make up a significant part of the post 9/11 Afghan government (Winter 2002c).

Like other Islamist movements that have come after it and that have been inspired by it, the Muslim Brotherhood (often referred to simply as the Brotherhood) was a populist movement that prioritized social welfare and opposed both Western capitalism and cultural Westernization. Sayyid Qutb, the Brotherhood's most prominent and right-wing ideologue, recalled Salafi philosophy when he stated that a return to the "age of purity" provided by the Prophet was the only remedy for "our sick, defiled, fallen age" (cited in Hoffman-Ladd 1987, 23). While some movements such as the FIS in Algeria have paid attention to social welfare more in their discourse than in their actions (Assima 1995), the Muslim Brotherhood did found hospitals, pharmacies, and, of course, schools, where the Qur'an and fundamentalist interpretations thereof were taught.

Apart from an assassination attempt on Nasser in 1954, for which the Brotherhood denied responsibility, resulting in the government banning the organization, the Brotherhood has largely been a nonviolent organization. Its branches in various parts of the world, however, have used violence at various times: Hamas, its Palestinian branch, is the most well-known example. It remains the main opposition group in Egypt, even though, like in many other Muslim countries, it is still banned. Standing as independents in the 2005 Egyptian election, its members won 20 percent of the vote and with eighty-eight seats form the largest opposition bloc, the legal opposition party having won only fourteen seats. It has branches in a number of countries, the first of which were formed by the Egyptian Brotherhood in Lebanon (1936), Syria (1937), and Transjordan (1946) (now Hamas, founded in 1987 in Palestine). Banned in some countries, such as Syria—where Hezbollah, Khomeinist-inspired Shi'a "party of God" and associated militia, is not banned—the Brotherhood is legal and highly successful in others, such as Jordan, where the Islamic Action Front (the Jordanian Brotherhood's political party) holds the parliamentary majority.

Islamist groups have often risen to success, within the framework of their "anti-Western decadence" stance, on anticapitalist or antiglobalization platforms that share some elements with secular left-wing anticapitalist or antiglobalization movements and others with Western fascist movements. Organizations such as the Muslim Brotherhood and their ideological inheritors have been clearly hostile to capitalism and to "Western" systems of government and political parties, including the very non-Western monopartite systems that were set up in "Islamic Socialist" states such as Nasser's Egypt and postliberation Algeria. Ironically, however, many of those same groups have used the political institutions and processes they criticize in order to attain power, such as was demonstrated by the FIS's use of the multiparty system and electoral process in newly democratized Algeria between 1990 and 1992. These groups are also financially and technologically savvy. Even as they outspokenly reject the evils of capitalism (for example, Gresh and Ramadan 2002; Ramadan 2003a), they have proved very adept at using the financial and technological means provided within world capitalist systems to gain power and influence and distribute their message, through the use of modern media, the funneling of petrodollars and even U.S. dollars into Islamist organizations, and so on (Geadah 1996; Béji 1997; Labévière 1999).

Islamism, Women, and Veiling

The Brotherhood's attention to social welfare did not, however, extend to support of trade unions and most certainly did not extend to support of feminism. Like all Islamist movements that have come after it, the Brotherhood's attitudes to women have been extremely conservative and based on the most fundamentalist interpretations of the Qur'an and hadiths. Feminism is deemed to be the agent of Western decadence, as is clearly indicated by the title of the 1978 proceedings of a 1952 Islamic conference in Egypt, *The Feminist Movements and Their Connections with Imperialism* (Hoffman-Ladd 1987, 32). This imperialist plot is also, depending on which version of it one reads, Christian or Zionist, or both. For Iranian Shi'a Islamist Jalal Al-i Ahmed in 1982, who coined the term *gharbzadegi* (literally, a plague from the West), usually translated as "Westoxication" or "Westitis," to describe the colonial plundering of Muslim countries by the West, imperialism is definitely Christian. It created a desire for modern technology among the countries of the pillaged "East" that the "East" did not have the means to produce (Al-i Ahmed 2002; See also Winter forthcoming 2009). For the Jihadist group al Jama'a 'l-Islamiyya, also founded in Egypt, after the Muslim Brotherhood renounced violence in the 1970s, it is Zionism. Al Jama'a 'l-Islamiyya is active in various forms throughout the Muslim world and diaspora, and is currently on the hit list of the United States and its allies as a terrorist organization, although it officially renounced violence in Egypt in 1998. Hoffman-Ladd refers to an undated tract distributed by this organization in which Zionism and feminism are bizarrely linked in a discussion of *The Protocols of the Elders of Zion,* a document now widely denounced as a hoax. The international Zionist conspiracy is deemed to have as its goal to "corrupt the youth of the whole world, and especially Muslim youth, and to destroy its morals and values" (Hoffman-Ladd 1987, 32).

For yet other Islamist organizations, such as the FIS in Algeria, the West is equated with the Jahilia, a pre-Islamic dark age where women supposedly had fewer rights. For the FIS, the West's "moral depravity" and "decay" are equivalent to the pre-Islamic "oppression" and "humiliation" of women (Bouatta and Cherifati-Merabtine, 1994). This notion that Islam improved women's lot is a common argument made by Muslim conservatives that does not, however, stand up well to historical scrutiny, as Ahmed (1992), among others, has noted.

Islamist movements have also, however, paradoxically tapped into certain modernist discourses on women's "emancipation," particularly in the postrevivalist phase. Lila Abu-Lughod has pointed out with relation to contemporary Egypt, for example, that Islamists characteristically "stigmatize sexual independence and public freedoms as Western but much more gingerly challenge women's rights to work, barely question women's education, and unthinkingly embrace the ideals of bourgeois marriage" (Abu-Lughod 1998, 243). Indeed, most Islamist movements advocate women's education, referring to the Qur'an as authority on this (Ramadan 2001, 2004). In many cases, they also support some form of appropriate paid employment for women and are even not averse to their active political participation: six out of the seventy-four seats in the 2006-elected Hamas majority in the Palestinian parliament are held by women.

Whatever the relationship of Islamic revivalists and Islamists to modernity, however, what is clear is that their discourse of a return to a supposed Islamic authenticity and morality in opposition to "Westernization" resides very firmly on the shoulders, or one might say the heads, of women. Not only is the nation the extension of the family (as, indeed, it was for the modernists), but if the nation is to return to "authentic" Islamic values to rediscover the core of its identity and morality, then the nation's wives, mothers, and daughters are the key to that Islamic fortress. They are, literally, its embodiment and its bodyguards, the emblems of its identity and the keepers of its traditions, through their own appearance and behavior and through their role in socializing its offspring.

Veiling and unveiling have come to symbolize that relationship of guardianship and espousal of a specific conception of what a modern Islamic nation or society might look like. And it is indeed a modern Islamic society: even the return to the home and family is conceptualized in modern terms, as the "home and family"—particularly in middle-class urban settings—underwent significant transformations in the twentieth century:

> To "return" to the home after the world has become fundamentally divided
> between a domestic and public sphere, after wage labor for all has trans-
> formed social and economic relations, after kin-based forms of social and
> economic organization have been attenuated, and after being a wife and
> mother has come to be thought of by some as a career, is to go to a new
> place and take on a radically new role. (Abu-Lughod 1998, 263)

The hijabi is, in fact, a thoroughly modern woman. As a ticket to social, educative, and professional interaction, as well as upward mobility, reveiling is
frequently represented as liberating in ways that, it is claimed by some, make
Western secular feminists uncomfortable (Franks 2001; Mahmood 2005).

Reveiling is, however, less liberating than some may claim, when considered within the context of Islamist ideology. In fact, Islamists couch purist
traditionalist discourse and imagery of appropriate women's behavior within
modern settings and social behaviors and a sort of neomodernist discourse on
women's progress. They systematically push the "different-but-equal" thesis,
which is Shari'a-based and set out clearly in the 1981 Universal Islamic Declaration of Human Rights (also known as the Cairo Declaration). According
to this declaration, the primary role for a woman is to be a good wife and,
especially, a good mother, in exchange for her husband's protection.[11] Islamists also insist heavily on the necessity for women to be modest exemplars
of Qur'anic virtue.

As scholars such as Fatima Mernissi and Valerie Hoffman-Ladd have
pointed out, the Islamic conceptualization of women's sexuality is of an
aggressive sexuality that is highly dangerous to men, and indeed liable to
create *fitna* (chaos or discord) (Mernissi 1975). The idea of *'awrat* (pudenda:
literally, weak and vulnerable parts), applies to a woman's whole body: hence
the need for covering it as it is both vulnerable and a dangerous temptation
(Hoffman-Ladd 1987, 28). Compare this with the Ancien Régime (pre-
revolutionary) French practice of referring to women as *le sexe* (shortened
from *le beau sexe*). *Le sexe* in French means both sex (as in male/female) and
visible sexual organs (vulva for women, penis for men). Christian conceptu-
alizations of women's sexuality, however, are of a polarized hypersexualized

---

11. http://www.alhewar.com/ISLAMDECL.html.

whore (bad) versus asexual virgin (good), with various hybrid forms such as the imagery of the Devil as a blond virgin or the myth of the toothed vagina. All Muslim women, on the other hand, are sexual, even the eternal virgins (houri) reserved for the pleasure of the good male believer in his heaven (there is no equivalent paradise for women).[12] Unlike Christianity, where sex is frowned upon, sex is good in Islam, as long as it is within marriage and, for women at least, procreational. The Qur'an stipulates that marriage is a duty of all good Muslims and polygamy (up to four wives) is only allowed if the husband can fairly attend to the needs of all his wives.[13] A good Muslim woman is thus not asexual but controls her dangerous sexuality, reserving her treasures (*zina*) for her husband.

Where Islam, especially in its fundamentalist interpretations, does resemble Christianity, and indeed patriarchal societies more generally, is in its attribution of the entire responsibility for the moral fabric of the family and by extension, society, to women's modesty. Women are the danger, they must be contained, controlled, covered. Women dressed in "degrading" Western clothing and adopting decadent "Westoxified" lifestyles within Muslim countries where Islamist movements are active have reported being harassed, policed, and in some cases such as that of urban Algeria in the 1990s, threatened with or subjected to violence (Boussouf 1995; Assima 1995). There are also many reports of Islamist women systematically policing other women in Muslim countries, particularly since the mid to late 1980s (Taarji 1998; Rozario 2006).

As numerous feminist scholars have pointed out, however, women have a range of reasons for reveiling. A number are making deliberate and conscious political choices when others are just as readily available to them, just as rightwing and/or fundamentalist women throughout the world make deliberate or conscious choices. These choices are invariably bound up with views on the role of religion in society and in their own lives, as well as on the particular interpretation to be made of the Qur'an concerning women's place in the world and appropriate behavior when moving about within it. They may also be bound up with negotiation of status and power, and in some

---

12. See Sura 44, v. 54, and Sura 56, v. 36–38.
13. Sura 4, v. 3.

contexts—especially post-9/11—may be part of a pro-democracy identity-politics movement. They may even embrace some feminist ideas: for example, the association Ak-der in Istanbul overtly campaigns against both Turkey's anti-hijab law and domestic violence.[14]

At the same time, it is at best naïve and at worst intellectually and politically dishonest to seek some "feminist" justification for any women's pro-religion activism in the name of "agency," anticolonialism, or whatever. Practically all activists for a reinscription of religion in public life are religious conservatives, and some are active members of fundamentalist movements, even if the majority of supporters and ideologues of right-wing and fundamentalist movements throughout the world are men, for reasons that appear to me to be logical, as men have much more to gain than women from participating in them. Though Islamist women have flirted with feminist movements in the past, they have been every bit as important as ideologues within their Islamist movements as men have; they are often leaders of women's groups and exercise considerable influence. This was the case, for example, of Zaynab al-Ghazali, of middle-class rural background, who was founder of the Association of Muslim Women and personal supporter of Hassan Al Banna, and who, as a teenager, was briefly involved with Huda Sha'rawi's Egyptian Feminist Union. According to Islamic Web site http://jannah.org, Ghazali, who died in 1988, found even Saudi Arabia to be insufficiently close to Islam, but was an enthusiastic supporter of the Khomeinist revolution in Iran.[15]

Reasons for reveiling can also, however, be more complex—as, for that matter, are women's reasons for making any choices that are demonstrably gender-marking within a male-supremacist system anywhere. Many women in the public sphere have reveiled simply in order to be able to move about in the world without fear of harassment, thus paying, as did their mothers or grandmothers, the price of crossing the boundary between private

14. For example, the organization's International Women's Day activities for 2008 foregrounded both of these issues. See Web site at http://www.ak-der.org/?lang=eng&p=&m=d 41d8cd98f00b204e9800998ecf8427e. Further information from Ak-der vice president Fatma Benli, interview with author, July 16, 2008.

15. http://www.jannah.org/sisters/zaynab.html.

and public. Others, however, have embraced the "politics of piety," to use Saba Mahmood's term (Mahmood 2005), advocated by Islamic revivalist movements, in an affirmation of female dignity, religiosity, and anti-Western cultural affirmation. And in many cases the lines between those who reveil simply to have peace and quiet, or literally be out of danger, those who seek solace and renewed individual empowerment and group identification in a world that has, for them, lost its familiar landmarks while failing to deliver on its new promises, and those who are "true believers" in the Islamist politico-religious agenda, can be indistinct. There are, in fact, many overlapping reasons for reveiling, which have been explored at some length in the literature, by feminist or women's studies scholars approaching the topic from a range of points of view.[16] Taarji in particular has noted, with relation to Egypt in the late 1980s, that the "diversity of styles of the Egyptian hijab" is "stupefying" (at least for her, a Moroccan, used to the more austere garb of local "Muslim sisters"). This variety "testifies to the incredible capacity of women to adapt to or get round a situation, or harness it to their advantage, no matter how constraining it may be" (Taarji 1990, 26). For many if not most, modern reveiling appears to be associated with a mix of factors that are difficult to separate out neatly: varying degrees of religiosity from the quietly pious to the fundamentalist, class including upward class mobility, access to greater freedom of movement and autonomy, freedom from harassment, peer group acceptance or pressure, participation in a group identity (national, ethnic, or religious), and access to various forms of power: religious, cultural, political, economic—and even, such as in the French hijab debate, media-driven overnight stardom.

Cloaked in Respectability

The politics of reveiling are seductive. On one hand, veiling appears to restore dignity and a sense of individual purpose to women who have found themselves the biggest casualties of the so-called "crisis of modernity." On the other hand, it provides a sense of group belonging and upward mobility

16. For example, Haddad 1984; Taarji 1990; McLeod 1992; Zuhur 1992; Badran 1995; Hessini 1994; Moghadam 1994, 2004; El Guindi 1999; Moghissi 1999; Franks 2001; Mahmood 2005; Rozario 2006.

in societies that, notwithstanding the inscription of many of them within a supposedly egalitarian modernist project, remain deeply class-stratified as well as divided along urban versus rural lines. Moreover, the political and intellectual elites of the decolonizing and postcolonial periods in many Muslim countries, especially although not solely in the Middle East and North Africa, are both descendants of precolonial ruling classes and Western-educated and Western-acculturated. The Khomeinist revolution in Iran in 1978–79 was fueled largely by opposition to the Westernized elite of Reza Shah, and the success of the FIS in Algeria was fueled by a feeling of disenfranchisement and disenchantment with the FLN and army-controlled one-party state during a period of severe economic crisis, reconfigured as a "crisis of modernity."

Periods of rapid and significant change have always had a "crisis" aspect. The "crisis of modernity" would appear to be the crisis of (post)industrial capitalist society and the liberal ideology accompanying it. In particular, it denotes fractures in the idea of linear progress toward a greater good for all in a world of government-regulated capitalism and social-contract egalitarianism. The promise of emancipation for the lower middle and other upwardly mobile classes has not held. Socioeconomic elites are doing relatively well, as elites generally do, to varying degrees, but the main social product of "modernity," a mushrooming urban lower- to mid-middle class, has found itself with unrealized aspirations, while displaced peasant classes and urban working classes, only barely in the game to start with, are now piling up on the social rubbish heap (as essayist Viviane Forrester noted so emphatically in her book *L'horreur économique* [1996]; See also Boltanski and Chiapello 1999).

As usual, the main losers are women, although they are rarely discussed as a specifically vulnerable population in general socioeconomic analyses of recession and class, even when disadvantaged racialized minorities are discussed. In France, as concerns socioeconomic exclusion among Maghrebian-background populations, most studies that are not explicitly feminist deal with the socioeconomic disadvantage and cultural ghettoization of young *men* and their fathers, but much more rarely with that of young *women,* and almost never that of their mothers. Which is curious, given the extraordinary amount of attention given to the hijab debate: the young women at the center of this debate are mostly, albeit not exclusively, from poorer urban areas and are daughters of recent immigrants.

One persistent misapprehension concerning the rise of extreme-right and fundamentalist movements in response to a "crisis of modernity" is that these movements were somehow born of such crises. While periods of economic downturn have always provided fertile terrain for extreme-right movements, and new groups may and do indeed emerge from the socioeconomic ruins, as was demonstrated most spectacularly by the rise of National Socialism (Nazism) under the Weimar Republic, they do not in themselves create these movements. Many of them, or individuals within them, have emerged from previous formations, as is the case of the Front National (FN, National Front) in France, whose leader, Jean-Marie Le Pen, was a member of an extreme right-group led by Pierre Poujade in the years after World War II and who is widely believed to have been associated with the extreme-right paramilitary group Organisation de l'Armée Secrète during the Algerian war, although he has always denied this. The economic downturn and ensuing social crisis that came with the end of the "Thirty Glorious Years" in the mid 1970s (see chapter 3) may have provided Le Pen with new opportunities to obtain popular support for his ideas, but the ideas, the people advocating them, and the groups these people belonged to were already there in one form or another. It is simplistic and dangerous to portray Islamist movements, or any other fundamentalist or extreme-right political movement, as born solely of a situation of victimhood. Many of the followers of such movements are indeed victims of socioeconomic crisis, but its founders and particularly its main ideologues almost never are. The latter are, however, very skilled in manipulating the ideology of victimhood, notably, as we will see in the case of France (see part III), to justify, among other things, violence and control of women.

As we saw above, the ante-Islamic origins of veiling, reaffirmed in the Qur'an, were to house higher-status women, normally confined to the home and family, in a sort of personal portable tent for their forays into the public sphere, marking them as socioeconomically distinct from slaves, peasant laborers, and prostitutes. This class attribution of veiling has not changed. Arlene McLeod's 1992 study of reveiling among often recently urbanized lower-middle-class women in Cairo revealed that the practice had little to do with piety for them and even less to do with Islamism. As women who worked in badly paid unsatisfying jobs for mainly economic reasons tied to the desire to purchase the trappings of upward social mobility (a bigger apartment, modern appliances, better education for the children), reveiling for them was largely to do with identification with an upwardly mobile lower middle class, by following the fashion associated with that class. It was also a way of conciliating their paid work outside the home, often performed more for economic reasons than for individual satisfaction, with the traditional role of wife and mother to which most of the women were still fundamentally attached: "This dress says to everyone that I am a Muslim woman, and that I am here working because my family needs me to!" (cited in McLeod 1992, 549). Paid work, for nonprofessional classes, is seen as demeaning to women and as taking them away from their primary responsibility of home and child care. Women interviewed by McLeod also cited the need to assert their dignity and regain men's respect in public, despite the fact that the clothing was hot, heavy, and impractical. As McLeod puts it, "Veiling presents a double face; it both symbolizes women's protest against a situation that threatens valued identity and status, and signals women's acceptance of a view of women as sexually suspect and naturally bound to the home" (1992, 552). These women's "consent" to veiling as a strategy of empowerment or resistance is thus ambiguous at best, as there "is no clear-cut other to confront directly," but a "layered and overlapping round of oppressors" (McLeod 1992, 553). Nor is there a particularly great range of choices open to them.

More recently, hijabs, jilbabs, and burqas have been popping up in unexpected places. Writing of the "new burqa" in universities in Bangladesh, where reveiling is a more recent and marginal phenomenon than in many other countries, Santi Rozario notes that "the student body is now much more mixed in class terms than it used to be, and veiling provides women from poor and non-elite backgrounds a way to raise their status" (Rozario 2006, 376). It also, however, provides the predominantly middle-class population in the university system with a way of reasserting its own class status.

In North Africa and the Middle East, as in Bangladesh, contemporary Islamist movements are doing their recruiting in high schools and universities, that is, among the current and future intellectual and professional elites

(Taarji 1990, 321). These people are also young and may, more than others, be suffering from the so-called "crisis of modernity," where the usual apparatus of citizenship and participation is failing them (a similar argument has been made with relation to Muslims in the West; see chapter 2).

Islamist women in university milieux congregate in relatively homogenous groups. They study together: they are very, very studious, according to Taarji (1990, 321). They pray together and read the Qur'an together, doing, in fact, little else as most secular pursuits are forbidden to rigorously pietist Muslims (Rozario 2006). In Cairo, women's "Islamic salons" emerged among the middle classes during the 1990s, founded by the "wealthy and pious" Suzie Mazhar, and in 1999 the Islamic university Al-Azhar opened a special section for training women muftis (Kristiansen 2005). Some estimate that 80 percent of women in Cairo are now headscarved, notably in the chic bourgeois areas and Cairo's "café society," although Taarji (1990) comments on the levels of poverty as well. Thirty years ago, it was the opposite (Kristiansen 2005; Chartier et al. 2006).

According to some observers, Islamist women are far less inclined than their male counterparts to engage with political-party Islamism or other forms of Islamist intervention at government or institutional levels. In its discussion of women of the FIS, *Maghreb-Machrek* reports that they are more likely to refer frequently to the Qur'an, with which they appear to be far more familiar than their male counterparts, and focus on re-Islamicization of society rather than political power as such (September–October 1994, cited in WLUML/FSLM 1995, 235). Lætitia Bucaille of that journal reported earlier the same year, following her 1993 meeting with female Islamist students at the Algerian university of Bouzaréah, that "each of the girls felt herself to be entrusted with a mission to propagate Islam and understanding of Islam" (September–October 1994, cited in WLUML/FSLM 1995, 234).

While these women's adherence to religious piety may be profoundly and personally felt, they are also embracing modern agendas. Even as they denounce "Western decadence" and advocate Islamicization of society and in particular sex segregation, they are educated, consider themselves the different-but-equal peers of men, and aspire to exercise an independent profession—a position that puts them at odds with many a male Islamist leader in their own movements.

Education and workforce participation, even at a professional level, do not, however, in themselves buy liberation. Women in post-Khomeinist Iran are among the most highly educated in the Muslim world and actively engaged in professional activity; this has not saved them from the severely restrictive personal laws to which the Khomeini regime subjected them and to which they continue to be subjected today, despite some measure of liberalization (Chafiq 1991). The situation of the veiled elite or upwardly mobile female population in Muslim societies is perhaps in some respects not so different from that of the English "daughters of educated men," those women whose constrained situation Virginia Woolf lamented (Woolf 1938).

In any case, their situation is far from liberation and even farther from feminism, which is a broader social and political project than equal access to education and female workforce participation, or even individual empowerment. Many right-wing women in the world are highly educated and may feel personally empowered in all sorts of ways. This does not in itself make their politics feminist, as "empowerment" or "agency"—or even equal access to some of the things men do in the world—are hardly, in themselves, a sound and comprehensive definition of "feminism" (Winter 2001a, 2001b, 2002a, 2006d). The latter concerns analysis of the ideology, structures, and impacts of male domination in all areas of life and the struggle to end it, and cannot be reduced to whether some women are individually empowered or whether there is sex equality in access to education.

When authors such as Myfanwy Franks, who studied women converts to Protestantism and Islam in the United Kingdom, claim that a reading of veiling as "a means of entering the public domain rather than as an exclusion from it is unpopular in some secular and Western feminist circles" (Franks 2001, 129), they are missing the point. (It is also an odd comment, seeing that the converts Franks is studying are Western.) Many in "secular and Western feminist circles" have no difficulty with the idea of veiling as a *strategy* of gaining access to public space for women whose "veil" has traditionally been their enclosure within the private circle of male family and community members, or who are operating within a modern context where veiling is made to appear attractive for the many reasons I outlined above. Whether veiling as *a symbol of certain values or ideologies* is "popular" or "unpopular" with secularists is another question entirely.

Women engaged in "bargaining with patriarchy," to recall Kandiyoti's famous term (Kandiyoti 1991), use a number of strategies that may combine elements that are demonstrably feminist with others that are demonstrably not, or may even be antifeminist. A hijab does not in itself transform the wearer into a feminist or an antifeminist, no more than it automatically makes her either empowered or disempowered. In any case, the fundamental question with which I am concerned here is less the diverse individual motivations of hijab wearers than the wider political manipulation of hijabization by a range of individual, collective, institutional, and civil society actors.

2

The "Cornerstone of the Republic"

Secularism and the Regulation of Religion

IT HAS OFTEN BEEN SAID that the French idea of laïcité, enshrined in article 1 of its constitution, is impossible to translate. Even though Western countries are, to varying degrees, secular, in practice if not always formally in law, and even though there is some debate as to how unique French secularism really is (Baubérot 2004), nowhere else in the West has secularism been a political and nation-forming battle in the way it has in France. Nowhere else has that nation-building secularism been so explicitly linked to both women's emancipation and schooling and been so strongly informed by a centuries-old battle for religious pluralism. Nowhere else has a law explicitly and firmly guaranteed not only the religious neutrality of the public space but also the political neutrality of the religious space.

To make things more complicated, within the context of the hijab debate, two new terms have emerged: *laïcisme* and *laïcard,* which are not synonyms for atheist either, but something else again. It is these terms, in fact, that are the most difficult to translate. If one can comfortably translate *laïcité* by secularism, although Baubérot has made a distinction between *laïcisation* as a formal legal process and *sécularisation* as a societal one, how does one find an English equivalent to the French *-isme? Laïcité* implies a state philosophy and practice, whereas *laïcisme* and *laïcard,* the latter being a person pejoratively designated as dogmatically secularist, imply an ideology. These two terms are in particular used by those who favor a more flexible or "tolerant" interpretation of *laïcité* to denigrate those who have a more rigorist or "intransigent" one (Baubérot 2004,

53

225). I will thus keep these two terms in French when necessary to make the distinction.

Separation of Church and State: A National Consensus?

The foundational document of French secularism is the 1905 law on the separation of church and state, although, as the Stasi Commission of 2003 noted, "Far from being a well-ordered whole, the legal regime of secularism is, rather, a disparate group of texts, enacted on the basis of the founding principles of the 1905 law, as issues related to the law of separation emerged" (Stasi et al. 2003). These include ministerial circulars, which are guidelines providing interpretations of law but do not carry the force of law, such as those of 1936 on the wearing of religious insignia, 1937 on the outlawing of religious proselytism in schools, and 1944 on neutrality of schools. The Republic was to become formally proclaimed as secular in the Fourth Republic Constitution of 1946; this was maintained in the Fifth Republic Constitution of 1958.

Article 1 of the 1905 law declares that "the Republic assures freedom of conscience. It guarantees the free exercise of faiths under no other restrictions than those set out hereinafter in the interest of public order." The first key restriction is contained in article 2: "The Republic does not recognize, remunerate or subsidize any faith." The second key restriction is article 26, which prohibits the holding of political meetings on religious premises. The third is article 35, which prohibits religious personnel, through speeches or posters within religious buildings, from inciting resistance to the law or attacks on other groups of citizens. Finally, article 28, which is at the core of the hijab debate, outlaws any display of religious signs or emblems on public monuments or in any other public place, with the exception of religious buildings, cemeteries, funereal monuments, and museums or exhibitions.

Much of the law deals with transitional and transfer arrangements for Catholic personnel, property, education, and other initiatives financed by the state. Articles 12 and 13 stipulate that church buildings (including synagogues) "put at the disposal of the nation" and used for public exercise of religious faiths under the law of 18 Germinal Year X (April 8, 1802), which reestablished the Catholic Church in France, remain at the disposal of those faiths at no charge to them. Article 25, however, stipulates that religious celebrations held within these premises are public and can be subjected to surveillance "in the interest of public order." Article 21 subjects religious organizations to government fiscal auditing, and article 22 provides for those organizations to maintain financial reserves that are (a) capped and (b) only to be used in the exercise of the religious faith in question and for no other purpose.

The law thus protects both freedom *of* religion and freedom *from* religion, not only by ensuring the neutrality of public space but also by, first, sanctioning persecution or harassment of others in the name of religion or by officers of religion, and second, limiting the enrichment of religious organizations and prohibiting the use of religious funds for secular purposes. It also establishes formal structures for state regulation of religious institutions, which has been highlighted as another peculiarity of French secularism (Bowen 2007).

While other Western nations are secular, then, France is secula*rist,* or *laïque* as opposed to "merely" secular, and secularism has been called the "cornerstone of the Republic." There is even a chair in the history and sociology of secularism at the prestigious Ecole Pratique des Hautes Etudes (Practical School of Higher Studies, specializing in applied natural, historical, philological, and religious sciences, attached to the Sorbonne); it is occupied by Jean Baubérot. Nowhere in the Western English-speaking world, to the best of my knowledge, does such a chair exist, although there are innumerable chairs in studies in religion and theology in secular universities.

If society and culture shape laws, laws also shape society; in fact, Olivier Roy argues that secularism in France is "first a body of laws before being a system of thought" (Roy 2005, 37). At first glance, the 1905 law and the practices that are governed by it would appear, a century down the track, to have produced a relatively strong consensus. Surveyed either regularly through local opinion polls usually based on small sample sizes of a few hundred, or less regularly but in more detail through studies such as that conducted in 1998 by the International Social Survey Program (ISSP) (1,133 respondents to a written questionnaire), most French citizens and residents believe that the French model of secularism is a good one or that it should be reinforced (46 percent and 28 percent, respectively, in the ISSP survey, discussed in Bréchon 2001 and Lambert 2001). Conversely, most believe that the Catholic Church either has just about the right amount of power or that its power should be reduced (49 percent and 25 percent, respectively). Predictably, these numbers are greater among left-wing voters and among irregularly practicing or nonpracticing Catholics or among nonbelievers. More generally, pro-secularists are more likely to be progressive on other matters that range from women's rights and homosexuality to the death penalty. The French have greater confidence in the school system than in any other institution (68 percent for schools, followed by 61 percent for the legal and court system, and 47 percent for religious organizations), and are overwhelmingly of the opinion (over 80 percent) that religious authorities should not involve themselves in influencing governments or voters. Almost two-thirds also believe that religion is more likely to be at the source of conflict in the world than of peace. Admittedly, the 1998 survey happened in the context of the already ten-year-old hijab debate as well as in the wake of the so-called "undeclared civil war" in Algeria between the state and the FIS, and of a wave of terrorist attacks in France in the mid-1990s, associated with another Algerian Islamist group, although the survey question was about religion in general. Also, respondents are identified only as Catholics or without religion, which indicates either that those practicing other religions were not included in the survey or their presence among respondents was so small as to be statistically insignificant.

What *is* significant, however, in the ISSP data—which are relatively consistent with local opinion poll data collected over the preceding ten years—is that, even if pro-secularist positions were more pronounced among nonbelievers, they were also very strong among Catholics, even regularly practicing ones. Moreover, slightly over half of those surveyed overall, notwithstanding their attachment to secularism and their confidence in the French school system, also believed that "fundamental truths" can be found in all religions, which indicates that pro-secularism is not "antireligion" per se. Contrary to the conflation that is often operated by critics of secularism—notably its Muslim religious critics and their supporters, both within and outside France—secularism, even French secularism, notwithstanding its more dogmatic expressions, is not the same as atheism, nor is it the same as outlawing of religion altogether and state persecution of those practicing it. Henri Pena-Ruiz, a fervent defender of secularism (some would even call him *laïcard*), has called the conflation of secularism with atheism and the latter either with the crimes of Stalinism or "the icy waters" of selfishness, "one of the most widespread forms of denigration" of secularism (Pena-Ruiz 2003, 191).

It is, however, certain that French secularism is the product of its dialectical relationship with Catholicism. That relationship is not only evident in the historical idea of "two Frances"—clerical and anticlerical—in the nineteenth century, notably in the early decades of the Third Republic (Baubérot 2000, 2004), but also within the tensions and contradictions within the practice if not the principle of secularism in France, as I have noted elsewhere, and will discuss further below (Winter 1995a, 1995b, 2006c). Baubérot has argued, in the introduction to his book marking the centenary of the 1905 law, that the idea of a French consensus around secularism, as it appears through surveys such as the one conducted above, is a myth. If slightly over half of regularly practicing Catholics (admittedly a small minority these days) support secularism, 48 percent of that group surveyed in 1998 still considered it should be watered down or abandoned (Bréchon 2001). If today, Islamist lobbies are campaigning to modify secularism in France, they are following in the wake of significantly more powerful and more numerous Catholic ones. As Baubérot puts it, "Since the Revolution, secularism has sparked passions in this country . . . very few people are really indifferent to it" (Baubérot 2004, 9). Léon Gambetta, Third Republic secularist statesman and, briefly, head of its government (1881–82), articulated, in 1872, the terms of the nonconsensus:

> Our adversaries say that we are the enemies of freedom of conscience, that we persecute consciences. This is, once again, slanderous: we are, on the contrary, champions of freedom of conscience and of the freedom of religious faith. (cited in Pierrard 2000, 159)

One hundred years after the 1905 law, despite a broad overall attachment to the philosophy and institutions of French secularism, this same argument is going on. Those who defend the 2004 law outlawing "conspicuous" religious insignia argue passionately that it protects freedom of conscience; those who oppose it argue, just as passionately, that it does the opposite.

Bon Anniversaire, Laïcité

On February 14, 2005, the prime minister's department launched the official commemoration of the 1905 law through a series of four colloquia organized by the Académie des sciences morales et politiques, one of the five academies of the Institut de France (of which the best known is the Académie française).[1] Speaking at the February 14 event, the then prime minister, Jean-Pierre Raffarin, described the 1905 law as "protector of the freedom of conscience," but pointed out, in a fairly obvious allusion to the headscarves debate and the 2004 law, that the relationship between religion and politics remained, or had become anew, "a major issue at stake for [French] society." As a consequence, "Reflection on the role of religions in French society, one hundred years after the 1905 law, appears . . . to be very important."[2]

Other fora were organized by a range of public institutions and non-governmental organizations, such as a conference on December 9 and 10, 2005, at the Université de Toulouse-le-Mirail, or an all-day conference held on December 9 by the Masonic Lodges, under the auspices of the largest of them, Le Grand Orient, or a debate organized by the Paris Centre Lesbien Gai Bi et Trans in late 2005.[3] "Secularism" rubrics proliferated on the Web sites of most nonprofit associations involved in any way, shape, or form with the debate.

The centenary, in conjunction with the hijab controversy, also provided a context for opening debate on the continued relevance of the 1905 law. If this debate was signaled from the time of the first headscarves affair of

1. The Institut de France was set up in 1795, under the Directoire, the post-Robespierre government headed by five directors, which ended with the Napoleonic coup d'état of 18 Brumaire Year VIII (Nov. 9, 1799). The Institut self-describes as a "Parliament of the learned world" whose aim is to "perfect arts and sciences according to the principle of multidisciplinarity." It is funded by roughly one thousand bequests, donations, and foundations.

2. Details of these colloquia can be found at http://www.canalacademie.com/article545 .html.

3. Freemasonry in France has a different history and contemporary connotation to its equivalents in the United Kingdom and particularly the United States. It is associated with bourgeois but progressive Protestant liberal rationalism, and many center-left and liberal right politicians, including France's first Women's Rights Minister Yvette Roudy (Socialist Party), are members of one or other of the lodges.

1989, it remained for many years largely a debate over the interpretation of the law. It was not until 2003, with the rekindling of the hijab controversy and the setting up of the Stasi Commission, and the centenary approaching, that possible revisions to the law began to be considered. Public discussion of this occurred in various fora, such as conferences and online discussions organized by the association Islam et laïcité,[4] or published by the national information service and government publisher La Documentation Française, in its series *Regards sur l'actualité* (Looking at Current Affairs) (Documentation Française 2004). In the party-political arena, however, it was mainly a question of reaffirmation of the law and the philosophical principles and historical origins that underpin it, with an occasional concession to the idea of tweaking the law to accommodate the presence of about six million Muslims (roughly 10 percent of the population) on French soil.

A number of politicians cited in the center-left daily *Le Monde* on the day of the anniversary itself, December 9, put their particular spin on the links between la laïcité and la République. Dominique de Villepin, who replaced Raffarin as prime minister on May 31, 2005, placed the law "At the heart of the Republican pact," even though no particular official event was organized on the actual day of the centenary. His colleague Nicolas Sarkozy, then minister for the interior, wanted to "tidy up" the 1905 law to provide for government regulation and financing of mosques, along the lines of the arrangements regarding the Catholic Church. The president of the National Assembly, Jean-Louis Debré, saw the presence of large numbers of Muslims lacking "our Republican conception of secularism" as a problem and characterized secularism as a "permanent combat." On the left of the political spectrum, François Hollande, national secretary of the Socialist Party, and then "PaCSed" partner of Socialist 2007 presidential candidate, Ségolène Royal, saw no need to change the law that had maintained "peace" between church and state for a century.[5]

He considered those who wished to change it to accommodate Islam as having never accepted the law in the first place. Like Sarkozy, however, he saw

---

4. http://www.islamlaicite.org.

5. For a discussion of the PaCS, see section of this chapter titled "'Ecumenical Secularism'? Or, *Plus Catho-Laïque que Moi, Tu Meurs*."

no difficulty in introducing regulations concerning the funding of mosques. Hollande's colleague, Jean Glavany, known as Monsieur Laïcité, neatly, or perhaps for some, not-so-neatly, tied in the theme of secularism to that of the riots of the previous month. According to Glavany, the riots expressed a "spectacular need for secularism," characterizing the latter as being fundamentally about respect for others (*Le Monde*, December 9, 2005).

For Pierre Lévy, writing in the online publication *La Revue Républicaine* a couple of weeks later, "The question is simply one of power: do we accept the re-emergence within the political order of other legitimacies than that of the sovereign people, external to the nation?" (Lévy 2005). In writing this phrase, Lévy evoked the Jacobin version of Republican nationalism, a key component in the history of the development of secularism, as we will see presently. André Laignel, member of the European parliament and general secretary of the Mayors Association of France, even more directly linked secularism with the philosophical bases of the Revolution and the Republic. Laignel claimed that the strength of the 1905 law was "the foundation of our Republican culture, the attachment to the social contract . . . It is the height of Enlightenment philosophy, of Kantian morals, and the affirmation of human rights [*Les Droits de l'Homme*] with freedom of conscience and freedom of expression" (Laignel 2005). These core foundational concepts of the revolutionary decade (1789–99) come up again and again in public declarations on secularism by French politicians and political commentators. Their message is clear: without secularism, there is no Republic.

A Centuries-Old Combat

France continues to be known today as the "eldest daughter of the Catholic Church" because of the conversion of its founding monarch, the Frankish conqueror Clovis, to Roman Catholicism in 496. Clovis was the first European monarch to embrace Roman Catholicism and as such, became known as the "only son of the Church." The land of the Franks became, by extension, the Church's eldest daughter. Clovis was also instrumental in laying the foundations of Gallican Catholicism: shortly before his death in 511, he convoked the first Council of Orleans, a synod of Gallican bishops, which established strong links between the Frankish crown and the Catholic episcopate. Among its decrees was that conferring the right of sanctuary on churches and ecclesiastical residences. That right is still invoked today, as was seen in Paris during 1996 when several hundred illegal immigrants, mainly from Mali, occupied first the St. Ambroise and then the St. Bernard churches, the latter providing them sanctuary until a brutal police raid forced them out. Most of the immigrants concerned were regularized in 1997.

The post-Clovis relationship between the French throne and the papacy alternated between cozy—at the time of the Crusades, for example, when the French throne was a leading combatant in Rome's so-called Holy War, or during the French Inquisition in the thirteenth century—and fraught—as in the early days of the Avignon papacy in the fourteenth century, when the secular power of the northern throne competed with an increasingly secularized papal power in the semi-autonomous south. Such tensions as existed between the papacy and the French throne were due, as they always had been, to the assertion by the "eldest daughter" of some autonomy in matters Gallican, including the right to tax the clergy—and to criticize Rome. Pope Boniface VIII (1294–1303) was even accused of heresy by King Philippe IV of France. Later in the same century, however, France found itself siding with the Avignon papacy against the Italian and Pisan claimants in the Great Schism that began in 1378, and the following century was to be marked by the consolidation of "modern" central monarchical power in France, notably via Louis XI (1423–83).

In 1516, the year before Martin Luther published his *Ninety-Five Theses On the Power of Indulgences,* that marked the start of the Reformation, a Concordat established a division of powers between the King and the Pope. This sowed the seeds of French "Divine Right" absolutism and of one of the most violent periods of religious persecution in France during and after the period of Reformation and Counter-Reformation. It is here that the battle for secularism can be truly said to find its roots.

In France, the Reformation is associated with the name of Huguenot, by which French Calvinists came to be known. They numbered an estimated two million at their peak, or a little over 10 percent of the population, which is ten times more, in percentage terms, than today: a combination of persecutions and exile, as well as final outlawing at the end of the seventeenth century, kept their numbers down. Between 1562 and 1598 there were eight religious wars in France, the most notorious event of which were the massacres that began in Paris on St. Bartholomew's Day (August 24) in 1572 and lasted until the middle of the following month, killing over 100,000 Protestants in Paris and elsewhere in France. The perpetrators were pardoned the following year. Between the wars came various forms of monarchical protection: Francis I during the early part of the century; Edict of Orleans 1561, three years after their first national synod; Edict of St. Germain formally recognizing them in 1562; and, most famously, the 1598 Edict of Nantes. This edict, signed by so-called good king Henri IV, a Protestant who converted to Catholicism to marry Marguerite de Valois ("Queen Margot"), of the Medici family, and to accede to the throne, granted equality and a degree of religious freedom to the Huguenots but restricted further development of Protestant churches.

Under the absolutist reign of Louis XIV and the influential Cardinal Mazarin in the second half of the seventeenth century, Protestants were once again persecuted and the Edict of Nantes revoked in 1685, rendering Protestantism illegal. Jansenism, a dissident form of Catholicism deemed heretical by the Pope, was also outlawed, in 1712. Louis XIV also severely restricted papal control of the French Catholic Church with his 1682 Declaration of the Clergy of France, which encapsulated the principles of Gallican Catholicism. In fact, the latter has, curiously, played a crucial role in the development of French secularism, in providing a model for state regulation of religion.

But it is in particular the history of French Protestantism that is inextricably tied to the history of French secularism. Perhaps more than anywhere else, Protestantism in France remains symbolically associated with the "protest" through which it originally got its name, and those coming from a Protestant tradition are today among the most fervently attached to secularism.

The history of secularism is also tied, of course, to resistance by a rising bourgeois intelligentsia to the Catholic absolutism of the monarchy and associated political and economic power of the Catholic Church and the aristocracy, culminating in the 1789 Revolution. In other words, one form of nationalism, associated with a notion of individual citizenship and rights and secular worldly enterprise, emerged from, and in opposition to, another.

A series of laws passed in 1789 and 1790 confiscated Church property (representing between 10 and 15 percent of all French land at that time), abolished tithes, forbade the taking of monastic vows, and dissolved most existing ecclesiastical orders, with the exception of those providing care for the sick and teaching. The culmination of these laws was the Civil Constitution of the Clergy, adopted on July 12, 1790, which formally subordinated the Roman Catholic Church in France to the French state, wresting its control as much from the monarchy as from the Pope. These measures at first reinforced Gallican Catholicism, in that the Catholic Church did not disappear as national religion, but nonetheless fulfilled the revolutionary government's main aim of weakening the monarchy by removing its religious legitimacy.

At the same time, religious freedom was formally constituted as a right under "freedom of conscience," which, as we have seen, is the guiding principle of the 1905 law. Jews in particular enjoyed some measure of religious freedom for the first time in France; under Napoleon's rule, this freedom was extended elsewhere in Europe.

The true formal beginning of secularism occurred with the creation of the first Republic in 1792, at which time not only were remaining ecclesiastical orders abolished but registers of births, deaths, and marriages passed from the clergy to the municipality, marriage became a civil ceremony and divorce became legally possible. Even priests were given the legal right to marry. While secularization of schooling did not follow seamlessly, as it logically might have, the secularization of marriage had great symbolic importance. Also during this period, figures such as Condorcet, who looms large in the history of public secular schooling in France, were writing treatises on egalitarian public education and citizenship, including their extension to women, that provided the philosophical underpinnings for the measures that Jules Ferry was to introduce a century later (Condorcet 1791; Kintzler 1984; Badinter and Badinter 1990).

This Republican movement culminated in the so-called Jacobin Constitution of 1793, the name coming from the Club des Jacobins where the Jacobins first met. This constitution, while never applied, developed many of the more radical Republican principles that continue to serve as a reference to many today, and were regularly evoked during the debate over the first headscarves affair of 1989–90. Seen by some as a sort of proto-Communist movement, Jacobinism is, at worst, associated with authoritarian nationalism, and at best, with radical opposition to the power of the monarchy and the Church and intransigent defense of Republican values of freedom of conscience and equality for all—which at the time, of course, meant white men. The 1793 constitution's articles set out rights to freedom of expression and conscience, the right—and even duty—to resist oppression, equality before the law, the right of all to public education, access of all to property, the requirement for state assistance to the poor, and, of course, sovereignty and unity of *le peuple*. This last—which means "the people" in the sense of a national or citizenship group and is seen to be just as indivisible as individual rights—was a key concept in the formation of French so-called political nationalism.

The battle against the duo of Church and monarchy was accompanied by a battle on another front, which would be similarly important to the creation of the modern Republic and its centralized education system. The fight against regional identities, already begun under Louis XIV's absolutist regime in the seventeenth century, was given legislative shape in 1790 with the creation of the modern *départements* (administrative divisions), designed to break up the unity of regions and thus their identity, with the consolidation of national power as a result (Ozouf 1984, 27ff). The breaking up of regional identities was also increasingly linked to undermining the oppositional power of the Church and the aristocracy, given that the counter-revolutionary movement found a great part of its strength in the linking—and mythicizing—of religious and Ancien Régime regional identities, as exemplified in the Vendée uprising of 1793–96.

Religion thus became tied up, as an oppositional force, with resurfacing regionalisms and the reethnicization of identity, and this connection continues today. Extreme-right politician Philippe de Villiers played extensively on the Vendée myth during his ephemeral career in the 1990s: blending aristocracy, rurality, and a "moral renewal" that was essentially based on Catholicism (Rechniewski 1995). Another extreme-right leader, Jean-Marie Le Pen, founder of the National Front, has made much of his Breton background, rural Brittany being another Catholic stronghold.

Napoleon Bonaparte nonetheless sought to make peace with the Catholic Church, which he rightly recognized as a formidable enemy, with the laws of 10 Messidor Year IX (July 15, 1801, the Concordat) and 18 Germinal Year X (April 8, 1802). The first reaffirmed Catholicism as France's major religion and restored some of its civil status, while still maintaining the balance of control in the hands of the French State. The second reestablished the Catholic Church in France.

Bonaparte was just as conscious, however, of the role of education in consolidating his new Empire. From the creation of high schools and student bursaries (law of 11 Floreal of Year X [1802]), as well as the first appointment in French history of a minister overseeing public education (1802), to the setting up of a secular university and teaching staff (laws of 1806 and 1808), Bonaparte's measures were designed to consolidate state power through training its governing, military, and intellectual elites.

The key to this was in the Grandes écoles system. The first of these had been set up as royal engineering schools in the mid–eighteenth century, with another two being set up in 1794 by the Convention, the first French government to be elected by universal suffrage of free men. The first of these was a civil engineering school, given a military status by Napoleon in 1805, and the second, the Ecole Normale Supérieure, trained future high school teachers to the level of the *agrégation,* which remains France's highest teaching diploma. The first Republican institutes of public education were thus training grounds for its elite, or, as Pierre Bourdieu was to put it in his well-known book of the same name, the *noblesse d'État* (state nobility) (Bourdieu 1989).

The more egalitarian purpose of state-run education as described by Condorcet faded into the background against these more immediate nation-building needs of Napoleon's empire. Public education took the shape it was to retain as the agent of reproduction and mystification of state power and the ideological premises on which it was built.

Ironically, the firm legal bases of free public schooling, and of today's relationship between state and private education, were established not during the revolutionary decade nor by Napoleon, but in 1833, under the July Monarchy (so named because of the month of an 1830 coup by Louis-Philippe, ally of the wealthy bourgeoisie, against his less liberal cousin Charles X).

The Guizot Law of that year required all municipalities of more than 500 residents to set up a school for boys (parliament did not vote for education for girls at that time and was to consistently reject it until the Ferry laws of the 1880s). It also, among other things, legalized private schools.

Also ironically, it was during the years of the Second Republic (1848–52) that the Church regained some terrain in the battle for control of education. Even though proposals put forward by Hippolyte Carnot, briefly minister for public instruction, foreshadowed the Ferry laws, the Falloux law, voted in 1850, established a partnership between Church and state in the delivery of education that endures today, notwithstanding the 1905 law. The Falloux law legally enshrined the principle of "freedom of education," expanding the role of the Church to delivery of secondary as well as primary education, so that state and church schools existed side by side. It also provided for public funding of up to 10 percent of the expenses of private schools. While "freedom of education" extended in principle to secular as well as religious private schools, in practice, private education was monopolized by the Catholic Church, and remains so today, just as the Falloux law has remained a reference for defenders of Catholic education, as well as, more recently, for advocates of state-approved Islamic private schools. Subsequent legislation has built on the Falloux law, such as the 1959 Debré law, which granted considerable funding to private schools in exchange for the obligation for them to adopt the curricula of public education and accept pupils and students "without distinction of background, opinions or belief." Catholic schools have willingly complied with this during the hijab debate, accepting a number of headscarved girls who had been expelled definitively from public schools, although these girls still had the right to study by correspondence under legislation that renders education both accessible and compulsory for all up to the age of sixteen.

The Falloux law notwithstanding, the role of public education in nation-building was by that time clearly established, in the minds of its Republican politicians at least. It was not till the first decades of the Third Republic, however, that secular public schooling was to attain its full status as the symbol par excellence of La République. President of the chamber of deputies Léon Gambetta declared in 1881, in a speech given at Honfleur, that education was "the cornerstone of social renewal" (cited in Burdeau 1979, 116). It was thus, as the heartland of secularism, also set to become the cornerstone of the Republic.

The Cornerstone and Its Contradictions

Claude Nicolet, historian of the French "Republican idea," as he terms it, has observed that "secularism remains the most original trait of French political history, but also its most burning and hotly debated contradiction" (Nicolet 1982, 484). The principle of secularism groups the three key ideas of Republican philosophy: reason, freedom of conscience, and equality. One might also add a fourth: national unity. It has often been noted that these concepts exist more in the dreaming than the doing, which is why "the Republican idea" is such a paradox. The formal "equality" guaranteed to citizens did not extend from the beginning to women, nonpropertied men, foreigners residing on French soil, colonized subjects, or slaves, and the fight by disenfranchised groups to achieve citizenship has been a long and difficult one. Even once achieved, citizenship does not confer equality, as has often been noted in relation to a variety of national contexts and discriminated groups. For example, France was until very recently just about the worst performer in Europe concerning presence of women in political office, and is still far from the best, notwithstanding Ségolène Royal's much-touted 2007 presidential candidacy. France's supposedly neutral "universality" has similarly been much criticized, for its universal pretentions were inscribed within a specific national framework: indeed, the term "nationalism" was coined in relation to France (Ozouf 1984, 76). As for freedom of conscience, its precise meaning and enactment have been not only at the heart of the headscarves debate but, historically, the battleground on which church and state, and before them, Catholics and Protestants, have debated their claims to the term "freedom."

Secularism is inhabited by three major contradictions. First, while it is supposed to enable the exercise of freedom of conscience, this freedom is only acquired at the price of submission to the authority of a state, that is, the Republic. Freedom of thought is not only a right but an obligation of citizens; it is acquired not merely through the exercise of individual will but through adherence to the values of the Republic and obedience to its laws. In fact, for the founders of the Third Republic, what was at stake in secularization of schooling was less the securing of individual intellectual freedom for citizens than need for citizens to be schooled in citizenship. It was only within the secular school system, where religious and other particularisms did not have right of entry, that the national identity of future citizens could be constructed.

Which leads to the second contradiction: the principle of secularism, which spearheaded the ideological and political battle against the power and dogma of the Church, became infused, under the Third Republic, with other dogmatisms. The inculcation of Republican morality took over where that of religious morality left off or, rather, was checked. If the 1789 Déclaration des Droits de l'Homme had become a "national catechism," to use Stéphane Rials' term (1988, 335), then secularism, and the principle of national unity with which it is inextricably linked, became the "Republican catechism."

This in turn leads to the third contradiction of secularism: however much it was meant to be the "refusal of transcendence," anchoring the minds of citizens-to-be in the terre-à-terre preoccupations of national identity and civic responsibility, it nonetheless was, and remains, in a permanent dialectic with the main institutional manifestation of that "transcendence," namely, the Catholic Church.[6] The secular Republic remains "the eldest daughter of the Catholic Church" and to this day has to accommodate the Church's power and influence, which, surprisingly, remains considerable, given that French Catholics are more lapsed than practicing (see chapter 3). France has 45,000 churches, of which 95 are cathedrals; while the estimated regular attendance rate is well under a third of those declaring themselves Catholic, and roughly

---

6. The term "transcendence," generally associated with religious belief (or with Kantian idealism) has an added political and sociological heritage in France. Auguste Comte, founder of positivism as well as of Western sociology (a term he coined in 1838), rejected "transcendence" as associated with the first, "theological," stage of human history, the second being the "metaphysical" (or humanist), and the third, highest stage being that of positive science, where value judgments are ostensibly not admitted and only observable facts are the basis of knowledge. Comte rejected the notion of the individual so central to French Revolutionary thought in favor of altruism, which, together with the notions of order and progress, formed the basis of positivist philosophy. His influence on the development of sociology in the nineteenth century was profound, and some form of positivist epistemology still underpins much work in social sciences and particularly economics today.

half of those who are officially Catholic never set foot in a church (*Quid* 2006), the clergy and lay Catholic groups are able to mobilize very quickly to defend their interests or oppose legislation perceived to be against them.

Contradiction 1: The Obligation to Be Free

Whatever the French Constitution states on the subject, the existence of freedom, in Republican terms, is not a given and certainly not acquired by the mere fact of being born on French soil or to French parents. Freedom is acquired through citizenship, and to become a citizen, one must learn how to be one within the secular school system, which fulfils, as Nicolet has put it, "the function of learning the rules of free thought":

> Thinking freely is a veritable exercise, with its rules and conditions: for, to think freely, one must think soundly. Hence the compulsory and indispensable education that can only be assured or supervised by the power that belongs rigorously to all, that of the State. (Nicolet 1992, 65)

Being a citizen of the Republic (or even resident of its territory, according to Rousseau), is both to incarnate the universal individual invested with "natural and imprescriptible rights" (*Déclaration des Droits de l'Homme et du Citoyen*, 1789, article 2), and to blend into the collective identity of the people, in turn identified with the nation-state. Article 3 of the Declaration of 1789 places sovereignty within the nation as a unified body. This shifted somewhat during the revolutionary decade: by the time of the Jacobin Declaration of 1793, sovereignty had passed to the people (article 25), to settle within the "universality of citizens" by 1795 (article 17), by which time "rights" and "duties" had also become separate headings. By 1946, with the formation of the Fourth Republic, sovereignty, and the guarantee of rights, are firmly back with the nation—or rather, the Republic—which for the first time is explicitly secular and includes women on an equal basis.

As the incarnation of "the people," the nation-state is at the same time its creator, as without the nation-state, "the people" cannot exist as a discrete group possessing inalienable, indivisible, and imprescriptible rights. The Republic thus becomes the mold out of which the identity, the values, and, indeed, the freedom of the citizen are fashioned (Nicolet 1982, 485). This shaping of individual identity and allegiance is of course, a primary function of nations, for without this molding of individual and collective consciousness, there would simply be no nation. That said, French secular nationalism has been, since the Revolution and especially from the time of the Third Republic, particularly strong and particularly imbued with a sense of its own mission to bring rights and freedoms to "man," which would later become, with the development of colonialist ideology, the much-criticized "civilizing mission." Long before Benedict Anderson (1991) analyzed the imagining of communities, France imagined the people as a collective and indivisible entity unified around a common political project in which the concept of rights featured centrally.

Just as the nation-state is the mold out of which the people are formed, the function of the law becomes not merely to "express the general will" (Declaration of 1789, article 6), nor even merely to interpret it, but also to determine it. The law protects rights, but also implies duties. Citizens of the Republic have a right to freedom (as defined by the state), but this right is not optional to take or leave. To be a citizen of the Republic, one is, paradoxically, *obliged* to be free. Citizens have rights, but they also have duties—including the exercise of their rights.

Freedom is thus only acquired at the cost of discipline. Which is why, to return to Nicolet's analysis, "Education constitutes one of the functions, if not the main function, of the city" (that is, in the ancient Roman sense of the city of citizens) (Nicolet 1992, 106). This philosophy of "freedom through discipline" comes through strongly in many of the positions taken in defense of an "intransigent" secularism during the years of the hijab debates, and perhaps nowhere more strongly than in one of the most well-known statements to have been made at the time of the 1989 affair: that of the so-called five intellectuals (Badinter et al. 1989; see chapter 4).

Contradiction 2: Secularism as a "Republican Catechism"

To be free, one also needs to be a citizen. And to be a citizen, one has to learn one's "citizenship catechism." This role of schooling was paramount in the construction of the Third Republic via the formation of Third Republicans. Napoleon had wanted a well-trained elite class to build and then administer the empire, but Ferry had his mind on the Republic's citizenship mission at home and its civilizing mission in the colonies. The model citizen needed to be trained well, and trained young, at least as early as kindergarten, and even before:

> It is education that must give souls their national form, and so direct their opinions and tastes that they are patriots by inclination, by passion, by necessity. A child, on opening his or her eyes must see his or her country, and until death must only ever see that country. All true republicans suck, with their mother's milk, the love of their country, that is, of laws and liberty. (Nicolet 1982, 352)[7]

To properly perform this work of orienting miniature Republicans in their country's direction, school must have a uniform syllabus at all levels and in all areas. No particularism in Republic school: national identity is one-and-indivisible or it is nothing at all.

All of which, of course, apparently contradicts the conception of individual freedom as it appears in liberal thought generally and French Enlightenment thought in particular. This freedom, however, not only requires discipline, as we have seen above, but also has its limits. Article 4 of the Declaration of 1789 defined freedom as enabling one to do whatever does not harm others: those limits to freedom are determined by the rule of law. This is the social contract defined by Rousseau in his work of the same name (1762). Social-contract liberalism requires one to do right by one's fellow citizens; thus, citizens make a pact to respect each other's rights. Such a pact has, of course, been based on the separation of public and private spheres as well as on the conceptualization of the individual as male, both of which have disastrous consequences for women—and not accidentally so, as a wealth of feminist scholarship has pointed out (for example, Okin 1979; MacKinnon 1983; Pateman 1988).

Within the public sphere, however—that of politics, education, justice, employment, and business—the social contract applies. To exist socially, the free individual/citizen must accept certain constraints, and these are

---

7. The word "patrie" is used for "country" in the original French. It literally means "fatherland," but without the fascist connotations it automatically has in English (although it does have the male-supremacist ones). Hence the commonly used alternative translation of homeland/country.

imposed by the state through laws. As Montesquieu wrote in *De l'Esprit des lois* (Of the Spirit of Laws), freedom consists of being able to do "everything that the laws allow" (Montesquieu 1748, 1:162). The state, as legislator, thus plays the key role not only in protecting freedom but in interpreting its very meaning. The French Republic, as founder of the modern idea of the nation-state, gives a particularly important role to the state apparatus in this area, which has given rise to quite specific manifestations of the tension between individual freedom (and the ensuing need for "tolerance") and collective good (and ensuing need for "discipline"), as has been evident throughout the hijab debate. Some defenders of the "tolerance" approach at the time of the 1989 affair, such as Harlem Désir, then president of the well-known antiracist group SOS-Racisme (see chapter 3), maintained that there was a need to "combine being as self and being as collective" (*conjuguer l'être soi et l'être ensemble*). The "intransigent" inheritors of the Jacobin ideal of the Republic retorted, with Maurice Bensayyag, that it was first necessary to "proclaim the being as collective before the being as self" (*proclamer d'abord l'être ensemble avant l'être soi*). In saying this, Bensayyag maintained that "one does not build a nation by glorifying the cult of differences" (Bensayyag 1989, 14). To be a citizen, one must be free. To be free, one must be a citizen. To be a free citizen, one must identify with the indivisible nation-people.

Which is why the Third Republic's schools taught, along with French, history, and geography, "morals" (ethics), civics, and the love of country (Prost 1968, 335–40; Baubérot 2004, 124ff). The elementary history manual of the time exhorts pupils to love the French Republic—"Republic and France, these are, my children, the two names that must remain engraved in the deepest recesses of your hearts"—and to be proud of it—"be rightly proud, you, children of the great French homeland" (Guiot and Mane, cited in Ozouf and Ozouf 1984). Even if this patriotic fervor has disappeared from today's school manuals, "morals" and civics are still taught—which is not altogether a bad thing, as children learn about the parliamentary system for example, and hold mock parliaments in primary school. Of course, all national education systems inculcate national ideology in their pupils and students; this is, after all, one of their primary functions. That said, the French secular school system has played, and continues to play, a particularly important role in the construction and internalization of the idea of citizenship of the Republic.

Contradiction 3: Secularism as Heir of Religion

Faced with the strength of Christian tradition, the Republic-daughter-of-the-Church was obliged to incorporate elements of Catholicism even as it rejected the latter's ideological foundations. We saw earlier that the institutions of Gallican Catholicism have informed the post-Revolution articulations of state-church relations. We have also seen above that the rhetoric of the Republican "catechism," particularly in the first decades of the Third Republic, recalls a religious zeal. The Catholic legacy is further felt, however, in institutions and laws such as those relating to marriage and the family as well as the organization of the Republic's calendar and of social life around Catholic festivals (out of ten public holidays in France, six are Catholic). The school system does not escape this influence; even today it bears the traces of the agreements made between the state and the Church. Some of these, like the midweek no-school day (only still fully observed in primary schools), originally to enable priests to hold catechism classes in schools but outside formal school hours, are fairly innocuous remnants. Others, such as continued state funding of private schools under the Falloux law, are much less so, and seriously undermine the idea of state education as a secular space.

Even the Napoleonic Concordat lives on in the twenty-first century. The Alsace-Moselle region, when it was taken back by France after World War I, was not subjected to the 1905 law—part of the reasoning being that it had not been French at the time that law was adopted—but was granted a specific status governed by the terms of the Concordat. This special status of Alsace-Moselle (including payment by the state of clergy's salaries), along with the existence of the Falloux law, has been used as an argument for a specific status for Islam in France. There was even a bill of law introduced into the National Assembly on June 28, 2006, by François Grosdidier (UMP), to this effect: to "integrate the Muslim faith into the Concordatory law of Alsace and Moselle."[8] The UMP is the Union pour un Mouvement Populaire, formerly named Union pour la Majorité Présidentielle, the successor to Jacques

---

8. http://www.assemblee-nationale.fr/12/propositions/pion3216.asp.

Chirac's Gaullist party Rassemblement Pour la République (RPR, Rally for the Republic). Chirac's successor as president, Nicolas Sarkozy, is UMP. It is the main right-wing party; until 2007 it formed a parliamentary coalition with the center-right Union pour la Démocratie Française (UDF). (Following the 2007 legislative elections, won by the UMP, the parliamentary political landscape has been reconfigured, with Sarkozy naming a number of former Socialist Party politicians, as well as centrist politicians, as ministers, and the UDF and other centrist groups now coming under the umbrella of the MoDem [Mouvement Démocrate], founded by François Bayrou, former major player in the hijab debate [see chapter 5] and third major contender for the presidency in 2007 after Sarkozy and Ségolène Royal.)

It is, however, at the level of ideology and rhetoric that the consequences of the Catholic legacy are the most problematic for secular schooling. Nicolet has called secularism the "spiritual power" of the Republic (1992, 65). During the 1989 headscarves affair, this "spiritual power" was much in evidence. Laurent Joffrin, in a reply to Harlem Désir's "tolerant" position, asserted that "religions do not have a monopoly on faith." For Joffrin, "the prohibition that frees," namely, the prohibition of religious insignia, constituted irrefutable proof of Republican "faith": "Without this, [religious] believers would never believe that we also believe in something" (Joffrin 1989, 35). Nation has replaced Church, the Declaration of the Rights of Man has replaced the Bible, the law has replaced the gospel, and secularism is the key element of the Republican catechism. Some, like Jean Lacouture and Jean Daniel (the latter being then editor of the current affairs weekly *Le Nouvel Observateur*), even saw the quasi-religious rhetoric within some of the pro-secularism statements as a kind of "secularist fundamentalism" (Daniel 1989a, 32).

Among the many opinion statements and analyses published in the French press during the 1989 affair, it is, once again, the statement by the five intellectuals that is the most striking manifestation of "Republican faith." In a tone as reminiscent of Sunday sermons as it is of the speeches of the revolutionary decade, the authors evoke the force of spirit necessary to fight the battle for secularism. They point out that the Republic also has its morality, with the rigors and constraints that this implies. When then education minister Lionel Jospin evoked a famous slogan from the May 1968 student and worker uprisings, "Forbidding is forbidden" (*Il est interdit d'interdire*), in stating that it "Exclusion is excluded" (*Il est exclu d'exclure*), the five intellectuals replied (their italics) with a phrase attributed to Mohammed Harbi: "*Forbidding is permitted*" (*Il est permis d'interdire*) (Badinter et al. 1989, 31). Such prohibition even represents, for the five intellectuals as for Joffrin, the road to freedom, necessitating its own discipline and sacrifices, as they state in crusading terms:

> Secularism is and remains by definition a battle, as are public schooling, the Republic and freedom itself. Their survival imposes discipline, sacrifices and a little courage on us all. No one, nowhere, defends citizenship by benevolently throwing in the towel. (Badinter et al. 1989, 31)

As another well-known intellectual, Bernard-Henri Lévy, put it, in a reply to the five intellectuals: "I don't see any reason . . . to go off on a crusade like this" (Lévy 1989, 18).

If secularism is a Republican invention, the idea of a liberating discipline and a salutary sacrifice come to us straight from the Bible: the road to salvation is the road of difficulty (Matthew 13–14). Except this time, the crusade is for the freedom of the people and the identity of the nation; it also recalls the colonial "crusade" to export the Revolution and later, to carry out the Third Republic's self-named "civilizing mission." France, "soldier for humanity" (as then prime minister Georges Clémenceau put it in a speech to parliament on November 11, 1918), fights not only to defend citizenship, but also to preach it. Clémenceau used this expression in his victory speech to parliament with reference to the returning soldiers: "Through them, France will regain her place in the world to pursue her magnificent course into the infinity of human progress, once soldier for God, now soldier for humanity, forever soldier for the ideal."[9]

A secular mission remains nonetheless a mission, with all the moral connotations that the term presupposes. The French nation must serve as a beacon to illuminate those who remain plunged into darkness. Such rhetoric, so prevalent in colonial discourses of the early decades of the Third Republic (and indeed in Clémenceau's 1918 victory speech), is equally abundant in the passionate arguments for secularization of schooling, then as now. The

9. http://www.senat.fr/evenement/archives/discours2.html.

reward for the crusaders of the Republic is no longer eternal salvation but "infinite human progress." It is no longer God but reason that will deliver us. Secularism thus appears as a "civil religion" in the Rousseauldian sense, as Baubérot, among others, has argued: it is the faith of each citizen that makes that citizen a willing and dutiful participant in the collective project (Rousseau 1762; Baubérot 2004). It is a new form of transcendence.

Hence the paradox. For, even if the Revolution was far from closing the religious chapter of French history, it did turn an important page, setting off the process that culminated in the 1905 law. Even if the Republic is on a mission to "convert," its "faith" is not mystical, not connected to a power that sits above and outside humanity, but is of the world and humanist. Christianity is thus at the same time a founding element and the main enemy of secularism. The relationship between French secularism and Catholicism is more complex than one of a simple diametrical opposition, even if that opposition is clearly present. It is also a relationship of co-optation, of reformulation, of compromise. It is both dialectical and equivocal.

"Ecumenical Secularism"? Or, *Plus Catho-Laïque que Moi, Tu Meurs*

"No one gets to out-*catho-laïque* us." This could have been the mantra of Napoleon, or Falloux, had they spoken that way. And no doubt it was the mantra of the more than a million people who demonstrated in Paris for *l'école libre* (that is, private schools) in June 1984, against then Socialist education minister Alain Savary's plan to establish greater state control over private schools. This protest led to a government backdown and resignation a month later of the entire government led by then prime minister Pierre Mauroy (Leclerc 1985; Teese 1986).

It certainly could have been the catchcry of RPR (right-wing) education minister François Bayrou in 1993, the year before he issued the famous "Bayrou circular" of 1994 on "ostentatious" religious insignia in schools (see chapter 5). In 1993, Bayrou put forward a bill to enable municipal governments to raise funding to private schools for the construction and maintenance of premises above the 10 percent limit decreed by the 1850 Falloux law. The bill was adopted by the assembly but on January 15, 1994, the provision removing the cap on funding was deemed antiequality and thus anticonstitutional by the Constitutional Council. That ruling occurred the day before a one-million-strong demonstration against the law—a sort of "symbolic revenge" against the 1984 demonstration (Baubérot 2000, 115).

It might also have been the mantra of the mayor of Lièvremont (and also Senator), Jean Pourchet, of the center-right party UDF. In 1992, in this small town in a region close to Alsace, primary school teacher Claire Bretin removed a crucifix from the wall of her classroom, where it had been installed by the mayor, as she rightly deemed its presence to be incompatible with the religious neutrality of the school environment. The mayor had it replaced on the wall. The teacher appealed to her union, the Socialist-aligned Confédération Française Démocratique du Travail (French Democratic Work Confederation, CFDT), which carried out enquiries in the region and discovered crucifixes in other schools. It requested of central school and government authorities that these crucifixes be removed. The story hit the national press—and was perhaps timed to do so—just after the release of the 1994 Bayrou circular on "ostentatious religious insignia" in schools (see chapter 5). Various excuses were found by local government and Catholic representatives: the region, which had been very loyal to the Catholic clergy during the Revolution, remained deeply Catholic; it was heavily populated by Swiss immigrants, who were used to having crucifixes in schools; the crucifixes were considered part of the area's cultural heritage and removing them would push the local community into identity politics, this last being an already familiar refrain in the hijab debate. The region's archbishop, Monseigneur Daloz, was of the opinion that "of course, the law should be respected everywhere, but gently, taking into account local specificities" (cited in *Le Figaro*, September 22, 1994). A month later, Pierre Kahn and André Ouzoulias, two philosophy professors from a primary-school teacher-training college in Versailles, published an opinion piece in the daily *Libération* on the necessity for equal treatment in cases of hijabs and crucifixes and advocated "dialogue" as the best solution to ensure a gradual passage toward full application of secularism (*Libération*, October 24, 1994).

Or "Plus catho-laïque que moi, tu meurs" could have been the slogan of the parliamentary right in 1999 (then in opposition), when it voted against the Civil Solidarity Pact (Le PaCS), the civil union law put forward by deputies from the Socialist Party, then in power (and subsequently adopted). The PaCS does not apply solely to homosexual unions nor does it confer the same rights and obligations as marriage. In particular, *pacsés* (those having entered into a PaCS), are prohibited from adopting children. It was nonetheless heralded as a "gay marriage" law, and Catholics were stridently opposed to it. When opposition deputy (member of Parliament) Roselyne Bachelot crossed the floor to vote for the law with the government, she was subjected to a vicious Catholic hate campaign (Bachelot 1999). In fact, apart from the issue of schooling, it is in the areas of family and sexuality that right-wing Catholics are the most actively and sometimes violently hostile to secularism and indeed to individual rights, notably those of women.

The catho-laïque mantra certainly seemed to be in evidence among large sections of the political class when Pope Jean-Paul II died. On the day of the Pope's death on April 2, 2005, the UMP-UDF French government issued a directive that all French flags were to be flown at half-mast for twenty-four hours—which immediately led to an outcry from the left (the Socialist Party and the Greens, among others, issuing a statement of protest) and from sections of the media.[10] The somewhat spurious logic behind this directive was that the Vatican (Holy See) has the status of a state, and when a state leader dies, flags are flown at half mast. (The Vatican also, and for the same reason, continues to occupy a seat at the United Nations, and thus has voting rights in the General Assembly. This has long been the object of vociferous protests from feminist nongovernmental organizations.) A number of mayors refused the governmental directive and flew the flag as normal.

President Chirac attended the special mass for the Pope's passing in Notre Dame de Paris on April 3. A large banner showing a photograph of the Pope was displayed in front of the crucifix over the altar, and relay loudspeakers broadcast the mass to crowds gathered in the square in front of the church, giving the whole thing an aura somewhat reminiscent of a rock concert. Chirac was also much in the news after shaking Condoleezza Rice's hand at the Pope's funeral in Rome, as if this event were an indication that the Pope was responsible beyond the grave for healing the rift between France and the United States over France's nonparticipation in the 2003 Iraq war. As for then prime minister Jean-Pierre Raffarin, the Catholic daily *La Croix* published a piece by him titled "Le pèlerin exigeant de la liberté" (The

10. For example, *Le Canard Enchaîné*, Apr. 6, 2005.

Demanding Pilgrim of Freedom), in which he sang the praises of a Pope who was apparently the main mover and shaker in destroying the Communist bloc (this supposedly being an unequivocally good thing) and more generally uniting the world (Raffarin 2005). Unsurprisingly, Raffarin remained silent on Jean-Paul II's sympathy for the Opus Dei faction (less pronounced, however, than that of his successor Joseph Ratzinger, Pope Benedict) or for extreme-right regimes in South America, notably that of Pinochet in Chile. Raffarin similarly remained silent on the Pope's dreadful record concerning women's and homosexual rights.

A little over a year earlier, the same government was ardently defending the religious neutrality of public space and equality of all before the law, as it voted in its law against conspicuous religious insignia in schools.

The following year, even sections of the Socialist Party joined in the Popemania (or at least, Jean-Paul II-mania). On June 13, 2006, the Socialist-led Paris city government decided to change the name of the square in front of Notre Dame from Parvis Notre-Dame to Place Jean-Paul II, even though at the national level, the Socialist Party is an ardent defender of secularism and now advocates a much more intransigent line in relation to religious insignia in schools than the Socialist government had in 1989.

On one level, this name change could be considered to be part of a raft of place-name changes in Paris under openly gay Socialist Mayor Bertrand Delanoë that reflect a broad political sweep, including many nods to the history of feminism or even lesbianism in twenty-first century Parisian geography. For example, Paris now has a Place Olympe de Gouges (a small crossroads not far from Place de la République, it was renamed in 2004 in honor of the author of the 1791 Declaration of the Rights of Woman), a Place Renée Vivien (renamed in anticipation of the 2009 centenary of the death of a lesbian literary icon whose favorite color, purple, has become a universal lesbian color), and a Passerelle Simone de Beauvoir (a footbridge in the Bercy area erected in 2006). Even so, the renaming of such a highly visible and oft-frequented public place after a world religious leader was seen by many as offensively in contradiction with France's secular values, and it generated significant polemic.

The change of name occurred at a ceremony on September 3, in the presence of Delanoë and amid a demonstration called by, among others, l'Union des Familles Laïques, the Greens, Brigade Activiste des Clowns (an activist group that performs clown acts at demonstrations), feminist groups such as Ruptures, and a number of gay organizations such as Act-Up, Sisters of the Perpetual Indulgence (international organization of gay male "nuns"), and the Panthères Roses. Some demonstrators reported an unnecessarily aggressive police response and in particular, homophobic remarks.[11]

The repositioning of Catholicism in relation to secularism, or secularism in relation to Catholicism, or, perhaps more accurately, the state in relation to both, notably during the hijab debate, has been referred to by Baubérot as signaling the development of "ecumenical secularism," or even *catho-laïcité*— or *christiano-laïcité* at the European level (Baubérot 2004, 2005). Indeed, religion seems to be set to make a comeback in European public life with the reference in the controversial Lisbon treaty's Preamble to Europe's "cultural, religious and humanist heritage" (Sarkozy would have preferred "Christian" in the place of "religious"). It is perhaps ironic that one of Europe's staunchly Catholic countries, Ireland, was one of the few to put the treaty to referendum, resulting in the "No" vote that hit world headlines on June 13, 2008 (even if the Treaty's mention of religion was not what led to this vote).[12]

According to Baubérot, the development of "ecumenical secularism" has been in response to a disillusionment with the idea of progress and a "recentering of identity" within "retrogressive thought" (2004, 263). It is also a component of the so-called Franco-French response to an Islam deemed to sit uncomfortably with Republican values. For it is clear from the examples cited above that the same state that falls all over itself to be secularist in the face of Islam also falls all over itself to be Catholic in the face of Rome (Gallicanism notwithstanding).

Relations Between the French State and the Islamic Faith

Within the context of the debate over immigration, racism, the hijab, and "France's second religion" (Islam), the French state has made moves to

11. For example, a written statement by journalist and former member of the European parliament, Aline Pailler, dated Sept. 3, 2006. Forwarded to me by Monique Dental.

12. The full text of the Lisbon Treaty can be found at http://europa.eu/lisbon_treaty/full_text/index_en.htm.

regulate Islam and establish formal consultative structures via its establishment of a much-discussed French Council of the Muslim Faith (Conseil Français du Culte Musulman, CFCM).[13] On some levels, this fits in with a double Franco-French secular imperative: that of granting equal status to all religions and that of keeping a watchful eye and even a controlling hand over what religious organizations are doing. On other levels, however, it both ties in with similar albeit mostly more recent initiatives in other Western countries (such as the United Kingdom and Australia), within a so-called post-9/11 geopolitical context, and reflects France's ambiguous and often fraught precolonial, colonial, and especially postcolonial relationship with the Muslim world and diaspora. Many French political observers have commented, however, that the setting up of the CFCM has addressed a serious inequality between the treatment of other faiths and that of Islam in France, from the granting of building permits for places of worship to matters pertaining to schooling, funeral rites and places of burial, and so on (Sevaistre 2005). They have further commented that the CFCM regulates state relations with the Islamic faith and not French Muslims, and the two should not be confused (Alaoui 2005).

These formal moves have nonetheless occurred within the context of a philosophical and political debate over the compatibility or otherwise of Islam with secularism. The argument is often put, on all sides of the debate, that there is no separation of religion and state in Islam: *umma* has both the religious meaning of community of believers and the modern secular meaning of nation, that is, a political community organized around common laws, language, customs, history, economic organization, philosophical and political principles, and so on. Moroccan Islamic modernist scholar Abdou Filali-Ansary notes, however, that the fact that the same term has these two meanings does not denote any necessary or automatic link between the two in Islam (Filali-Ansary 2002, 28). Filali-Ansary also debunks the argument that Islam, not being organized into an official "church" with official leaders, has never needed secularism. In practice, Islam has always had its ulamas and its imams, who have exercised considerable sociocultural and sometimes

13. For an easily available example of the discussion on CFCM, see the dossier of articles on the subject in issue 23, no. 1, of *French Politics, Culture and Society* (2005).

political power (see, for example, Lazreg 1994 and Daoud 1996 on the political influence of ulamas in Algeria).

As I have argued elsewhere, religions do not exist outside human history and its political imperatives, and religious texts, however purist one attempts to be, are open to interpretation (Winter 2001a, 2001b, 2006a). In relation to Islam in particular, Leïla Babès has similarly argued:

> I do not think that the Koran has produced law: the latter is the result of centuries of human elaborations. It is not a pure emanation, exempt from borrowings. . . . Which is why Muslim law is positive law. The *'usúl al-fiqh* (foundations of law) have been constituted after the fact, to legitimize law and give it a sacred character by referring it back to the Prophet and his companions. (Babès 2004)

Filali-Ansary similarly notes that even if Islam shares with Judaism a series of prescriptions and proscriptions designed to regulate the lives of individuals (women in particular, I add in passing) and maintain social order (*shari'a* and *halakha*, respectively), nowhere in the Qur'an is there any suggestion that what is contained therein should be the basis for a political system (Filali-Ansary 2002). Moreover, as we have seen above in the case of France, at other moments in history the concept of separation of religion and state has been equally unthinkable in Catholicism, and indeed much *more* unthinkable than it is in Islam today. Filali-Ansary has even argued that even if Muslim nations "have not experienced secularization as an internal or autonomous move," there have been, as early as the eighteenth century, oppositional moves toward secularization within Muslim societies that were independent of Western influence (Filali-Ansary 1996, 79; 2002).

All of which also means that Islam, like Catholicism or any other religion, does not speak with one voice, and is no more intrinsically hostile to secularism than any other religion. This would appear self-evident, but it needs restating within the context of agitation in France over the compatibility of an apparently monolithic "Islam" with an equally monolithic "laïcité." Neither is monolithic, in fact (Baubérot 2004; Roy 2005).

At different times in its history, then, in different parts of the world, variations in compatibility between religion and state become evident. If religious fundamentalism is gaining prominence today (and not only within

Islam), this, argues Roy, is in part a function of secularization and of a failure of the secular institutional apparatus (state, laws, and so on) to claim the same degree of adherence in the wake of economic doldrums and political crises (Roy 2005, 117ff). Baubérot makes a similar argument with relation to religion-linked identity politics and the breakdown of national identities more generally (2004, 19ff). This, on one level, is not necessarily new: as we saw above, the Vendée counterrevolutionary movement linked regional identity and Catholicism. Moreover, as we saw in chapter 1, the very terms "fundamentalism" and "integrism" come from Christian sources. On another level, however, it *is* new, as the debate is no longer Franco-French or Euro-European. First, it involves a largely albeit not entirely postcolonial population that is racialized and enclosed within a "difference" that is constructed as irreducible even as state and other actors make much of its "integration" (see chapter 3). Second, it is linked, as both Baubérot and Roy note, with issues of globalization and European Union supranationalism, which have rendered possible the development of transnational ethnic and religious identities. Third, as I discussed in chapter 1, Islamism is an international phenomenon (French Islamist organizations are discussed in chapter 3).

While the question of "Islam and secularism" is not—or should not be—synonymous with that of "Islam*ism* and secularism," discussions of a supposed need to reframe secularism to accommodate "France's second religion" tend to arise with relation to Islamist expressions of Islam and not others, as is demonstrated by much although certainly not all of material produced by the quite prolific association Islam et laïcité. Set up in 1997 by, among others, Alain Gresh, as part of the Ligue de l'Enseignement (Education League), an association for the support of public secular schooling in France, Islam et laïcité was created with the precise brief of discussing the presence of Islam within secularist France.[14] Yet Islamist or even more broadly revivalist expressions of Islam in France are far from representative. François Grosdidier's bill to extend the Alsatian Concordat to the Muslim faith does not correspond to a majority demand among French Muslims, and were a referendum on this bill to be conducted among all French citizens and residents who identify as Muslim, it is unlikely that the majority would vote

14. http://www.islamlaicite.org.

in favor of the proposal. Even French Islamist movements that may be seeking greater Concordat-style "flexibility" in French secularism are not for the most part integrist, as I noted in chapter 1; that is, they do not seek religious control over the state and do not even seek political representation (Roy 2005, 118ff). Political participation of this sort in the West is not their concern at this point in history: their concern is to ensure that they have enough maneuvering room and influence within the secular state to enable them to wield religious power within their communities. In this, their agenda is not dissimilar to that of the 48 percent of "hard-core" Catholics surveyed by the ISSP. In the face of the secular state, their argumentation is thus usually articulated around greater "flexibility" within the secular school system, along with support for Islamic schools.

Technically, under the 1905 law and the 1850 Falloux law, mosques and Islamic schools are, or should be, regulated in the same way as Catholic churches and schools and have the same rights and freedoms. More broadly, Muslims have recourse to both UN and European human rights conventions on nondiscrimination, civil and political rights, and freedom of religion (to which the 2003 Stasi Commission also explicitly referred). On the ground, however, local practices have been idiosyncratic, leading to more concerted lobbies for equal access of the Muslim faith to freedom to practice and infrastructural support for doing so: as we will see in chapter 6, some of the Stasi Commission recommendations speak directly to this issue.

The first formal state response to these lobbies, apart from the already-existing and already-regulated Grand Mosque of Paris, closely linked to Algeria and inscribed within the "1905 tradition," was the establishment of a Council for Reflection on French Islam (Conseil de Réflexion de l'Islam de France, CORIF). CORIF was set up at the beginning of 1990, amid the polemic following the first headscarves affair of 1989, by Pierre Joxe, then minister for the interior with the Socialist government. It was composed of fifteen designated or co-opted members and had a double brief: to advise the government on matters pertaining to the exercise of the Muslim faith in France and to reflect on the setting up of a representative body for French Islam. After three years of meeting, CORIF's activities had resulted in only two concrete outcomes: provision for designated Muslim plots in French cemeteries and halal food for soldiers (Maurer 2005, 9; Terrel 2004, 72). The CORIF episode was generally agreed to be unremarkable both because of the relatively few outcomes and its lack of representativeness (Cohen 2001, 324; Hafiz and Devers 2005, 82). It nonetheless had the merit of opening the conversation concerning institutional representation of French Islam and formalization of dialogue between the Muslim faith and the state (Maurer 2005, 9).

CORIF Mark II was the National Coordination of French Muslims (CNMF), set up in 1993. Although supposedly made up of representatives of Muslim associations rather than government appointees, it was even more short-lived and ineffectual: it did not last the year out. The reason for this was the withdrawal of the Morocco-linked National Federation of French Muslims (FNMF; see chapter 3), which claimed that the CNMF gave too much voice and power to the Algeria-linked Paris Mosque (Hafiz and Devers 2005, 82). Following the demise of the CNMF, the Consultative Council of French Muslims (CCMF) was created, once more through government co-optation and still giving the Paris Mosque significant influence. It subsequently changed its name to the Representative Council for French Muslims (CRMF). This organization managed to publish, in 1994, a "Charter of the Muslim Faith in France," written by a group of intellectuals associated with the Paris Mosque. The need for a more broadly representative organization continued, however, to be felt, and, within the context of social unrest in the *banlieues* (suburbs) and the ongoing debate over the hijab, the government's need to regulate French Islam became ever greater (Hafiz and Devers 2005, 82–83). All the more because the right was now in power and the minister for the interior was the hardline Charles Pasqua (RPR), author of infamous 1993 laws on immigration and nationality (see part II).

In October 1999 began the process leading to the creation of the current CFCM, the official interlocutor of the government in matters Islamic. At that time, minister for the interior with the then Socialist government, Jean-Pierre Chevènement, set up a fairly representative consultative group of major mosques and Islamic organizations, along with some individuals deemed to have an authoritative voice (Hafiz and Devers 2005, 83; Maurer 2005, 9). The deliberations of this group led to the 2001 signing of an agreement setting out the structure and status of the future CFCM; the structure provided for election by representatives of mosques, the size of the congregation determining the weight given to the vote.

The first elections took place in 2003, under the auspices of minister for the interior Nicolas Sarkozy, with a participation rate of almost 90 percent, electing the membership of both the CFCM and 25 regional bodies. Elected members of the CFCM were FNMF, 18; Union des Organisations Islamiques de France (UOIF), close to the Muslim Brotherhood, 13; Grand Mosque of Paris, 6; Comité de Coordination des Musulmans Turcs de France (CCMTF), 2; Ile de la Réunion, 2; nonaligned Al-Islah Mosque of Marseille, 1 (Hafiz and Devers 2005, 86). The Fédération Française des Associations Islamiques d'Afrique, des Comores et des Antilles (FFAIACA) did not obtain a seat.

From the outset, the CFCM was the subject of some polemic over its composition, its representativeness, and its role. Its first two years were not particularly illustrious, and it struggled with a double brief that was at once administrative (halal abattoirs, yearly *hadj* or pilgrimage to Mecca) and religious (training of imams, appointment of Muslim chaplains in prisons and the army). As far as the regional bodies are concerned, some have successfully established a relationship with local government and administrative authorities, but others have not (Maurer 2005). In 2005, a second election took place, following vigorous campaigning, with an 85 percent participation rate. It was seen as a victory for the FNMF, which increased its representation to 19 seats, but so did the Paris Mosque, with 10 seats. The UOIF dropped to 10 seats and the CCMTF to 1; the others maintained their seats. Dalil Boubaker, rector of the Paris Mosque, retained his presidency in what was seen as a coup for more secularist Islam against Islamist pressure, with the UOIF and the FNMF (see chapter 3) each retaining their vice presidencies.

The most recent CFCM election, at the time of this writing, was in June 2008, and saw, as widely predicted, the replacement of Boubaker as president by Mohammed Moussaoui, who is a mathematics professor at the University of Avignon as well as a local imam, and advocate of a "consensual" Islam (*Le Figaro,* June 22, 2008). Moussaoui, who was born in Morocco, is vice president of the Rassemblement des Musulmans de France (Rally for French Muslims, RMF), an organization founded in 2006 out of internal divisions in the Fédération Nationale des Musulmans de France (see chapter 3) and supported by Morocco. In a communiqué issued on June 14, 2006, this relatively new player on the French national Islamic stage affirmed that it wished to "contribute to the emergence of a moderate and tolerant Islam that respects the laws of the Republic, an Islam of the middle way."[15] According to the media, including Muslim media, the RMF may well be a "consensual" organization, but it is also an ambitious one, wanting from the outset to take over primary responsibility for training imams, deciding the start of Ramadan, and so on. Mouassoui's election as president of CFCM and the new RFM majority with 20 seats seems likely to help realize these ambitions, although the UOIF remains influential with 13 seats and won the majority of the vote in the Parisian and Lyons regions. (The CCMTF won 4 seats, with one seat each going to the independent Musulmans des Antilles, Afrique et Comores, Algerian group, and Tabligh pietists, while the FNMF dropped to only one seat.)

The CFCM has been considered too "fundamentalist" for some and too tightly under the yoke of a "neocolonial" power for others (Fernando 2005; Maurer 2005). At the same time, it came into existence in response to lobbying by Islamic organizations themselves, and it is arguably no more nor less representative of French Muslims overall than Archbishoprics are of Catholics. It was reputed to have been beleaguered by the Algero-Moroccan conflict, but this seems set to change to a UOIF-RFM power play following the most recent election.

What the CFCM's role and influence will be long term is hard to predict at this stage. It has, however, already attracted trenchant criticism from pro-secular French Muslims:

> What is sure and certain is that integration will never be through the CFCM nor through the automatic attachment of this community with Islam. Of all communities, it is only this one that has been obliged to have religious representation. The silent majority . . . is much more representative, with its nuances and wealth [of experience and views] respectful of secular principles. This majority has been working for years, silently but efficiently, to overturn the order and to reduce this integrist and fanatical minority to silence. (Labidi 2004, 13)

15. Cited in a June 20, 2006, report by Muslim news Web site Saphir News. http://www.saphirnews.com/RMF,-un-nouveau-mouvement-musulman_a3672.html.

What is also "sure and certain," however, is that Islamist organizations, notably the UOIF (and in the background, Tawhid), and FNMF, have well and truly established themselves as a certain "voice of Islam" in secularist France, and they have done so, ironically, with the support of the French state.

3

French Muslims

Between "Integration" and "Muslimism"

THE DEVELOPMENT during the 1970s and 1980s of a postcolonial French population that had, now that the postwar boom was over, become associated with socioeconomic problems, gave rise to a sort of national identity crisis and concerns over "immigration," which were in part manufactured by the extreme-right party Front National and its leader, Jean-Marie Le Pen. Indeed, the economic recession and its associated social crisis provided the ammunition necessary for the extreme-right to regroup under the National Front's banner and rocket to a political stardom of sorts during the 1980s. Another key player in the 1980s debate over racism and immigration was the new national organization SOS-Racisme (from which the leadership of Ni Putes Ni Soumises—Neither Whores Nor Submissive—emerged two decades later), which mobilized hundreds of thousands of young people around racism and police brutality. It was, however, also much criticized for its closeness to the Socialist Party and was perceived by many as having co-opted and sanitized an already-existing antiracist movement.

Also gathering force within the context of the 1980s debate over racism and "integration," to emerge during the 1990s in particular, largely via the hijab debate, was French Islamism, represented by a number of organizations of varying radical or moderate tendencies. These organizations, most of which have links with Maghrebian Islamist groups, the Muslim Brotherhood, the Saudi-controlled World Islamic League, the Turkish Islamist group Millî Görüs, or with Hamas in Palestine, have been accused, with good reason, of manipulating and escalating the hijab debate and even of manufacturing it, much as Le Pen manufactured the "problem" of immigration.

Yet, many studies of the French hijab debate, notably most of those published in English, completely ignore or considerably downplay the role played by Islamist groups and their sympathizers within the debate (for example, Ardizzoni 2004; Scott 2005; Bowen 2007). Which is all the more reason to pay these groups some attention here.

Who Are "French Muslims"?

This is a less straightforward question than might be assumed, for two main reasons. The first of these is that disaggregation of census data by religious and political belief is prohibited under a 1978 law on "information technology and freedom," unless the person surveyed gives written consent (Kaltenbach and Tribalat 2002, 55). Estimates are thus extrapolated from survey data as well as existing census data about country of origin of immigrant populations, which have to be looked at in historical perspective, as a significant number of today's French Muslims were born in France. The second reason is that the term "Muslim" is polysemic: it can refer to a religious belief, to an ethnic background, or to an ethnic or cultural identification. Although these may often overlap, they do not do so systematically. Once again, a paucity of disaggregated data makes analysis difficult, but in this second case, there are little such data anywhere. In Muslim countries, given that in most cases there is no formal separation of religion and state, (a) there are unlikely to be demographic studies of degree of religious and cultural identification with "Muslimness," or (b) even if there were, respondents would be foolhardy indeed, in many national contexts, to respond that they were nonbelievers, as this could incur some degree of personal risk for them, ranging from social stigmatization to death. In non-Muslim countries, either the state assumes all Muslims to be religious (which is curious, because such assumptions are not made with relation to Christianity) or does not invest in research that might provide information about religious and ethnic identification. Fortunately, however—and despite the abovementioned prohibitions on census data—France is one country where a lively interest is taken in the degree of religiosity of its citizens, and a number of surveys, some small, some quite large, have provided some indications as to what "Muslimness" might mean. That said, as Kaltenbach and Tribalat have pointed out, many strongly expressed opinions about "French Muslims" by those participating in current debates are often just that: opinions, not facts, even if they are often expressed as certainties (2002, 55ff). Moreover, they argue, citing Franck Frégosi, that this "totalizing" tendency to categorize everyone into religious groups, on the part, I add in passing, of an ostensibly secular Republic, is part of a colonial strategy of group marking (Kaltenbach and Tribalat 2002, 56–57; See also Haut Conseil à l'Intégration 2001).

What we do know with relative certainty, however, is that France has one of Western Europe's largest Muslim populations and possibly the largest, in both numerical and percentage terms, and one of its oldest. Estimates vary considerably, however, and two of the lowest are provided by two surveys conducted in 2005 and 2007, the first by market research firm Ipsos and published on June 11, 2005, by Catholic daily *La Croix,* and the second conducted by the firm IFOP, for another Catholic publication, *La Vie* (published in issue 3209, March 1, 2007). According to these surveys, only 4 percent of France's population declared itself Muslim. According to the government's national immigration Web site, France's Muslim population has remained relatively static since 1994 at five million, a figure confirmed by the 2007 edition of the yearbook *Francoscopie* (Mermet 2006).[1] The reputable yearbook *Quid* puts the figure higher, at 5.98 million or roughly 10 percent of the French population.[2] This is not inconceivable, as France has Western Europe's highest birthrate and its fastest-growing population, with some suggestion that populations that are ethnically Muslim are the main driver of this. The ethnically Muslim percentage of the population is estimated as being significantly higher among the under-25s. Most Muslims also live in the Parisian region (which corresponds to immigration destinations).

Whatever the exact figure, however, even the most conservative estimate securely places Islam in second place among France's religious or cultural traditions (observed or not), although it is still well behind Catholicism, identified as the religion of an estimated forty-five million people in France. Next in line after Catholicism and Islam is Protestantism (between one and

1. http://www.histoire-immigration.fr.
2. http://www.quid.fr.

two million), with Judaïsm and Buddhism following. Survey figures cited in the 2005 and 2007 editions of the yearbook *Francoscopie* place France's Jewish population at a little under one million—Europe's largest—but the author notes that "Jewish" is as much if not more an ethnic category than a religious one (Mermet 2004, 2006). But then, so is "Muslim," as we will see. Only 15 percent of French Jews are regularly practicing and most of these are of Sephardic (Maghrebian) background. Forty percent identify as secular or atheist (Mermet 2006, 253).

France also has the most diverse of Europe's Muslim populations, and the most closely linked with the history and prehistory of European colonialism, as well as, for some, with the French ideal and practice of political asylum. As an indicator of background, according to the 2004 Census of the Institut National de la Statistique et des Etudes Economiques (INSEE), 8.1 percent of France's population, or 4.9 million people, are born overseas, and of these, half are now women (a balance reached for the first time in 1999, as opposed to 45 percent in 1946), mainly because of family reunion immigration. While 35 percent of immigrants come from other European Union countries, the largest single national group comes from Algeria (almost 14 percent), followed by Morocco (roughly 12.5 percent), and Portugal (roughly 11.5 percent). Tunisian and Turkish immigrants each represent roughly 4.5 percent of the immigrant population, with the Turkish group now being slightly higher. Sub-Saharan African immigrants are now 570,000 or 12 percent of all immigrants, an increase of 45 percent since 1999, although still only around 3 percent of the total diasporic population worldwide. Seven out of ten sub-Saharan African immigrants come from former French colonies, most of which are Muslim, but to date this population has not figured at all in the public debate over Muslim identity in France. Most of the remaining immigrants come from Asia, representing 14 percent of the total. INSEE includes Turkey in the Asian group, which is interesting, given Turkey's application to join the European Union. Other Middle Eastern countries, including Iraq, Iran, and Lebanon are also included in the Asian group. Turks are the only "Asian" immigrants numbering more than 2 percent of the total immigrant population. Of the 250,000 immigrants from Eastern Europe, a tiny percentage would be Muslim.

Significantly, those born in Algeria, Morocco, Tunisia, and Turkey have the highest unemployment rate: at over 20 percent, it is almost triple the average for nonimmigrants, the rate for Algerians being the highest and for Tunisians being the lowest. Sub-Saharan African unemployment rate is also, at slightly under 20 percent, higher than the immigrant average of roughly 16.5 percent (Tavan 2005; Borrel 2006).

A great many French Muslims today, however, particularly of Maghrebian and most particularly Algerian background, were born in France, although roughly three million remain nonnaturalized immigrants (Mermet 2006, 251). Most French Muslims are postcolonial, although a growing number are not. This number, apart from immigrants and children of immigrants from Turkey, Iraq, Iran, Pakistan, and other nations not colonized by France, includes an estimated 60,000 converts, of whom many are presumed to be formerly nonpracticing "ghetto youth yearning for recognition" and as a result embracing Islamic identity politics (Mermet 2006, 251). Some estimates even go as high as 100,000 (Mermet 2002, 280).[3]

Over 90 percent of French Muslims are Sunni (compared to 85–90 percent worldwide), and most of these are Malekite, as they are of Maghrebian background: an estimated 60 percent of all French Muslims and over 30 percent of all immigrants. Sunni Islam has four schools of thought and jurisprudence, all named for their founders: Hanafism, the largest (45 percent of Muslims worldwide) and most liberal school, dominant in South and Central Asia, also practiced in Eastern Europe and present in many regions of the Middle East; Malekism, the second largest and the least reliant on the hadiths, practiced by 25 percent of the world's Muslims and dominant in North and West Africa; Shafiʿism, one of the more conservative schools, heavily reliant on the hadiths, dominant among Kurds and in Southeast Asia and also practiced in some other areas of the Middle East and East Africa; and Hanbalism, a very conservative branch practiced by less than 5 percent of the world's Muslims but disproportionately influential given that it is dominant in the Arabian peninsula and in particular, in

3. See also http://www.portail-religion.com/FR/dossier/Pays/France/index.php; Haut Conseil à l'Intégration 2001.

the form of ultraconservative Salafi-influenced Wahhabism, in Saudi Arabia. (For more detailed information on the development of the four schools, see Coulson 1964.)

Malekite jurisprudence refers, instead of the hadiths, to the custom and practice of the people of Medina, the Prophet's residence during the period of the *hijra* or *hégire* (flight from Mecca), as "living sunna." Imam Malik, the founder of the Malekite school, is also reputed to have been scrupulous in authenticating sources. This, in combination with the limited reliance on hadiths, is no doubt the source of a fairly widely held opinion that the Malekite school is one of the most purist and least fanatical. From this point of view, it is thus somewhat odd that it is the supposedly "least fanatical" Muslims of Maghrebian Malekite backgrounds who have been the object of national debates about immigration, "integration," racism, culture, and religion. It is all the more peculiar as it is Maghrebian-background Muslims, especially of Algerian background, that are the most "integrated" into French society and customs, as we will see presently.

As indicated earlier, figures on the French and religion are somewhat rubbery, especially when one takes into account people's actual adherence to religious faith. The percentage of survey respondents claiming to be nonbelievers, agnostics, or "without religion" ranges from under 20 percent to over 50 percent, depending on the survey. The yearbook *Quid* extrapolates the following information from surveys conducted in 2003 (in particular one by the CSA Institute, based on a large sample of 18,000 people) and 1994 by market research companies in conjunction with the press (the 1994 figures are in parentheses, and the italics are mine):

- religious belief (as percentage of people surveyed): Catholic 62 (67); *no religion* 26 (23); Muslim 6 (2); Protestant 2 (2); Jewish 1 (1); other 2 (3); no opinion 1 (2)

- religious practice: attendance at religious ceremonies more than once a week 13 (12); once a week 9 [Catholics 11, Muslims 27] (12); once or twice a month 7 (6); occasionally, for specific festivals 24 (23); only for ceremonies such as marriage, baptism 10 (7); *never* 47 (48)

Results for nonbelievers and nonobservance of religious practice are mostly not disaggregated by religious faith, although a large survey conducted by CSA in October 2006 and published in *Le Monde des Religions* in

January 2007 indicates that of the roughly 50 percent of French people that identify as Catholic, only one fifth are actually believers (CSA 2006).

Similarly, a 2004 survey by market research company IFOP estimated that 44 percent of French people do not believe in God, as against 20 percent in 1947.[4] Even those who do are unlikely to be practicing, and the younger the age group, the greater this tendency becomes. Another survey conducted by IFOP for the Catholic daily *La Croix,* in July 2006, showed that only 4.5 percent of Catholics attend weekly Sunday mass, and they are very unlikely to be young.[5] Moreover, Catholics are, unsurprisingly, overwhelmingly concentrated in rural areas.

One can thus reasonably assume that roughly half of the French population today does not engage in any religious practice whatsoever and of those, at least half, possibly more, do not believe in any religion. Demographers and sociologists have further noted an individualization of religious belief and practice, with an increasing diversity of modes of expression; some link this to a more general preoccupation with a search for individual identity and autonomy (Kaltenbach and Tribalat 2002, 57; Mermet 2004, 265–66). More importantly perhaps, especially for discussions of what constitutes "Muslimness," declaration of religious identification is not necessarily an indicator of either religious belief or religious practice, but rather an often hybridized cultural or customary identification (Wihtol de Wenden 2005). As some prominent Muslims put it: "One can be 'born Muslim' and choose to be atheist." (This sentence is the title of themed issue 31 of *Prochoix,* 2004, with contributions by Ibn Warraq and Taslima Nasreen as well as by a number of French Muslim intellectuals.) Moreover, close to 70 percent of those who identify as Muslim, whether believing or not, or practicing or not, consider the separation of church and state to be important, and some of those supported the 2004 law (Winter 2006c). According to data extrapolated from surveys, only around 42 percent of Muslims declare themselves to be believers, which is on the increase since 1994, but 70 percent claim to have fasted during Ramadan (Mermet 2002, 280). Religious identification is particularly strong among young Muslims, in an opposite trend to that of

4. http://en.wikipedia.org/wiki/Demographics_of_France#Today.
5. http://www.ifop.com/europe/universite/un_fr.htm.

young Catholics. It is also strong among blue-collar workers; it is highest among the unemployed (Mermet 2004, 271). Once again, this is the opposite of the trend among Catholics, which suggests a definite link between class, race, and religious identification. Some even note that among younger French Muslims, religiosity is becoming the new ethnicity (Khosrokhavar 1997; Djavann 2004; see below). Sex-disaggregated data are harder to come by for Muslims than for Catholics, but according to *Francoscopie* 2005, more men than women declare themselves to be Muslim (6 percent of the total French population for men as opposed to 5 percent for women), which is, once again, the opposite of the case for Catholics (60 percent as opposed to 65 percent) and Protestants (1 percent as opposed to 3 percent) (Mermet 2004, 271).

More generally, the data suggest that religious categories are national, historical, or cultural as much as religious or even, in some cases, ethnic, and not by themselves illuminating as concerns the debate over the relationship between "Muslimness" and hijab-wearing in France. The statement that there are six million (or five million, or seven million) Muslims in France is, within the context of this debate, more opaque than revealing. The intensity of the polemic over Islam in France indicates that there is a need for further wide-ranging surveys of sample populations of Muslims that are more statistically significant than a few hundred or couple of thousand people and that are disaggregated and cross-referenced according to ethnicity, national background, class, age, sex, sexual orientation, geographical distribution, political persuasions, religious beliefs and practice, education levels, and whether born and educated in France or not.

The largest relevant study done to date, conducted in 1992 by demographer Michèle Tribalat for the Institut National d'Etudes Démographiques (INED), did not specifically concern Muslim populations but immigrant populations in general and their descendants (Tribalat 1995). It is nonetheless useful for our discussion here, in particular because it is one of the rare large studies to discuss religious belief and practice among Muslims in any statistical detail. The study surveyed 13,000 people of immigrant background, and one of its findings was that young French people of Algerian background in particular were just as indifferent to religion as young French people of European or Catholic background (Tribalat 1995, 93–98, 217).

Another study of this type would be needed today to see if this remains the case, although Tribalat and Jeanne Kaltenbach, in referring several years later to this survey, noted that these data had not so far been contested by smaller polls conducted by private survey firms (Kaltenbach and Tribalat 2002, 19).

More research on converts is also needed, given the visible presence of converts within the hijab debate, whether as protagonists (three expulsions in 1999 concerned converts or the children thereof), as commentators (female converts often turn out for public debates on the hijab question, where they are almost always the most conservatively dressed and generally adopt the most purely religious arguments), or as "advisers" (some key Islamist agitators during headscarves affairs, including the first one in 1989, have been converts).

A Long History

France's relationship with the Arabo-Muslim world, and in particular the Middle East and the Maghreb, goes back a very long way. It is a multileveled relationship—at once military, political, economic, sociocultural, intellectual, and artistic—and its power dynamics have shifted throughout the course of history. Certainly, the terrible weight that European colonialism has placed on modern history continues to be carried through the contemporary hijab debate in France and the other debates on national and ethnic identity, religion, women, and racism, of which the hijab debate has to a disproportionate extent become a symbol. It would, however, be as serious an error to ignore the historical shadow of precolonial or extracolonial interactions between France and the Arabo-Muslim world within the current debates, as it would to ignore that of the Franco-French history of the creation of the Republic and the battle for secularism. Likewise, it would be an error to ignore the Muslim world's own history of internal debates on modernism, tradition, secularism, and Islamic revival and Islamism, despite the common "it's not the same in the West" mantra deployed in the French hijab debate.

France has often been called "the most invaded country in Europe." One of those invasions occurred under the Umayyad dynasty, of which the power center was Damascus, during the period of rapid expansion of the new Islamic Empire. During its westward and then northward expansion into the Maghreb then Europe via Spain, the Umayyad army, led by Abd el Rahman, made it as far as what is now Vouneuil-sur-Vienne, on its way from Poitiers (in the Poitou region, south of the Loire valley), toward Tours, situated some 250 kilometers southwest of Paris in the Loire Valley. It was at this midway point, in 732, exactly one century after the death of the Prophet, that the Umayyad army was routed by the Frankish army led by Charles Martel, in what is known in French as the Battle of Poitiers and in English as the Battle of Tours (no doubt so as not to confuse it with the Battle of Poitiers in 1356, during the Hundred Years' War).

The first major contact between France and the Muslim world was thus military and involved an invasion of France, not the other way around. It did, however, set in train an interaction that has been marked by both cultural and intellectual exchange and political and military conflict ever since. From the Crusades in the eleventh century to the storming of Algiers by France in 1830 and the Algerian War of Independence some 125 years later, the conflicts have been significant and costly and have left an indelible mark on collective memory and consciousness on both sides of the Mediterranean.

In counterpoint, however, the intellectual and cultural exchanges have been rich and diverse. The most banal but frequently overlooked evidence of this today is in the large number of French (and English) words, many originally Europeanized via Spanish, that come from Arabic—from "algebra" to "orange." Behind this incorporation of vocabulary is, of course, an incorporation of new knowledge and new customs. A more complex and fraught legacy comes from the development of orientalism, which, despite its well-documented flaws leading to its bad name today (notably as popularized through the work of Edward Saïd [1978]), also comprised a significant body of scholarly erudition and cultural interaction. At a scholarly level, "orientalism" was once what would be called "Middle Eastern and North African Studies" today. That said, as many feminist scholars have noted, orientalism also came to operate as a political and cultural tool of nineteenth and twentieth century colonialism, one of its key aspects being the sexual fantasizing of Arab and Middle Eastern Muslim women.[6]

---

6. For an overview of the history and controversy over the "orientalism" debate, including polemic over Saïd's work, see MacFie 2000. For some feminist perspectives, see Brahimi 1984; Knibiehler and Goutalier 1985; Croutier 1989; Enloe 1990; Ahmed 1992; Lazreg 1994.

France and the Middle Eastern and (in particular) Maghrebian Muslim worlds thus have a love-hate relationship that is almost 1,300 years old. Even today, as the main former European colonizer of the Maghreb and Muslim sub-Saharan Africa, as well as of parts of the Middle East between 1918 and 1939, under the post–World War I punitive breaking up of the Ottoman Empire, France makes much of its "privileged" relationship with the Arab world.

It was within that already long-lived historical context that the French army stormed into Algiers on July 5, 1830, a move ordered by beleaguered monarch Charles X just weeks before he was overthrown by his cousin Louis-Philippe in the July monarchy coup, thereby commencing the colonial story that was to impact so significantly on today's postcolonial story of Islam in France. This is so for many reasons, the first being chronological. Algeria was the first Maghrebian colony of France (and indeed, its first Arab, or rather, Arabo-Berber, colony), and as such marked a beginning of a new era in Franco-Muslim relations, as they became from that point both inscribed within the nineteenth-century ideology and practice of colonization and materially present in France through the beginnings of immigration (Liauzu 1990, 65).

Second, Algeria was unique among French colonies in that from the outset, its colonization was imbricated with the project of nation-building in the *métropole* ("mainland" France) (Silverstein 2004). From 1848 when it was officially annexed and divided into three départements by the newly formed Second Republic, it was formally considered part of France, rather than a colony like any other. As such, it formed the object of a specific policy of settlement in ways that other colonies did not. This included land grants and other encouragements to settlers, as well as some deporting of French "undesirables"—although most of the latter, if convicted of an offense, went to penal colonies in New Caledonia or French Guyana. By the time of the start of the Algerian War of Independence (1954–62), there were more than one million white French in Algeria, constituting roughly 12 percent of the total Algerian population. In particular, the "expatriate" French Algerian population, known as *pieds noirs* (literally, "black feet," a term with obvious racializing connotations), comprised a significant number of poor whites, many of whom, by the time of the War of Independence, were several-generations-Algerian and some had never, or rarely, set foot on *la métropole*. At the end of the War of Independence, these pieds noirs were "repatriated" to a country they had never thought of as home.

"Algeria is France" became the official French battle cry for the French state during the war. François Mitterrand, later to become Socialist president in a landmark 1981 election victory, was minister for the interior in 1954. In a speech to the National Assembly on November 12 of that year, Mitterrand set the tone by stating that Algeria was France, that Algerian law was French law, and that the French nation, including the départements of Algeria and French overseas territories, was one and indivisible and would remain so. Tellingly, a survey conducted among 930 people by the glossy magazine *Paris-Match* in 1990, almost thirty years after the end of the war, found that over one-third of respondents considered the Algerian war to have been a "civil war" (cited in Stora 1992, 284).

Third, Algeria was for France a primary source of cheap labor in the post–World War II boom, known in France as the Trente Glorieuses (thirty glorious years), from 1945 to 1974. The latter date was when the French government, reacting along with other European governments to the first oil crisis, began to introduce restrictions to immigration known as the *fermeture des frontières* (closure of borders). During the Trente Glorieuses, recruiters from French industry conducted roundups of male workers in Algerian villages. Mostly illiterate and from rural backgrounds, these men became the unskilled workers in French factories, the human fuel that fed the boom. They were housed in dormitory-style lodgings built by a company created especially for that purpose, SONACOTRA (Société Nationale de Construction de logements pour les Travailleurs Algériens), a name that has become an evocative reference in the collective memory of Algerian-background French. It was a practice that continued even during the Algerian war and that was to extend throughout the Maghreb. Even at the end of the war, the Evian Accords (the treaty signed by France and Algeria) provided for 50,000 Algerian "temporary" workers per year to be recruited to go to France for three years, at the end of which they would presumably return to Algeria. Many did not, however, and in the twelve years between the end of the war and the *fermeture des frontières* the number of Algerian immigrants residing in France more than tripled, even though everything possible was done to discourage them from settling permanently (Benguigui 1997, 20). This included severe restrictions on family reunion migration, which created hardship for both the workers and their wives, who had no legal status in France except as spouses of (often naturalized) migrant workers. During the war, the Algerian workers that French companies had brought to provide cheap and docile factory labor were treated with suspicion and were subjected to both state-sanctioned and nonsanctioned violence, and police brutality was reported to be widespread, including the never-solved drowning in the Seine of a couple of hundred Algerians during a demonstration for Algerian independence in Paris on October 17, 1961.

Algeria might well have been "France" for Mitterrand and many others in 1954, but clearly, Algerians were not as French as white French.

Fourth, the Algerian war was to divide France and bring down the Fourth Republic. Its history, on both sides of the Mediterranean, is filled with silences and brutal internal repression of dissent, and remains a deep scar on the French collective psyche and that of its Algerian-background citizens (Stora 1992; Benguigui 1997; Silverstein 2004). Many white French were members and supporters of the FLN, many engaging in illegal resistance against the French government (Hamon and Rotman, 1979). In doing so, they called upon Jacobin notions of the duty of citizens to resist an unjust government, as in the case of the *Manifeste des 121* in support of those arrested for producing false papers and otherwise assisting Algerian FLN members. Many, however, were also avid supporters of *l'Algérie française*: a right-wing "Manifeste des intellectuels" was produced in opposition to the *Manifeste des 121* (Rioux and Sirinelli 1991).

The story of Algerian colonization also brought a new political connotation to an old term: *indigène*. The *indigènes* were the "native" Algerians, as opposed to the settlers (*colons*) or *pieds noirs*. The term, associated in English with the cultural affirmation and rights of peoples to self-determination, and positively connotated, is considered racist in French: it is a little like saying "the natives" in English. This term was to be used deliberately and ironically during the post-2002 rekindling of the hijab debate, to draw attention to French "neocolonial" racism (see chapter 8).

Among the many instances of physical and symbolic violence by the French state or the French military against the *indigènes* was the staged public unveiling, on May 13, 1958, of a group of women in Algiers, orchestrated as part of a demonstration in opposition to the by then foundering Fourth Republic by rebel right-wing generals opposed to Algerian independence. Naming themselves Committee for Public Safety, recalling the committee of the same name formed during the Revolutionary decade (1793–95) and associated first with Danton and subsequently with Robespierre and the Terror, these generals called for a return of de Gaulle to the political scene to save the day. This incident ended up being the final blow bringing about the downfall of the Fourth Republic and the creation of the Fifth, with de Gaulle at its head. Ironically for the rebel generals, de Gaulle and his government moved toward negotiation of independence, and the rebel generals subsequently formed the Secret Armed Organization, an extreme-right paramilitary organization responsible for some of the most violent acts of repression and torture against Algerian nationalists. Even though the unveiling was committed by rebel right-wing generals, it was experienced by Algerian women as an act of extreme symbolic violence by a colonial state that had hypocritically manipulated a discourse of women's "emancipation" to colonialist ends (Lazreg 1994, 135–37).

This unveiling incident was also evoked in the post-2002 hijab debate, by more or less the same people as those who were redeploying the term *indigènes,* which indicates that even though Algerian-background girls are probably the least likely of French Muslims to be donning the hijab today, the history of Algerian colonization remains an emotive historical reference in the French debate around race, ethnicity, religion, and national belonging.

At the same time, however, colonized men were also harnessing women to their anticolonial (and then postcolonial) nationalist project. Although women willingly participated in this, as they had a common interest with their "brothers" in getting rid of the colonizer, they were also subjected to considerable political blackmail in a nationalist cause that became synonymous with serving the interest of men and the latter's control over women (Hélie-Lucas 1990; Moghadam 1993; Daoud 1996). This scenario is not, of course, unique to Algeria: it has been played out time and again in anticolonial struggles and postcolonial nation-building, as it had been in colonial nation-building. It continues to be played out in diasporic situations, with the formerly colonizing state and men from postcolonial ethnic minorities once again vying to appropriate and instrumentalize women, through various forms of co-optation on one hand and political blackmail on the other, as is amply demonstrated throughout the hijab debate.

As a consequence of this colonial relationship, France's Algerian-background population is its biggest and oldest Maghrebian population, as well as being its most deprived socioeconomically (Tribalat 1995). It has also—at least until relatively recently—been its most problematized racially, particularly during the 1980s debates about "integration," which is curious, as Algerians are less likely than many other Muslim minorities to exhibit troublesome markers of "difference." We shall see in part II that few of the over one hundred hijab incidents in French schools leading to expulsions between 1989 and 2003 concerned Algerian-background French, and those that did, even if high profile, were relatively atypical, Algerians being France's most secularized Muslims.

Which is why a word of caution must be noted with relation to discussion of connections between the story of French Algeria—and Algerian France—and the hijab debate. It seems to have become almost de rigueur for scholars in the English-speaking world to evoke, often in passing and without much contextualization or historicization, the legacy of French colonization of Algeria and the Algerian war (and, more recently, the 2005 riots) in their discussions of the hijab debate, and vice versa, thus implying, willingly or not, some sort of direct connection between them (for example, Killian 2003; Jones 2004; Wing and Smith 2006). The association of the 2005 riots with the hijab debate is particularly puzzling, as the rioters, while largely of Maghrebian background, were male, not remarkable for their religious or Islamist connections, and certainly not clothed in hijabs. Socioeconomic exclusion is related to these riots, certainly, as is male violence. Islamic revivalism and hijabization, however, are not. Moreover, this is far from the first time that Maghrebian-background youths have died or been injured within a context of altercations with the French police or that such incidents have sparked riots, as we will see presently.

Elliptical and decontexualized references to the colonization and "postcolonization" of Algeria within discussions of the hijab debate have tended to create the impression that resentful postcolonized French descendants of formerly colonized Algerians have been suddenly turning to religion and the girls among them donning the hijab, and in doing so, have become the major protagonists of hijab affairs and drivers of the accompanying debate. This is, however, not the case. More accurate is the assumption that Algerian-background French have participated centrally in the surrounding debate, but in doing so, they have often—albeit not exclusively—come down on the side of secularism and against religious extremism. Discussion of French colonization in Algeria is certainly relevant, but its relevance is more to do with historical, socioeconomic, political, and symbolic framework setting of the French race debate more generally than with the positioning of Algerian-background individuals as key actors in the hijab events.

Finally, and significantly, as concerns the hijab debate, the history of the colonization, decolonization, and postcolonization of Algeria is also the history of colonized, decolonized, and postcolonized Arab and Berber Muslim women, of the ways in which they have been constructed by men on both sides of the Mediterranean as well as by white French women, and thus of their specific battles for a voice.

This is not to say that Tunisia and Morocco have not also been part of this sorry colonial and postcolonial story, but they were never considered to be part of France in the same way as Algeria, and their struggles for independence did not divide a European Republic in violent internal conflict, finally bringing it to its knees. Nor were Tunisia and Morocco painted in their apartment by Delacroix, even if today, Morocco in particular is more likely to be donning a hijab in French schools, we will see.[7]

The Postcolonial Problematization of "Muslims" in France

The 1974 "closure of borders" during the beginnings of the economic recession signaled the end of legal (but ostensibly temporary) work-related entry of

---

7. *Women of Algiers in their Apartment* (1834), by Eugène Delacroix, is one of the most famous orientalist paintings. It shows a rare "insider" view of Algerian women "at home" (Delacroix was actually invited into private rooms in a home in Algiers). Algerian Francophone feminist writer Assia Djebar famously gave this title to a series of short stories about Algerian women, during and after the War of Independence, and the anthology is post-scripted by Djebar's essay providing a feminist analysis of the Delacroix painting and Algerian women's voice or lack thereof (Djebar 1980).

non-French citizens, although 100,000 people per year continued to migrate under family reunion and refugee legislation. Many more entered illegally, and there have been periodic "regularization" initiatives such as that of the newly elected Socialist government in 1981, and that which followed the occupation of churches by illegal immigrants in 1996, although it has been noted that processing of regularization applications in the latter case has been slow. There were also, however, initiatives that moved toward further restriction, notably in 1984, 1986, 1993, 2003, 2006, and 2007, with further measures likely at the time of this writing. Many of these measures have impacted more significantly on women, such as increased requirements in terms of minimum income and size of accommodation for family reunion immigration. Moreover, the residency status of women who have migrated to France under family reunion legislation has depended on that of their husbands, as well as on them remaining married for a minimum period; this is also the case for foreigners marrying French citizens. This is despite directive 76/207 and 1986 and 1987 resolutions, of the then European Community, which provided for independent residency and work permits for immigrant women.[8]

Many have noted—among them Madjiguène Cissi, elected spokeswoman of the illegal immigrants who sought refuge in Paris's St. Bernard Church in 1996—that 1974 marked the start of the production of legislative and administrative documents and procedures that were to manufacture this new category of immigrants: the *sans papiers* (without papers) (Cissé 1997). Simultaneously, in shifting emphasis from the importing of immigrant workers to integration into French society of those who were already there and by this time, it was clear, were mostly there to stay—often swelling the ranks of the unemployed—1974 marked the start of the creation of a problem hitherto of little concern to the French: the problem of "integration."[9]

Integration was to become the buzzword of the 1980s within discourse and debates concerning France's racialized minorities and in particular its

8. *Le Monde*, May 15, 1985; Collectif des femmes immigrées 1984; Les Yeux Ouverts 1984; SAFIA 1992; Lesselier 2003.

9. I discuss the "integration" debate, and women's role therein, in considerable detail in Winter 1995a, chapter 4. I do not have the space to reproduce that entire discussion here, but its main elements can be found in Winter 1994a and 1998.

Maghrebian-background minority. Discussion of the issue and the related question of immigration (also assumed to refer primarily to Maghrebian immigrants) filled the pages of much journalistic and scholarly literature at the time, as did, more generally, racism and antiracism and the rise to prominence of the National Front in a newly Socialist-led nation. Also in sharp focus was the growing presence of *beur* culture—also closely linked to "Algeria in France" (Silverstein 2004). This culture was given enhanced prominence through the 1980s emergence of *le mouvement associatif* (community associations and other nongovernmental organizations of all descriptions) as a privileged form of young people's political and community organization, rendered high profile and trendy by SOS-Racisme among others (see below).

Beur, a term common in France through the 1980s and 1990s, is French back-to-front slang for *arabe,* and referred originally to those born in France of Algerian background; it was quickly generalized to refer to any French people of Maghrebian background. (French back-to-front slang is called *verlan,* which is [*à*] *l'envers* [the wrong way round], that is, said back-to-front.) During the 1990s the *beurs,* and children of *beurs,* developed a new *verlan* form of their nickname: rebeu—a sort of *double verlan,* often used ironically, and arguably more frequent today than *beur.* Both terms are invariable, although there are feminine forms of both—*beurette* and *rebeuse,* respectively—generally used with some condescending, infantilizing, or otherwise diminishing effect (see discussion of *beurettes* below).

The idea of integration was deployed in France during the 1980s in some ways to put a more positive spin on the idea of "assimilation," associated with French colonialism and the notion that immigrants must be Frenchified at all costs. Integration supposedly represented a more holistic and respectful way of looking at things, although in practice it was often the same idea dressed up in new language. Many sociologists and legal scholars writing at the time, however, made the distinction that assimilation was something that happened long term in any case, whatever the politics of governments, as generations of descendants of immigrants blend into the national community and become like—and equal to—everyone else (Costa-Lascoux 1989; Khellil 1991). Even here, however, some used the term integration to describe this process, as continual and constitutive of a nation (Schnapper

1991), while for the former group, integration was more to do with a conscious process, informed by a political will on the part of the state.

Whatever the terms used, and whatever the debate about their precise meaning, there seemed to be a widespread concern that although France had historically been an integrationist (or assimilationist) country, this French "integration machine" had "suddenly jammed" (Stora 1989; See also Stasi 1984). There was also, however, an equally widespread concern—sometimes emanating from the same people—that this "integration breakdown" and the polemic around the supposed problem of integration more generally was a smokescreen to obscure the more substantive and difficult debate on (postcolonial) immigration and racism in France (Gaspard 1992; Bonnafous 1992).

The term integration was indeed obfuscating, as it was used—by politicians, representatives of government agencies, the media, and a number of intellectuals—in a number of misleading ways. First, it was used in relation to a postcolonial population that was perceived as "Arab" (although in reality both Arab and Berber), that was Muslim and that was highly visible and vocal. Asian postcolonial immigrants, for example, were not targeted by the integration debate, even though Vietnamese communities in France's cities were as insular as any others and perhaps even more so. But they were not unemployed factory workers and they were not Muslim.

Yet, as we have seen, the majority of this "problem" Muslim population was not particularly religious and certainly not Islamist, even if Islamist networks in France were already beginning to manipulate the resentment of the racialized and marginalized (Kepel 1987; Zéghidour 1990). This population was constructed anew as fundamentally different and "culturally" unassimilable, racialization in France often tending to be expressed as a question of culture rather than color or ethnicity. Concerns over integration became a new way of racializing a specifically marked population. The population so marked was increasingly that described by the oxymoronic expression "immigrants of the second generation." If one is of the "second generation," one is, in general, born in France and thus is neither immigrant nor in particular need of integration.

Second, the problem of integration was not posed in relation to Maghrebian-background journalists or intellectuals or lawyers or doctors.

It was posed in relation to a newly postindustrialized and postcolonized French underclass of Maghrebian (primarily Algerian) immigrant men who were losing or had lost their factory jobs and their teenage children and grandchildren. The problem of integration was, in fact, first and foremost a problem of class and of socioeconomic exclusion, as many noted at the time (Furet, Julliard, and Rosanvallon 1988; Désir 1991; Wieviorka 1992).

Finally, the term integration was combined with another, the *moteur de l'intégration* or "driver of integration," in a by-now familiar state instrumentalization of women's "emancipation." Even Maghrebian-background (usually male) commentators were of the view that

> while in these dark years of unemployment Muslim men without work are seeking a gleam of hope on the horizon of Mecca, from where their gaze could wander to refocus on Ryad or even Tehran, women can only congratulate themselves on their sojourn with Marianne [the feminized symbol of France], who, without hesitation, economic doldrums or not, reassures them as to her rights and her dignity. (Zéghidour 1990, 155)

As those who ostensibly had everything to gain from embracing the values of the Republic and much to lose from not doing so, women were thus the driving force of an integration in which their brothers were more reluctant to participate. Or, as Adil Jazouli quipped, "No one gets to out-French the beurettes" (*Plus français que la beurette, tu meurs*) (cited in Fohr 1993).

During the 1980s and early 1990s I spoke with a number of Maghrebian-background women activists working within organizations such as Les Yeux Ouverts (eyes open), Les Nanas Beurs (beur chicks), SOS-Racisme, Solidarité Avec les Femmes d'Ici et d'Ailleurs (Solidarity with Women from Here and Elsewhere, SAFIA), Expressions Maghrébines au Féminin (EMAF), and the Mouvement contre le Racisme et pour l'Amitié entre les Peuples (Movement against Racism and for Friendship among Peoples, MRAP), including relatively high-profile figures such as Souad Benani (president of Les Nanas Beurs), Chérifa Benabdessadok (editor-in-chief of the MRAP's national magazine *Différences*) and Shéhérazade Ouarem (vice president of SOS-Racisme). Almost unanimously, these women agreed, along with a number of authors writing at the time (such as Assouline 1992; Lacoste-Dujardin 1992), that school, the workplace and wider French society offered better options for Maghrebian-background women than the narrow world of family-based religious and patriarchal traditions that are typical of rural families anywhere as well as of immigrant families from poor rural or urban backgrounds. At the same time—and again, almost unanimously—they rejected the "beurette craze," as Benabdessadok put it, as being simplistic and suspect. Well-known Franco-Maghrebian author Leïla Sebbar similarly criticized the generalization of the image of integrable beurettes as creating monodimensional "good girls" on the one side and "bad boys" on the other, the latter being locked into the role of delinquents, failures and so on (Sebbar 1990). Such stereotyping recalls colonial discourse on "emancipable" women and "backward" men, and we will see later, in relation to the 2003–4 rekindling of the hijab debate, that it continues to provoke strong reactions.

What was also perverse and manipulative from the outset, and particularly in the wake of the first headscarves affair in 1989, was that the female "drivers of integration" were also contrasted with the backward and oppressed women who were presumably under the yoke of Islamic patriarchy. Pre-1989, the latter had mostly been the mothers: those women, mostly illiterate and with little to no French, who came to France under the family reunion program and once there, carried on the patriarchal tradition in relation to both their sons and their daughters. Post-1989, the focus shifted toward the young hijab-clad girls, although the mothers had not entirely left the picture. Once again, the Frenchwardly—and upwardly—mobile beurettes came out on top in both cultural and socioeconomic terms.

The question here is not one of whether it is a good idea for women to embrace values of freedom, equality, and secularism, however flawed their application might be, as I am convinced it is. So are the vast majority of Maghrebian-background women in France, by their own accounts and by the accounts of those scholars having conducted demographic and qualitative studies. The question is rather one of how that movement by women in their own self-interest is then instrumentalized by other political and social actors to their own ends and how women's collective struggles for liberation are co-opted to other agendas. The question is also, conversely, one of how opposition to this co-optation is then in turn harnessed to "antiracist" agendas in which men's interests dominate, and in which men's behavior, including toward women, is exempted from scrutiny. These tensions informed feminist and antiracist reactions to the "integration" debate in the 1980s and have continued to inform them throughout the almost two decades of the hijab debate.

The Front National, SOS-Racisme and Le Mouvement Associatif

The tensions around integration emerged in the context of the rise of a muscular and populist extreme-right in the guise of the FN (also often referred to as *le Front*), alongside the "pale-pinking" of the left, as the Communist Party's support base had diminished and the center had largely triumphed over the left within the Socialist Party. (The symbol of the French Socialist Party is a rose and its color is pink; the color of the Communist Party is red. The idea of "pale-pinking" is thus an apt metaphor for the increasing shift of the left toward the center at this time, and indeed the term *rose pâle* was increasingly invoked to ironic effect at the time, the word *rose* meaning both the flower and the color pink.)

In 1981, when François Mitterrand was elected president and a Socialist government came to power in the legislative elections, the optimism that followed the defeat of decades of right-wing government was quickly dampened. Not only did the Socialist Party withdraw fairly rapidly from its more progressive stances, particularly after the fall of the Mauroy government in 1984 (see chapter 2), but various extreme-right formations also emerged as strong oppositional forces, the most enduringly successful of these being the FN. The FN was formed in 1972 out of the remains of preceding and largely disorganized extreme-right groups, notably Ordre Nouveau (new order) (Chebel d'Appollonia 1987, 314ff). Jean-Marie Le Pen, who was quickly to become the Front's leader, and had been part of Ordre Nouveau, had a long extreme-right pedigree, as we saw in chapter 1.

After its formation, the FN spent a decade in virtual obscurity, which was at its lowest ebb in 1981, when Le Pen was unable to obtain the 500 signatures necessary to become a presidential candidate. Two years later, however, the Front shocked the nation by its success in a municipal by-election in the formerly Socialist stronghold of Dreux, an industrial town with high unemployment and a significant Maghrebian-background population on the outskirts of the Parisian region. The Front obtained 16.7 percent of the vote in the first round, and in the second, the mainstream right joined forces with it to defeat the left, with three councillors ending up being FN (Mayer 1998). It went on to obtain more than 5 percent of the vote in the 1984 European elections, almost 10 percent in the 1986 legislative elections, with thirty-five deputies elected, and 14.7 percent in the 1988 presidential election, which "confirmed the existence of a new political force and made everyone forget Dreux," as former Socialist mayor of Dreux and feminist scholar Françoise Gaspard has put it (Gaspard 1990, 20). These successes were, however, less significant than those of the mainstream right during the same period (Perrineau 1996, 42).

The Front managed to rise to prominence by playing the usual extreme-right cards: security (playing on economic downturn and "law and order") along with race and immigration, a theme that, as Piero Ignazi notes, was *first introduced* into the party-political landscape as a problematic issue by the Front (Ignazi 1996, 73). In the campaign leading up to the 1974 presidential election, only the National Front featured immigration in its platform, although the issue did not take off until the beginning of the following decade, partly as the result of being picked up by the mainstream right, in government in the 1970s, partly as a convenient scapegoat during the recession. The Front played heavily on this, contributing significantly to the manufacturing of a French "identity crisis," in which the "problem" of immigration, and, subsequently, of Arabs and Muslims more generally, became associated with ills ranging from AIDS to delinquency and unemployment. The Front's slogan, La France aux Français (keep France for the French), "de-Frenched" nonwhite non-Christian French citizens and residents in a more direct and arguably more internally coherent way than the mainstream discourses on integration. Le Pen also worked hard on giving the Front a respectable veneer to bring it out of lunatic fringe marginality, citing Reagan and Churchill, among others, as inspirations (Chebel d'Appollonia 1987, 336). Moreover, he cultivated a sophisticated and cultured persona attractive to a country used to a political class largely trained by the Grandes Ecoles. He also became skilled at trotting out the occasional token Maghrebian, who was usually well-paid to give the National Front a nonracist veneer.

Originally, the Front's supporters came from the traditional support groups for the extreme-right: men, petty bourgeoisie, rural populations. Rumors that Communist Party voters had massively defected to the National

Front were not true in the first instance, despite the Dreux result; it was more that blue-collar and other left-wing voters had stopped voting altogether. This disaffection with the electoral system, along with fractures within both the left and right—resulting in a record number of sixteen candidates— was evident in the first round of the 2002 presidential election, when the abstention rate reached a record high of almost 28 percent. It appeared that the abstentions came largely from the left, as the second-round runoff was between Le Pen and Chirac, resulting in the left, bizarrely, rallying support around Chirac so Le Pen would not become president. As the years went on, the Front did, however, recruit more and more poor whites living in areas with high-density racialized populations.

The 1989 headscarves affair gave the Front new ammunition. In its 1990 platform appeared the following:

> There were 50 mosques 15 years ago. There are almost 1,500 today and every month tens of new ones are being built in every region in France. Yesterday immigrants refused our culture, today they want to impose their own on us. (cited in Les Marie-Jeannes 1993)

The following year, Le Pen spoke of a "probable invasion of our territories by foreign crowds," which could "result in a logic of war"; this would cause grave risks to national security and justify the use of armed forces by the government (speech at a meeting of European Right Wing parties at the European Parliament in Strasbourg, cited in *Le Monde,* July 6, 1991).

More disturbing, however, was what Pierre Tévanian and Sophie Tissot have called the "lepenization of minds" (Tévanian and Tissot 1998, 2002). This process had started well before they were writing about it and even well before the 1989 headscarves affair, although it became more evident through the 1990s. For example, in 1990, Jacques Chirac, then leader of the opposition, was saying, in terms closely resembling those of Le Pen:

> The more we allow immigration, the greater the insecurity. This is not a question of ethnicity, but our immigration is a "bottom of the range" one. We are moving towards serious racial conflicts that will be the consequence of the French people's refusal to be invaded by other cultures. (cited in *Le Nouvel Observateur* 1363, December 20, 1990)

This was, of course, before he felt a sudden preelectoral concern for those "on the margins" in the lead up to the 1995 presidential election.

The National Front had thus succeeded, during the 1980s, in dictating part of the national political agenda.

In response to this and to socioeconomic marginalization of postcolonial minorities, in response as well to a wider disillusionment with traditional party-political or trade-union forms of political organizing, a variety of new antiracist and ethnic minority formations emerged, as part of the *mouvement associatif* referred to earlier. This was also facilitated by new financial support from the Socialist government elected in 1981, which, under the 1981–83 Mauroy government at least, was generous in its allocation of grants to nonprofit associations and to community cultural initiatives. Moreover, alongside the partly media-driven fascination with "integration," "second-generation" immigrants and beurettes appeared a fascination with beur culture more generally: Radio Beur was founded in Paris, the "multicultural" publisher L'Harmattan, among others, published a number of beur autobiographies and novels (see Hargreaves 1997), the rock group *Carte de Séjour* (which means "residency card"; the band was a sort of Franco-Maghrebian answer to UB40) shot to fame with its mixture of rock, reggae, and raï (Algerian music), and *merguez-frites* (Maghrebian spicy beef sausage with French fries) were sold from city street stands alongside the more traditional *crêpes* (pancakes). In short, Maghrebian "ethnic" became as "in" as the carriers of these cultural traits were themselves marginalized.

At the beginning of the 1980s, another new phenomenon was also developing in France: riots in urban ghettos. The first significant riot was in Vaulx-en-Velin, in the Lyons area, in 1979 (others were to occur in 1990–91, generating extensive media coverage), and the second and third occurred in 1981 and 1983, in a housing project called Les Minguettes in the Lyons suburb of Vénissieux. The 1983 riot, which was the subject of intense media focus, both at the time and subsequently, was in response to one of the growing numbers of police "errors": on June 20, Toumi Djaidja was shot point-blank when he intervened in an altercation between police and local youths. This shooting was to become the rallying call for the first national march "for equality and against racism" organized by the newly formed SOS-Racisme. The march, inaccurately but tellingly nicknamed the *marche des beurs,* began in Marseilles on October 15, 1983, and ended in Paris with a demonstration of an estimated 100,000 people. The march's coordinators, including Djaidja, met with President Mitterrand at the end of the march, and all those present who were not French citizens and not long-term residents received from him a work and residency permit valid for ten years.

Thus began the career of SOS-Racisme. From the outset, this organization captured the imagination of large numbers of young French people of all backgrounds, organizing national rallies, concerts, and other events. It also, however, attracted a great deal of criticism for being too pally with the government and in particular with the Socialist Party, and more generally for demagogically co-opting and sanitizing the struggles of the racialized and appropriating antiracist work done over many years by a number of organizations, "emptying them of their subversive content" (Boubeker and Beau 1986, 96; See also Amara and Idir 1991; Laïdi and Salam 2002, 129ff). Its highly media-genic and politically ambitious president, Harlem Désir, was similarly criticized as being the too middle-of-the-road face of a "trendy" antiracism. Those of us active in the feminist movement at the time shared these concerns and observed that the masculine gender of "pote" in SOS-Racisme's slogan *Touche pas à mon pote* (hands off my buddy), written on a little green hand held up to signal "stop," reflected an absence of gendered analysis in SOS-Racisme's platform (Winter 1995a).

The organization nonetheless managed to make some waves and rally large numbers of people around issues of race, culture, and social exclusion, in ways that obviously had the National Front worried. In response to SOS-Racisme's *Touche pas à mon pote,* the Front retorted with *Touche pas à ma France* emblazoned across a blue-white-red map of France (part of the Front's logo).

From Beurism to Muslimism

SOS-Racisme and the "beur(ette) craze" were not, however, the only expressions of Maghrebi-Muslim identity politics in France in the 1980s and 1990s, and the National Front was not the only extreme-right group that the beurs (or their rebeu successors) were to face. Islamic revivalist and, subsequently, Islamist movements were also active in France in the 1980s and were, along with a certain post-9/11 Americanization of the race debate in France, to be instrumental in what Chahdortt Djavann (2004) was later to call the emergence of "Muslimism" (see chapter 6). It was an identity where religiosity was the new ethnicity, and the difference-affirming hijabi replaced the driver-of-integration beurette. These movements found willing members among disenfranchized beurs for whom the promise of democracy and human rights, blended with various mixes of "right to difference" and "right to integration" discourses, held out by the distant and more privileged leadership of SOS-Racisme and other organizations such as France-Plus, had not materialized.[10] Moreover, the associations that had in the 1980s ridden a wave of government funding and public interest found themselves in financial trouble, and by the end of the 1980s, successive governments were becoming less supportive of community antiracist movements, and had even begun to court Islamic revivalist and Islamist movements that were attracting new recruits (Laïdi and Salam 2002). The Rushdie affair, the 1989 headscarves affair, the 1991 Gulf War, and the development of Maghrebian Islamism all contributed to this rightward Islamist shift in France—as they did (particularly the last) to a harder line taken by the French government.

We saw in chapter 1 that Islamist movements have varied in their attitudes to women—and how far they go toward advocating equality of the sexes, within the logic of their own religious precepts, will to some extent be determined by how far women's rights are already advanced in the wider political environment. In marked contrast to the FIS in Algeria, organizations such as Al 'Adl Wal Ihsan and the Justice and Development Party in Morocco, Hamas in Algeria, and Ennahda in Tunisia have encouraged active participation by women, and Ghannouchi in particular has criticized Islamists who continue to advocate strict segregation of the sexes and oppose women working (Lamloun 1998). Most Islamist groups in France have a comparable stance in favor of education, workforce, and even political participation for women.

It has been argued, including by many of the headscarved protagonists in the French hijab debate, that the situation in the West is completely different from that in the Muslim world and one cannot equate prescriptions

---

10. France-Plus was founded by Algerian immigrant Arezki Dahmani with the primary aim of encouraging beurs to enrol to vote and become involved in France's party-political life.

concerning women's rights, duties, and appropriate behavior and attire in Muslim countries with choices made by thoroughly modern young Islamic women in the democratic West and the discursive space in which they move. In most of the non-Western examples given here and in chapter 1, however, the hijabization of women is similarly not a state-imposed practice but an oppositional one, and apart from Algeria, women have mostly not been overtly and physically coerced into wearing them. There may be many forms of psychological and social coercion, but this is also the case in the West.

French scholars of Islamism such as Gilles Kepel (1994) and Olivier Roy (2001, 2004) point, among other more direct influences, to immigrant-channeled influences that have aided the development of French Islamism, such as agitation within France by outlawed Maghrebian Islamist political parties. It is certain that the Muslim Brotherhood is a central part of the "genealogy of (French) Islamism," to borrow Roy's title (2004). Its activity within France as elsewhere in Europe, like that of the Saudi World Islamic League, has been channeled through educative and cultural institutions. The Brotherhood also has direct family links with France. Hassan Al Banna, the founder of the Muslim Brotherhood, is the maternal grandfather of Tariq Ramadan, whose controversial presence and views have loomed large in the hijab debate in France, as will be discussed in chapter 8.

While Ramadan and his supporters have been quick to point out—and rightly so—that a family relationship does not of itself constitute a basis for analysis of someone's political position, Ramadan has nonetheless shown himself to be adept at carrying on what appears to have become a family tradition. In fact, he has unambiguously situated himself within it. In a book of "conversations" between himself and Alain Gresh, chief editor of the international affairs monthly *Le Monde Diplomatique*, Ramadan sings the praises of both his father and his maternal grandfather, as having passed on to him a "fundamentally spiritual and humanist" faith and sense of social justice, in particular as concerns the resistance of the Third World. He further states that he feels himself to be "close" to Al Banna's ideas and activist commitment and claims that subsequent positions and actions of members of the Egyptian Brotherhood have deformed those ideas (Gresh and Ramadan 2002, ch. 1). He thus manages both to reinvent Al Banna as the profoundly spiritual hero of the people's resistance and to situate himself within this romanticized heritage. Distancing himself from subsequent discourse and actions of some of the Brotherhood in Egypt, he manages to invest the European Brotherhood, as represented by himself and those close to him, as "the good guys." As Caroline Fourest has pointed out, however, Ramadan is highly selective about which parts of Al Banna's platform he highlights and careful about how he frames them (Fourest 2004).

If Islamist groups in France can be seen, like Islamist groups elsewhere, to be part of an "Islamist international," the contemporary development of which is closely tied to globalization (Roy 2001, 2004), their development is also specific to the French context, in particular as concerns their positioning in relation to secularism and to the French state. Relatively marginal in the 1980s, French Islamist groups have proved effective in using the hijab debate in particular to maneuver themselves into a prominent political position. Like Islamist and indeed other extreme-right movements everywhere, they have used socioeconomic marginalization of certain groups as a breeding ground, arriving with a demagogic discourse and offering a ready-made group and personal identity as a solution. In France, they have also used and manipulated both resentment by other Muslim and particularly Maghrebian constituencies against Algerian control of the Paris mosque and the supposedly cozy relationship between Algerian-background imams and the French state, and the state's attempts to regulate and control a moderate, pro-Republican, pro-secular "French Islam."

Through charismatic personalities such as Tariq Ramadan and his influential European-background allies such as the above-mentioned Alain Gresh, these movements are gaining considerable ground, although, in a not dissimilar way to the conservative Catholic lobby, their visibility, vocality, and presence in positions of influence are disproportionate to their actual level of support among French Muslims. Unfortunately, as is demonstrably the case elsewhere in the West, white French supporters have been instrumental in the development of the high profile of some of these charismatic leaders and the religious or supposedly "antiracist" movements in which they are involved, as we will see in part III. Without that support, they would not enjoy the same level of access to a public forum and spheres of cultural and political influence.

Catherine Wihtol de Wenden identifies three main tendencies in French Islam, associated with French Islamic federations that have been vying for the hearts and minds of France's Muslim youth for the past couple of decades: "fundamentalist" Islam, as represented by the UOIF, "Gallican" Islam, as represented by the FNMF (the term "Gallican" being an implied comparison with Gallican Catholicism), now in the process of disintegration and being replaced by the RMF as discussed in chapter 2 as well as below, and "Republican" Islam, as represented by the Grand Mosque of Paris. She also notes the rise of the youth organization Union des Jeunes Musulmans (Union of Young Muslims, UJM) and the "at once modern and fundamentalist seductions of Tariq Ramadan" (Wihtol de Wenden 2005, 17–18).

The main movements with which I will be concerned here, because of their central involvement in militancy around the hijab incidents and in the wider debate over "French Islam" and, more recently, "Islamophobia," are UJM, UOIF, FNMF, and Etudiants Musulmans de France (Muslim Students of France, EMF), formerly Union Islamique des Etudiants de France, and Conseil de la jeunesse pluriculturelle de France (Council of Multicultural Youth in France, Cojep). Other organizations include La Voix de l'Islam, led at the time of the 1989 headscarves affair by Aboul Farid Gabtani, a Franco-Tunisian convert to Shia Islam, which organized the 1989 anti-Rushdie demonstration in Paris, the French branches of Jama'at al Islami (not to be confused with pietist organization Jama'at al Tabligh), now on the hit list of many Western and non-Western governments as a terrorist group, and the WIL, the largest Saudi missionary and charity group (see chapter 1), which, among other things, controls a number of small mosques throughout the Muslim and Western worlds. Incidentally, the Muslim Brotherhood–related founding group of the WIL included Tariq Ramadan's father, Said Ramadan, who had lived briefly in exile in Saudi Arabia after having been expelled from Egypt by Nasser for Islamist activity. Apart from these, various Maghrebian and Middle Eastern extreme Islamist groups are or have been active in France, although many if not most are illegal in France and some are terrorist, such as the Comité de Solidarité avec les Prisonniers Politiques Arabes and the Groupe Islamique Armé, which were responsible for a number of terrorist attacks in Paris in the 1980s and 1990s.

The UJM was formed by so-called "third generation" Maghrebian-background French men in 1987, in the Lyons suburb of Les Minguettes: site of the shooting and riots of the beginning of that decade and remaining a "sensitive zone." It has also, increasingly, been a fertile site for the development of Islamist activism. Ten years after the 1983 March for Equality and Against Racism, Toumi Djaïdja, the former martyred hero of SOS-Racisme, became an adept of Islamic revivalism and set about transforming the premises of what had been SOS-Avenir Minguettes, where the idea for the march had been generated, into a mosque. In 1989 in Lyons, UJM set up the Islamist press and bookshop Tawhid, along with the Tawhid Islamic Center. Tawhid, which is, as we saw in chapter 1, a key concept in Salafism, is also—perhaps coincidentally, perhaps not—the same name as that of a supermarket chain in Cairo owned and operated by the Muslim Brotherhood (Labévière 1999, 142). The Lyons press is managed by Tariq Ramadan and his brother Hani and publishes the former's work. The group, which also organizes Tariq Ramadan's speaking tours in France, where he does not officially live (he has Swiss nationality), is close to the Muslim Brotherhood, the UOIF, and EMF and was active during the anti-Rushdie demonstrations and the hijab debates. It was centrally involved in a high-profile hijab incident involving an eighteen-year-old final year high school student in Grenoble in 1993–94 (see chapter 5).

The FNMF, connoted as "Moroccan," was set up in 1985 in opposition to the Paris Mosque because the latter was perceived to be too close to Algeria. Its founders were two converts: Daniel Youssef Leclerc and Strasbourg doctor Abdallah (Thomas) Milcent. Milcent, who had become close to Islamist movements during travels in Turkey, Pakistan, and Afghanistan, was later to become a "technical adviser" to many families of headscarved girls during hijab incidents, and Leclerc was stridently vocal at the time of the 1989 affair. The FNMF, which is also close to the World Islamic League, has played on intra-Maghrebian rivalries. It has, among other things, set up a training institute for imams: of France's estimated 900 imams in 2004, 90 percent were foreign-born (mostly Moroccan) and had attended Islamic universities in Egypt, Turkey, and North Africa (Mermet 2004, 272). In January 2006, in a move not dissimilar to those happening elsewhere in the West, then interior minister Nicolas Sarkozy expressed concerns about the development of "radical Muslim minorities" grouped around mosques and private Islamic training schools and announced measures to ensure that imams spoke French and "understood the European way of life" (BBC Radio Report, January 3, 2006).

The FNMF, which has been presided since 1992 by Moroccan Mohamed Bechari (with Abadallah Boussouf, rector of the Strasbourg Mosque, as vice president), has been in serious trouble in recent years. Internal squabbles led to Boussouf taking legal action against Bechari for falsification of records, use of forgeries and financial irregularities, but Bechari was cleared by the court. Even though it won the majority of seats in the 2005 election of the newly constituted CFCM, following a 2006 split it lost practically all of them to the RFM in the 2008 election, as we saw in chapter 2.

Cojep is a Turkish youth association reputedly close to the Turkish Islamist group Millî Görüs (national vision), which controls the Eyyüp Sultan Mosque in Strasbourg, the heartland of Franco-Turkish Islamism (Bowen 2007, 53). Founded in France in 1992 and based, from 1996, in Strasbourg (Alsace), where most of the Muslim population is of Turkish background, Cojep claimed by 1998 to group some 120–150 associations, mainly in Eastern France (Frégosi 2001, 104; Weibel 2006). It was also at pains to officially distance itself from Millî Görüs although it retains ideological links (Frégosi 2001, 104ff). Cojep demonstrates a perhaps more Ramadanesque Islamism inscribed within French citizenship; it has in particular participated in Islam et Laïcité since 1999, and its members have become active in the Socialist Party in the Strasbourg area. It also, however, has links with UJM/Tawhid and with Jeunes Musulmans de France (linked to the UOIF).

By far the most high-profile Islamist group in France is the UOIF, which was formed in 1983—the same year as SOS-Racisme's first national march—by two foreign students, Tunisian Abdallah Ben Mansour and Iraqi Mahmoud Zouheir, around the Groupement Islamique de France, headed at the time by Lebanese Sheikh Fayçal Al Malaoui, and the French members and allies of the Tunisian Mouvement pour la Tendance Islamique (later Ennahda). The UOIF was mentored into existence by Yussuf Qaradawi, well-known Muslim Brother, originally from Egypt and reputed to be close to Hamas in Palestine. The UOIF allegedly channels funds to Hamas through its Palestinian relief organization Comité de Bienfaisance et de

Secours aux Palestiniens, of which the Lyons address is the same as that of Tawhid (Venner 2005, 114ff).

Ben Mansour was refused French nationality in 1996 on the grounds of nonassimilation due to his association with extremist organizations "advocating the rejection of essential values of French society" (Council of State decision no. 178449 of June 7, 1999, rejecting Ben Mansour's appeal). As for Qaradawi, he is also part of the governing group of the Egyptian bank Al Taqwa, reputed to be the Muslim Brotherhood's main financial arm, and presides the European Council for Fatwa and Research (ECFR). The ECFR, now based in Dublin, was set up in London in 1997 and is the main English-language channel used by Qaradawi for publication of fatwas (Islamic legal opinions, and not "death sentences," contrary to what has become the popular Western belief since the Rushdie affair). The ECFR advocates strict shari'a law and opposes equality between women and men. It is in relation to Qaradawi's ECFR activities that the UOIF has in recent years distanced itself from him, in particular as concerns proposed French publication by Tawhid of a collection of ECFR fatwas.

In 1991, the UOIF assisted the Algerian FIS in setting up meetings in various locations in France to garner support for its cause in Algeria in the lead up to the 1991–92 legislative elections there (Sifaoui 2002, 50). Presided since 1992 by Lhaj Thami Breze, of Moroccan background, with Fouad Alaoui as general secretary, the UOIF now groups some 200 associations under its aegis and organizes yearly congresses at Le Bourget in the northern suburbs of Paris, attended by several thousand people. These meetings have been characterized as a sort of "Muslim *Fête de L'Huma*" (Kaltenbach and Tribalat 2002, 218; Sfeir 2002, 474), *L'Huma* being *L'Humanité,* the communist daily newspaper, and the *Fête de l'Humanité* being a big fair organized every Easter by the Communist Party at La Courneuve, also in the northern suburbs of Paris. The congresses are as a result nicknamed *La fête de l'oumma* (umma) as a play on words. Kepel (1994) documents at some length the structure and rise to prominence of UOIF, which has garnered support by actively engaging itself with local communities in the provision of mosques, religious instruction, youth networks, family assistance, and so on.

The list of UOIF's past and present leadership and high-profile associates reads like a who's who of French, Maghrebian, and European Islamism and its dynasties. Its French leaders are mostly Muslim intellectuals and hold doctorates in Islamic studies, philosophy, or political sciences from French universities. Ahmed Jaballah, formerly of FNMF, who was to become the UOIF's high-profile spokesman on Islamic law, holds a doctorate in Islamology from the Sorbonne, is now director of the Paris school of the Islamic Institut Européen des Sciences Humaines (IESH), a member of the ECFR, and vice chairman of the Union des Organisations Islamiques d'Europe (UOIE), based in London, and also Qaradawi-inspired via the UOIF. His wife Noura was outspoken during the 2003–4 hijab debate. The IESH was set up in 1990 by the UOIF in Saint-Léger-de-Fougeret in the Burgundy region, as a largely Saudi-funded private higher education institute of Islamic theological studies. Under the directorship of Ben Mansour, its first intake of students was in 1992. The IESH is now run under the aegis of the UOIE and a London institute was set up in 1997, with a Parisian one opening its doors in 1999. The IESH makes much of the fact that "more than 40 percent" of students are women, supposed proof that "in the area of religion and access to knowledge," "authentic Islam" does not discriminate against women.[11] The IESH today has circa 800 students from all over Europe; its teaching is done primarily in Arabic.

Internationally, apart from Qaradawi, who was guest of honor at the 2000 UOIF congress, the figure of Rachid al Gannouchi, leader of outlawed Tunisian Islamist organization Ennahda, looms large in UOIF's and UOIE's constellation. This has, along with Ben Mansour's background, contributed to a "Tunisian" connotation of the UOIF's leadership, although its current leaders are Moroccan. As guest of honor at UOIF's 1990 congress, al Ghannouchi proclaimed that France had now become a "land of Islam" (*dar al islam*). It is significant that in 1989, the year of the *Satanic Verses* ruckus and of the Creil headscarves affair, UOIF had changed its name to Union of Islamic Organizations *of* France rather than *in* France (Kepel 1994, 199; Kaltenbach and Tribalat 2002, 218). On December 27, 1993, left-leaning daily *Libération* reported on the annual congress of the UOIF, at which the organization refuted claims that it received significant foreign subsidies to push ideology close to Ennahda. The following year, an article in weekly

11. IESH Web site: http://www.iesh.fr.

newsmagazine *Le Nouvel Observateur* reported police concerns at the massive sums of money passing through UOIF, and at the time, its association with a number of members of the Muslim Brotherhood, as well as with Mahfoud Nahnah, head of Algerian Hamas (Aïchoune 1994).

All of these formations, however, appear moderate beside the extremely marginal and stridently anti-Semitic Parti Musulman de France (PMF), founded in 1997 by Mohamed Ennacer Latrèche, with the aim, apparently, of "liberating Muslims from the influence of the Zionist Socialist Party" *(Libération,* January 3, 2004). It is also the only French Islamist political party. Born in Tunisia of Algerian parents, Latrèche grew up in Strasbourg, where his father is an imam. He undertook religious studies in Damas at the end of the 1970s and on his return to France engaged in political activism, initially organized around support for the UMP and anti-Semitic agitating. He claims 2,000 members for the PMF but is quick to add that these memberships are not "formal" *(Libération,* January 3, 2004). According to Franck Frégosi, these members appear to have been recruited largely among Franco-Algerians, mainly harkis (Algerians who had fought on the French side during the Algerian war), although some right-wing Alsatian autonomists also appear to be members, and Turkish-background Muslims have participated in its demonstrations (Frégosi 2004). Since its creation, the PMF has regularly participated in, or organized, anti-Semitic initiatives, often ostensibly associated with support for Palestine, and has links with individuals on the French extreme-right, notably Shoah (Holocaust)-denying historian Serge Thion, who has spoken at PMF rallies and published a defense of Latrèche on the self-proclaimed "World's largest website for Historical Revisionism" (*Le Monde,* January 18, 2004; Thion 2004).[12]

The PMF is extremist and marginal, and other Islamic organizations, such as mosque associations, have distanced themselves from it. If I mention it here, it is because it has to some extent contributed to operating an Islamic equivalent of lepenization. First, it has attempted to co-opt resentment around the 2004 antireligious insignia law and occupy the main Muslim protest space around it, notably via a demonstration in Paris on January 17, 2004. Other Islamist organizations took the calculated risk of

12. http://www.vho.org.

not distancing themselves at that time, thus—according to journalists Blandine Grosjean and Olivier Vogel, writing in Libération—allowing the hijab debate to become more "radicalized" *(Libération,* January 3, 2004). Second, via its association with Thion and its repeated anti-Semitic statements dressed up in a rather see-through anti-Zionist and anti-Islamophobia cloak, the PMF represents the radical fringe of a growing anti-Semitic tendency within the anti-2004-law movement. Third, and following from this, it is the radical extreme of a growing association of some parts of this movement with Hamas and even Hezbollah. This conflation of anti-Zionism and anti-Semitism, and pro-Palestine and pro-Islamist activity, is hardly new, no more than is the deployment of victim status and accusations of anti-Semitism by the right-wing Israeli state and its supporters, in order to deflect any criticism of its occupation of Palestine. What *is* new, or has developed more strongly, in the rekindling of the hijab debate in recent years, is the imbrication of this debate, for a significant and highly vocal number of participants, with the Israel-Palestine issue. I will discuss this further in chapter 8.

Part Two | A Fifteen-Year Saga

THE POLITICAL, MEDIA, AND LEGAL POLEMIC about the hijab in France has been long and not entirely linear. It has had peaks and troughs, hardening and softening of stances. In particular, the ways in which it has been imbricated within wider national and international debates on race, nation, women, religion, "Muslimness," and secularism have changed significantly over the years, even if the terms of the underlying polemic over the interpretation and application of secularism have remained essentially the same. Interestingly, feminist voices, barely listened to in 1989, were suddenly the flavor of the month in 2003, but this does not mean that they were necessarily better heard, as we will see in part III.

Chapter 4 examines the 1989 affair and the political and media debate that ensued and that focused in particular on racism and on the appropriate interpretation of secularism. It also looks at the impact and implications of the Council of State ruling of 1989, which was to provide the yardstick for legal cases until the passage of the 2004 law. In particular, it does what the French media did *not* do to any significant extent at the time: it foregrounds feminist voices.

Chapter 5 traces developments from 1990 to 1995. These were punctuated by a series of Council of State rulings following appeals against expulsions, and by the Bayrou circular of 1994 prohibiting "ostentatious" religious insignia. This period was also marked by the rise to prominence of oppositional Islamism in Algeria in 1990–92 and by the Gulf War, the latter being extremely unpopular in France and leading to the protest resignation of defense minister Jean-Pierre Chevènement. By the time of the Bayrou circular, Islamist presence around many hijab incidents in schools had become much more prominent, and a wave of terrorist attacks associated with Algerian Islamists occurred in France the following year. The ante was also upped on the side of the French state: 1993–95 was a period of right-wing government and particularly discriminatory immigration and nationality laws were introduced in 1993. Another new development, in 1995, was the publication of two books on the hijab issue, both written by women with experience of the field and both taking explicitly feminist standpoints, but advocating two opposing positions.

Chapter 6 covers the decade from 1995 to 2004 and beyond. Although the late 1990s were relatively calm in hijab terms, notwithstanding a brief resurgence in 1999, the middle of the decade was marked by a number of incidents as well as by Council of State rulings upholding expulsions, contrary to those given earlier in the decade. The chapter will focus in particular on the 2003–4 period: the national and international contextual factors, the work of the Stasi Commission and the adoption of the 2004 law. It will also look at French Muslim reactions to the law and at other government measures concerning both immigration and the memory of colonial history at that time.

4

1989

Three Little Girls and a
Great Big "Psychodrama"

ON SEPTEMBER 18, 1989, Leïla and Fatima Achaboun, two sisters of Moroccan background (aged thirteen and fourteen), and Samira, their fourteen-year-old friend, of Tunisian background, were expelled from junior high school (*collège*) Gabriel Havez in Creil, for refusing to remove their hijabs. The school was around sixty kilometers north of Paris in a ZEP, that is, zone d'éducation prioritaire (priority education zone). These zones, set up in 1981, were defined as areas with particular needs due to socioeconomic problems and received extra government resourcing because of this. Such zones typically have a high immigrant population, high unemployment rate, and high teacher turnover; in Creil, this turnover was 30 percent and included two principals who had preceded Ernest Chenière, principal at the time of the affair. Ironically, a study of junior high schools conducted under the auspices of the National Statistics Institute INSEE showed that "the setting up of priority education zones had no significant effect [between 1982 and 1992] on the success of children" (Bénabou, Kramarz, and Prost 2004). In a study of the experience of girls of North and sub-Saharan African background in the socioeconomically disadvantaged Parisian suburb of Pantin, Keaton (2006) notes that ZEP has become a stigmatizing term, and some school principals have for that reason refused ZEP status and attendant extra funding as it gives their schools bad reputations. This fear of the ZEP label, particularly in the light of the INSEE finding cited above, is likely to be exacerbated by provisions introduced by the government in 2007 and effective from the start of the 2008 school year, which remove locality restrictions in parental choice of schools for their children. Unions and other associations fear that this measure will deepen the socioeconomic and racial divide in the school system as white and better-off families desert disadvantaged schools (see, for example, Hennache 2007).

In a scenario that subsequently became familiar, at the end of the previous school year in June 1989, teachers at Gabriel-Havez, reacting to religiously based obstructive behavior from students (absences in particular), had asked for rules to be elaborated concerning respect for secularism. The girls nonetheless turned up headscarved in September, keeping themselves in a close-knit group apart from others and resisting decisions by teachers to separate them from each other in class. Chenière had requested that they drop the headscarf to their shoulders during class times; they could wear it in the school yard during recreation. After several days absence, they reappeared, still headscarved, claiming tearfully that God had told them to wear the headscarf and they would rather die than remove it. A few days later, Chenière received a visit from Samira's father, accompanied by an imam:

> I was called a racist, [the imam] said that France was a country of freedom and that the schoolgirls thus had a right to wear the veil, that in any case the school's 260 girl students would soon be turning up veiled and that Islam would be the first religion in France, they were working on that. . . . A little later, young Muslim boys were distributing a petition in front of the school gates for the construction of a mosque in Creil. Samira's father returned to see me a few days later, explaining that the veil was not a religious object but a simple headscarf. And that I thus could not prohibit it. . . . We were in the process of contacting parents, associations, teachers in order to broaden the debate when the Affair broke out in the press. (Chenière 1989, 36)

And so began what the French center-left daily *Le Monde* was later to call both a "national psychodrama" and the "headscarves saga" (October 20, 1994). Early reports and media commentaries set the tone: on October 4, 1989, the left-wing daily *Libération*'s account of the Creil incident was titled "Le port du voile heurte la laïcité du collège de Creil" (Wearing of the veil conflicts with the Creil college's secularism) (cited in Gaspard and Khosrokhavar

1995, 12). The following day, the communist daily *L'Humanité* evoked the "quiet paranoia" of the Creil principal, Ernest Chenière, while a few days later, the center-right broadsheet *Le Figaro* upped the ante in referring to the "chadors of discord" (Gaspard and Khosrokhavar 1995, 13–14). A chain reaction followed: there was news of other incidents in other schools; some teachers went on strike against the wearing of the hijab; on October 19, direct intervention from Abdallah Ben Mansour and Ahmed Jaballah (cofounder and president of the UOIF—see chapter 3) led to the three Creil girls breaking an agreement that had been reached on October 9 after extensive talks with the wider community; three days later, on October 22, a few hundred Muslims demonstrated in the streets of Paris; and the media surpassed themselves in circus skills. The 1989 affair dominated national debate for the rest of the school year, in particular during the autumn and winter of 1989–90. It quickly became the framing mechanism for a wide-ranging polemic about national identity, involving secularism; the accommodation of "France's second religion"—Islam; the problem of "integration"; racism; religious fundamentalism; and so on. Occasionally, there were passing and generally tokenistic references to women's "emancipation."

Why did the behavior of three young teenagers, and their ensuing expulsion from school, provoke such a "psychodrama"? Part of the reason is to be found in the more general debate, throughout the 1980s, about socioeconomic and political conditions in France and its growing and increasingly problematized Muslim population, with accompanying attention to the issue of racism. Another part is to be found in the intensity of the battle for secularism. Most European-background French participants in the 1989 debate—that is, most of those contributing to the mainstream media debate at that time—referred explicitly and even at length to that battle, as in, for example, an article by well-known political scientist Michel Winock (1989), appropriately titled "La laïcité est un combat" (Secularism is a combat).

The headscarves affair in Creil was in fact the eruption of something that had been increasingly rumbling through the 1980s. Part of that 1980s context, as we saw in chapter 3, was the rise of Islamist "community" groups. Some of these groups were behind various incidents in schools during the 1980s, of which the most commonly cited occurred in a school in Noyon, symbolic heartland of French Protestantism, being the birthplace of Calvin, and coincidentally located in Oise, the same département as Creil. In 1985, a few girls turned up to school wearing hijabs, blocked their ears during natural science classes, and refused to attend swimming classes. By 1988, they were refusing music classes as music was "internal communication with Satan" (cited in Kaltenbach and Tribalat, 2002, 191). Similar incidents occurred elsewhere, and absences on the days of Muslim religious festivals became generalized in some schools. In Creil, however, the lead up to the headscarves affair was initially prompted by the systematic absence from the same school, not of Muslim girls, but of ten Jewish students who returned to class ten days later than everyone else at the end of the school holidays and did not attend school on Saturdays. In June 1989, the school board of the Collège Gabriel Havez made a ruling requiring the attendance of these students on school days, at which time the matter of the three protagonists of the headscarves affair was raised. The board and the regional school inspector both invoked the circular of 1936 and the decree of 1937 concerning religious and political proselytism in their negotiations with representatives of the Jewish and Muslim religious communities and parents of the children. The agreement reached was respected by the Jewish families but not by the Muslim ones, with the now notorious consequences.

If the 1989 eruption was the effect of an accumulation of ever more difficult incidents, it was also a question of timing. The year 1989 was, on one hand, the bicentenary of the French Revolution: it was a year of both national celebration and national introspection. On the other hand, it was the year of a number of high-profile events signaling a more militant presence of Islamism in France, Europe, and across the Mediterranean. On February 14, Iranian leader Ayatollah Khomeini issued a fatwa condemning Salman Rushdie to death for *The Satanic Verses,* published the previous year, forcing Rushdie into hiding in the United Kingdom. Later that year, a European Muslim conference was held in the Netherlands with a view to pressuring European Union governments to grant specific status to Muslim communities, on the basis of a particular interpretation of article 27 of the UN Covenant on Civil and Political Rights (Kaltenbach and Tribalat 2002, 188ff). Across the Mediterranean, in Algeria, the FIS was granted legal status as a political party, roughly a month prior to the Creil expulsions.

So 1989 was both a symbolic year in the French national calendar, and a year in which both Muslim identity politics in Europe and the rise of Islamic political extremism more generally were gathering extra attention. The headscarves debate, within that context, became the catalyst for a debate in which the combat for secularism—and interpretation and application thereof—became inextricably linked with the national angst over "integration" of "immigrants" and the place, in a country that combined both Catholic and secular traditions, of France's second religion. The focal point for that debate was, as former center-right president Valéry Giscard d'Estaing put it, "what French identity is for us" (cited in *Le Figaro,* October 23, 1989).

As concerns the issue of women's rights, while the welfare of the Creil girls in particular and Muslim women in general was often mentioned, it was mainly as a vehicle through which the Republic could be held up as a shining example. The participation of women themselves in the debate was thus more as symbols than as social actors in their own right. Feminist voices in particular were marginalized, and the only Muslim-background or Maghrebian-background commentators cited in a roundup of quotes by prominent figures, published by the center-right daily *Le Figaro,* were three men (*Le Figaro,* October 23, 1989). The first two were Cheikh Tejini Hadam, then rector of the Paris Mosque, and Daniel Youssef, one of the leaders of the FNMF (see chapter 3), both of whose reactions were predictably religiously conservative defenses of hijab-wearing in schools. (The Paris Mosque position was to shift in subsequent years.) The third was Michel Hannoun, former deputy with the RPR, and author of a 1987 report on immigration to the state secretary on human rights, titled, significantly, *L'Homme est l'espérance de l'Homme* (Man is the hope of Man). Hannoun, as might be expected from the author of this report, which adopted a positive "integrationist" line, called for calm rather than passion as the latter would only lead to an increasingly confrontational debate.

The absence of female, and in particular feminist, voices was somewhat curious, given the ambient discourse during much of the 1980s, according to which Maghrebian-background teenage girls and young women were the "driver of integration," as discussed in chapter 3. Some observations were, however, made at the time, and continue to be made up to the present, about the fetishizing focus on the girls while the behavior of boys in schools, and toward the girls, was left unpoliced and largely unexamined.

Jospin and the Council of State *Avis* of 1989

At the level of the state, the "hijab problem" landed first in the lap of Lionel Jospin, then education minister with the ruling Socialist government. A little over a month after the September 18, 1989, expulsion of the three Creil schoolgirls, on October 25, he reminded the National Assembly of the fundamental principles of Republican secularism, namely: "confessional neutrality," prohibition of religious or political proselytism, and the requirement that "pupils and parents respect the rules by which establishments operate" (cited *Le Monde,* November 6, 1989). The following day, he announced his decision to prohibit the expulsion from public schools of girls who continued to wear the hijab, advocating "dialogue" as a means of treating individual cases and emphasizing that "no child should be deprived of his or her right to an education" (cited in *Le Monde,* October 28, 1989). The announcement of Jospin's decision caused a major stir within the government, already somewhat shaken about by a rather badly received public comment by Danielle Mitterrand, wife of then President François Mitterrand. Some days prior to Jospin's announcement, Mme Mitterrand, who was the only woman cited in *Le Figaro*'s October 23 roundup of public comments, had advocated respect for all traditions, "whatever they may be." The then prime minister, Michel Rocard, supported Jospin, stating that he refused "the reductionist choice that would lead, in concrete terms, to an opposition between secularism and refusal of exclusions" (cited by *Le Figaro* under a November 10 front-page headline "Rocard supports Jospin"). Jack Lang, then minister for culture, also came down on Jospin's side; he was one of the many who were to change their position some years down the track. This conception of the "flexible" and "tolerant" secularism of a public school system adapted to a modern multicultural age, accepting all children with all their differences, opposed the more "rigorous" or "intransigent" conception defended by, among others, Jean-Pierre Chevènement (minister for defense, who was to resign from his post some fifteen months later because of his opposition to the Gulf War), Henri Emmanuelli (Socialist Party vice president), Pierre Mauroy (former prime minister, who had been forced to resign following the 1984 crisis over public funding of Catholic schools), and Laurent Fabius (also a former prime minister during the same Socialist Party term in government). According to this "rigorous" (Jacobin) conception, secularism was not to be compromised: the prohibition of religious insignia was applicable to all, without exception. Once again, a French "national identity crisis" was perceived to be at the heart of this conflict within the Socialist Party, as in the broader debate (*Le Monde,* October 28, 1989). Was "being French" primarily a matter of principles or of culture, or both? To what extent could principles be deemed neutral, culture-free? To what extent could they be made to bend without breaking, and what would be the consequences for the Republic?

It was not only within his own party that Jospin's decision caused a stir, as is demonstrated by the November 2 statement by the "five intellectuals" (Badinter et al., 1989), so called because it was penned by five well-known white French intellectuals. Three of them were among the rare women to be granted media access on the issue. The five were Elisabeth Badinter, much criticized over the years by feminists for her antifeminist writings, in particular in the book *Fausse route* (2003; for critiques see Audet 2003; Chiennes de Garde 2003); Régis Debray, Marxist intellectual who was to reappear as a member of the Stasi Commission during the 2003 hijab polemic; Alain Finkielkraut, well known for his work on post-Shoah Jewish identity in France and the problem of Shoah denial; he was later to become controversial over comments relating to the 2005 riots; Elisabeth de Fontenay, philosophy professor at the Sorbonne, known for her defense of animal rights; and Catherine Kintzler, author of work on Condorcet and on Republican identity and values, including secularism (Kintzler 1984, 1996).

Their open letter to Jospin was in response to the latter's original decision, taken on October 26 (the expulsion of the three Creil girls having occurred on September 18), to "exclude exclusion" of the three girls. The text by the five intellectuals was one of the most emotively worded statements amid the headscarves outcry. In their open letter, that was titled "Teachers, let us not capitulate!" and commenced "the future will tell us whether the year of the Bicentenary [1989] will have seen the Munich of the Republican school system," the authors made a clear comparison between Jospin's capitulation to Muslim religious interests and President Daladier's capitulation to Hitler in 1938, via the signing of the Munich Accords (Badinter et al., 1989). They were not, however, the first to make this analogy. A week earlier, anthropologist François Pouillon had, in the pages of left-wing daily *Libération,* referred in passing to a possible government backdown in the face of the Islamist lobby as a "derisory Munich" (Pouillon 1989). The five intellectuals went on to emphasize the necessity of "authority" and "discipline" to defend secular schooling: the firm Jacobin hand of strong government (the historical comparison with Daladier being, of course, de Gaulle) versus a weak offering of a lame paw (Badinter et al., 1989).

The publication of this statement marked a significant escalation of an already lively media polemic, with many well-known intellectuals—most of whom, contrary to the five intellectuals cited above, were men—now moving to the center of the media circus ring. A number of them echoed the "crusading" battle-cry rhetoric of the five intellectuals (for example, Winock 1989), focusing strongly on intransigent application of secularism as integral to the survival of the Republic. The position of the authors was, in fact, supported by a number of prominent members of the intellectual, artistic, antiracist, and feminist community, as demonstrated at a public meeting organized on November 28 by Gisèle Halimi and her association *Choisir* around the slogan: "For the Defense of Secularism; For Women's Dignity" (Rochefort 2002, 153).

Media humor accompanying this polemic focused similarly on religion versus secularism. A cartoon published in *Le Monde* on October 28 showed three school pupils side by side: on the left, a boy dressed in the black suit, hat, and face-framing ringlets of ultra-Orthodox Jewish men, reading the Old Testament; in the middle, a girl in full chador, reading the Qur'an; and on the right a boy holding a very large crucifix, reading the New Testament. Over them stood Lionel Jospin, smiling anxiously and sweating profusely, saying: "And your maths books? Where are your maths books, you little scoundrels?" The three are shown replying in unison: "One more word, and we'll call the TV stations!" A few days later, in the issue of *Le Nouvel Observateur* containing the article by the five intellectuals, appeared another article reporting "Lionel Jospin's crazy week" (Bazin 1989), accompanied by another cartoon on the theme of multiple religious onslaught. On the left, three school children: a boy scout with a cross on his hat, a Jewish boy clothed as in the cartoon discussed above, and a girl wearing hijab and jilbab. In the middle, with his back to us, a male adult, probably intended to be Jospin, saying angrily: "No! *That* is not just tradition [a fairly obvious reference to Danielle Mitterrand's comment], it's propaganda!! Get out!!" indicating the exit to a forlorn-looking pupil on his, and our, right, dressed in the Republican *bonnet phrygrien* (Phrygian cap) adorned with a *cocarde* (tricolor rosette), symbols par excellence of the Revolution and the Republic (see chapter 8). The point being, of course, along the lines of that made by the five intellectuals, that Jospin had sacrificed Republican values to the diktats of religion.

Confronted with this polemic, with divisions in his own party and with the specter of the 1984 crisis—with which the 1989 headscarves affair was now being liberally compared—looming large, Jospin referred the matter to the Council of State. Set up in 1799, with its role redefined by an 1872 law, the Council of State (*Conseil d'état*) is the highest administrative authority in France. It has the power to make determinations on the constitutionality of new legislation and is the highest court of appeal on matters of public administration. Its *avis* no. 346.893, handed down on November 27, 1989, would become the reference point for courts and government alike for close to fifteen years.[1] In making it, the Council of State referred to many national and international laws, including the 1905 Law on the Separation of Church and State, the European Convention on Human Rights (1950, ratified 1981), and the two 1966 UN International Covenants on Civil and Political Rights and on Economic, Social and Cultural Rights. It also referred to two French laws adopted just months previously: law 89-486 of July 10, 1989, on orientation in education, and law 89-548 of August 2, 1989, concerning the conditions of entry and residence of foreigners in France. The relevant articles of the former concerned the right to an education and freedom of expression of school students within the context of respect for "neutrality and plurality," and their requirement to attend classes and respect teaching activities (article 1). The law further mentioned that schools provided an environment favoring equality between men and women (article 1). The relevant articles

---

1. The term *avis* means advice or opinion, but I have kept the original French term as the use of either of these English terms could convey the impression that the *avis* is not legally binding, which would be incorrect.

of the latter law concerned nondiscrimination by public authorities against individuals or groups on the basis of nationality, ethnicity, or religion (article 1) and the responsibility of schools to "inculcate in children respect for the individual, for his or her origins and differences" (article 2).

The key paragraph of the Council of State's *avis* reads as follows:

> In schools, the wearing by students of signs by which they intend to manifest their religious affiliation is not by itself incompatible with the principle of secularism, insofar as it constitutes the exercise of freedom of expression and freedom of manifestation of religious beliefs, but . . . this freedom should not allow students to sport signs of religious affiliation that, due to their nature, the conditions in which they are worn individually or collectively, or their ostentatious character or display as a protest, would constitute an act of pressure, provocation, proselytism or propaganda, or would jeopardize the dignity or freedom of the student or of other members of the school community, would compromise their health or safety, or would perturb the conduct of teaching activities or the educational role of the teachers, or would disturb order in the establishment or the normal operation of the public service. (Conseil d'Etat 1989)

A small vocabulary note is warranted here. The French term *ostentatoire*, used by the Council of State, translates as ostentatious, conspicuous, or visible. It does not, however, have in French the connotation of pretension that it does in English. It means highly conspicuous or showy. The economic term "conspicuous consumption," for example, is expressed in French as *consommation ostentatoire*. I will nonetheless use "ostentatious" here to make the distinction clear between *ostentatoire* used in the 1989 Council of State ruling, and later, as we will see in chapter 5, in the 1994 Bayrou circular, and *ostensible* (conspicuous, highly visible), the term that was used in the wording of the 2004 law.

In the following paragraphs, the Council of State explicitly left it to school boards and local education authorities to determine their own regulations concerning the application of the principles outlined in the ruling, according to procedures for school governance set out in ministerial decrees of 1976 and 1985. Local administrative tribunals would have the power to determine the necessity or otherwise of an expulsion and any student so expelled would have the right to attend a private school or follow correspondence classes. The latter right is also open to any other student suspended or expelled from school for whatever reason, in accordance with the 1959 law on compulsory schooling for all children up to the age of sixteen.

The Council of State *avis* was at once perfectly clear and perfectly vague, and as such, appeared to satisfy everyone—and no one. On one hand, it appeared to support Jospin in maintaining that wearing of religious insignia did not per se violate the 1905 law on the separation of church and state, but on the other, it empowered schools to discipline students whose wearing of religious insignia was perceived to jeopardize the political and religious neutrality of the school environment. The definition of what constituted "ostentation," "provocation," "pressure," "proselytism," or "propaganda," or of what might constitute a disturbance to public order, was, however, left open, which constituted a problem that was to become increasingly evident in the years to follow, as we will see in the next chapter.

Jacobins versus Girondins, Two Hundred Years down the Track

It was not only within the government, however, that the 1989 affair caused ructions. It divided most political and community groups, however tightly or loosely defined, notably those on the left. The 1984 debate over the funding of Catholic schools had created a political crisis, but it remained a Franco-French debate, in terms of both its participants and the matter under debate, with Republican secularism on one side and the Catholic Church on the other. The historical and political battle lines were clearly drawn. The 1989 debate, however, in introducing new elements into an old argument, blurred those lines, creating new contradictions and confusions. Hence its divisiveness, as the Franco-French political and intellectual players in the public debate grappled with questions that took them outside what had historically been the Franco-French arena. How did one argue for respect for cultural diversity without undermining secularism? How did one argue for freedom of conscience without encouraging Islamic proselytism? How did one refuse such proselytism without becoming intolerant of cultural diversity? How to defend women's emancipation without advocating exclusion on one hand or opening doors to Islamic fundamentalist wedge politics on the other?

Within the mainstream debate, many of those who had been on the side of Catholic schools in the 1984 debate now, curiously, opposed the hijab *in the name of Republican secularism*. This particular contradiction (or hypocrisy) was to recur throughout the debate, in particular at the time of the second and third "affairs" in 1994 and 2003–5, as we have already seen in part in chapter 2. It became clear, particularly in retrospect, that for many, race was a more important issue than religion. Charles Pasqua, for example, author of notorious 1993 laws that both restricted immigration and removed automatic "birthright" (*droit du sol*) that conferred French nationality to all those born on French soil, was in 1989 the leader of the opposition RPR group in the Senate. Pasqua's "instinctive reaction" in 1989 was "to say no to the veil, because it is a distinctive mark . . . and this is not normal within secular schools" (quoted in *Le Figaro*, October 23). Yet four years later he moved to reinforce "distinctive marks" of another sort: between those born in France of French parents and those born in France of non-French parents, with his 1993 nationality law.

Interestingly, however, the main conservative spokespersons for the three monotheisms demonstrated a rare moment of unity, which was coherent for the Catholic Church at least, given its centuries-old battle against secularism. (This unity was, however, subsequently to fracture considerably.) Thus archbishop of Lyons, Monseigneur Decourtay, declared that he was "not personally shocked" by women wearing the hijab, and Monseigneur Lustiger, archbishop of Paris, did not wish to wage "war against teenage *beurs*" (both quoted in *Le Figaro*, October 23, 1989). Even significantly more left-wing Catholics such as Monseigneur Jacques Gaillot, at the time bishop of Evreux, recognized the "Koranic veil" as a "cultural and religious sign" that "the secular school system should be able to integrate" (quoted in *Le Monde*, October 25, 1989). Protestants were somewhat more divided, but a number sided with the Catholic hierarchy. Pastor Jean-Pierre Montsarrat, for example, who was at the time vice president of the Protestant Federation of France, found it "unacceptable to make children pay, by expelling them from school, for adults' inability to deal with the problems of our society" (quoted in *Le Figaro*, October 23, 1989). This was, admittedly, a somewhat different argument to those of the Catholics in that it placed the accent more on the welfare of children than on the acceptance of religion. On the Jewish side, the then grand rabbi of Paris, Alain Goldmann, was of the opinion that "it is no longer religious representatives that are demonstrating intolerance . . . but the secularists," who "refuse Muslim children [curiously, the paper citing him used the word "children" in the masculine] the right to wear the chador, and Jewish children [the paper also, this time correctly, used the masculine form] the *kippa* [yarmulke] in schools" (quoted in *Le Monde,* October 21, 1989). This comment by Goldmann also demonstrates the terminological confusion between hijab and chador so often made at the time, as I noted in chapter 1, and as we will see elsewhere.

This collusion of the mostly conservative senior office bearers of the monotheistic religions is not, however, as rare as one might think. Jewish and Muslim leaders had supported the Catholic Church's condemnation of Martin Scorcese's 1988 film *The Last Temptation of Christ* and the following year, the Catholic Church supported Islamist condemnation of Salman Rushdie's *Satanic Verses* (Ragache 1990). More recently in the Middle East, senior Christian, Jewish, and Muslim religious leaders in Israel held a historic joint press conference, on March 30, 2005, to protest a plan to organize World Pride (a world gay, lesbian, bisexual, and transgender gathering) in Jerusalem later that year, saying that it would "offend the very foundations of our religious values and the character of the Holy City."[2] Muslim countries, the Vatican, and non-Western Catholic countries also find themselves on the same side at UN deliberations concerning homosexual and reproductive rights.

In France in 1989, however, the monotheistic consensus was not complete. The ultraright Monseigneur Lefebvre, who had been excommunicated in 1988 for his sustained opposition to liberalization within the Catholic Church and in particular to interreligious dialogue, advocated radical solutions to the hijab problem: either conversion or deportation to their "country of origin" (quoted in *Le Courrier Australien,* December 1989). Lefebvre of course found natural allies among the French extreme-right. Bruno Mégret, then one of the main figures of the National Front, was cited in the tabloid *Le Quotidien de Paris* as saying that "Islamic civilization is arriving. After its installation on French soil, it is now implanting itself symbolically through the wearing of the chador in schools" (cited in Gaspard and Khosrohkavar 1995, 18).

2. http://www.worldnetdaily.com/news/article.asp?ARTICLE_ID=43567.

On the ultrareligious end of the Muslim spectrum, the UOIF and the FNMF both weighed into the debate and were certainly active in behind-the-scenes agitation, as they had been in the opposition to Salman Rushdie earlier in the year. In an open letter to prime minister Michel Rocard dated November 21, 1989, the then president of UOIF, Ahmed Jaballah, claimed that wearing the hijab was an obligation for all Muslim women and took exception to a statement by Rocard that the hijab was a sign of women's alienation.

Elsewhere on the French political scene, however, the divisions were far greater, and it was on the left in particular that the debate between two conceptions of secularism, within the context of the wider debate on race and culture, was the most fiercely waged. While the left—and most of the center-right—staunchly defended *both* the principles of secularism *and* a "politics of integration," it was unable to reach consensus on what precise content to give either of these, and how they might interact happily. Two fairly distinct positions emerged that roughly corresponded to those in evidence in the Socialist Party, as outlined above, and that could be broadly characterized (setting aside historical nuances) as a latter-day Girondin-Montagnard (or Jacobin) opposition. On one side was the tolerance lobby ("Girondins"), those who wished to see a "flexible" interpretation of secularism that would be inclusive of "other" cultures (the position adopted at the time by SOS-Racisme, the Mouvement contre le Racisme et pour l'Amitié entre les Peuples, some of the Socialists, some intellectuals, and the Greens). On the other, the intransigents ("Jacobins") maintained that the equality and freedom guaranteed by secularism necessitated rigor and sacrifice, and that true integration could only be achieved through personal and collective discipline (some intellectuals, including Muslim; the Communist Party; and some of the Socialists). The five intellectuals, with their insistence on the Republic and on discipline, and their comparison of Jospin's tolerant position to the capitulation of Daladier at Munich, most clearly portray the latter position. For them, the basis of the Republic is its school system and the wearing of the hijab within schools was the thin end of the wedge:

> Negotiating, as you are ["you" is Lionel Jospin], by announcing that the government will yield, this has a name: capitulation. Such "diplomacy"

only serves to embolden those very people it claims to mollify—and if they ask tomorrow that *their* children be spared the study of all those Rushdies (or Spinozas, Voltaires, Baudelaires, Rimbauds . . .) that encumber our teaching, how are we to refuse them? (Badinter et al. 1989, 31)

The point about wedge politics is well made, but comparing Jospin's "capitulation" to that of Daladier in 1938, to the most frightening dictatorship of modern times, is problematic, for it was a hyperbolic shock tactic that on one level resembled the extreme-right "Muslim invasion" rhetoric. Consider, for example, the words of Creil principal Ernest Chenière, later to become an RPR deputy and one of the strongest advocates for a law outlawing religious insignia:

Imagine that it is no longer three young girls that pose a problem but a thousand, fifty thousand, this would be horrifying. It is well and truly time that democracy reacts, for otherwise it is doomed to very dark days. (cited in *Le Figaro*, October 21, 1989)

The identification of Islamism with the extreme-right is accurate; the identification of hijabization with Islamism, while hotly debated, is defensible. A call to vigilance, even in 1989, was, from that perspective, not an overdramatization. But the idea of an Islamism poised to eat away at secularism and in doing so, bring down the Republic, veers off into the realm of fantasy. It is entirely plausible in the Muslim world, which in 1989 had *at least* two clearly fundamentalist states (Saudi Arabia and Iran), and where the separation of religion and state remains the exception rather than the norm. It is significantly less plausible in the West, particularly in a country like France, where the majority of Muslims support secularism. Some of the comments made at the time in opposition to the expulsions expressed similar views. Etienne Balibar, Marxist professor of philosophy and coauthor with Immanuel Wallerstein of *Race, nation, classe* (1988) wrote in the pages of left-wing daily *Libération* that it was illusory to think that school discipline in "the land of human rights," as France likes to characterize itself, was going to block Islamist extremism that was operating across the Muslim world: "Democratic humanism will have to find more efficient and intelligent paths by which to support liberation in the Middle East" (Balibar

1989). Balibar was of the opinion that the preoccupation with the "Islamic peril" obscured the reality of racism in France, which was expressed less through the Creil incident than through other restrictions placed on Muslim freedom of religious expression or through the refusal of some municipalities to enroll children of immigrants (Balibar 1989).[3] Balibar echoed the words of Jacques Berque, renowned scholar of the Muslim world, who in his 1985 report *L'Immigration à l'école de la République,* denounced French paternalism, folkloricization of cultures, and the "exclusion of children that are being enclosed within their cultural specificity" (Berque 1985).

Comments such as those by Chenière and the five intellectuals that Islamist wedge politics could bring about the "destruction of the [secular] school system," which in turn "would precipitate that of the Republic" (Badinter et al. 1989, 31), thus appeared, for some, closer to the scaremongering of the extreme-right than to a defense of secularism. Even if the basis of the argument is ostensibly not fear of invasion of Muslim hordes and the ensuing destruction of French culture and way of life, but defense of Republican values of liberty and equality, the tone adopted by Chenière, the five intellectuals, and others who expressed similar views took them sailing very close to the wind of racist assimilationism for which colonial France had been so often and so strongly criticized, from both without and within.

The tolerant faction did not hesitate to pick this up and in doing so pushed the debate firmly back into the arena of the already-existing 1980s debate on immigration, "integration," and racism. According to some, it was here, and not in arguments about the meaning and application of secularism, that the *real* problem underpinning the headscarves affair was to be found. Champions of this position included Jean Daniel, editor of *Le Nouvel*

---

3. Although Balibar did not specify why this was the case, two scenarios immediately come to mind: the children of immigrants without valid residency or work papers and the children of polygamous families. Polygamy was recognized at the time for the purposes of immigration (this was subsequently changed, in 1993), affecting mainly sub-Saharan African families, but not for the purposes of enrollment in public education, social security, and so on: only the children of first wives were so recognized. There was, however, no clear legal basis for exclusion of children from schooling in either case, given that school is by law free and compulsory for all children under sixteen.

Observateur, and Harlem Désir, the charismatic president of SOS-Racisme (which was later, under different leadership, to change its position, joining the call for a law against religious insignia). For Jacques Julliard, professor at the Ecole des Hautes Etudes en Sciences Sociales (France's leading social sciences university) and then regular editorial columnist with *Le Nouvel Observateur,* the debate over immigration had, with the headscarves affair, "undeniably taken a religious turn":

> So? Mohammed's fault? Let us be careful. The anti-Islamic argument has for a long time been a convenient alibi, dressing up hatred of Arabs and the refusal to welcome them in a cloak of respectability. Let us also note that the withdrawal into a community, based on an aggressive assertion of tribal identity, is a classic reflex of minority groups that do not feel entirely accepted or who feel this identity is threatened. (Julliard 1989, 33)

According to this point of view, then, the panic over three hijabs was attributable to an anti-Arab racism that is deeply entrenched in French society, politics, and culture. It also translated a refusal to deal with the identity crisis that was less the problem of France's Maghrebian-background population and its problems of "integration" over which politicians, the media, and intellectuals alike had agonized for the previous decade, than a problem of French society as a whole. The tolerants thus appeared to be more clearly preoccupied than the intransigents by the issue of anti-Arab sentiment in French society and many, like Daniel, tended to characterize the position of the intransigents as simply veiled racism. Opinion polls taken at the time of the affair tend to give credence to such a view. A poll conducted for the daily *Le Monde* by the market research company IFOP and published on November 30, 1989, indicated that 60 to 75 percent of those surveyed associated Islam with violence, regression, intolerance, and oppression of women, and roughly the same number were hostile to the building of more mosques in France (cited in Liauzu 1990, 65).

It is significant that the term "hostage" recurs frequently in public commentary by the tolerants, providing a sort of thematic link between people who would be in ferocious disagreement on other issues. For Protestant Pastor Monsarrat as for Marxist-leaning philosopher Etienne Balibar, for Claire Bataille of the Trotskyist-feminist magazine *Les Cahiers du féminisme*

(Feminist notebooks) as for philosopher Bernard-Henri Lévy, notorious in the feminist movement for his numerous antifeminist writings and comments, the three Creil schoolgirls were "hostages," "alibis," or even "victims" of a sociopolitical problem and debate that are situated at another level (Bataille 1989; Lévy 1989). Moreover, according to some of the tolerants, the intransigents, in penalizing the children, confused them with their parents, as Claude Allègre, then special adviser to the minister for education, put it (Allègre 1989, 33).

In response to such accusations of racism or pleas for inclusion or respect for other cultures, some white-European-background intransigents counterattacked. Journalist Serge Maury, for example, writing in the pages of the left-leaning newsweekly *L'Evénement du Jeudi* (main rival of *Le Nouvel Observateur*), some eighteen months after the 1989 affair commenced, considered it racist to tolerate from Muslims what would be intolerable from Christians, as if Muslims were incapable by definition of following "common democratic rules," arrested in their development, a combination of "big kids and archaic beings" (Maury 1991).

The intransigents also returned against the tolerants the accusation of confusing the children with their parents. According to them, the hijabization of the girls was, as one Maghrebian-background feminist supporter of the expulsions put it, "an Islamist setup," with the girls being pawns in the Islamist game of wedge politics.[4] While few feminists of Maghrebian background who held this view were cited in the press, a few Muslim-background men were. One of them was Arezki Dahmani, president of the "integrationist" immigrant/multicultural association France Plus. According to Dahmani, "500 integrists of Turkish background have imposed their law on 56 million French people, among them 4 million Muslims, who want nothing either of this integrism or of this way of acting" (quoted in newsweekly *Le Point,* November 30, 1989). Similarly, Maurice Benassayag, who, like Michel Hannoun was an "integrated" Algerian, a member of France's political elite (but on the Socialist side), stressed that "one does not build a nation by glorifying the cult of differences" (1989, 14). Like Dahmani, he stressed that hijabization was a marginal phenomenon, involving a very small group

4. Fatéma Mezyane, personal communication, August 28, 1992.

of students (a pro-hijab demonstration in Paris on October 22 was attended by only 500 people, according to the police). Where Dahmani placed the blame at the door of a "defective political system" in France, Benassayag called to account the surprising "faculty for ignorance" of politicians, saying that France had "waited for the very photogenic veiled girls from Creil to discover the problem of an integrist threat in France" (1989, 14). According to Benassayag, if there was such a threat now, it was because of political neglect in France and a piecemeal approach to dealing with issues. He pointed in particular to the number of mosques in France run by foreign imams with conservative and even fundamentalist views, rather than more representative French Muslims.

It was, of course, somewhat more difficult to accuse a Dahmani or a Benassayag of racism than it was to accuse a Badinter, but Ernest Chenière, the Creil principal, found himself at the center of such accusations. Interviewed on October 12, 1989, by *Le Nouvel Observateur*, he commented that the previous year, when he did not allow students be absent on Jewish shabbat, he was accused of anti-Semitism, and now was accused of racism. The journalist interviewing him commented that at that, he laughed, and added that he was from Martinique: the assumption being that if one is of Afro-Caribbean background, one cannot be racist (Chenière 1989). There are, however, pecking orders in racisms: even if Chenière is himself racialized, he sits higher up the pecking order in both class and race terms than a sub-Saharan African street-sweeper or an unemployed Maghrebian factory worker. That said, this observation does not in itself make Chenière either racist or antiracist, and accusations of "racism" certainly appear much more absurd when leveled at someone who is himself racialized, even if not in the same way.

Liberty, Equality, and, *Still*, Fraternity

One point on which the tolerants and the intransigents apparently agreed was their concern for the welfare of the girl "hostages," which would be ensured by removal of their hijabs. The five intellectuals maintained, for example, that secular school was also a place of "emancipation" where "equality between the sexes" would be respected. Admitting a symbol of "female submission" into this emancipatory space would be to undermine the principle of equality

(Badinter et al. 1989, 30). On the tolerant side, Allègre was of the opinion that "the best way to remove the veil" was to "admit the girls into secular schools, where they can learn, compare, understand and in the end make up their own minds" (Allègre 1989, 33). Even if, in 1989, speaking of women's rights and equality between the sexes in the context of a debate featuring girls and schooling could be assumed to be relatively unextraordinary, it is noteworthy that almost all left-wing participants in the debate referred to the "oppression" or "emancipation"—and, occasionally, "liberation"—of women, although they usually employed the singular *la femme*, long-criticized by feminists in France as a symbolic abstraction that negated the experience of flesh-and-blood women. As Christine Delphy put it in 1980:

> Ten years after the appearance of the Women's Liberation Movement, there are still people like Georges Marchais [at the time leader of the Communist Party], who speak of "the liberation of *la Femme*," who forget the "s" that makes all the difference between a myth and flesh-and-blood beings. (Delphy 1980, 3)

Notwithstanding this annoying persistence of references to that mythical *la femme* in the 1989 hijab debate, the rhetoric used by participants in that debate concerning her "oppression" and "emancipation" was persuasive, and the sentiments expressed appeared sincere (whether one agreed or not with the generally expressed view that the "veil" was the symbol of the oppression of women).

With few exceptions, however, it was not the welfare of the girls but *the interest of the Republic* that was central for these commentators. For the tolerants, for example, the main goal was to find a solution that provided the greatest chances of "integration." As Daniel put it:

> I wager on the Republican school system. . . . [I]t is possible—not certain but possible—in keeping the young Muslim girls at school with their head-scarf, to exert an influence over them that will be greater than that of their families. (Daniel 1989a, 32)

Similarly, for Elisabeth Badinter, one of the intransigents, what was unacceptable above all was not so much the oppression of women but "the flouting of two principles as precious as Republican secularism and equality among human beings" (Badinter 1989, 37). Even if the latter point was a reference to equality between men and women, it was also a reference to equality between people of different cultural backgrounds and religious faiths. On the tolerant side, Jean Daniel showed himself to be every bit as good a Republican by insisting that the alternative of private Islamic schools (advocated by Badinter among others) would "result in these girls being lost to the Republic" (Daniel 1989a, 32). Daniel's words echo those of Jules Ferry, who a little over a century earlier, in advocating public schooling for women, had urged his parliamentary colleagues to decide that *la Femme* should "belong" to Science and not to the Church.[5]

In some respects, then, the tolerants and the intransigents of the 1989–90 debate appear less far apart than the intensity of the debate would have led one to believe. The fundamental difference between the two camps is not over the meaning of secularism nor over the road to the "emancipation" of women, nor indeed, for the most part, the bases of "French identity," but over the primary frame of reference. The intransigents remained firmly on the Jacobin terrain of Republican values that must be defended, almost at all costs, while the tolerants placed themselves on the contextual terrain of the "problem" of "integration," advocating what appeared to them to be the best means of resolving it. On both sides, the responsibility for the "oppression of women" was presumed to lie at the door of Islamic fundamentalists and, by implied extension in many cases, the whole Muslim world, but it was definitely *not* the Republic's problem. Its institutions, starting with its school system, were presumed to be *by definition* egalitarian and liberating of women. I will once again use the examples of Daniel and Badinter, as their rhetoric is fairly representative of that deployed within the mainstream debate and has the advantage of being extremely clear.

Three years prior to the 1989 headscarves affair, Badinter had authored a much-publicized book that was much criticized by feminists, in which she claimed that the French Revolution had put an end to patriarchy (Badinter 1986; Martinet 1987). Her 1989 words concerning the values of the Republic and the "emancipation" of women were necessarily framed within the context of this previous work. For Daniel, it was the *mission civilisatrice*:

5. Speech at the Salle Molière, Apr. 10, 1870. Cited in Mayeur 1985.

> We must do all we can to encourage men who, within Islam, are fighting
> for the modernization of their religion and in particular for the emancipa-
> tion of woman. (Daniel 1989a, 33)

The use of *les hommes* (men) and *la femme* (woman) is telling. It has been
argued that the generalization of the masculine plural to mean "humanity"
has a specific historical connotation in French that it does not in English,
namely, the reference to *Les Droits de l'homme,* encapsulated in the 1789
Declaration of that name, among other things. Its replacement by "people"
is thus a less straightforward linguistic exercise in French than in English,
as neither "les personnes" nor "les gens" fits this purpose very well in many
cases. The feminist counterargument is that continued use of the term *les
hommes* is also the result of entrenched misogyny that likewise dates back
to the time of the Revolution, as Olympe de Gouges' authoring in 1791
of the *Déclaration des droits de la femme* attests. Replacement of *Les Droits
de l'homme* by *Les Droits de la personne* or the "generic" "les hommes" by
"l'humanité," "les hommes et les femmes," or another suitable expression has
been an even harder battle for feminists in French than in English, and one
that largely remains not won. The use here by Daniel of "les hommes" defines
"people within Islam" as being male, and disappears women's fight for their
own emancipation. The implicit message is clear: women are not agents who
"emancipate" themselves, but symbolic representations ("woman") whose
status can be altered only by the actions of men.

Seen in such a light, the various arguments in favor of women's "emancipation" begin to appear specious. They do not originate within a feminist
analysis of the French Republic as male supremacist but, on the contrary, are
put to the service of defending that same Republic as liberator of Muslim girls.
So, if the hijab is the "symbol of the oppression of a sex" (Badinter 1989), then
to remove the oppression, one must remove the hijab. It was not, however, so
much "the oppression of a sex" that was bothersome for these 1989 defenders
of the Republic, whether tolerant or intransigent, but a particular manifestation thereof. It was the symbol that was bothersome, much more than any
oppression it might represent: a Muslim woman who walks about bareheaded
is not *always* or *necessarily* in less danger of oppression than one who wears a
headscarf, as testimony, then and now, by Maghrebian-background women of

violence against them demonstrates (Bellil 2002; Amara 2004). (That said, some nuancing is required with relation to the age of girls, a point to which I will return in chapter 7.) In 1989–90, activists with Maghrebian-background feminist organizations active at the time, such as Les Nanas Beurs and Expressions Maghrébines au Féminin, pointed out that the absence of a headscarf did not stop men taking their daughters back to the "country of origin" and marrying them off by force, for example.

It was thus the *image* of oppression, rather than the reality, that disturbed the majority of participants in the mainstream debate at that time. Through that imagery, including illustrations that accompanied various articles and features at the time, runs a neo-orientalist combination of fascination, desire, fear, and repugnance. As Rachel Bloul has noted, apart from the stereotypical "world-behind-the-veil" images that appeared in the French press at the time, there was a proliferation of sexualized imagery in the various cartoons that also inevitably appeared (Bloul 1994). One of these cartoons, published in the satirical weekly *Le Canard Enchaîné* on October 25, 1989,[6] shows a nun saying angrily: "Give them an inch, they take a mile!" indicating the length of the "mile" with her hands, while a young, trendily dressed hijab-clad woman with a typical pretty-girl face walks casually away with a large pair of scissors that she has just used to cut a corresponding amount of material for her hijab out of the back of the nun's skirt, exposing the nun's unflattering underwear and large buttocks. Bloul writes:

> By fantasizing young Muslim women as autonomous libidinal actors, it establishes an imaginary alliance with them in the ridiculing of the old, repressive, patriarchal orders represented paradoxically by the figure of the nun. Thus, the French, male viewer can accomplish, in fantasy at least, the complicity of the forbidden woman. . . . This cartoon is also highly ambiguous in its illustrations of the links between sexuality and representations of the Other in two highly derogatory images of women. (Bloul 1994, 124)

6. The word *canard* (literal meaning, "duck") is used colloquially to describe a tabloid, low-quality paper. The addition of the adjective *enchaîné* (chained/bound) evokes various literary sources, including *Prometheus Bound* and Alfred Jarry's satirically grotesque character of King Ubu, in the play *Ubu enchaîné*.

Bloul further points out that it is only via a sexuality defined and controlled by men that women are able to appear as autonomous social actors within French society. The hypersexualization of the young Muslim woman in the cartoon thus has a double meaning: she is at once "forbidden" and "liberated" and as such, doubly seductive. Moreover, in exposing the buttocks of the nun, showing her hairy legs and dowdy undergarments, the cartoon uses the hypersexualized Muslim girl as the agent of mocking sexualization of a supposedly asexual figure. Finally, the cartoon overlays a supposed Catholic-Muslim hostility with a female-female hostility, taken to the extreme of old, ugly woman versus young and beautiful one.

Seen but Not Heard: Women in the Margins

Cartoons such as this, along with endless photographs of the three Creil schoolgirls or headscarved participants in the October 22 demonstration, were the main ways in which women, particularly of Maghrebian background, "participated" in the mainstream media debate. They were the image accompanying the words of men. The only woman who made it into *Le Figaro's* October 23 roundup of quotable quotes from representatives of government, political parties, associations, trade unions, and religious organizations was Danielle Mitterrand, wife of the then president. This was also due, of course, to the conspicuous absence of women in any positions of political power in these organizations. Not even Michèle André, then state secretary for women's rights, merited citing, although a short interview with her appeared in *Vendredi* some two weeks later, on November 10. Around the same time, the daily *Le Quotidien* cited comments by former women's rights minister, Yvette Roudy, that "to accept veiling would come down to saying yes to women's inequality in French Muslim society," and by prominent feminist lawyer Gisèle Halimi (November 6 and 2, respectively, cited in Gaspard and Khosrokhavar 1995, 195). The latter had organized a petition and meeting in Paris in support of the five intellectuals and resigned from SOS-Racisme because of its opposition to the Creil expulsions, saying that the SOS-Racisme slogan "Touche pas à mon pote" (hands off my mate) obviously referred only to men. These comments were, however, rare exceptions, for the major broadsheets and newsmagazines largely ignored what women had to say, leading to the comment by Jeanne-Hélène Kaltenbach and Michèle Tribalat some thirteen years later that at the time "few women expressed themselves" on the subject, implying that this was the choice of the women rather than the media (Kaltenbach and Tribalat 2002, 204). In a lengthy supplement to a July 1990 issue of *L'Evénement du Jeudi* devoted to the affair and to the issues of secularism and Islam, a number of commentators from 1989—political, religious, and intellectual—were quoted. This time, no Danielle Mitterrand. Not even an Elisabeth Badinter. And certainly no female ministers, ex-ministers, or representatives of Muslim women's or feminist groups. No woman was considered to have anything memorable enough to say.

This is not, however, to say that commentary by women was completely absent. Apart from the obligatory photographs of the three teenagers at the center of the affair and other hijab-clad girls, the papers occasionally cited the girls, often to sensationalizing effect. For example, following Danielle Mitterrand's comments on "respecting traditions, whatever they are," *Le Figaro* of October 23 sported the headline: "'We'll keep it on until we die': the Creil integrists do not want to give in; Mme Mitterrand's declarations reinforce their determination." The article starts by citing Leïla and Fatima Achaboun, two of the three Creil girls, as saying, repeatedly and determinedly: "We've always worn the headscarf, even at home. We'll keep it on until we die! We can wear it at school: Mme Mitterrand said so on television" (cited in *Le Figaro,* October 23, 1989). *Le Figaro,* which characterizes the girls as using Danielle Mitterrand's words as a protective shield, does, however, join most of the other dailies in portraying the girls as pawns in a power game among adults.

Commentary by other Muslim-background women was relatively rare. There were of course commentaries by male "experts" reminding the French public of the difficulties encountered by women targeted by Islamists in Algeria or Iran. Among these were an interview with Tunisian minister for culture Habib Boulares ("Non à l'uniforme politique!") in *Le Nouvel Observateur* (Boulares 1989), and an interview with Syrian doctor and anthropologist Haytham Manna, resident in France, who recalled what is actually written in the Qur'an about veiling and denounced the dishonesty of some fundamentalist "translations" (Manna 1989, 38). Manna also referred at some length to Egyptian modernists and to the feminism of Huda Sha'rawi (39).

Rare, however, were articles featuring commentary by Muslim-background women, and these took a little time to appear. *Le Monde* of November 24 quoted Sultana Cheurfa of the Cercle des Socialistes de Culture Musulmane (Circle of Socialists of Muslim Culture), who supported prohibition of the hijab in schools as the best ally of young women in resisting its imposition by their fathers. A couple of articles appearing a little later featured such resistants. In December, *Le Figaro* featured Iranian women exiles in France who expressed surprise that the Council of State did not simply ban the hijab in schools *(Le Figaro,* December 11, 1989). The following July, during the wave of "roundup" articles of the year's debate, the women's monthly magazine *Marie-France* focused on a young Maghrebian-background French woman, in her final year in high school in the northern suburbs of Paris, who rebelled against a hijab imposed by her father by living a "double life": headscarved in her neighborhood, but bareheaded at school or out with her friends (Legrand 1990). The article also featured a photograph of the massive 1990 demonstration against the Islamic Salvation Front in Algiers on International Women's Day (March 8).

Remarkable by its virtual uniqueness in the mainstream press was a November 9, 1989, article by Algerian-born journalist Florence Assouline in the newsmagazine *L'Evénement du Jeudi.* Assouline subsequently published a book: *Musulmanes: Une chance pour l'Islam* (Muslim women: a chance for Islam), (1992), a study of Maghrebian women's fights for their rights in Algeria and in France. Titled "Paroles de musulmanes" (Muslim women speak), the 1989 article is remarkable not only because it features the voices of Muslim women but also because it foregrounds feminist voices, in a media debate in which the latter were largely silenced. The article is accompanied by a photograph of young Maghrebian-background women, dressed, made-up and nail-polished in Western feminine style, together in a group that looks at once festive and activist. One, smiling, has one arm round a friend's shoulder and the other raised in the air in a fist. They appear to be watching or looking at something outside the frame. Assouline interviewed spokeswomen for three women's groups: Les Nanas Beurs, EMAF, and L'Eveil (the Awakening), an Iranian women's group. Les Nanas Beurs and L'Eveil explicitly identified as feminist, although this is not discussed in Assouline's article, and both had close associations with the autonomous feminist movement.

The position of EMAF, while feminist, was more ambiguous in terms of its relationship with the broader women's movement. Both EMAF and Les Nanas Beurs, represented respectively in this article by their presidents Alima Boumediene—whom we will meet again later as an ally of Une Ecole Pour Tous-tes and Les Indigènes de la République—and Souad Benani, opposed the expulsion of the students. This was not, however, unanimous in the case of the Nanas Beurs, as we will see. For Benani, "We are plunged into the middle of a paradox. How can feminists oppose exclusion without supporting the wearing of the veil?" Benani, who then taught in a LEP (Lycée d'enseignement professionnel), one of the technical high schools for students not envisaging academic or professional careers, and widely considered "difficult" by teachers who worked in them, described the Muslim girls who made up 80 percent of her female student population:

> They arrive at school, wan and subdued. After morning recreation, back they come all made up and spruced up. As if by magic, their skirts are shorter and their appearance less strict. It is only through school that they escape from their families. It's a big breath of oxygen [for them]. I've tried to get a debate going on the veil, but they're not interested! All they know is that they do not want to be like the girls from Creil. (cited in Assouline 1989, 22)

Benani told Assouline, as she told me in conversation three years later, that les beurettes are mostly like her students, *"very* trendy, you don't find trendier than them."[7] Firmly opposed to private religious schools, Benani was against leaving the headscarved girls to choose between correspondence classes and private Islamic (or Catholic) schools. She was also firm on the necessity for the headscarved girls to follow the whole curriculum without exception (most of the problematic cases, then as in the years to follow, involved some sort of attendance problem or supposed religious objection to parts of the curriculum). Boumediene, for her part, was not opposed to the creation of "Franco-Muslim" schools that would be co-financed by the state and subject to strict regulation, like Christian or Jewish Schools. Her explanation as to why the affair had been so inflammatory was that "it concerns the

7. Personal communication, Jan. 20, 1993.

driver of integration: women"—thus picking up the by this time hackneyed expression concerning the apparently huge integrative potential of young Maghrebian-background women. She noted her concern that on both sides of the debate, "Once again, they have silenced us on the pretext of protecting us. They need to stop infantilizing us, we have paid a high enough price to know what is good or bad for us" (cited in Assouline 1989, 23). Given the small amount of public discursive space given to women of any background, let alone Maghrebian, during the months of the headscarves debate, Boume-diene's comment was most appropriate.

The person from L'Eveil, who did not wish to be identified by name, commented that:

> Putting the issue of racism before that of the rights of women would be to commit the same error that was fatal in Iran. In 1979, we said to ourselves: if we need to don the chador to fight the Shah and American imperialism, why not? After all, it's only a piece of cloth. Mistake! For the first decision the government made to consolidate its power was to make the wearing of the veil an obligation. . . . Everywhere, fanatics are taking advantage of the slight-est backsliding by secularists to progress their laws. If the Republic yields, all those families who are still resisting integrism will yield. We have paid too high a price for such simple "negligence." (cited in Assouline 1989, 23)

The position of Iranian women, as presented here in feminist form by the representative of L'Eveil, and in more mainstreamed form in the article from *Le Figaro* cited earlier in this chapter, while perhaps unsurprising, given the direct experience of Islamism as described by L'Eveil, has been noteworthy in its relatively consistent intransigence throughout the two decades of the headscarf debate. Their particular defense of "Republican values" is, how-ever, articulated in very different terms from those used for the most part by European-background French. While the latter are concerned about the Republic per se, Iranian women such as those from L'Eveil are concerned about the Republic *as the line of defense for women against fundamentalism*. Unfortunately, the fact that Iranian women are coming from the particular perspective of their experience of state-imposed Islamism has been used to diminish their arguments by pro-hijab French Muslims, who have claimed that "in France, it's not the same."

Assouline's article was to the best of my knowledge the *only* article in the mainstream daily and weekly press at that time to exclusively feature explicitly feminist voices from women of Muslim background. As such, it was both of key importance and insufficient. The only other relatively mainstream article at that time to feature women of Maghrebian background was a Round Table discussion in the January 1990, issue of the monthly magazine *Arabies,* in which two Muslim-background women, intellectuals this time, participated. The first, Leïla Sebbar, a well-known Franco-Maghrebian author and at that time a high school literature teacher, expressed astonishment both at the questioning of secularism and at the fact that it came from Muslims. At the same time, "as a secularist and a daughter of a secularist," and as someone who had "been active in the women's movement," she felt a need to defend the girls:

> I still have trouble in analyzing these contradictions and in seeing how I can resolve them. And not just for me. (Sebbar et al. 1990, 12)

The other woman, sociologist Rabia Abdelkrim, also found herself faced with contradictions:

> All of a sudden there appeared a confrontation between two clans where I, as a woman, was called upon to take a side. . . . You're a woman, you're for women's rights, so obviously, automatically, you're against the headscarf. If you say that there's a need to discuss, to understand, then you're an archaist. In a debate where I attempted to nuance things, I was told "You're scorning the Republic." (in Sebbar et al. 1990, 15)

Abdelkrim was one of those who maintained that it *wasn't* the same thing as in Iran. For her, a prohibition of the headscarf was reminiscent of the right-wing demonstration organized in Algiers in 1958 when women were publicly unveiled (discussed in chapter 3). "That was violence," she commented, "and violence provokes a withdrawal into identity politics. While in Algiers or in the Maghreb I am fiercely opposed to the veil, here the headscarf does not mean the same thing." At the same time, Abdelkrim stressed that, unlike the yarmulke, which is worn by men and boys only, and unlike Christian crosses, which are worn by either sex, the hijab "cannot mean anything other than *underneath,* is a woman. There is absolutely no question of saying that it is a simple scarf, just another item of clothing" (in Sebbar et al. 1990, 16).

On this point, feminists, whatever their position concerning the advisability or otherwise of expulsions from school, were unanimous. But why were we not hearing from them? This was the question asked by Sylvie Caster, writing in the pages of *Le Canard Enchaîné*, in an article just as satirically titled "Le Torchon ne risque pas de brûler." This title, which means, literally, "no risk of the dust cloth/teatowel burning," and figuratively, "no risk of any running battle" is a reference to the first newsletter of the so-called "second wave" of the feminist movement: *Le Torchon brûle* (a feminist play on the literal and figurative meanings), of which the first issue appeared in May 1971. Caster noted that "the famous voice of women" had remained "desperately mute" and called feminists to account over it (Caster 1989).

Yet, as a collective open letter to the media, written by feminist organizations in protest at the media silencing of their voices, puts it:

> A section of public opinion is wondering about our silence.
>
> If our voices are no longer heard, it is not because we have lost them, but because they are not allowed through. This did not begin yesterday. For all we write you letters, communiqués, articles, they are hit with a veritable censorship.
>
> Muslim integrists veil women. Western liberals unveil their bodies. The symptom has merely shifted.
>
> You have thrown a veil over a certain feminist voice, the troublesome one. (Dialogues des Femmes et al. 1990, 8)

The censorship continued: not one mainstream newspaper or magazine published this letter either. Yet it was signed by a number of well-known feminist organizations—including L'Eveil, one of the few to have been contacted by the press, as noted above.

Moreover, as its authors noted, this was far from the first or the only feminist comment to be made; the hypocrisy of the media in silencing feminist voices, while sections thereof deplored that same silence, was flagrant. It was also all the more astonishing in that many of the individual and collective signatories of feminist comments were themselves well known and their opinions would have been of interest to the public. They included press communiqués all issued in the last week of October by L'Eveil, the Mouvement Français pour le Planning Familial (MFPF, French Family Planning Movement), Les Nanas Beurs, EMAF, and by Femmes Sous Lois Musulmanes (FSLM, Women Living Under Muslim Laws); the European bureau of WLUML/FSLM was at that time in Grabels, near Montpellier. They also included a number of individual letters to the press, to political parties, and to Jospin. Finally, the media were sent a collective communiqué authored by several prominent women, including Leïla Sebbar; another two famous authors—the late Marguerite Duras and Algeria's leading female francophone author Assia Djebar, who in 2005 became the fifth woman and the first of Maghrebian background to be elected to the prestigious Académie Française; Hayette Boudjema and Shéhérazade Ouarem, vice president and treasurer of SOS-Racisme; Nora Zaïdi, member of the European Parliament; Noria Allami, social psychologist, whose book *Voilées, dévoilées* on the historical and social background to the practice of veiling in the Muslim world had been published the year before (Allami 1988); high-profile French feminist activists such as Maya Surduts, of the Paris Women's Center among other roles, Souad Benani, president of Les Nanas Beurs; and various other professionals, public figures, and politicians including Socialist deputy Segolène Royal, future candidate for the French presidency.

The press could thus not claim that the authors of the feminist texts were not well known enough to be of interest to the general public. These and other feminist letters and communiqués—including a short article by Fiammetta Venner, later to become a well-known feminist intellectual, journalist, and activist and, with Caroline Fourest, a prominent contributor to the 2003–4 hijab debate—made it into print in a small Parisian feminist publication, the Women's Center newsletter *Paris féministe*.[8] At the time, like many feminist publications in the days before Web sites, *Paris féministe*

---

8. Co-founded as *Paris féministes* in 1982, by Geneviève Prost and myself, and renamed *Paris féministe* in 1985, this publication was produced as a bimonthly by the Paris Women's Center. Another publication, *Ruptures*, started appearing toward the end of *Paris féministe*'s life and continues to appear today. The communiqués cited are Matine 1989; MFPF 1989; Les Nanas Beurs 1989; EMAF 1989; Boudjema et al. 1989; Venner 1989; Femmes Sous Lois Musulmanes et al. 1989.

was produced by largely volunteer labor on a typewriter, stencils, and a roneo machine, but in a national context in which feminist voices were determinedly and deliberately marginalized, it was a precious source of information and comment. The only nationally and newsagency-distributed nonacademic feminist magazine at the time was the Trotskyist-feminist quarterly *Cahiers du féminisme* (its winter 1989 issue contained a five-page spread on the headscarves affair [Bataille 1989]): this was as close as feminism got to mainstream press at the time.

Similarly silenced—apart from occasional shock headlines such as "we'll wear it until we die," or the Assouline article or *Arabies* round table, both cited above—were analyses, by women or girls who wore the hijab or by others, whether feminist and/or of Muslim background or not, of why the hijab was worn more generally and why girls were wearing it in France. There was no discussion of whether or how the girls themselves were complicit, or willing, or forced, or otherwise, beyond what were largely opinion pieces; in later years, this discussion developed more, notably after the publication of various books on Maghrebian-background girls more generally (such as Assouline 1992; Lacoste-Dujardin 1992), on immigrants (Tribalat 1995), or the hijab debate in particular (Altschull 1995; Gaspard and Khosrokhavar 1995). By 2003, the media were falling all over themselves to capture the words and actions of headscarved girls and women, but not necessarily in ways that were any more constructive than their silence of 1989.

As for feminist positions, feminists were as divided as the mainstream/malestream left on the question of whether to expel the headscarved girls or not. As indicated above, the debate caused splits in some groups; at least one activist, who supported the expulsions as a means to check Islamist wedge politics, left the Nanas Beurs because of the group's position against expulsions.[9] Françoise Gaspard, prominent feminist and erstwhile mayor of Dreux, alienated many feminist friends and coactivists by speaking out strongly against expulsions (Gaspard and Khosrokhavar 1995). The "celebrity" collective statement, authored by Boudjema et al. (1989), also came out strongly against expulsions, contrary to L'Eveil and many other feminists.

9. Fatéma Mézyane, personal communication, Aug. 28, 1992.

As noted above, the public debate had referred in passing to "women's emancipation," although, as Hélène Augé commented, it was not until October 24, in the pages of *Le Monde*, that "women's alienation" was explicitly associated with the wearing of the "chador" (Augé 1989, 35). The debate's primary focus nonetheless remained elsewhere: secularism, cohesion of the Republic, racism, "integration," Islam or Islamism, or a combination of these. On the face of it, feminists appeared to fall into line with the tolerant position on one side or the intransigent position on the other, but their arguments were very different, in that the primary focus was the *best interests of the girls,* whether those at the center of the affair or Muslim schoolgirls more generally.

Consider the following extract from a statement by the late Hedda Jullien:

> [The public school system] is not only secular, but also Republican.

So far, it would sit happily alongside the words of the five intellectuals. The following sentences, however, are very different in tone:

> It must then conscientiously apply at least the first two mottos inscribed on
> its pediment (the third being contradictory to the second and inapplicable
> in mixed schools): Liberty, Equality. Especially equality of opportunity in
> life. (Jullien 1989)

Here, in providing a feminist critique and refusal of a *fraternité* that by definition excludes women, Jullien's text, for all its secularist "intransigence," departs fundamentally from most of those published in the mainstream press, although, unsurprisingly, it is argued along similar lines to the statement made by L'Eveil in the Assouline article cited above.

Similarly, those feminists opposing expulsion did so in the name of women's liberation: "Without [public secular schooling], women would remain even more enclosed within tradition, under the parental yoke and religious obscurantism, which would throw them straight into the arms of integrists" (EMAF 1989).

The "troublesome" aspect of feminist voices in 1989 was not to do with *whether* feminists aligned themselves with the intransigents or the tolerants, but with *why* they did so. The sin of feminists, whatever side they took, was to refuse the tokenization of "Muslim women's emancipation." Instead, they placed women *at the center* of the debate, linking women's rights and women's freedoms with secular schooling and stressing that for the most part, the media did not make this link but focused on polemic around Republican values or racism. In doing so, argued feminists, it "masked a fundamental aspect of this affair, namely that the veil is the symbol of a 'separate development' reserved for women and of inequality between men and women that results" (Femmes Sous Lois Musulmanes et al. 1989). It was feminists' refusal of the use of women as symbols or vehicles to carry on a debate that was largely not about them, while women themselves were excluded from participating in it, that condemned the "famous feminist voice" to silence.

5

1990–1995

From Psychodrama to Saga

ESTIMATES OF THE TOTAL NUMBER of headscarf incidents between 1989 and 2003 vary according to the source, as do those of total numbers of headscarved girls: there are a range of opinions on the subject and hard data, outside cases that went to court, are hard to come by. Hanifa Chérifi, appointed in 1994 by the then right-wing government as a government mediator with families in problematic cases of headscarf wearing in schools, estimated that the number of headscarved girls had dropped from approximately 2,000 at the beginning of 1990 to 400 in 1999, with around 100 being problematic (cited in *Libération,* January 9–10 , 1999). In 1994, she had dealt with around 300 headscarf conflicts; by 2003, this had fallen to 150 (cited in *Le Monde,* December 10, 2003; See also Zouari 2004, 23; Myard ed. 2003, 71). According to a Department of Education census cited by *Le Figaro* on October 20, 1994, there were 1,032 hijabs in French schools at that time. Geographically, most of the incidents were concentrated around the areas of Lille/Amiens, Versailles/Paris, and Lyons, in high-density immigrant ghettos, most of the schools being, as in 1989, in ZEPs (see chapter 4). By the beginning of the November 1994 midsemester school holidays, then education minister François Bayrou (UDF) estimated that numbers had dropped from 2,000 at the beginning of the year to under 600, with a total of 52 expulsions throughout France, including 17 in the northern industrial town of Lille and 18 in Strasbourg, with a further 30 cases in Mantes-la-Jolie and 20 in Goussainville, both in the outer suburbs of Paris, awaiting decision (*Le Monde,* November 26, 1994).

A police intelligence document issued by the Service des Renseignements Généraux (RG) on September 29, 2003, and reported in *Le Monde* on October 9, put the number of hijabs in schools at a few hundred at that time, as against 1,123 in 1994 and 446 in 1995. In 1994, however, according to an unconfirmed report cited by *Le Monde,* the RG had put the figure much higher, at 10,000 to 15,000, leading to *Le Monde* declaring that "since 1993, the figures appear to have taken off" (cited in Gaspard and Khosrokhavar 1995, 29).

Reports such as this have led some commentators to point out that the extent of the hijab phenomenon in France has been overestimated. During a conference held on May 23, 2003, Hanifa Chérifi stressed that in Creil, where the headscarves saga started, three girls out of a Muslim student population of 500 were wearing the hijab, while in 2002, in the largest secondary school in Lyons, with a population of 2,500, one student was wearing it. She added that the marginality of the phenomenon did not mean it was unimportant—on the contrary, there was a real problem—but that it was nonetheless important to remember that the actual number of conflictual situations was very small (Myard 2003, 71–72). In 1995, Françoise Gaspard and Farhad Khosrokhavar, in one of the first of what would become many books in French dealing exclusively with the subject, estimated that fewer than one percent of French Muslim schoolgirls were likely to be wearing the hijab (Gaspard and Khosrokhavar 1995, 30–31). Contrary to Chérifi, they considered that not only was the number of headscarved schoolgirls being inflated but that the importance of the phenomenon was also being grossly overdramatized.

An exhaustive search through sites such as Légifrance has produced no single document containing an overview of all cases of expulsion during the 1989–2003 period, or even comprehensive lists of tribunal decisions, but one could say without fear of exaggeration that well over a hundred contentious incidents occurred during that period, some concerning a single student, others concerning two or more. Expulsions also appeared to follow a pattern of peaks and troughs, clustering during certain periods. Most cases of expulsion went to court, resulting in a little over half of the expulsions being overturned. Muriel Frat, writing in the pages of *Le Figaro* on September 19, 1995, mentions that forty students were reinstated in "recent" tribunal decisions. Christine Guimonnet, writing on the Web site of Reconstruire l'école (Rebuilding the School System), put at 92 the number of cases appearing before administrative tribunals during a "peak" period of the 1994–95 school year, with 74 decisions resulting in 44 expulsions being overturned and 30 upheld.[1] (Administrative tribunals are special courts dealing with state and public service administration, the only areas in which case law is given significant weight in France.) Nicky Jones provides a lower estimate, documenting "approximately 83" cases that appeared before tribunals between 1992 and 2003, with the majority of rulings occurring in 1996 and 1997 (Jones 2004, 315). There were, according to Jones, few affairs heard after that date; my own searches confirm this. In most cases appearing before tribunals in 1996 and 1997, the expulsions were overturned, but most of these concerned individual students. Those cases where expulsions were upheld concerned groups, with the result that in purely numerical terms, around 40 percent of expulsions were upheld by the courts (Jones 2004, 315–16). The fact that courts tended to uphold expulsions in the cases of groups is significant, as it suggests that the girls exhibited obstructive or proselytizing behavior in groups that they did not manifest individually.

The key legislative and discursive developments in the headscarves saga, however, largely predated this apparent mid-1990s flurry of court cases. The main markers of these developments were the two ministerial circulars issued in 1993 and 1994 by education minister François Bayrou and those legal cases that prompted Council of State rulings: the Kherouaa affair in Montfermeil in 1992, the Yilmaz affair in Angers in 1994, the Aoukili affair in Nantua in 1995, and, in 1996, a series of rulings, four of which were responses to appeals lodged this time by Bayrou.

These developments were framed within others occurring both nationally and internationally during the period between the 1989 affair and the 1996 Council of State rulings. Across the Mediterranean, the FIS in Algeria,

---

1. Guimmonet's text is undated; it was consulted on Oct. 16, 2006, at http://www.r-lecole.freesurf.fr/laic/voile1.html. Reconstruire l'école is an association set up in the late 1990s in opposition to the policies of then Socialist education minister Claude Allègre, said to be heavily influenced by "third way"–style think-tank Fondation Saint-Simon (dissolved in 1999). See http://www.r-lecole.freesurf.fr/Asso/Historique.htm and Laurent 1998.

legalized during the 1989 democratization wave, had had significant wins in municipal elections and had been poised to win a national election when the second round of legislative elections was canceled by the ruling FLN at the beginning of 1992. One consequence of the FIS activities was an influx of temporary and permanent Algerian asylum seekers to France, including, initially, members of the FIS itself, once the FLN outlawed it anew. France had also been involved in the unpopular Gulf War in 1991, provoking a minor political crisis with Chevènement's resignation as defense minister and considerable public protest. Two years later, in 1993, a right-wing government came to power and wasted no time in taking a harder line on immigrants, with the notorious laws introduced by new minister for the interior Charles Pasqua.

1989–1992: A Problem That Would Not Go Away

The Creil incident was not the only headscarves affair to occur in 1989—nor was it the first in France, as we saw in chapter 4—but its high public profile obscured the others from view, which was somewhat ironic, given that it also to some extent provided the inspiration for them. Individual hijab-wearing students aged from fourteen to eighteen were suspended in the suburbs of Montpellier, Marseilles, and Avignon during the month of October 1989, and on November 6, sixty-five teachers at a junior high school in Poissy, in the western suburbs of Paris, refused to teach their classes as long as one of the students kept her headscarf on—which lead to a rapid backdown on the part of the student (Chikha 1990, 1–2, 6). Ten days later, teachers went on a rolling strike in Montmargny, in the outer suburbs of Paris, against one of their number, a European-background French woman who had married an Algerian and converted to Islam, turning up in a hijab. The teacher in question arrived bareheaded the following day (Chikha 1990, 7–8). And on November 22, another incident occurred in Noyon, which had been the site of a pre-"affair" incident in 1985. Approximately thirty junior high school students, mainly of Moroccan background, refused to attend classes, such as physical education, drawing, and natural sciences, that they deemed incompatible with Islam, leading to sanctions against them (Chikha 1990, 8). Three of them were expelled the following January for refusing to remove their hijabs. And then, on December 2, a few weeks before the publication in the national education department's newsletter of a relatively lengthy and detailed ministerial circular by Jospin explaining the Council of State *avis*, Leïla and Fatima Achaboun turned up to school in Creil bareheaded. Their father, a Moroccan immigrant, had been summoned by the Moroccan Consulate the previous day and advised to remove his daughters' headscarves: an indicator that "home country" interference was sometimes on the secularist and not the Islamist side. It would take their Tunisian-background friend, Samira, another month and a half to remove her headscarf; in the meantime, she did her schoolwork in the school library.

Despite the backdowns in most of these 1989 cases, including by those at the center of the Creil affair that had started the whole saga, the headscarf was not about to disappear from the young heads it covered, even if, then even more than now, it remained a very marginal phenomenon. It even continued to find some interesting allies. Consistent with the support by Catholic archbishops for reinstatement of the Creil girls in 1989, some Catholic schools started accepting headscarved Muslim girls who had been expelled from public schools. Thus, at the start of the 1990–91 school year, four young headscarved Muslim girls (described in the pages of *Le Figaro* as "four young Isla*mists*" [my italics]) were accepted into the Jeanne d'Arc (Joan of Arc) school in Reims (*Le Figaro,* September 25, 1990), while Nour Ali Khadim, daughter of an Iraqi political refugee, found herself studying at the Sacre-Cœur junior high school in a town in the department of Ain, not far from Lyons (*Libération,* October 3, 1990).

The next high-profile affair to lead to Council of State intervention occurred during the same period. At a meeting in September 1990, the governing board of a junior high school in Montfermeil, in the northeastern suburbs of Paris, decided to prohibit the wearing of "all distinctive signs, worn as clothing or otherwise, of a religious, political or philosophical nature" (this replaced a former article prohibiting only the hijab). This decision became article 13 of the school rules two months later and led to the December 14 expulsion, by the school's disciplinary board, of three headscarved girls: Samira Kherouaa and two sisters Hatice and Ayse Balo. The Creil rector (regional director of education) upheld this decision on March 11, 1991, as did the Paris Administrative Tribunal on July 2 the same year. The parents then appealed to the Council of State, which is the second-last stop in appeals

procedures, the last being the European Commission of Human Rights leading to a final and binding decision by the European Human Rights Court.[2]
In what became known as the Kherouaa affair, and the second landmark
in the headscarves saga (and the first to give high-profile cases a Turkish
aspect), the Council of State ruling no. 130394 of November 2, 1992, reaffirmed the terms of its 1989 *avis,* not only in overturning the Administrative
Tribunal's decision and reinstating the students but in revoking article 13 of
the school rules used as the basis for excluding them. It ruled the provisions
of the article to be illegal because too general and absolute, as they prohibited *all* distinctive signs regardless of whether or not they disrupted order or
teaching activities, constituted proselytism or propaganda, or endangered the
dignity, freedom, health, or security of students. Decisions made on the sole
basis of article 13 thus went beyond what the school was, at that time, legally
empowered to do. Other behaviors exhibited by one of the girls (as reported
by school principal Ali Boumachi), such as refusing physical education classes
and calling Muslim girls who did not don the hijab "bad Muslims," which
could have been interpreted as disruption or proselytism, were not on record
as a basis for their expulsion and were thus legally inadmissible (Kaltenbach
and Tribalat 2002, 218).

The 1992 ruling introduced two additional and linked elements: explicit
clarification that "general and absolute" restrictions on all religious insignia
were illegal, which had already been implicit in the terms of the Council of
State's 1989 *avis,* and made explicit in Jospin's 1989 circular explaining the
ruling (Jospin 1989), and the Council of State's use of its powers to quash
not only school disciplinary and Administrative Tribunal decisions but also
school rules.

These clarifications and reinforcements of the Council of State's 1989
position did not, however, relieve individual schools of the responsibility
for managing and resolving conflicts locally on a case-by-case basis (*Libération,* November 6, 1992). The 1992 ruling thus did not satisfy teachers'

---

2. Kaltenbach and Tribalat note that only one hijab case made it to the European Human
Rights Commission between 1989 and 2002, and this case was thrown out as inadmissible
because one step in the appeals procedure —at the level of the school disciplinary board—had
been missed (2002, 215fn3).

unions, among them the Fédération de l'Education Nationale (FEN), which called for "a clear bill of law establishing rules for behavior that would be permanent and valid for all schools, and would put an end to the polemic orchestrated by integrist groups." The union did "not accept that religious pressure groups question respect for the rules by which school collective life functions, the principle of secularism of the State and of its institutions, and the principles of equality between girls and boys" (cited in *Le Figaro,* November 5, 1992). Already in 1989, the general secretary of the FEN had stated that he was "expecting a regulatory text from the government" (cited in *Le Monde,* October 27, 1989).

The FEN was, in 1992, to find itself some prominent allies. One of these was Ernest Chenière, whose right-wing politics were to become well-known: in his calling for the law he had the support of most of his RPR colleagues (*Libération,* September 12, 1994). Another was SOS-Racisme under new president Fodé Scylla, which, on October 23, 1994, adopted a recommendation calling for a law, reversing the position it had taken in 1989. But even before Chenière moved back into the center ring of the hijab circus, two of his colleagues were attempting to introduce legislation. In mid-November, Robert Pandraud and Eric Raoult, RPR deputies from Seine-St-Denis, a département of suburban Paris, had tabled a bill "reforming the 1989 law on the orientation of education [see chapter 4] and reaffirming the concept of secularism in public schools" (*Le Figaro,* November 17, 1992).

The second appeal to the Council of State, by the Turkish immigrant parents of Zehranur and Neslinur Yilmaz, also concerned a case involving school rules. In June 1991, following several months of negotiations with the elder sister, Zehranur, the school board of the Joachim du Bellay high school in Angers adopted the rule that no student would be admitted into the classrooms, study rooms, or refectory with his or her head covered. The girls' father signed the school rules document at the start of the 1991–92 school year, when Zehranur's younger sister Neslinur was to start at the school, but refused his permission for the girls to go to the swimming pool, dance, sing, participate in school excursions of longer than one day's duration, eat any animal flesh in the school canteen other than fish, or remove their hijabs under any circumstances (cited in Jones 2004, 322). The principal suspended Zehranur and refused to enroll her sister. The Administrative

Tribunal in Nantes, to which the father appealed, upheld the principal's decision in its ruling of February 13, 1992, but the Council of State overturned it on March 14, 1994, giving the reason that the school rule constituted a "permanent prohibition" applying to the majority of school premises, and it had not been adequately demonstrated that this rule was justified by particular circumstances. The students' freedom of expression was thus not respected. Once again, as well as reinstating the students, the Council of State annulled the offending rule.

1993: Government Changed, Ante Upped

Encouraged by these rulings and the *avis* of 1989, as well as by Islamist groups, parents kept sending their daughters to school in hijabs, and some parents of expelled students took their cases to court. In a pattern that had, by 1992, become typical and thus predictable, things gathered steam at the start of the school year. Girls as young as eleven were turning up to school in their hijabs and starting to adopt more obstinate behavior in relation to attendance at some classes, particularly although not solely physical education, swimming, and other sports. (In subsequent years, there were reports of headscarved eight-year-olds, although such cases were rare.) Of those cases that went to court, in some cases the courts reinstated students; in others, it upheld the expulsions.

The beginning of the 1993–94 school year was no different. In the Xavier-Bichat junior high school in Nantua, near Lyons, four girls, of Moroccan and Turkish background (which once again, was typical), refused to remove their hijabs during physical education classes; by October 12, the majority of teachers at the school were on strike. In a statement delivered to the school management, they wrote:

> The wearing of the headscarf calls into question the freedom of students, compromises their safety during the practice of scientific subjects, physical education and sport, is discriminatory toward the girls and is segregationist. . . . It is a provocative act contrary to the values of the Republic which are freedom, equality, fraternity and secularism [*liberté, égalité, fraternité et laïcité*], and that jeopardizes integration of students into French society. (cited in *Le Monde*, October 13, 1993)

On October 26, François Bayrou, minister for education with the newly elected right-wing government headed by prime minister Edouard Balladur, issued ministerial circular no. 93-316 on "respect for secularism," motivated by incidents "that have arisen in a certain number of schools frequented by young girls wearing an Islamic veil" (Bayrou 1993). The circular reminded school rectors, inspectors, and principals of three principles. First, the objective of secularism was "to unite all young French people and not separate them," and the role of schools was to "favor integration and not division." Respect for this principle was "imperative." Second, the circular reminded its addressees of both the Council of State *avis* of 1989 and the Jospin circular of the same year, and instructed them to ensure that school rules were in accordance with the terms of the ruling. It went on, as had Jospin's circular, to stress the responsibility of principals, following dialogue with the students and their parents and consultation of the relevant school authorities, to take action in cases where a student's behavior constituted "an act of pressure, provocation, proselytism or propaganda, [or] disturb[ed] order in the establishment or the normal functioning of a public service." Finally, it stressed that attendance at school was compulsory; the only allowable absences were for medical reasons. Bayrou finished by recalling the links between secularism and the Republic:

> From the outset, the Republic has passed on its values through schooling. Freedom and secularism naturally appear among these values. Principals must rank respect for this heritage first among their concerns. (Bayrou 1993)

This was exactly what the disciplinary board of Xavier-Bichat junior high did. Following a week's suspension at the end of which they still refused to remove their headscarves, the four girls in question were expelled on December 4, a decision confirmed by the Lyons rector's appeals commission on December 22. Their case presented some significant differences from that of Kherouaa or Yilmaz. Not only had the girls distributed religious tracts within school grounds, they had also staged protests outside the school, with the "support" (or policing) of a network of Islamist adults "responsible for ensuring that they remain veiled at all times" (*Le Figaro*, November 7). Central to the group was the girls' "Islamic adviser," one Hassan Moulay, a pseudonym for Turkish Islamist Konus Hüsseyin. Moulay, sixty-two years old at the time, was known to the French authorities as an "itinerant Islamist activist" and illegal immigrant (sous-préfecture of Nantua, cited in *Libération*, November 16, 1993), having made declarations against the laws of the Republic.[3] He was arrested in Nantua and subsequently deported by order of the minister for the interior, Charles Pasqua (*Le Figaro*, November 11; *Libération*, November 16). The press even started reporting the Nantua affair as the "affair of the Nantua Isla*mist* headscarves" (*Le Monde*, December 22), and *Le Figaro*'s tendency to use the incorrect term *tchador* was particularly pronounced at this time (for example, October 22, November 18).

On December 22, 1993, *Le Monde* reported that a girl, in her final year at the Emmanuel-Mounier high school in Grenoble and thus preparing her *baccalauréat* (bac, high school graduation), expelled a few days earlier for refusing to remove her hijab for physical education (the only time she was asked to by the staff), was now distributing leaflets in front of the school. In the outer suburbs of the same town, at the Aristide-Bergès high school, a school rule was adopted, not unlike that adopted in the Yilmaz case, allowing the headscarf in the corridors and school yard, but not in classrooms and other study areas. The student whose behavior had prompted the adoption of this rule immediately ceased coming to school (*Le Monde*, December 22, 1993).

Notwithstanding the overt Islamist presence during the Nantua affair, not all were convinced. For example, Dominique Julia, in a letter to *Le Monde*, wrote of the "humiliated children" of Nantua, the adjective being used, rather bizarrely, in the masculine form. Julia referred in particular to the invasive media treatment of the affair, with "two little Moroccan girls" being held up on national television as an example, and to the "dangerous generalization" that assimilated "all headscarves to Islamist activism," transforming all Maghrebian or Turkish immigrants into potential Islamists (*Le Monde*, November 20). Unfortunately, in this particular case, that assimilation happened to be accurate. The Nantua affair was, in fact, perhaps the first case in which it was very publicly and unambiguously so, taking the shape

---

3. The *préfecture* is the administrative center of each département, where its police headquarters are located. A *sous-préfecture* is, as the name suggests, a subregional police/administrative branch within the département.

of things to come in 1994. Even if the UOIF had been involved in the Creil affair, its involvement had been less overtly militant.

Some recognized the signs. Dominique Ducher was one of them. In a letter to *Le Monde* on November 13, Ducher wrote:

> A widely accepted interpretation tends to make the wearing of the veil into a habit that is anchored in female Muslim mentalities from their childhood and as old a practice as Islam itself. This is a flagrant falsehood. I was a cultural "cooperant" [French public employee working in an aid-related capacity in former French colonies] in Algeria . . . teaching in three different high schools: I never saw a single student wearing the veil inside the school! This phenomenon is thus recent: far from being a religious practice, it is in fact ideological and an obvious manifestation of an active proselytism put to the service of fanaticism.

At the same time, there was some indication of media disinclination to engage in the same level of hype as it had in 1989, which may have been motivated, among more left-leaning press, by critical distance from the right-wing government. In 1989, the left had been divided. In 1993, it had a common governmental enemy: the right-wing Balladur government, including the extreme racism of Charles Pasqua's agenda. So, when Ernest Chenière, now an RPR Deputy in Oise, where the school in Creil was located, stated publicly that there were 700 veiled students, adding a comment about an "insidious jihad," the press citing an estimate by the ministry for education of fewer than ten problematic cases at that time (*Libération,* November 6–7, 1993), considered Chenière's comments to be a "dangerous overstatement" (*Le Monde,* November 11, 1993). *Le Monde* further proclaimed that "by mixing up the wearing of the headscarf, violence and checking of residency papers in schools, part of the majority [party in government] is playing the sorcerer's apprentice" (*Le Monde,* November 11, 1993).

The comment on the "checking of residency papers" was a reference to incidents such as that reported a couple of weeks earlier in Montreuil, an inner-eastern suburb of Paris. A high school principal had written to students to inform them that those without residency papers in order by the end of the All Saints' school vacation (October/November) would not be admitted back into school. The Créteil rector, furious, instructed the principal to write a second letter declaring the first to be null and void (*Libération*, October 29, 1993).

In a report in December that year, *Libération* again played down the idea of a headscarf "crisis" by reporting on Lamartine junior high school in Villeurbanne, in the Lyons region, where some twenty students attended school wearing a variety of styles of hijab. The principal, Pierre Grannec, was cited as prioritizing attendance above all else, and as engaging in dialogue with parents, in particular as concerns swimming classes, which girls were tending to avoid via the deployment of medical certificates. In Grannec's opinion, however, "the real causes of absenteeism appear to us to be connected to the girls' relationship to their bodies at this stage in their lives and to a reluctance to engage in physical effort." The gym teacher, Thierry Garnier, backed him up: "It's too easy to reduce the phenomenon to a religious prohibition: we know very well that certain teenage girls, who are terrified of the water, use religion as a pretext to get out of swimming classes" (both cited in *Libération*, December 6, 1993). This rather begs the question of what excuses non-Muslim girls (or indeed boys) who shared such "well-known" fears were using; Garnier did not, however, offer comment on this. The principal, Grannec, emphasized that in any case, hijab-wearing remained a very marginal phenomenon in a school of 610 students, of whom 49 percent came from seventeen different foreign backgrounds. Grannec's view was backed up by the relative paucity of court cases during the five years following the 1989 affair (only five according to *Le Monde* [October 10, 1994]).

1994: Year of the Islam*ist* Headscarf?

By the beginning of 1994, however, the Islamist muscle-flexing was hard to ignore and was to lead up to what would become known as the *Affaire bis* (literally, the "repeat" or "encore" affair) at the start of the following school year in September. Earlier that year in Grenoble, on February 5, the UJM, with the support of the FNMF, rallied between 1,000 and 1,500 school and university students, mostly men, to a sit-in to support eighteen-year-old Schérazade Ben Larbi, a final-year high school student who had been expelled for refusing to remove her headscarf for physical education. Ben Larbi, who went on hunger strike following her expulsion but later enrolled in another high school in the Grenoble area, maintained in a television interview at the start of the 1994 school year, following the publication of the second Bayrou circular, that she had decided on her own to don the hijab, and that neither her father nor anyone else had manipulated her.[4] That may be the case, and, given that Ben Larbi had reached the age of majority by the time of the events in question, it would be difficult to argue otherwise, at least in any legal sense. The UJM was nonetheless the main agitator, with few female faces present at the demonstration, and, apart from Ben Larbi herself, zero female voices.

According to a February 7 report in *Libération,* "In a few months, the UJM has become the obligatory interlocutor of school principals, police and certain mayors of the Lyons suburbs as soon as these need a contact point for young Muslims or Muslim families" (*Libération,* February 7, 1994). Even though the association, and its bookshop and publishing house, Tawhid, run by Hani and Tariq Ramadan, claimed to be independent of Islamic "integrism," it was equally distanced from any idea of French integration. Opposed to secularism and in favor of a community-based identity politics, UJM also played overtly on the memory of the Shoah and the sensitivities of the French State with relation to the history of official collaboration with the Nazi regime, by having demonstrators at the February 5 rally wear black armbands with a yellow crescent on them. Given the anti-Semitic positions of Islamist groups, which would become more and more overtly displayed in years to come, this playing on the imagery of the Shoah was hypocritical and manipulative.

French schools and courts, were, however, no closer to finding an overall solution to the problem in 1994 than they had been in 1989. In May 1994, within one week of each other, two cases went before administrative tribunals, with completely different outcomes. According to some press sources, the families who brought these cases to court had been encouraged by the Council of State decisions in the Kherouaa and Yilmaz cases, in November 1992 and March 1994 respectively. On May 3, the Orleans Administrative Tribunal overturned the expulsion of two headscarf-wearing sisters, of Turkish background, from the Ronsard high school in Vendôme, citing article

4. Interview broadcast on Antenne 2 national television news, as reproduced in a monthly newsmagazine *France-TV Magazine* 66, Oct. 1994.

10 of the 1789 Déclaration des Droits de L'homme et du Citoyen, which was also central to the 1989 Council of State *avis*: "No one shall be harassed on account of his opinions, even religious ones, provided that their manifestation does not disturb public order as established by law."[5] The tribunal also noted the "perfect discipline" of the girls within school grounds (cited in *Le Monde,* October 20, 1994).

Exactly one week later, the Lyons Administrative Tribunal upheld the expulsion of Fouzia and Fatima Aoukili, aged thirteen and eleven, respectively, the previous year from the Xavier-Bichat junior high school in Nantua. The decision was based on two elements: the "systematic" refusal of the girls to attend physical education classes dressed in clothing "compatible with the normal exercise of this activity," and the behavior of the girls' father, a Moroccan immigrant, who "refused any compromise that would have ensured respect for the girls' freedom to manifest their religious convictions without undermining teaching activities, indulged in making public statements in which he manifested his opposition to the principle of secularism, and these actions brought about serious disturbances to school life."[6] Aoukili had, among other things, distributed leaflets written by Abdallah Milcent, the French convert of FNMF fame.

Meanwhile, at his daughters' old school in Nantua, their Turkish friends turned up on June 9 bareheaded, while others, also of Turkish background, turned up to local schools wearing the hijab (reported in *Le Figaro,* June 10, 1994). Further north, other Turkish-background girls turned up headscarved at the junior high school André-Malraux in Saint-Jean-de-la-Ruelle, a ZEP near Orleans: they told the press that they thought the law had changed, according to what they had heard on television (*Le Monde,* June 4, 1994). They were, apparently, referring to the Orleans Administrative Tribunal decision in May. On May 31, around ten girls arrived at school headscarved and carrying placards bearing the names of Turkish students, chanting "we want the headscarf!" Both the school principal and the local mayor claimed

---

5. Even though French possessive adjectives agree with the gender of the noun possessed and not that of the possessor, I have chosen to use the masculine possessive pronoun in translation in this case because in 1789, it definitely *was* "his."

6. Tribunal Administratif de Lyon, summary of unnumbered judgment, May 10, 1994.

that although the local Turkish community was very insular, there had to date been good relations, and they suspected Islamist agitation behind the headscarf incidents. One of the girls involved had left for two years to go to a religious school in Turkey; she returned to class headscarved and was one of the most obstinate. The school rules had banned the hijab, but following these demonstrations and various negotiations the school board decided to allow it within school grounds and in all classes except science laboratories and physical education and sports.

Other, pro-secular, parents were outraged at what they saw as a cowardly backdown by the board and spoke of launching a petition in the town against the hijab in schools. Their spokeswoman, Christiane Radakowski, spoke of four or five headscarved girls and another four wearing a full-length black tunic. The school board's response was to say that its hands were tied: it could not, by law, expel girls on the sole basis of hijab-wearing (reported in *Le Figaro,* June 7, 1994). In Vendôme, in the same region, the fellow students of the reinstated Yilmaz girls, mainly those in senior years, expressed their views by organizing a protest action against "religious integrism" at the school. The municipal council shared their concern: in a statement dated May 29, the councillors expressed their concern at "the rise of politico-religious integrism that risks annihilating the entire politics of integration that has been developed with success over several years within the town's Turkish community" (cited in *Le Figaro,* June 7, 1994). According to the report in *Le Figaro,* petitions calling for a law to block the development of religious fundamentalism within schools were circulating in both towns.

They were not alone. By 1994, Jean-Pierre Chevènement, who had been in 1989 among the intransigents in the Socialist Party and prior to that had been minister for education (1984–86), had joined Chenière, teachers' unions, and SOS-Racisme in calling for a law. Chevènement told *Le Figaro* on June 11 that the "lax" attitude of the left had imperiled Republican values. He attributed the left's laxism to naïveté or "misplaced sensitivity" following a history of colonial and postcolonial neglect:

> The rejection of the West in the Arab-Islamic world feeds off two ingredients: poverty and humiliation. In closing off the road to modern development to the Arab world, the West has historically fed a sentiment of

injustice and humiliation. More recently, the Gulf War has whipped up integrism. France's position in the Maghrib would be much better today if it had not compromised itself at the side of the US. (interview with *Le Figaro,* June 11, 1994)

Circular Conversations

On September 12, 1994, *Libération* featured a full-page article with the large-print headline: "Cinq ans après, la croisade anti-foulard de Bayrou" (Five years on, Bayrou's anti-headscarf crusade). The choice of the term "crusade" recalled the language used in the 1989 debate. The article, which featured a large photograph of headscarved students at the aforementioned "tolerant" Lamartine junior high school, where the hijab had "posed no problem whatsoever," announced Bayrou's intention, communicated first to the right-leaning newsmagazine *Le Point* on September 10, to "forbid [religious] signs that are so ostentatious as to separate young people from each other," so as to avoid the development of juxtaposed communities with different customs, which would "break up the national community" (*Libération,* September 12, 1994). This was, as the authors of the article did not hesitate to point out, a complete about-face from the position Bayrou had expressed five years earlier, when he was a young center-right deputy on the opposition benches. At that time he had said that "any gesture of exclusion could bring about the development of Koranic schools, which would be much more detrimental to integration than the wearing of the veil over hair." He went on to point out that he had had, as a teacher, male Jewish students in yarmulkes who did not attend classes on Saturdays, and it "never would have occurred" to him to set an important piece of homework on that day (cited in *Libération,* September 12, 1994). Even the year before, in his 1993 circular, Bayrou had basically reiterated the terms of the 1989 Council of State *avis,* leaving it up to individual schools to make decisions on a case-by-case basis.

But, as the authors of the *Libération* article pointed out, much had changed in a few short months. The two contradictory judgments handed down in May by the Orleans and Lyons tribunals led to murmurs within parliamentary ranks of "incoherent judgments," leading Bayrou to adopt the view that such uncertainty was not "healthy" and school principals should not be left on their own to deal with it (*Libération,* September 12, 1994). He was also helped along in his change of position by the strong-arm tactics of minister for the interior Charles Pasqua, whose 1993 nationality laws had fueled resentment, and by the sometimes explosive situation in immigrant ghettos.

Ten days after his interview with *Le Point,* Bayrou issued his second circular, the one that would be remembered as the *Circulaire Bayrou,* in which he stated that:

> In France, the national project and the republican project have merged around a certain idea of citizenship. This French idea of the nation and the Republic is, by its nature, respectful of all convictions, in particular religious and political convictions and cultural traditions. But it excludes the breaking up of the nation into separate communities, that are indifferent to each other, only considering their own rules and their own laws, engaged in mere coexistence. The nation is not simply a group of citizens who have individual rights. It is a common destiny.
>
> This ideal is built first and foremost at school. School is, par excellence, the place of education and integration where all children and all young people meet, learn to live together and to respect each other. The presence, within this school, of signs and behaviors that show that they cannot comply with the same obligations, nor attend the same lessons and follow the same curricula, would be a negation of this mission. It is at the school gates that all discriminations must stop, whether they are based on sex, culture, or religion. (Bayrou 1994)

The circular included a proposed article for insertion in school rules:

> The wearing by students of discreet signs, manifesting their personal attachment to convictions, religious among others, is allowed in the school. But ostentatious signs, that in themselves constitute elements of proselytism or discrimination, are forbidden. Also forbidden are provocative attitudes, noncompliance with requirements concerning attendance and security, behaviors liable to constitute pressure on other students, to disrupt the conduct of teaching activities or to disturb order in the school. (Bayrou 1994)

The reaction to Bayrou's circular was immediate and widespread. Not only did headscarved students at a number of schools demonstrate vociferously, but various individuals and associations issued statements to the press. The UOIF, through its then president Abdallah Ben Mansour, spoke of its "extreme disquiet" in the face of the rise of discriminatory attitudes and called for an "Estates General of Islam," while the more pro-secular Dalil Boubaker, then rector of the Grand Mosque of Paris, interpreted Bayrou's circular as an "invitation to principals to convince rather than force" (both reported in *Le Monde*, September 22, 1994). Teachers vented their frustration: "This half-measure doesn't solve anything . . . it lights the fire but doesn't provide the means to extinguish it" (cited in Fohr and Chouffan 1994).

Two months later, in a lengthy interview with *Le Monde*, Marceau Long, vice president of the Council of State, expressed concerns that the reopening of this debate by Bayrou would only lead to "new misunderstandings," noting that Jospin had understood this risk in 1989 in saying that he was not sure that a religious sign could of itself be "ostentatious" (Long 1994). Long articulated the double problem that had been at the center of the hijab debate from the beginning and would underpin the campaign for, and the adoption of, the 2004 law. First, a circular does not have the weight of law and is open to interpretation as well as to overruling by the Council of State if it does not remain within the bounds of existing law. The responsibility for decisions thus remains with individual schools and as we have seen, this not only causes often severe stress to school administrations, teachers, students, and local communities, but also leads to legal wrangles with contradictory outcomes. Second, where is the line to be drawn between respect for religious freedom, guaranteed by the constitution, and respect for the religious and political neutrality of the school space, guaranteed by the 1905 law? When *Le Monde* put this question to Long, he replied:

> These questions are not new in France. Council of State case law during the period of Third Republic anticlericalism is swarming with rulings on disputes that were as passionate as they were quaint. The Council of State established its position at that time: the freedom of religious expression can only by limited for reasons of public order, which are determined on a case-by-case basis. (Long 1994)

It was a position that the Council of State's 1989 *avis* had reiterated and reinforced. Long added, however, somewhat prophetically:

Only the extreme solution of a law prohibiting the wearing of religious signs, whatever they may be, would make it possible to get past these obstacles. Politically difficult to get up, this outcome . . . could be referred by the parliament to the Constitutional Council [which] would make a judgment concerning the compatibility of the text with constitutional principles such as freedom of conscience and of religious expression. (Long 1994)

Long's final point was made with his other hat on: the one he then wore as president of the Higher Council for Integration:

Integration is a phenomenon that demands time. Any policy that forces people to make premature choices is bad. . . . I am not naïve with respect to the dangers of Islamism but it is better to let time work. Ultimatums can provoke withdrawals and fortify closed communities. (Long 1994)

Both at the time and retrospectively, this comment appeared at once sensible and more naïve than Long professed to be. It was sensible, especially in the political climate of the time when decided anti-immigrant government policies in other areas were exacerbating precisely the sort of humiliation and rejection of which Chevènement had spoken some months earlier. At the same time, Long appeared to underestimate the extent to which Islamist networks were already driving the agenda, which is somewhat surprising in the light of the latest chapter in the headscarves saga that had been played out in the preceding months.

L'Affaire Bis

Everywhere headscarves affairs occurred at the start of the 1994 school year, the scenarios were similar: headscarved students turned up to their high schools in defiance of the Bayrou circular and demonstrations were organized, at the instigation or with the support of local Islamist agitators, in front of the school gates. In some places, a new presence was emerging among the usual crowd of headscarved girls, their friends, families, and "advisers": splinter extreme-left groups, believed to be breakaways from the Trotskyist Ligue Communiste Révolutionnaire (LCR). The LCR had loomed large in the 1968 student and worker actions and remains a significant leftist political presence in France, notably within the ranks of antiglobalization groups such as Association pour une Taxation des Trans-actions Financières pour l'Aide aux Citoyens (ATTAC) and the European Social Forum. In Mantes in particular, members of the Jeunes contre le Racisme en Europe (Young people against Racism in Europe, JRE), who were not local residents, demonstrated with twenty-four headscarved students of the Saint-Exupéry high school and their friends, families, and "advisers" in early October and, along with some hardline Islamist agitators, engaged in provocative behavior that led to some of them being arrested (which was their intent, according to Joël Fily, under-prefect of Mantes) (*Libération*, October 6, 1994; *Le Monde*, October 6, 1994). This group waged a cam-paign against the Pasqua nationality laws, the Bayrou circular, and racism and "policing" more generally, in a conflation of issues that foreshadowed what was to develop in the 2003–5 debate. In Lille, also in early October, there was a standoff at the gates of the Faidherbe high school between police and around twenty headscarved girls, and their "djellaba-clad entou-rage," who had called for a general student strike (*Le Monde*, October 5 and 12, 1994). (The djellaba is a long traditional and usually hooded Moroc-can tunic worn by both men and women; many wear it only for special occasions.) The girls were not allowed entry to the school as long as they maintained their demand. Later that month their demand escalated to a call to a hunger strike, following the expulsion from the school of nine of their number on October 24 (*Le Monde*, October 25, 1994).

In the Mantes case, the ringleader of the girls, Sonia, was, fairly atypically for these incidents, of Algerian background, but more typically, the daughter of immigrants and herself born in the country of origin (*Libération*, October 11, 1994). Most of her headscarf-wearing friends, however, were of Moroc-can background and apparently more subservient to paternal authority than Sonia, who, according to press portrayals, was acting more independently (*Libération*, October 11, 1994). Some commentators noted that older stu-dents were more likely to be inflexible, although some of the younger girls proved just as intransigent. In fact, reports were increasingly showing that it was difficult to generalize—or to make accurate assessments—concerning the degree of autonomy from parental authority exercised by the girls. At the André Chenier junior high school in Mantes, where nineteen out of twenty-two headscarved students removed their hijab at the end of October after several weeks of negotiations with the school administration, principal Luce Le Bars expressed her surprise at the degree of autonomy exercised by her young charges in deciding to don the headscarf:

> I thought the parents were behind it; I was wrong. . . . I discovered that they were really attached to their headscarves, that it wasn't simply a matter of public display but something deep and personal. . . . Some parents even told me they were hostile to it, but it was impossible to get their daughters to remove their hijabs. (cited in *Libération*, October 28, 1994)

When asked what had decided the nineteen to remove their hijabs, she spoke of six weeks spent doing "practically nothing but" negotiating with the girls; she also reported reactions of the girls after participating in a demonstration in front of the Saint-Exupéry high school two weeks earlier. They discovered that some of the demonstrators were not there at all for the hijab but to push other agendas, and "some confided to [her] that they felt a bit manipulated." Similarly, at the senior high school in the same town that had been the site of so much agitation, most of the headscarved students gave in either before, during, or after disciplinary interviews in late November. Here, it was indeed the oldest students that proved the most intransigent.

As in some other cases, the hijab was not necessarily a new phenomenon in these schools: the deputy principal of the Saint-Exupéry high school in Mantes pointed out that there had been a few hijabs in class as early as 1977, and even though that number subsequently grew to around thirty, any incidents were resolved through dialogue. It was when headscarved students started refusing to attend certain excursions and classes that problems began (cited in *Le Monde*, October 6, 1994). The implication was, as many school staff were at pains to point out, that new elements were being introduced into the equation, and, notwithstanding the autonomous judgment observed to be exercised by some girls as described above, they were not acting in isolation from a wider political movement. This movement included the UOIF and FNMF—the former often acting through local imams and the latter largely through Abdallah Milcent's aforementioned "advisory" role during hijab incidents. One of the Lille girls, Leïla, told a journalist from *Le Monde* that she had been wearing the hijab since she was twelve, against her will; even now that she had reached the age of majority, she still was pressured by her parents to wear it, and "perpetually under surveillance" by headscarved girls and their male entourage in school. She was one headscarved student who welcomed the directive of Faidherbe high school to remove her hijab: "Removing the veil is being free" (cited in *Le Monde*, October 12).

The existence of Islamist involvement and parental and peer-group pressure was perhaps most evident at the Romain-Rolland high school in Goussainville, in the suburbs of Paris. This school was reputed to be on the pet hate list of French secondary school teachers as one of the most difficult in the country. At the end of the 1993–94 school year in June, the principal had managed to convince one of his headscarved students, Samia, to replace her hijab with a more religiously neutral French provincial-style headscarf. The school board, however, decided to override the principal and ban all forms of head covering, effective from the start of the new school year in September. At the start of the 1994–95 school year, on September 15—and thus five days before Bayrou issued his circular on "ostentatious" religious insignia—four girls arrived wearing garments reminiscent of the Iranian chador and were surrounded by around twenty male "bodyguards." They included the same Samia who the previous June had reached agreement with the principal. One of Samia's friends had apparently approached a teacher to ask her to "do something for this girl who has fallen into the hands of the fundamentalists." But what exactly could a teacher do in such a case? The teacher reported to the press that "Samia said some weird things, in particular about the situation in Algeria" (cited in Fohr and Chouffan 1994). In another by now familiar pattern, it definitely seemed that Samia and her friends had fallen into the hands of something or someone during the summer vacation, for their behavior and dress had changed to such an extent that teachers no longer recognized their own students.

In successive negotiations with various representatives of school and community groups, including SOS-Racisme, the girls, always accompanied by some of their "bodyguards," maintained the same refrain: they chose the hijab, why was Islam being attacked when other students wear yarmulkes and little crosses around their necks? Their words, on the face of it, seemed perfectly reasonable and positioned the girls as victims of racist and anti-Muslim discrimination, but Nasser Ramdane, representative of SOS-Racisme present at the negotiations, commented that "whenever one of them appeared about to give in a little, one of the boys would elbow her, and she would resume her original position" (cited in Fohr and Chouffan 1994). In yet another familiar pattern, the girls spoke little in public, and the main participants in the pickets of the school and in media interviews were male.

A newly enrolled student, Rachid Amaoui, set up the Committee for the Right to an Education, called for student strikes, and organized successive demonstrations and pickets in front of the school: Maghrebian-background students crossing the picket lines were called "collaborators," a term heavy with the memory of Vichy France. A few years previously, Amaoui had co-founded, in a nearby suburb, Rappel (recall or reminder), an association aimed at recalling straying Muslims to the "right" path. While the association had impressed local police by transforming a few delinquents into upstanding citizens, its discourse was a little too close to that of the Algerian FIS for the comfort of most. According to activists with other community rights and antiracist associations, the headscarf issue was perfect for the Rappel activists: they could play on sentiments of injustice to infiltrate suburban immigrant communities (Chouffan 1994; *Le Monde,* September 30, 1994).

During the period of the *Affaire bis* in September–December 1994, over seventy girls were expelled for wearing the hijab, primarily in the school administrative areas of Lille, Versailles (where Mantes-La-Jolie is located), Créteil (in the inner southeastern suburbs of Paris), and Strasbourg. The youngest was ten, the eldest was sitting for her *baccalauréat,* and their national backgrounds were primarily Moroccan and, contrary to what had to date been the case, Iranian and Algerian.

There was also, during this period, renewed significant media coverage of the hijab issue, with the press publishing numerous editorials and commentary pieces as well as large quantities of outraged letters to the editor, the object of this outrage being alternately government racism and Islamist infiltration. There was, however, a shift in tone in the press commentary. While the 1989 debate had been essentially about racism, "integration," and interpretations of secularism and its role, the 1994 debate seemed more about the usefulness or otherwise (mostly otherwise) of the Bayrou circular in resolving the problem and about the extent to which Islamists were manipulating the girls and the debate.

The right-leaning press was generally more inclined to highlight the latter issue. For example, *Le Figaro* carried an article "Quand le voile devient une arme" (When the veil becomes a weapon) on October 18 and then "Foulard islamique: la manipulation" on October 20, and *L'Express* sported, on the cover of its November 17, 1994, issue: "Foulard: le complot. Comment les islamistes nous infiltrent" (Headscarf: The conspiracy. How the Islamists are infiltrating us). The headline was accompanied by a photograph, which the left-leaning daily *Libération* exposed on December 10 as being of a young model from an extras agency, wearing an Iranian chador, taken especially for the cover of that issue by Marianne Rosenstiehl, photographer with an agency by the name of Sygma. This revelation, predictably, caused a mini-scandal around media manipulation of hijab imagery.

The left-leaning press focused more on the Bayrou circular. *Libération,* for example, accused Bayrou of "flirting" with teachers' unions, which were generally in support of a prohibition of the hijab (September 12). It accused him in particular of keeping a weather eye on the upcoming 1995 presidential elections in finding "the right political dosage" that both advanced the principle of prohibition while leaving interpretation of this principle flexible and open to local school boards, even if that carried the "risk of once again conflating Muslim and integrist" (September 21). How that particular risk was exacerbated by Bayrou's hybrid solution was not, however, made entirely clear.

The *Affaire bis* was also a stocktaking moment, with the press publishing special themed supplements or providing a roundup of "the story so far." Various surveys were cited, such as one carried out for *Le Figaro* by market research company Sofres the previous June, according to which 86 percent of French were favorable to prohibition of the hijab (cited in *Libération,* September 12). In a special supplement on October 20, *Le Monde* published the results of its own survey, conducted by IFOP, on attitudes by non-Muslim French toward Islam and by Muslim French toward France. While, as in 1989, non-Muslim French were inclined to associate Islam with fanaticism and rejection of Western values, their attitudes were decidedly more open when asked specific questions about day-to-day reality in their neighborhoods, such as the construction of a local mosque or interfaith marriages. French Muslims showed themselves to be just as open: over three-quarters saw no problem with interfaith marriages, and two-thirds saw Islam as compatible with French values, including as concerned secularism and the relegation of religion to the private sphere. Those favorable to the creation of private Islamic schools and to the granting of a "special status" to Islam were even fewer than in 1989. As concerns the FIS—a question uppermost in everyone's minds at that time—most expressed their disagreement with the FIS's ideas and actions and their desire to keep the French Muslim community separate from the Algerian debate, although an estimated 10–15 percent nonetheless were open to dialogue with the FIS. In general, the image conveyed of French Muslims was consistent with that of 1989, and with the one that would also appear in 2003: the majority were "integrated" into French society insofar as they supported Republican values, including the separation of religion and state, and were very far from being receptive to the theses of Islamist agitators.

This curious tension between the public image of an Islam incompatible with "French values" and the day-to-day reality of "integration" and generally positive interaction between Muslims and non-Muslims, at least on a noninstitutional level, has informed the hijab debate throughout, but was perhaps the most accentuated during the period leading up to and following the *Affaire bis*. This was due in great part not only to the more obviously muscular tactics of the Islamist entourage of the headscarved girls, but also to the situation in Algeria on one hand and, on the other hand, hostility among most French Muslims (not to mention the non-Muslim left) to the right-wing French government in place at the time, particularly to the nationality and antiterrorism laws introduced by the much-disliked Charles Pasqua.

Various "experts" were once again brought in to comment on the question, mostly male sociologists and political scientists who had written books on Islam, immigration, and race debates in France, such as Bruno Etienne, Patrick Weil, Olivier Roy, and Slimane Zéghidour. And once again, few women, apart from the occasional headscarved girl, were asked what they thought. One exception was Khadidja Khali, president since 1976 of the French Union of Muslim Women, which provided, among other things, various social services and advice to Muslim women who had fled their homes or were being subjected to violence. According to Khali, the headscarves issue was being manipulated from abroad for political reasons, and she stressed that "what Arab men want is not necessarily what Islam is." She also pointed out that the polemic around the hijab was reinforcing racist discrimination against Maghrebian and Middle Eastern women in search of work: even very highly qualified women were turned away as soon as potential employers learned their name (Khali 1994). This tallies with anecdotal evidence provided to me at the time and subsequently by women of Maghrebian background in France, as well as through a series of interviews I conducted in 1997 with Algerian women fleeing the FIS.

1995: A Turning Point?

1995 was a busy year in French politics. Jacques Chirac, who was personally in favor of a hijab ban, was elected president of the Republic, and Jean Tiberi replaced him as mayor of Paris. Jacques Gaillot, bishop of Evreux, was removed from office on January 13 for his left-wing activities: opposition to the Israeli occupation of Palestine, to apartheid in South Africa, to war in general and the Gulf War in particular, and to French nuclear testing in the Pacific. Later that year, when Chirac resumed testing on the Mururoa Atoll, Gaillot sailed on one of the protest boats to the area. On July 15, an Islamist terrorist bombing occurred at the suburban express underground train station at St-Michel, on Paris' famed Left Bank, killing eight people and injuring 117. The previous significant attack had been on department store Tati in Paris's rue de Rennes on September 17, 1986, killing seven people and injuring 55, during a wave of bombings that year all linked to an Iranian organization. The St-Michel attack was committed by the Algerian Islamist terrorist group Groupe Islamique Armé, also responsible for a number of other bombings that year.

During the same period, solidarity organizations with Algerian exiles, notably intellectuals and, in particular, women, such as the Réseau International de Solidarité avec les Femmes Algériennes (International Solidarity Network with Algerian Women, RISFA) or Association de Solidarité avec les Femmes Algériennes Démocrates (Association of Solidarity with Algerian Democratic Women, ASFAD) were very active, and the situation of Algerian women was much discussed in the press (WLUML/FSLM 1995, 1996). The Franco-Algerian left and intellectual community had already been rocked by the death of a number of well-known Algerian intellectuals since the assassination of poet, fiction writer, and journalist Tahar Djaout in 1993: the total death toll during what became known as the "undeclared civil war" in Algeria between 1992 and 2002 is estimated at 100,000. The UN High Commission for Refugees issued a guideline identifying Algerian women as a social group in danger and unprotected by their state, in accordance with the 1951 Geneva Convention on Refugees, and thus eligible for political asylum (UNHCR 1995a, 1995b). The French government declined to follow this guideline, partly because of pressure from then Algerian president Bouteflika to counter a "brain drain" from Algeria. This resulted in significant hardship for Algerian women exiles (Winter 2002b). A number of book and article publications, both mainstream and activist, on the situation of Algerian women appeared, or had already appeared (Bouatta and Cherifati-Merabtine 1994; RIFSA 1996; Daoud 1996; Taarji 1998; Amnesty International et al. 1998). These included personal testimony (Fatès 1993; Assima 1995; Boussouf 1995).

The question of whether or not to "negotiate" with the FIS, once it had abandoned terrorist tactics, was at that time being hotly debated in France, and to some extent mirrored the Franco-French debate on whether "dialogue" was possible between the French state and Islamist groups and individuals in France in the case of the hijab. A Western-sponsored attempt at negotiation had been held in late 1994 and early 1995 under the auspices of the Catholic community of Sant'Egidio in Italy, between the FLN, the FIS, and "democratic" Algerian opposition parties, represented at Sant'Egidio mainly by the Front des Forces Socialistes. This initiative, and in particular the FFS's participation, were roundly criticized by left-wing Algerian parties such as the Rassemblement pour la Culture et la Démocratie and Ettahadi, as well as by autonomous feminist groups, such as ASFAD, and certain prominent individuals such as Djaouida Djazaerli, Algerian-background businesswoman, former private secretary to the rector of the Paris Mosque and devout Muslim, who commented in 1997:

> The problem is not who the French government dialogues with, the problem
> is how the Algerian people is going to live. And I have a strong feeling that
> this people does not want to live in terror. You know what the democratic

leader who was in Paris last week told [journalists]? He said to them: "Why, then, don't we come here and dialogue with the National Front?"[7]

Djazaerli was also at that time critical of the hijabization movement in French schools.

Within this context of a shift to the right in France and the escalation of violence in Algeria, three unprecedented things happened with relation to the French hijab debate. First, the Council of State upheld an expulsion, in the notorious Nantua case. Second, the first major comprehensive demographic study of immigrant populations and their descendants was published, giving, among other things, key information about school orientation and success rates and degree of identification with religion (Tribalat 1995). Third, two books were published that were not only specifically on the French hijab debate but also authored or coauthored by women, and explicitly feminist.

On March 10, 1995, the Council of State rejected the appeal lodged by the parents of Fouzia and Fatima Aoukili, the students at the center of the 1993–94 Nantua affair, stating as reasons that the evidence submitted clearly established that the teaching activities of the school had been "very seriously disrupted by the attitude" of the two sisters, that their behavior had breached order in the school and breached the prohibition of proselytism. Particular behavior cited was the refusal of the girls to remove their hijabs for physical education classes and the behavior of their father during demonstrations at the school gates. It further noted that the rules of Xavier-Bichat high school did not—contrary to what was claimed by the Aoukilis—impose a "general and absolute" prohibition of religious insignia and were thus not illegal.

This ruling marked a turning point in that it signified that it had become impossible, even within the generous and somewhat imprecise legal parameters that the Council of State had laid down in 1989, to ignore the increasingly evident link between hijabization in schools and politico-religious proselytism by Islamist groups. Even if a report issued the following year by the Council of State's Rémy Schwartz, reviewing four years of legal cases on the hijab issue, was subsequently criticized for its ongoing woolliness on

---

7. Interview with the author, Sept. 1997.

the question (Kaltenbach and Tribalat 2002, 224–26), the 1995 decision reflected a growing intransigence.

As for Tribalat's study, while it may not have caused a seismic shift in public opinion, it did provide significant research data to counter ambient speculation and hyperbolic assumptions, first, about the "Islamist tidal wave" that was sweeping France, and second, about the supposed academic success story of Maghrebian-background girls. Not only were young beurs as indifferent to religion as white French "Catholics," but beurettes, particularly of Algerian background, were disadvantaged within the school system. The findings of Tribalat and her research team confirmed what a number of other commentators and researchers had already proclaimed: first, "French Muslims" were also, by and large, "French secularists," and second, the main issue at hand was not religious intolerance but socioeconomic exclusion. The roots of the hijab "psychodrama" were to be found, on one hand, in French racism and structural and systemic disadvantage and, on the other, in activity by transnational Islamist movements already established in France, who took advantage of this climate of resentment to recruit their foot soldiers in France's urban immigrant ghettos. This tactic paralleled that used by the French National Front during roughly the same period to recruit disgruntled members of the white French petty bourgeoisie as their own foot soldiers. Islamist recruitment, however, happened largely among recent immigrants to France, including, as we have seen, non-postcolonial Turks, which is another reason to exercise some caution in establishing direct and exclusive causal links between the legacy of the Algerian war, disenfranchised beurs and the development of hijabization. Such links exist but they are neither straightforward nor unique.

The two 1995 books on the hijab debate were noteworthy for a number of reasons. First, as mentioned above, they were authored or coauthored by women, and, second, they were overtly feminist. Third, unlike preceding feminist works on Maghrebian-background girls and young women in France (Assouline 1992; Lacoste-Dujardin 1992), they were specifically devoted to the hijab debate. Fourth, they provided two opposing feminist perspectives on the issue. Finally, like much of the preceding work on immigration and "integration" but unlike much of the media commentary on the hijab debate over the years, both were the result of fieldwork or personal experience on the ground, rather than simply being opinion pieces. There had of course been some general works published on Islamism, including in France (such as Roy 1992 and Kepel 1987, 1994), and a large number of books and scholarly articles on race, immigration, and "integration," including on women. Slimane Zéghidour's *Le Voile et la bannière* (1990) had even provided a background to the politicization of the hijab in the Muslim world and diaspora, with commentary on the French hijab and "integration" debates. But even this book was not specifically on the French hijab debate and was not written from a feminist perspective centered on protagonists in the debate.

The two 1995 books were *Le Voile contre l'école,* by Elizabeth Altschull, herself a high school teacher with direct experience of the issue, and *Le Foulard et la République,* by Françoise Gaspard and Farhad Khosrokhavar, both of whom are professors at the Ecole des Hautes Etudes en Sciences Sociales (France's leading social sciences university). Gaspard, who is at the time of this writing the French governmental delegate to the UN Committee on the Elimination of Discrimination Against Women (CEDAW), is a prominent feminist activist, notably in the Parity campaign for equal representation of men and women in parliament that led to the adoption of a law in 2000, and was, as mentioned in chapter 3, Socialist mayor of Dreux at the time of the 1983 National Front win.

Altschull's thesis was along "intransigent" lines. Arguing that the hijab issue was being manipulated by both Islamist movements and the French racist right to advance a political position that had nothing to do with women's "choice" or their best interests, she called for the prohibition of all religious insignia in schools. Gaspard and Khosrokhavar took the "tolerant" line, downplaying the importance of the hijab phenomenon and its links to Islamist agitation and opposing expulsion.

Altschull's book was prompted by her own experience in 1992, as a teacher in a junior high school in a "problem suburb" (Altschull 1995, 11–32). The debate that ensued at her school following her request that a thirteen-year-old student, Aïcha, remove her hijab in class highlights the many underlying tensions and contradictions of the various hijab affairs of the time. Those who had at first grudgingly given support, such as the school principal, later withdrew it; some fellow teachers started making nondirected vague statements about "racism"; and others started coming out with stereotypes of Muslim girls who were "different" from "us," who are "married off by arrangement at sixteen and happy about it." Representatives from the Ministry of Education intervened, advising against prohibition and urging "dialogue." Aïcha accused a male teacher of sexual harassment, and her father, who had refused to shake Altschull's hand on meeting her because "his religion forbade him shaking hands with a woman," complained to the school of physical violence against his daughter by teachers' aides (most of whom were themselves of Maghrebian Muslim background). He also started a campaign against a teacher who taught Darwin's theory of evolution to first-year students, claiming that it was "not objective" because it did not present the Qur'anic view as well. Another student, who was part of an Islamic study support group in which Aïcha's parents were active, lodged a complaint against the school for "racism" in assessment procedures. He had copied, word-for-word, an encyclopedia entry on Mecca for homework and as a result was given a zero. Wholeheartedly supported by some fellow teachers and in particular by the teachers' aides, Altschull came to realize that "they" had declared war on her, as the local grocer, also of Maghrebian background, put it ("they" being the parents of Aïcha and their Islamist associates). She found herself in the bizarre situation of being supported by many Maghrebian-background members of the school and local communities, among others, and *not* supported by white French people in positions of authority.

Altschull described the isolation at that time of teachers dealing with a "headscarf situation": either they were accused of "sensationalizing" or, if they remained quiet, others would assume there was no problem (Altschull 1995, 74). She further commented on the girls' refusal to socialize, not just with boys but with any non-Muslim students, resulting in their social isolation.

As concerns colleagues who advocated "tolerance" for the hijab and tried to work with the student to prevent the latter's social isolation, Altschull took the view that such an attitude, while commendable, was naïve. It was difficult, she argued, to accept the hijab and not then come under other pressures to selectively censor one's teaching. The "tolerant" teachers were more likely to be found in the senior high schools than the junior or technical high schools, for reasons Altschull attributed to a certain intellectual hierarchy among teachers: senior high school teachers believed themselves to have a more "nuanced" position. Overall, however, Altschull estimated in 1995 that the teachers who supported a "preventive" prohibition of the headscarves formed a slight but growing majority (87).

Altschull was also one of the few at that time to focus on the behavior of boys in the school environment. Here, once again, she demonstrates sympathy for teachers such as those at the Faidherbe high school in Mantes who did not want to penalize the girls when the aggressive and proselytizing behavior of the boys was at fault (76). She had stressed this point a year previously, in December 1994, during a television panel discussion in the wake of the Bayrou circular and the Goussainville incident.[8] The expression of an opinion, however, even offensively put, is governed by laws on freedom of speech, and cannot be prohibited legally unless accompanied by behavior that is unambiguously violent or bullying, obstructive of teaching, or constituting religious or political proselytism or incitement to racial hatred.

Altschull's book was important because, contrary to the "My Republic Right or Wrong" theses of the five intellectuals and others, it was both based on extensive field research and personal experience and framed within an explicit feminist concern for the welfare of girls and women. One might take issue with Altschull's supposition that feminists showed a wishy-washy failure to react during the headscarf debate—we saw in chapter 4 that this was clearly not the case—but her feminist thesis is unmistakable. She maintains that just as women's oppression is universal, so must feminism be, and "cultural tolerance" of what is a sign of women's oppression is unacceptable.

Gaspard and Khosrokhavar are equally concerned by the welfare of girls, but they are less concerned about Islamist manipulation of the affair than about white French manipulation. Their research involved two-hour interviews conducted in 1993 and 1994 in the Paris and Dreux regions with roughly a hundred young women, of Algerian (both Kabyle and Arab and including some daughters of harkis), Moroccan, and Turkish (including some Kurdish) backgrounds—of which five, chosen as representative, are transcribed in the book. They found little evidence of Islamist proselytism

8. Remarks during the program *Droit de savoir: Les Musulmans de France*. TF1, Dec. 1994.

or pressure among these interviewees. They identified three types of "veil": the traditional head covering worn in the country of origin, mainly worn by older women or the girls' mothers; the head covering worn to keep the parents happy and have peace and quiet at home and in the local community; and that worn as a form of identity politics. In all cases, they found that a dominant theme in reasons given for wearing the hijab was "individual freedom of choice." The wearers claimed, as did the authors, that this is what differentiated the "French hijab" from that "imposed" in Muslim countries. Some girls in the third group even wore the hijab in opposition to their fathers, who were against it.

In a footnote, Gaspard and Khosrokhavar described the only real case of religious proselytism that they encountered, but downplay this as a nonpolitical identification with a "pious Islamist community" in the style of the Muslim Brotherhood rather than a militant political Islamism such as that of the Algerian FIS. I find this distinction somewhat unhelpful. It is true that the Muslim Brotherhood and organizations close to it are not political parties in France nor are they associated with terrorist activity, and that the FIS is both. It is thus certainly wise not to conflate different manifestations of Islamism and to stress, as do the authors, that the FIS goes well beyond the stated aims and practices of the Brotherhood. That said, it is erroneous to claim that the religious proselytism in which this interviewee was engaged was not militant, just as it is erroneous to say that the Brotherhood is simply a "pious community" in the style of the Tabligh, without any wider militant agenda.

While Gaspard and Khosrokhavar recognized that the hijab was the sign of a barrier between men and women, they also saw it, in the French context, as being a sign of connection with a local community and a block to interaction with the wider world that is not dissimilar to that found in the behavior of young Muslim men, in a climate of growing racism and the absence of a nation-state that appears relevant to them (Gaspard and Khosrokhavar 1995, 62). The authors—rightly, to my mind—saw the hijab as an ambivalent garment: a sign of cultural identification that is a specific engagement with modernity (63). They further claimed that "French feminists" refused dialogue with hijab-clad women as they immediately wrote them off as alienated and separated, with the result that the girls were "thrown into the arms" of Islamic associations that provided no support to them in defending equality between men and women (62fn). (I note in passing that Gaspard was also favorable to the Sant'Egidio initiative for "dialogue" with Algerian Islamist parties, discussed above.)

On all of these points, I see both merit and flaws in the authors' arguments. They are certainly based in an observable reality, and the authors correctly note that identity politics play an important role in hijabization, which, whether through obedience to family and community pressure, religious conviction, ethnic affirmation or Islamist politics, or a combination of these, is a modern response to a modern situation. In my opinion, however, Gaspard and Khosrokhavar underestimated the influence of transnational Islamism in France, and similarly, and surprisingly, underestimated the significance of the hijab as a subordinating gender marker. Muslim men do not wear the hijab. Their sexuality is not under scrutiny and they are not considered a danger to other Muslim men and to the community by their very existence, even if they *are* considered dangerous within white racist logic and incidences of racist violence against Muslim men have been well documented. As I argued in chapter 1, however, racism and social exclusion did not create Islamist movements, they simply provided a fertile terrain for the latter to cultivate a new following.

Both books provided more detailed and in-depth analysis of the hijab debate than had to date been available in the mainstream media and both in particular gave feminist perspectives. Their publication, along with that of Tribalat's demographic study, in the year following the Bayrou circular and the Goussainville incident, were a stocktaking moment of sorts: a time of reflection in the context of a debate that had if anything become more fraught than in 1989, as it settled from the psychodrama it had been back then into the saga it had now clearly become.

6

1995–2004 and Beyond

How Ostentatiousness Became Conspicuous

DURING THE YEARS between 1995 and 9/11, the hijab issue neither went away nor showed any particular signs of escalating beyond what was already in place, and it tended to occupy less space in the public arena than it had during the 1994–95 peak. It continued, however, to be an irritant, more acutely so at some moments than others, with both the white French and Islamist extreme-rights using each incident to score further points, while governments, school administrations, teachers and their unions, and feminist, antiracist, and other progressive associations remained as perplexed and divided as ever, as regular opinion canvassing in the press revealed. By 2000, however, there were few reports of hijab incidents and in 2001, there was a virtual political and media silence on the issue. The renewed focus on the issue from late 2002 thus appeared odd, 9/11 notwithstanding, and the agitation from that time around the introduction of a law has been characterized as an exaggerated hype prompted by the political class on one hand—particularly the newly elected right-wing government—and the media on the other (Tévanian 2005; Ezekiel 2006). While this is to some extent true, these were neither the only actors nor the only factors involved, and the seeds of the 2003–4 debate and the 2004 law had already been sown well before the turn of the millennium.

1996–2002: Not Really So Quiet on the Hijab Front?

During 1996 there was some softening of the tone toward the hijab, and this year marked the end of a period called the "second veil crisis" by Kaltenbach and Tribalat (2002, 218). In March of that year, the Senate Commission for Cultural Affairs made public its opposition to a law, despite repeated calls for one from various quarters, expressing concerns that it could be unconstitutional. It considered the 1989 Council of State *avis* to be sufficient and noted that the hijab phenomenon remained a marginal one.

As concerns teaching staff, according to a report in *Libération* on December 12, 1996, at the time of voting for union representatives in schools, teachers' unions were not in agreement over the need for a law, despite regular petitions and occasional industrial action by teachers in schools where hijab-wearing students had become a problem. Breaking with previous positions, Hervé Baro, general secretary of the Fédération de l'Education Nationale, and Jean-Michel Boullier, of the Socialist-affiliated Confédération Française Démocratique du Travail, both at that time opposed a law, which would block "dialogue" with "the" Muslim community. Monique Vuaillat, of the Fédération Syndicale Unitaire (Unitary Union Federation, which was, by the end of the last century, France's largest teachers' union), had no firm position on the issue, although she expressed a concern that a law would further encourage *communautarisme* (communitarianism), that is, hardline, insular, and antisecular Islamic identity politics. Finally, leftist union Force Ouvrière (Force of the Working Class, formed in 1948 as the result of a split within the Communist Confédération Générale du Travail) was firmly in favor of a prohibition of all religious insignia in schools.

A few days later, on December 16, *Le Monde* published a number of letters to the editor on the hijab theme, representing a range of opinions. In the same issue, it cited the president of the Conference of French Bishops, Monseigneur Louis-Marie Brillé, who claimed that pushes for a law on the veil would lead to a risk of endless theological and moral debates. He argued that the hijab was qualitatively different from a crucifix in a classroom as the latter can be easily removed, but a piece of clothing is a different matter. In a manner reminiscent of the arguments of Gaspard and Khosrokhavar, Brillé argued that it was all the more difficult in the case of the hijab, which is "for us, a sign of submission," but "perhaps for those who wear it, a sign of identification and even emancipation" (cited in *Le Monde,* December 16).

In 1996 there were two significant Council of State rulings. In the first, the so-called Northern Islamic League ruling, it upheld the 1994 expulsion of seventeen students from the Faidherbe High School in Lille. The decision was once again based, as the Nantua ruling had been, on "disturbance to public order" in the school. In the second, or rather, the second series, of rulings, the petitioner was, for the first time, not the parents but the minister for education himself, who applied for a series of decisions by the Strasbourg Administrative Tribunal, overturning the expulsions of a number of students, to be annulled and for the expulsions to be upheld. This time, the minister's petition was denied, the claim of proselytism being considered unfounded and the claim of absenteeism during sports classes, while being found a legitimate reason for expulsion, had not been the basis of the school administration's decision and was thus inadmissible in this case.

During subsequent years, things seemed to quiet down somewhat, with an emerging focus on the issues of absenteeism and "appropriate" clothing for certain activities, notably science classes and physical education, but this was not necessarily more likely to result in expulsions being upheld in the courts. Kaltenbach and Tribalat (2002) note that out of forty-nine hijab cases brought before the Council of State between 1992 and 1999, only eight resulted in the decision of a school administration being upheld, simply because in legal terms, most of the expulsions were on spurious and indeed illegal grounds. Only in those cases where there was obvious political proselytism and explicit refusal, for religious reasons, to attend certain classes, or to dress appropriately for certain types of classes, were expulsions upheld by the Council of State. Kaltenbach and Tribalat, whose position is critical of Islamist involvement in whipping up the hijab controversy and favorable to prohibition of all religious insignia in schools, provide a scathing critique of the use by schools of danger to students in science or gym classes and absenteeism as arguments to get round the 1989 Council of State ruling. In the first case, they note that British schoolgirls happily play sport and conduct chemistry experiments with their hijabs on and wryly comment that if headscarves truly represented a danger during physical activity, "How many nurses, Augustine sisters and sisters from St-Vincent-de-Paul would have been injured, strangled by their cornets or burned alive inside ambulances during wars?" (Kaltenbach and Tribalat 2002, 225–26).

The Council of State, in another landmark ruling on October 20, 1999, upheld an expulsion because of a refusal to remove the hijab during sport and gym classes, basing its arguments not on danger but on the right of schools to require a particular form of dress for specific activities (reported in *Le Figaro,* October 21, 1999; *Le Monde de l'Education* 276, 1999). This ruling became the general yardstick: from then on, schools had the right not to prohibit the hijab overall, but to require its removal—and indeed the removal of any other inappropriate clothing—for physical education activities.

As concerns absenteeism, Kaltenbach and Tribalat note that it does not concern only hijab-wearing girls but is "*the* problem in junior and senior high schools." The Ministry of Education estimated in 2000 that close to 100,000 students regularly were truant from schools (Kaltenbach and Tribalat 2002, 226). They thus claim that expelling only hijab-wearing girls using absenteeism as a reason—but not other students who are regularly absent—is hypocritical, as the real reason for the expulsion is the hijab. On this question, there seemed to be some unanimity between the anti-ban and pro-ban camps. For example, anti-ban political science professor Yves Sintomer, writing in the opinion pages of *Libération* on October 25, 1999, condemned an October 8 decision by the Caen Administrative Tribunal upholding the expulsion of two twelve-year-old Turkish-background girls from Jean-Monnet junior high school in the Norman town of Flers for absenteeism during gym classes, a decision he deemed to be hypocritical.

Flers, which was at the center of a minor resurgence of the hijab debate in 1999, had been in the news since January 8 of that year, when the majority of high school and junior high school teachers at Jean-Monnet school went on strike. They were sixty-eight in number, according to Jérôme Host's 2004 documentary *Un racisme à peine voilé* (A Barely Veiled Racism), which featured the Flers affair among others. The reason for the teachers' strike was the four-month-long refusal of one twelve-year-old to remove her hijab, despite the school's refusal to enroll her at the beginning of the school year the previous September, and the subsequent donning of the hijab by one of her classmates. The teachers told the press that it was less the hijab in itself, "but everything behind it." Roughly fifty co-students organized a counterdemonstration, one of them, Salima, telling the press "It's not her parents who are forcing her, they are her own convictions." The principal, Eric Geoffroy, noted that the young girl at the center of the dispute was born in France, but that her family was "relatively isolated in the Turkish community" (all cited in mainstream Communist daily *L'Humanité,* January 9, 1999). Extreme-right politician Bruno Mégret, who had split from the National Front in 1998 to form the Mouvement National Républicain (subsequently receiving 2.33 percent of the vote in the first round of the 2002 presidential elections), complicated matters by attempting to co-opt the teachers' demonstration. After negotiations brokered by Ségolène Royal, then state secretary for junior high schools, under education minister Jack Lang, the striking teachers agreed to accept the girls back into their classes on the condition that they followed the whole curriculum, including natural sciences and physical education. This did not happen and the girls were subsequently expelled. In an on-screen interview in the film *Un racisme à peine voilé,* Pierre Tévanian accused government mediator Hanifa Chérifi of having put pressure on the girls' parents.

The hijab found itself much less frequently in the headlines, however, between 1996 and 2001, than it had in the first half of the 1990s. Occasional reports provided news of what was happening elsewhere, sometimes with humorous intent, such as a January 8, 1998, report in *Libération,* taken from the UK newspaper the *Independent,* about the British navy's attempts to recruit Muslim women, with a uniform similar to the Pakistani salwar kameez and a specially designed headscarf. The newspaper titled the article "Le navy met le voile," in a deliberate play on words: *"la* voile" means "sail" (and *mettre les voiles* means "to set sail" as well as, figuratively, "to run away/ escape"), while *"le* voile" means "veil" (and *mettre le voile* means "to don the veil"). There was also occasional news of another strike, or another expulsion, in France, frequently in the "news in brief" column. It seemed that the hijab issue, if not exactly in a holding pattern, had become somewhat of a fact of school life, set to trundle along in unresolved fashion for the time being. The nation, meanwhile, turned its attention to other matters such as terrorist attacks, illegal immigrants (*sans papiers*), the homeless, the implementation by the Socialist government, reelected in 1997, of a reduced minimum working week (from 39 to 35 hours), and the PaCS (1999) and law no. 2000-493 of June 6, 2000, favoring equal access of women to elected office (*tendant à favoriser l'égal accès des femmes et des hommes aux mandats électoraux et fonctions électives*), commonly known by the much briefer title of the parity law, not to mention the long lead-up to the next presidential elections in 2002.

This did not, however, mean that all was quiet on the hijab front or in relation to the nest of issues it called up. Social exclusion and racism, especially concerning Maghrebian-background populations, are never far from the spotlight in postcolonial, postrecession France, even if in the mid to late 1990s it turned briefly to shine on sub-Saharan African–background *sans papiers*. This was also the period during which government consultations that ended in the creation of the French Council for the Muslim Faith were reactivated in earnest. Finally, it was during this period that the *mouvement associatif* found a new way of organizing: via the Web. Whether Islamist, racist, Zionist, anti-Semitic, antiracist, feminist, or just interested in having a chat, associations found a new virtual meeting space and unprecedented means of publication and national and international networking.

Among those making use of this tool were emerging antiglobalization movements, in which Islamist movements and in particular Tariq Ramadan became involved around the turn of the millennium. Ramadan and like thinkers succeeded in attracting considerable support among a certain French left intelligentsia, notably although not solely that grouped around the newspapers *Le Monde* and *Le Monde Diplomatique,* through the influence of Alain Gresh and Xavier Ternisien in particular. Ramadan became the face of a certain "European Islam," supposedly anchored in a modern and "integrated" Muslim faith. The audience given to Islamist discourses such as those of Ramadan in world and European social fora has been increasingly criticized by feminists as well as by some of the broader secular left. One notable critic is Bernard Cassen, co-founder of antiglobalization organization ATTAC in France and former chief editor of *Le Monde Diplomatique,* who criticized Ramadan as one of the unrepresentative self-proclaimed Islamist spokespersons of Muslim minorities who "think for them, without them" (Cassen 2003).[1]

By the new millennium, however, a large part of the national political debate was beginning to turn toward the presidential and legislative elections planned for 2002. In September 2000, the proposed constitutional reform reducing the presidential term from seven years to five, to bring it in

---

1. See also Correa 2002; Rebick 2002; Mansouri and Michelini-Beldjoudi 2003; WLUML 2005.

line with the legislative term, was approved by referendum and applied from 2002. The 2000–2002 period was characterized by instability and division in political parties, but the impact of this was to be particularly marked on the left, which advantaged the right, as we have seen in the case of the 2002 presidential election when the left vote was splintered (see chapter 3). The worrying outcome of the first round, which opened the possibility of an extreme-right president being elected in a country that still carries the painful memory of Vichy and collaboration during World War II, prompted Pierre Tévanian and Sylvie Tissot to update and republish their *Diction-naire de la lepénisation des esprits* (Dictionary of the lepenization of minds) (1998). As they wrote in their preface to the new edition, not only had voter abstention reached record highs, especially among the working class and the unemployed, but the media and the political class were continuing "as if nothing had happened on April 21" (2002, the date of the first round of the elections) (Tévanian and Tissot 2002, 20–21).

"Post-9/11" or "Post 4/21"?

In France as elsewhere, 9/11 produced an immediate heightened focus on terrorism and security: the very next day, the then Socialist government led by prime minister Lionel Jospin, who had been education minister at the time of the 1989 headscarves affair, reactivated and deployed the Plan Vigipirate, a security measure created in 1978 under the presidency of Valéry Giscard d'Estaing during a wave of terrorist attacks in Europe, but only deployed for the first time in 1991.[2] The government was also obliged, by police protests in particular, to back down on a proposed law on the presumption of inno-cence of suspects.[3] The first arrests of suspects believed to be close to the Bin Laden network were made in Paris on September 21, but the impact of 9/11 was quickly both overshadowed and amplified the same day by a violent

2. The plan has four levels of alert: yellow, orange, red, and scarlet. It was raised to orange, and to red for railway stations, after the Madrid bombing of Mar. 11, 2004, and to red following the London bombings of July 7, 2005.

3. Under French law, this presumption does not exist, contrary to what is the case in Western English-speaking countries, even if the rights of suspects have also been eroded by a raft of antiterrorist laws in the United States as elsewhere.

explosion of warehoused ammonium nitrate at the fertilizer factory AZF, run by French transnational petrochemical giant Total, in Toulouse. This explosion, equivalent to a small earthquake, killed thirty people, seriously injured over 2,500 (many ending up permanently disabled), and slightly injured another 8,000. It also destroyed a working-class residential area and a number of buildings of the nearby Université de Toulouse-le-Mirail. Forty thousand people were made temporarily homeless, many of them for several weeks. A lengthy enquiry ensued to determine whether the explosion was the result of negligence or error or whether it had been deliberate, a "terror-ist attack" of sorts: a Maghrebian-background employee fell under suspicion. The official verdict reached by the government was of an accident, but both the government and Total were widely criticized for insufficient and tardy action in support of the victims and the damaged community. The focus thus turned toward local questions of capitalism, class, environment, and political responsibility—and indeed, racism, both because of the immigrant background of many residents in the area and of the factory workers and because of the accusation of "terrorism" leveled against one of the workers. The "terrorism" association was amplified when a pseudo-terrorist group adopted the name AZF, which is short for Azote Fertilisant (nitrogen fertil-izer). The group attempted to extort money from the French government by threatening to place bombs on railway tracks. Hype from 9/11 was thus somewhat bizarrely and obliquely caught up in a purely local tragedy.

That said, France and some other countries in continental Europe, nota-bly Spain, were not as immediately and thoroughly prepared to embrace the U.S. agenda as was their neighbor across the English Channel. On one level, the French state had no difficulty in engaging with the concept of "war against terrorism," for in reacting to 9/11, it was in part saying "welcome to the club." French cities, Paris in particular, were already familiar with terrorist attacks, although admittedly none had been on the scale of the World Trade Center attack. On another level, however, France was unwill-ing to engage with the concept of the "axis of evil" on George W. Bush's terms. This was partly due to a deep-seated Franco-American hostility and different geopolitical focus. It was also due, as became evident in the case of France's refusal to engage with the Iraq war, to French political and eco-nomic interests in the Middle East as well as its own internal relations with the Arab World through the presence of significant Arabo-Muslim minorities in France.

France's Arab neighbors and minorities, as well as many others on the so-called third-worldist left, felt vindicated that the arrogant United States had had its comeuppance, and on one level cheered Al-Qaeda and Bin Laden. This was characterized by Farhad Khosrokhavar, writing in *Le Monde* in November 2001, as "The Victory of Osama Bin Laden" (Khosrokhavar 2002).

Third-worldist (*tiers-mondiste*) is a French term of denigration referring to a certain antiracist and antiglobalization left that naïvely, or self-interestedly, uncritically supports anti-Western discourses emanating from non-Western countries or individuals. It is a stance that is also associated with the dominant discourses of the World Social Forum; in this context, however, the term *altermondialiste* (other-worldist) has taken over. Many on the French left, of a variety of ethnic backgrounds, including a number of feminists, are critical of such third-worldism, and some of them have dubbed the international affairs monthly *Le Monde Diplomatique,* and to a lesser extent the daily *Le Monde,* as third-worldist because of the positions taken by their editors, Alain Gresh and Bernard Cassen, as well as many of the journalists writing for them.

The French state's reluctance to engage fully with Bush's agenda was, however, also due to a different strategic reading of the situation, as Olivier Roy suggested in 2002:

> First . . . the threat is exaggerated. . . . Second . . . even if terrorists attempt to procure weapons of mass destruction, it will not be via rogue states but via organized crime networks, in states that are not considered enemies (such as Russia) . . . and even within the Western bloc . . . or U.S. allies (the only Islamic bomb to currently exist is in Pakistan). . . . Third . . . the externalization of the threat ("us" and "them") sidelines the fact that terrorist radicalization is as much an internal problem in the West and its close allies (Saudi Arabia, Pakistan) as an export from problem countries; this radicalization is, moreover, maintained by regional crises that the new American policies exacerbate rather than quietening. . . . Most cadres involved in terrorist acts associated with Al Qaeda are re-Islamicized and recruited in the West, and even include converts. (Roy 2002, 23–24)

206 | A FIFTEEN-YEAR SAGA

For all of these reasons, it is far from certain that 9/11 had the same instant political impact in France as it did in the Anglo world. France had been living with the issues for a long time; in many ways 9/11 was just more of the same. The AZF disaster arguably did as much, if not more, to scratch at the sores of French racism and social exclusion.

The aftermath of 9/11 nonetheless amplified the tensions in the already existing political landscape, including the debate over the hijab. Fawzia Zouari argues that the post-9/11 level of re-hijabization internationally, including in Maghrebian countries Tunisia and Morocco, was such that it was possible, including within France, to speak of a "pre-9/11" and "post-9/11" hijab (Zouari 2004, 32). Anecdotal evidence in France indicates that 9/11 did prompt a new wave of hijab-donning that was as much anti-American as anti-French: it is a proclamation of belonging to, and solidarity with, a worldwide community of vilified Muslims (Winter 2006c). This is perhaps one of the most significant impacts of 9/11. In increasing, and to a great extent creating, the international polarization between the "West," as proclaimed and defined by the United States, and its new enemy of choice, Islamic "terror," 9/11 not only exacerbated an existing rightward shift in the French political landscape, but also contributed to a further "Muslimization" of the race debate. Before the 1990s, *Islam* was much discussed in France, but *Muslims* as a supposedly coherent group, much less so. Post-9/11, the "Muslimization" of references to immigrants (of the "second generation" or not), Maghrebians, Arabs, Turks, and so on, already in evidence during the 1990s hijab debates, increased dramatically, in a discursive shift that privileged religious identity over ethnicity. I will return to this in chapter 7.

All of this said, the chronology of events nonetheless tends to indicate that the resurgence of the "Franco-French" hijab debate in France in 2003 is as closely and directly related to the 2002 presidential and legislative election result, the hard security and anti-immigrant line taken by then interior minister Nicolas Sarkozy, and the setting up of the Stasi Commission, as it is to 9/11, and perhaps even more so. The seismic shock of the 2002 presidential runoff between Chirac and Le Pen after Le Pen's success in the April 21 first round was perceived by many as evidence of a political crisis. Just prior to that election, the siege of Ramallah in Palestine exacerbated the effects of the rightward shift, reigniting tensions that were never far from the surface in a country with such an ignoble history of both anti-Semitism and anti-Muslim racism as France. It is arguable that the Ramallah siege, along with Sarkozy's law and order agenda, were more instrumental than 9/11 in the resurgence of the hijab debate in France. As we will see in part III, the third headscarves affair became tightly enmeshed with the Palestine issue among sections of the antiracist movement, in particular those grouped around the MRAP and the Indigènes de la République.

As elsewhere in Europe (Germany in particular), a wave of anti-Semitic attacks by individuals and groups of Muslim background occurred in France after the news of the Ramallah siege broke: a synagogue in Marseilles was burned to the ground, individuals were shot in the street, kosher shops and restaurants were bombed or hand-grenaded. The "traditional" enemies of French Jews are—and remain—the white extreme-right, but in 2002 the most violent attacks came from men of Muslim background (CNCDH 2004; Mayer 2004). In some of the testimony to the Stasi Commission (discussed below), such as that of Louise Arvaud, principal of a junior high school in central Paris, teachers spoke of anti-Semitic verbal and physical attacks in schools, with regular cries of "*sale juif!*" (dirty Jew) and "*vive Bin Laden!*" being heard. The rise of Muslim anti-Semitism has in turn provided a pretext for the Jewish right to increase its vocal support for Israel. Within such a polarized context, the Muslim and Jewish left opposed to both Islamism and anti-Semitism, as well as to Israeli occupation of Palestine, had some difficulty in occupying a public space.

It is unsurprising that toward the end of 2002 Sarkozy, then interior minister with the newly elected right-wing government, introduced a raft of security measures, as well as a new law further restricting immigration (2003), which pulled the focus back toward both homegrown Islamism and institutional racism.

A further element was introduced by a new focus on violence against women in the *banlieues* (suburbs) where racialized and particularly Maghrebian-background populations lived. On October 4, 2002, in Vitry-sur-Seine, a poor inner suburb of Paris largely populated by Maghrebian-background residents, Sohane Benziane, daughter of Kabyle immigrants, was burned to death on the eve of her eighteenth birthday by gang leader Jamal Derrar, who had had an argument with her former boyfriend. Three years later, on the anniversary of her death, the Vitry City Hall inaugurated Sohane Benziane Esplanade, along with a stela bearing plaques to her memory. The following January, a Sohane Benziane youth and cultural center was inaugurated in the 15th arrondissement of Paris. Finally, on April 8, 2006—three-and-a-half years after her murder—Derrar was sentenced to twenty-five years in prison, and an accomplice, Tony Rocca, to eight years.

Also in late 2002, the late Samira Bellil's autobiography *Dans l'enfer des tournantes* (In the Hell of Gang Rapes) was published. (Bellil died of stomach cancer on September 7, 2004.) This book, a grueling story of paternal violence, teenage homelessness, and gang rapes in the immigrant ghettos of Paris—and their combined effect on women—was also a story of survival, hope, female solidarity, and emancipation. Not only did Bellil finally manage to leave the *cités* (housing projects) and train as a youth worker, returning to work with young people in the same ghettos from which she herself came, but her mother finally stood up to her husband on her own and her daughters' behalf. This had been achieved only after a long process involving growing awareness of the price paid by her eldest daughter and the need to protect her younger ones and the independence brought by paid employment outside the home. Bellil, who was twenty-nine at the time, dedicated her book, written with the assistance and support of Josée Stoquart, to her "sisters doing it tough so that they know there is a way out. It is long and difficult, but it is possible" (Bellil 2002, 7). She also dedicated it to her family, as well as her foster family, and in particular to her two younger sisters. In her postface to the book, Bellil stressed that everything written in the book was "scrupulously accurate," and that she was tired of hearing claims that the problem of gang rapes in the immigrant ghettos was exaggerated or that girls were willing participants in them (279).

Bellil's words and Benziane's violent murder became the focal point and rallying cry for a nationwide mobilization of *femmes des quartiers* (literally, women of the local areas, but the implication is "women of the ghettos," organizing at a grassroots level). Following the model of SOS-Racisme, which twenty years previously had organized the first nationwide Marche pour l'égalité et contre le racisme (see chapter 3), the women held a nationwide Marche des femmes des quartiers contre les ghettos et pour l'égalité (against ghettos and for equality) from February 1 to March 8, 2003. A number of them had been activists with SOS-Racisme or its offshoot La Maison des Potes (House of Buddies) and had been meeting in local groups since 2001.

Using Vitry as its starting point in memory of Sohane, the march visited 23 towns throughout France to finish in Paris for a 30,000-women-strong International Women's Day march. The march, using the slogan *Ni Putes ni Soumises* (NPNS; Neither Whores nor Submissive), the name adopted by the association created at the end of the march, rallied women around the objectives:

> To denounce omnipresent sexism, verbal and physical violence, forbidden sexuality, rape organized in gangs, forced marriage, and fratricide in the name of guarding family honor or imprisoned suburbs. (cited in Amara 2004, 148)

Close to SOS-Racisme and, like SOS-Racisme, to the Socialist Party, NPNS rallied women from the banlieues around the issue of violence. It was, however, to come under heavy fire from sections of both the feminist movement and the antiracist left. Both, for different reasons, accused it of being co-opted and of having too narrow a focus (see part III). Much of the criticism was focused on NPNS president Fadéla Amara, who had been national president of La Maison des Potes since 2000. This increased following the 2007 legislative elections, when Amara, as a socialist deputy, accepted a junior ministry with the right-wing government headed by François Fillon, widely thought to be President Sarkozy's puppet. Amara, secretary of state for town planning policy, attached to the Ministry of Housing and Town Planning, has now been written off by most of the left as an opportunistic sellout.

Also in 2002, French bookstores started displaying a range of post-9/11 books, some of which dealt with 9/11 but many of which dealt with Islam and Islamism in France or the hijab issue, or both (for example, Zouari 2002; Kaltenbach and Tribalat 2002; Laïdi and Salam 2002; Sifaoui 2002). The date of their publication is arguably in part an effect of lead time and the nature of the research which in some cases was conducted over many years, but in a number of cases it was surely planned.

From Headscarf Affair to Bandana Affair

At the end of 2002, it was not in the school but the workplace that the hijab started once again to come under intense public scrutiny. The case of

Dalila Tahri, sacked for wearing her hijab to work at transnational telemarketing company Téléperfomance, hit front page headlines on December 4. Tahri appealed to the Council of Prud'hommes (the French Industrial Tribunal), which ruled on December 17 that her sacking was illegal. While article L120-22 of the *Code du Travail* (French workplace legislation) provides for employers to impose specific restrictions to individual freedoms if this is justified by the type of work to be performed, article L122-45 prohibits discrimination on the basis of appearance and religious beliefs. It is on the basis of this second article that the Prud'hommes ordered Tahri's reinstatement. Even article L120-22, introduced in 1992, puts the accent on the individual freedoms of employees; employers must prove that any restrictions are truly justified. This case reactivated a workplace debate that, although present for the duration of the headscarves saga, was largely overshadowed by the issue of the hijab in schools. Questions were raised about the neutrality of the workplace and the extent to which the latter was a public or private space, as the separation of church and state in France concerns public institutions (schools, hospitals, Parliament, the public service). Indeed, previous workplace cases had concerned health workers and other public servants. In 1994, for example, a student nurse had been suspended from her practicum in the psychiatric section of a Bordeaux hospital for refusing to wear the same uniform as the other nurses. On September 27, 2002, in rejecting an appeal from a hijab-wearing health worker sacked from a public clinic for the homeless, the Paris Administrative Tribunal clearly stated that tolerance for religious insignia such as the hijab concerned school students only, and employees of the public service were bound, by the principle of secularism of the state and strict religious neutrality of public institutions, to refrain from expressing their adherence to a religious faith in the workplace.

At the time the Téléperformance conflict hit the headlines, *Le Figaro* claimed that young hijab-wearing women were more numerous in French streets than ten years previously but observed that, paradoxically, there was a significant reduction in the number of hijab incidents in schools, and sociologists, politicians, and media had overall lost interest in the matter. It asked "why this paradox?" and then failed to suggest an answer to its own question (*Le Figaro*, December 4, 2002). Notwithstanding the political climate in

France at the time and an apparent renewed focus in the publishing industry on the hijab and related issues, it was true that 2001–3 were relatively quiet years in terms of actual hijab incidents. At the end of the 2002–3 school year, government mediator Hanifa Chérifi reported that in contrast to the average of 450 cases per year that she had been dealing with five years previously, only 150 cases were now coming her way each year. Most of these were resolved through discussion and no more than ten resulted in expulsions (Hafiz and Devers 2005, 202).

It was also in late 2002, however, that a new type of hijab began to come under scrutiny in French schools: the Islamic bandana. It was later to become the quintessential "French" hijab, notably via the high profile case of the Lévy sisters (discussed below). Knotted behind the head and worn in conjunction with high-necked clothing such as turtlenecked sweaters, it was originally worn as a way of being a hijab without being a hijab, to get round school rules about appropriate dress or "ostentatious" religious insignia. Tolerated in some cases, as its predecessor the hijab had been, the bandana came up against its first official sanction at La Martinière-Duchère high school in Lyons. This school is one of the largest in the Lyons area with 2,500 students and situated in one of its "difficult" suburbs. During Ramadan, in December 2002, a sixteen-year-old student turned up in a scarf tied behind the head bandana-style, covering neither forehead nor ears. When asked to remove it, she refused, for religious reasons. The school authorities declined to hold a disciplinary hearing, upon which the teachers went on strike. The authorities referred the matter to government mediator Hanifa Chérifi, who met with the parties in early February 2003. Chérifi did not manage to convince the girl to remove her bandana and she continued wearing it in class, a decision to which the majority of teachers were hostile, petitioning school authorities to hold a disciplinary hearing as they held the bandana to be an "ostentatious" religious symbol (*Le Monde,* February 24, 2003). According to their spokesperson, Jean-Claude Santana, they feared that Islamist movements would use tolerance of the bandana to disrupt the "fragile equilibrium" in the school (*Le Monde,* February 24, 2003; *Lyon Capitale,* March 19, 2003). The director of education was reluctant to hold a disciplinary hearing, asserting that, despite what the student herself had claimed, her bandana was "not an Islamic veil," and expressing concern that a prohibition would provoke a strong identity-politics reaction that would quickly escalate (*Lyon Capitale,* March 19, 2003). He even advised the teachers demanding an expulsion to discuss the matter with Kamel Kabtane, rector of the Lyons mosque (Conan 2003).

These two reactions reveal a key element in the shift in thinking since 1989. In 1989, the media-fueled debate within the political and intellectual class and school administrations was around inclusion versus exclusion and the meaning and appropriate enactment of secularism. By 2003 the institutional and political focus had shifted to a more strategic, terre-à-terre peacekeeping agenda, in order to avoid a *dérive communautaire.* This term, literally translated, means "communitarian drift": its sociopolitical meaning is a withdrawal into intransigent and semiseparatist group identity politics, with the generally understood reference being to Muslim identity politics in particular. Sometimes the term *dérive intégriste* is used instead, to put the accent on Islamist agitation, but one or the other term became increasingly common in the hijab debate throughout the 1990s. The term *dérive multiculturaliste* has also been used (for example, Barthélemy 2001, 311), recalling an ongoing polemic concerning the perceived practice in what the French call "Anglo-Saxon" countries, in a contemporary reconfiguration of the opposition between French "assimilationist" and English "laissez-faire" colonialist approaches. This "Anglo-Saxon multiculturalism" is deemed by many French to be nothing more than a ghettoization of racialized minorities through a logic of "separate development."

The relative interchangeability of three quite distinct terms is revealing of the intellectual and political confusion surrounding the issue. As Chahdortt Djavann points out, for example, the use of the term *communautariste* is technically incorrect:

> That immigrants from such and such a region of China tend to live side by side, that they resolve in their own way a certain number of problems concerning their communal life, *that* is *communautarisme.* One could indeed be concerned about it in a country ruled by law and consider that everyone should be subjected to the same jurisdictions. But with Islamism, it is something else entirely. Here is it a matter, to revive an old term, of *confessionalism. . . .* Islamist confesssionalism does not pay any particular

attention to Turkish, Algerian or other communities . . . it intends to unite
Muslims independently of their national origins. (Djavann 2004, 42–43)

Djavann uses the term "Muslimism" to refer to a new Muslim identity politic
among young French people whose parents immigrated from a Muslim country. It is a combative identity, and according to Djavann, "built in great part
around the Israeli-Palestinian conflict" (42). It is also, as I suggested earlier,
in part the consequence of a post-9/11 "clash of civilizations" polarization.

In the above bandana affair, both teachers, in favor of an expulsion, and
the director of education, opposed to an expulsion, defend opposite positions for the same reason: their desire to maintain what is often a fragile
calm in difficult schools and avoid a *dérive communautaire*. The extent of
the *dérive* and its institutional provocation is characterized by a fairly minor
but heavily symbolic incident. In April 2003, then interior minister Sarkozy
was booed and whistled at the annual congress of the UOIF, for reminding
attendees of the requirement, established by a ministerial decree issued by
the previous Socialist government on November 25, 1999, to pose bareheaded for identity photos (all French citizens and residents must carry an
identity or residency card with a photo).

The Legal and Political Framing of Conspicuousness

As we have seen, the lead-up to the 2005 centenary of the 1905 law on
the separation of church and state, in the context of well over a decade of
wrangles over the hijab issue, sparked a discussion within the political and
intellectual class over whether the 1905 law should be revised, or tweaked.
For example, Jean-Arnold de Clermont, who was at the time president of the
Protestant Federation of France, was of the opinion that it should be, and,
perhaps curiously for a Protestant, invoked the special concordatory status
of Alsace-Moselle to support his argument (Clermont 2004). Former education minister François Bayrou (interviewed, ironically, by Catholic daily
La Croix), and historian of secularism Henri Pena-Ruiz both were of the
opinion that it should not (Bayrou 2003; Pena-Ruiz 2004). The press also
continued to send up the debate via its cartoons and satirical articles. For
example, *Le Monde* published a cartoon on June 19, 2005, showing young
headscarved girls entering school, followed by boys who were pulled up by

teachers, with the header: "Yes to the veil in schools . . . "; and the footer: ". . . without distinction as to sex," the latter phrase being contained in the French constitution.

Calls for a law explicitly banning the hijab in particular or religious insignia in general in public schools increased, with many turnarounds from a previously tolerant stance to an intransigent one. At the end of 2003, public opinion polls showed 57 percent of those surveyed to favor a law (Zouari 2004, 33–34). Among those hardening their line was Socialist Party deputy Jack Lang. Minister for culture with the 1981–86 and 1988–93 Socialist governments and later minister for education (1992–93 and 2000–2002), he had, in 1989, supported Lionel Jospin's tolerant stance on the hijab. He had even made a notoriously silly comment, with neo-orientalist overtones: "I find these headscarves very becoming. They highlight the lovely faces of these young girls" (cited in Conan 2003). Then, following the Socialist Party's 2002 defeat in both presidential and legislative elections, Lang changed his tune, and on January 27, 2003, in an interview on the television current affairs program *Complément d'enquête* (Follow-up investigation), called for a law banning the hijab in schools. He said:

> For a long time I thought that the *avis* of the Council of State . . . gave a relatively just indication . . . [but] my thinking has evolved over the past months, as Islamism has taken forms of penetration and propaganda that are sometimes unacceptable in our country. (cited by Agence France Presse, January 27, 2003)

Three months later, he told the weekly newsmagazine *L'Express* that what had influenced his change of heart was testimony by Muslim intellectuals and activists that the young hijab-wearing girls were being manipulated by extremist groups (Lang 2003).

Not to be outdone, Luc Ferry, then minister for youth and for education with the right-wing government elected in 2002, expressed similar concerns on the same day, in January 2003, on the occasion of the first national day for memory of the Shoah and for the prevention of crimes against humanity to be commemorated in French schools. Addressing the senate, he spoke of his concern about "the rise in community-group conflicts" within schools and universities and in particular about anti-Semitic incidents (cited by Agence

France Presse, January 27, 2003). The following week, he spoke to the press of his "personal" opposition to the wearing of the hijab by students within school grounds. "If there were no Council of State *Avis,* I would forbid the wearing of the Islamic headscarf in schools. . . . If the Republic prohibited this headscarf, this would help families and young girls to liberate themselves." He further recommended that school administrations interpret the 1989 Council of State *avis* in the "toughest manner possible" (cited in *La Croix,* February 6, 2003). In May, during a UMP conference titled "Schools and Secularism Today," he declared it would be "advisable" to legislate on the hijab in schools, stating that the "real problem" was *communautarisme,* with division of students into religiously identified subgroups being "unacceptable" (cited in Le Monde, May 24).

In fact, between August 2002 and November 2003, eight private members' bills on prohibition of religious insignia were presented to the National Assembly, half by members of the right-wing majority and half by members of the left-wing minority (of which three were from the Socialist Party, including one from Jack Lang, and one was from the Communist group). According to philosopher Pierre Tévanian, co-originator of the "lepenization of minds" thesis and strongly opposed to banning of the hijab—and thus, presumably, of other religious insignia—rekindling the hijab debate was a useful diversionary tactic for the ruling right-wing coalition in the face of considerable social protest. He further argued that for the Socialists, it was a means of recapturing an electorate that had been critical of its soft approach concerning immigration, "insecurity," and the hijab debate—in particular, teachers and white working-class voters (Tévanian 2005, 30). I have considerable sympathy for Tévanian's arguments on this particular point, as the sudden political agitation around the hijab during a relatively hijab-free period in schools does seem suspect. At the same time, while hijab incidents in schools may have diminished, cultural relativist and Islamist lobbying had not.

The extent of political pressure, however, resulted in President Chirac constituting, in July 2003, a Commission to Reflect on the Application of the Principle of Secularism in the Republic (Stasi Commission). The commission was given the brief of looking not only at schools but also at the public service more generally, notably hospitals and prisons. Its chair, Bernard Stasi, was at that time ombudsman for the Republic (1998–2004). Stasi had

had a long career as a deputy with the center-right formation that eventually became the UDF, and had been at various times, among other things, minister for overseas departments and territories (the DOM-TOM) (1973–74), vice president of the National Assembly (1978–83), and member of the European Parliament (1994–98).[4]

The commission comprised twenty people and was far from being a right-wing grouping, although as is invariably the case with such committees of "experts," all members were part of the political and intellectual elite. They were also all pro-secularism, but the brief of the commission was not to debate the desirability of French secularism, as it was already firmly established in law and in the constitution, but to debate its application in the contemporary context. The full list of members can be found on the official presidential Web site.[5] They included

• high-ranking academics: Maurice Quenet, rector of the Paris Academy and chancellor of Paris Universities; René Rémond, president of the prestigious Fondation Nationale des Sciences Politiques

• scholars specializing in the Muslim world and issues of race, immigration, and "integration" in France: Islamic modernist Mohammed Arkoun; political scientist Gilles Kepel, specialist on Islam, Islamic revivalism, and Islamism in France and in Europe; law scholar Jacqueline Costa-Lascoux, specialist on France's postcolonial and Muslim minorities; and Patrick Weil, specialist in the study of the history of French nationality, immigration, and integration in the twentieth century

• specialists on *laïcité*: Jean Baubérot, chair in history and sociology of *la laïcité*; and Henri Pena-Ruiz

• members of the Haut Conseil à l'Intégration, an advisory and research body set up by the government in 1989: Gaye Petek, president of Elele:

---

4. Départements d'Outre-Mer: Martinique, Guadeloupe, French Guyana, Réunion Island, and Territoires d'Outre-Mer (now called Collectivités d'Outre-Mer although the "TOM" acronym remains in use): French Polynesia, Wallis and Futuna, St-Pierre and Miquelon and Mayotte. New Caledonia, now semi-autonomous, is officially referred to simply as New Caledonia: it has no formal DOM, TOM, or COM appellation.

5. http://www.elysee.fr/elysee/francais/actualites/a_l_elysee/2003/decembre/liste_des_membres_de_la_commission_stasi_sur_la_laicite.6707.html.

Turkish Culture and Migrations; and government mediator in hijab incidents, Hanifa Chérifi

• other intellectuals: philosopher Régis Debray, former active Communist close to Che Guevara in Cuba and Bolivia, who works on the idea of religion and on media—a field he has dubbed "mediology"—and one of the signatories to the five intellectuals' text of 1989; sociologist Alain Touraine, who coined the term "postindustrial society" and is specialized in the study of social movements

• political figures: Michel Delebarre, former Socialist deputy and deputy-mayor of Dunkirk at the time of the Stasi Commission; Nicole Guedj, lawyer, municipal councilor in Pantin in the inner suburbs of Paris and regional councilor for the Ile-de-France and national secretary of the UMP with responsibility for human rights; Nelly Olin, UMP senator, mayor of Garges-les-Gonesse; Marceau Long, honorary vice president of the Council of State

• management consultant Raymond Soubie, former social affairs adviser to Raymond Barre, center-right prime minister during the 1970s, and now chief executive officer of Altédia, a management consultancy firm specialized in "human resources and communications"

• high school principal Ghislaine Hudson, for many years principal of the French High School in New York

The nineteenth and twentieth members were the chair, Bernard Stasi, and the rapporteur, Rémy Schwartz, of the Council of State, who had in 1996 prepared a report on the hijab-in-schools cases that had come before the Council of State.

Three of the committee were of Muslim background (two Kabyle Algerian: Arkoun and Chérifi; one Turkish: Petek). This is more than proportional to the Muslim-background percentage of the French population, although in terms of the main population concerned by the debate, perhaps a little less so, although two of the three were women. There were only three other women (25 percent of the commission), one of whom was also Algerian, but Sephardic Jewish (Guedj). This low percentage of women was clearly *not* proportional to the percentage of the French population. Moreover, at least two of the female members of the commission were close to the government (Guedj and Olin; Olin was also the only member of the government on the commission), one was a government appointee (Chérifi) and one sat on several government-constituted committees (Petek). Only one female academic sat on the commission, amid a crowd of male ones: Costa-Lascoux.

The commission heard submissions from some 140 individuals and representatives of groups over three months, with roughly 100 of these being public. Those making submissions included numerous members of the government, including many ministers; representatives of political parties of all persuasions, including the National Front, and of several trade unions; religious authorities, including Dalil Boubaker, pro-secular Rector of the Paris Mosque and then president of the newly created French Council for the Muslim Faith, and highly conservative Catholic Archbishop Lustiger, as well as Protestant, Jewish, Greek Orthodox, Hindu, Buddhist, and Baha'i representatives; representatives of associations such as the Union des Familles Laïques, SOS-Racisme, and Ligue contre le Racisme et l'Antisémitisme (one of the rare antiracist associations to have adopted the intransigent position in 1989); feminist and women's organizations such as NPNS, the French division of the European Women's Lobby, International League of Women's Rights, Lyons-based Femmes Contre les Intégrismes, and the French Union of Muslim Women; school principals and teachers (including a delegation from La Martinière High School in Lyons, site of the above-discussed bandana affair); prison and hospital directors; company directors (such as the general manager of large supermarket and retail chain Auchan); academics such as Jean-Paul Willaime, director of the group Sociology of Religions and Secularism at the Institut de Recherche des Sociétés Contemporaines and Gilles Delouche, director of the Institut National des Langues et Civilisations Orientales (more commonly known by its acronym INALCO, also frequently referred to as "Langues O"); some high school students from the Parisian region (some from the school of which Ghislaine Hudson was principal); prominent individuals such as Alain Gresh, editor-in-chief of *Le Monde Diplomatique* and opponent of a ban, Fodé Scylla, former president of SOS-Racisme and supporter of a ban, now a member of the European Parliament; prominent individual feminists such as Gisèle Halimi, lawyer and rights activist, Chahdortt Djavann, Iranian immigrant and vocal author of a pro-ban book called *Bas les voiles!* (2003), and Yamina Benguigui, director of a film on Algerian immigration, and author of a book on the same theme, as well as another on Muslim women, and subsequently to become one of the deputy mayors of Paris, holding the human rights and antidiscrimination portfolios (Benguigui 1996, 1997). These last three all supported a ban. There was even a submission from the women's Freemasonry Lodge, along with the other main lodges including the largest, the Grand Orient de France.[6]

Outside those already named, there were few verbal submissions or interviews with women's groups of any persuasion, locality, or ethnic background. In his opening statement presenting the report, however, Stasi noted that the commission had received over two thousand letters from individuals and associations wishing to put their point of view, share their experiences, or make proposals concerning appropriate action from the relevant authorities. He further noted the impressively large number of books that had appeared in recent months on the subject of secularism. Delegations from the commission had also visited Germany, the United Kingdom, Belgium, Italy, and the Netherlands to compare notes on the situations and approaches there. Finally, Stasi stressed the difficult conditions in which the hijab crises had developed: difficulties with "integration" that recent immigrants had experienced, the difficulties of living in many of France's suburbs, unemployment, feelings of suffering discrimination and rejection from "the national community," all of which explained how some might be tempted to "lend a benevolent ear" to extremist groups who oppose "what we call the values of the Republic" (Stasi et al. 2003, 6).

The commission's report, numbering some seventy pages, was handed down on December 11, 2003.[7] It was divided into four parts: the first was devoted to the history and philosophical principles of secularism, the second to the legal principles and framework, the third to considering the contemporary challenges of secularism, and the last to framing and making recommendations.

---

6. The Observatoire du Communautarisme Web site maintains a dedicated page on the Stasi Commission, with links to the report, to the transcript of a number of public submissions, and to articles and commentary. http://www.communautarisme.net/commissionstasi.

7. The full text of the report is downloadable in pdf form from http://lesrapports .ladocumentationfrancaise.fr/ BRP/034000725/0000.pdf.

The report made twenty-three separate recommendations, only one of which was immediately and officially adopted, although others, notably those concerning chaplains and some of the revisions to school curricula, have found their way into practice and some were already in train. Apart from that which led to the 2004 law, a key recommendation was that Yom Kippur (Jewish) and Eid-el-Kebir (Muslim) be added to France's public holidays, to be taken in addition to other holidays in schools and as alternatives to Christian holidays in the workplace. Within a country that arguably constitute's Europe's main meeting ground for the various branches of the monotheistic religions, but where most public holidays remain Catholic, this was a coherent and positive recommendation. Another key recommendation that went along the same lines of religious recognition was the creation of a National (secular) Institute of Islamic Studies, no doubt as a secular, state-run alternative to the Islamist-controlled Institut Européen des Sciences Humaines. The commission further recommended that the fight against racial discrimination and impoverishment and ghettoization of immigrant areas in cities be made a national priority, with measures to include the creation of an Anti-Discrimination Authority. This last recommendation did end up being actioned, with the creation, via the passage of a law on December 30, 2004, of the Haute Autorité de Lutte contre les Discriminations et pour l'Egalité (known by its acronym la HALDE). La HALDE is empowered, among other things, to bring cases of discrimination before the public prosecutor, but the jury remains out, among antiracist and homosexual rights organizations, on its effectiveness to date.[8]

These recommendations placed the hijab issue firmly within a sociopolitical context of socioeconomic marginalization and structural and systemic racism and laid responsibility for resolving these problems just as firmly at the door of the government.

Along the same lines were other recommendations concerning changes to the school curriculum to make the history of slavery a compulsory part

8. For example, conversations in June 2008, with the president and some members of the newly opened Centre Lesbien, Gai, Bi et Trans in Paris, indicate that, notwithstanding La HALDE's publication of some reports on discrimination against homosexuals, members of the lesbian and gay community are not convinced of la HALDE's effectiveness in taking up discrimination cases. For more information see http://www.halde.fr.

of the history curriculum and to expand the section of the curriculum on the history of colonization, decolonization, and immigration. The commission also recommended that teaching on religions as "facts of civilization," already starting to be incorporated into French and history curricula, be expanded to become a separate subject and that there be better provision for the teaching of Arabic and other Muslim community languages.

The commission also, however, recommended measures to reinforce secularism and outlaw culturally justified discrimination against women. Apart from what was to become the 2004 law, it recommended that the principles of secularism become a major theme in already existing civic instruction programs in schools and that there be strict rules of attendance, including following the curriculum as taught. It further recommended that France oppose any international convention recognizing polygamy or repudiation and change its own laws that allow the application of Algerian, Tunisian, or Moroccan personal laws for immigrant couples from those countries. (Feminists in France have for many decades campaigned against legislation and bilateral agreements enabling the application of Maghrebian personal laws in France for women citizens of those countries; See also chapter 8.)

Finally, the commission recommended that regulations concerning the use of hospitals and other public services include provisions that all employees of and subcontractors working with the public service must maintain neutrality and, conversely, members of the public cannot refuse to interact with employees or representatives of the public service on the basis of the sex, race, religion, or ideas of the latter.

The commission further noted that teachers in so-called problem schools were given insufficient support in difficult situations and remarked on violence, coercion, and segregation imposed on girls in some minority communities. It stopped short, however, of making specific recommendations to address either of these issues, apart from those mentioned above concerning the strict application of religious neutrality and attendance rules, antidiscrimination measures, and attention to socioeconomic development in urban ghettos.

On the face of it, the Fillon government, elected in 2007, is finally making some moves to address the last issue. A much-touted Plan banlieue (officially called Espoir Banlieue, or "Suburbs-Hope"), introduced in January

2008 by Fadela Amara and strongly supported by Sarkozy, provides for monitoring and retraining of young dropouts and significantly improved public transport serving underprivileged ghetto areas. The plan has met with a lukewarm reception and six months down the track has not been considered an overwhelming success, with some noting that the overall agenda of the government is undermining any potentially positive impact of the Plan banlieue (see, for example, *L'Humanité*, July 10, 2008).

As I noted in 2006, the Stasi Commission did little more, in making these recommendations, than reiterate what many had been calling for since 1989, but in doing so, it lent official weight to these demands (Winter 2006c, 284). It was thus a great pity, albeit unsurprising, that the government focused first and foremost on a single restrictive and punitive measure and various low-cost rhetorical and image-building devices (such as the Cité Nationale de l'Immigration discussed below), at the expense, in particular, of comprehensive measures to address socioeconomic exclusion and sex, race, and cultural discrimination, both inside and outside schools. Although other recommendations were subsequently picked up, as we have seen above, progress has been slow and the impact minimal.

The recommendation that became the law contained a shift in vocabulary from the term "ostentatious." The fourteen years of administrative and legal wrangles that had taken place since the Council of State *avis* in 1989 had revolved in great part around the question of whether or not the hijab was sufficiently "ostentatious" to constitute provocation, proselytism, or propaganda. The difficulty in defining this troubling ostentatiousness, and varying degrees of manipulation of the concept on all sides, led many teachers in particular to call for the adoption of a law banning all *visible* religious insignia (Stasi et al. 2003, 57–58). The Stasi Commission stopped short of making this recommendation, but chose the word *ostensible* ("conspicuous") instead of "ostentatious," shifting the focus from degree of provocative display to degree of visibility. In recommending this term, it gave examples of conspicuous signs: "veil," large cross, or yarmulke, while inconspicuous signs included medallions, small crosses, stars of David, or small Qur'ans: generally the sorts of things that can be worn on a small chain around one's neck.

Hand of Fatma pendants were also included in the list of allowable inconspicuous signs, although technically, these are not religious symbols.

The *khamsa* (Arabic for five) or hand of Fatma is a talisman dating from pre-Islamic times, worn to ward off the evil eye. Usually made of filigree silver or gold, it is in the form of a stylized symmetrically designed hand with an eye (often blue) in its palm. It has over time become associated with the name of Fatima (the Prophet's daughter and wife of 'Ali, the Prophet's cousin and leader of Shi'a Islam).

On the basis of the Stasi Commission's recommendation, education minister Luc Ferry presented to the National Assembly, in January 2004, a bill to outlaw conspicuous religious insignia in French schools. This officially became law on March 15, 2004, applicable from the start of the new school year in September. Although the law bans all "conspicuous" religious insignia, it is perceived to target the hijab. As in 1989 and 1994, however, hijab wearing was a marginal phenomenon and the law has largely been followed without question (Winter 2006c). The then minister for the interior Nicolas Sarkozy claimed in October 2003 that out of 250,000 Muslim schoolgirls, 1,256 insisted on wearing the hijab, only 20 caused problems, and only 4 had been expelled (cited in *Le Monde*, December 10, 2003). He was basing his figures on a police intelligence service (Renseignements Généraux) report dated September 29. According to this report, only around 1 percent of schoolgirls were wearing the hijab: this was the figure given for Strasbourg, for example, which has a high Turkish population. Education authorities in Lille reported around 200 nonconflictual cases, fifty of them being in one school. Other sources suggested a higher number, however: according to some of those presenting reports to the Stasi Commission hearings, there were around a thousand hijab-clad girls in the Seine-St-Denis département alone (inner northern suburbs of Paris with a high Muslim immigrant population). It was consequently suggested that real numbers overall were four times higher than the figure given by Sarkozy (all reported in *Le Monde*, December 10, 2003).

At the start of the 2004–5 school year, however, it was claimed that the overall figure had dropped to 639, and according to the Education Ministry, 90 percent of cases had been "resolved through dialogue" (François Fillon, quoted in *Le Monde*, November 27, 2004).

Given the work done by the Stasi Commission and the mostly positive and coherent recommendations contained in its report, many of which would not have been difficult to enact (such as the symbolically important and goodwill-building recommendation that Eid-el-Kebir and Yom Kippur be made into additional school and alternative public holidays), the government's narrow focus on a ban was disappointing albeit predictable. The perception that its raison d'être was to specifically target the hijab was heightened by the fact that of the forty-eight cases of expulsion between September 2004 and April 2005 only three did not involve the hijab, but boys wearing Sikh turbans. This latter case gave rise to some discussion, as it was considered by some to be proof that the law applied to everyone but by many others to be a tokenistic attempt to hide the fact that the law was really about the hijab (*Le Figaro*, November 6, 2004; *Libération*, November 10, 2004; Winter 2006c). It is still, however, individual school boards that remain responsible for determining expulsions, not the central government. So the accusation of tokenism would need to be generalized to school principals and school disciplinary boards countrywide, presumed to be acting in concert. The Sikh boys appealed against their expulsion, but lost the appeal.

The 2004 Law, Race, and Islam in France

As concerns support for the law, when the bill was presented in January 2004, 53 percent of 402 French Muslims surveyed by telephone on January 21 by market research company CSA for the tabloid *Le Parisien* opposed the introduction of the law; 42 percent supported it and 5 percent voiced no opinion. This was significantly lower than the overall population, based on a survey of 1004 people conducted on December 15 and 16, 2003, which indicated 69 percent in favor (74 per cent among teachers), 29 percent against, and 2 percent without an opinion. Close to half of Muslims did, however, support the law, and among those who did not, many did support secularism. Those surveyed on January 21, 2004, were 93 percent in favor of the Republic and 68 percent in favor of the separation of church and state. Ninety-five percent supported equality between women and men, and 93 percent supported equal treatment of all individuals, whatever their religious beliefs. These last two findings are open to interpretation as to their correlation with opinions on the law.[9]

9. http://www.csa-tmo.fr/dataset/data2004/opi20044012b.htm.

Another telephone survey, of 970 people, was conducted by CSA on February 2 and 3, 2005, concerning the 1905 law on the separation of church and state. Thirty-two percent of respondents considered the principle of secularism to be above all about equality among all religions, while almost as many placed separation of religion and politics and freedom of conscience in first position (28 percent in each case). Only 9 percent considered it to be about reducing the influence of religion in society. Seventy-nine percent considered secularism to be important in schools (very important for 53 percent), and 75 percent considered it an important element of French identity. Fifty-eight percent considered secularism to be in danger today, 40 percent of these because of "more and more people wearing conspicuous religious insignia"; 39 percent considered that religious representatives were becoming more and more vocal about social issues; 35 percent found that different religious and cultural communities were mixing less and less; and 21 percent were concerned about state subsidizing of mosque construction.[10] The concern about "conspicuous religious insignia" would appear to be grossly exaggerated and no doubt informed by the law, as the number of headscarved girls and women in France would appear to be, at worst, stable and possibly declining. Even if one takes the high end of the 2003 estimates cited above, and then multiples this figure by twenty to arrive at a very generous estimate of all Muslim women in France who wear the hijab, these would still represent an infinitesimal proportion of Muslim women in France: 2 or 3 percent, but the real figure is probably less than 2 and perhaps even lower, as suggested by Gaspard and Khosrokhavar in 1995 (see chapter 5). Scott (2007) cites a survey conducted just prior to the adoption of the 2004 law according to which 14 percent of Muslim women were wearing the hijab at that time. This is a surprisingly high figure, and by all other estimates from various sources over the years, unrealistically so, which tends to indicate that the survey was conducted in areas known to have a high concentration of hijab wearing, perhaps with deliberate intent to artificially inflate figures. Even this high estimate, however, was still considered a low percentage by Scott.

The concern about the vocal intervention of religious representatives in social and political issues is perhaps closer to the mark, although there is no

---

10. http://www.csa-fr.com/dataset/data2005/opi20050203c.htm.

reason to believe that this has increased. The unrepresentative religious right has always made a lot of noise on social and political issues, particularly if they are to do with women or sexuality, as I noted in the case of the Catholic campaign against the PaCS. What has changed today is that the Muslim religious right is now an integral part of that landscape, whereas before, the Christian (particularly Catholic), and to a considerably lesser extent, Jewish, right had almost exclusively occupied that space.

What is certain, however, is that perceptions of a greater religiosity and lower "integrability" of Muslims within French society remain strong: 45 and 57 percent, respectively, of respondents to a survey of 1052 people conducted on behalf of the National Consultative Committee on Human Rights during the height of the renewed hijab debate in November and December 2003. The authors of the report note, however, that this hostility is slightly lower than it was in 1995, which would indicate, despite the "lepenization of minds" and the hijab debate, that attitudes in France generally to Muslims are not reflective of a supposed increase in "Islamophobia," much discussed in the 2002–5 period (see chapter 8) (CNCDH 2004, 220–23). The higher the education level and the lower the age, the less the hostility, to both Muslims and immigrants; blue-collar workers and business owners are more hostile than professionals. Hostility is also slightly lower among those with at least one parent born overseas, although the difference is less than one might have assumed. Catholics are more hostile than others, as, predictably, are those on the right of politics, and the petty bourgeoisie. The only Muslim religious practice, however, that is deemed to pose a problem for harmonious coexistence in society, is, unsurprisingly, hijab-wearing (81 percent). Religious observance through prayer, fasting, teetotaling, or eating halal food are, on the contrary, perceived as unproblematic (75–85 percent of respondents, depending on the particular practice). Oddly, however, the construction of mosques in one's local area appears to worry people much more than the practice of prayer, which, when correlated with results of other surveys, may indicate that mosques are perceived as markers of social segregation or right-wing proselytism. It may also reflect the trend toward individualization of religious and cultural identity (which is also the case for French Muslims), mentioned in chapter 3.

The hijab issue was, unsurprisingly, one of the most discussed by French citizens and residents during the months following the Stasi report being handed down. According to a survey conducted by opinion poll company IFOP, the hijab debate peaked in February 2004 as the top subject of conversation in a range of topics that went from sport to national and international politics (83 percent score, as opposed to a 68 percent score in January 2004) (Dabi and Parodi 2004, 4). The authors of the IFOP report attribute this to the political arena's bipartisan co-opting of a wider social debate, thus driving the agenda in this respect. A highly provocative demonstration in Paris on January 17, organized by the extreme-right Muslim Party of France, may also have contributed.

Other data of interest during this period are the increase in Muslim support for the Socialist Party, notwithstanding the fact that the Socialists also mostly voted for the 2004 law. An IFOP analysis published in December 2006 showed that Muslim support for the Socialist Party even increased in the months leading up to the passage of the 2004 law (from 43.7 percent in December 2003 to 47.9 percent in March 2004) and increased sharply again following the riots in October and November 2005, reaching 55.2 percent in April 2006, as the pre-presidential campaign started to get under way. This is almost double the support for the Socialists in the wider population at that time.[11] A CSA survey of 5,352 people conducted on April 21, 2007, on the eve of the first round of the presidential election, indicated that 64 percent of Muslims voted for Ségolène Royal, 19 percent for UDF candidate François Bayrou (which corresponded with the vote for Bayrou in the wider population), and only 1 percent for Nicolas Sarkozy. The survey also indicated that close to half of the French population either declares itself to be a nonpracticing Catholic (26 percent) or nonreligious (19.5 percent), with a further 13 percent expressing no opinion as to religion.[12]

Keeping in mind that most French Muslims are secular and even secularist, it is not surprising that it was the government's response to the 2005 riots, rather than the 2004 law, that prompted the increase in their support for the Socialist Party. It would seem that ultimately, the issues of structural socioeconomic inequity and the racist "law and order" agenda of the 2002–7

11. http://www.ifop.com/europe/docs/L'orientationpolitiquedesMusulmansdeFrance.pdf.

12. http://www.csa-fr.com/dataset/data2002/opi20020421d.htm.

French government, notably its minister for the interior Nicolas Sarkozy, are far more important for the majority of French Muslims than the hijab issue, regardless of the sound and fury of a minority of their number and the more general media hype.

"Them" and "Us"

Even where a priori positive steps have been taken by the government, they leave much to be desired. For example, the planned Centre de mémoire de l'immigration to which the Stasi report refers (article 4.1.2.3), came into official being as the Cité nationale de l'histoire de l'immigration through the publication of a decree on January 1, 2005.[13] This project, that was twenty years in the making, was originally an idea drawn up by immigration historian Gérard Noiriel. Officially opened (in President Sarkozy's absence) on October 10, 2007, and housed in the Porte Dorée Palace in Paris, the Cité was for some time a virtual one, with a Web site only, although various exhibitions and conferences had been organized over the years. One of these was a major conference in November 2003 with the title Leur histoire est notre histoire (Their history is our history). This title was subsequently to become the virtual museum's slogan, although at the time of my last consultation of the site on January 16, 2008, the slogan had disappeared, in favor of a header heralding a series of inaugural events for the first year of the museum's concrete existence.[14] It had been previously pointed out, however, that the "them" and "us" in the virtual museum's slogan begged the question of who counted as "us" (Jelen 2005). Judith Ezekiel has further pointed out that women were either completely absent from the site's imagery or most decidedly in the minority: in 2008, they remain largely absent from the site, so do not even seem to be part of "them."[15]

13. The term *cité* should no doubt be understood in terms both of the classical political idea of the city and its relationship to the concept of citizenship, and of the modern French idea of the *cité* as a street or residential estate—a space grouping people into a local community within a metropolis.

14. http://www.histoire-immigration.fr.

15. Post to French women's studies e-mail discussion list *Etudes féministes*, Jan. 9, 2005.

Having not yet had the opportunity to visit the new museum, I can only speculate on whether stories and images of women are more present than on the Web site or whether the othering implicit in the "them" and "us" slogan has disappeared or been diminished. The othering of postcolonial immmigrants, however, reverberates throughout the discourse of the French political elite, as exemplified, caricaturally, in the traditional July 14 television address given by President Chirac in 2004. First, he used the hackneyed and nonsensically self-contradictory expression "immigrants of the second generation" to refer to French citizens of immigrant parents. Second, he delivered an ambiguous and rather clumsy sentence, intended to be "inclusive," about "some of our compatriots" being attacked because they are Jewish, Muslim, or "just simply French." This sentence was almost instantly heard as yet more othering and widely misquoted as "Jewish, Muslim, or French."[16]

The supposed good intentions of the French government in acknowledging diversity through such measures as the Cité have been further belied by measures such as the law of February 23, 2005, imposing "recognition of the Nation and the national contribution in favor of the repatriated French."[17] This law was ostensibly adopted to formalize recognition of harkis in French colonial history, but it went much further than that. Article 4 of the law stipulated that "programs of university research [were to] give the history of the French presence overseas, notably in North Africa, the place it deserves," and that "school curricula [were to] acknowledge in particular the positive role of the French presence overseas, especially in North Africa, and give the history and the sacrifice of those combatants with the French army who came from those territories, the eminent place that is their right." This law was opposed by a number of historians such as the above-mentioned Gérard Noiriel, as well as by the Association Harkis et droits de l'homme (Harkis and human rights).[18] The historians' petition opposed the law on the grounds that it

16. http://www.cip-idf.org/IMG/rtf/allocution_14_juillet_2004_script_integral.rtf; http://www.nouvelobs.com/articles/p2073/a246755.html.

17. *Journal Officiel* 46 (Feb. 24, 2005): 3128.

18. http://www.ldh-toulon.net/article.php3?id_article=573.

imposes an official history, contrary to neutrality of the school system and respect for freedom of thought that are at the heart of secularism,

imposes an official lie concerning the crimes, massacres extending sometimes to genocide, slavery, and racism that are the heritage of [the colonial past],

legalizes a national communitarianism, giving rise in reaction to communitarianism among groups that are thus forbidden any past.[19]

This petition is particularly important in the context of the hijab debate. The first point above, in invoking the values of secularism, implicitly refers to that debate and shows up the hypocrisy of the government's defense of secularism in relation to the 2004 law.

The second point is all the more salient, given the timing of the law, because, one week before it was made public, the Commission d'Enquête Citoyenne pour la vérité sur l'implication française dans le génocide des Tutsi (the Citizens' Commission of Inquiry for the truth on French involvement in Tutsi genocide) released its preliminary report on French responsibility in the Rwanda genocide (CEC 2005). An independent commission appointed by the Rwandan government has since obtained similar findings to the CEC. The commission's report, handed down on August 5, 2008, includes recommendations that thirty-three senior French military and political officials be prosecuted. Those named include former Socialist president, the late François Mitterrand (d. 1996), and two former prime ministers, Edouard Balladur and Dominique de Villepin. The immediate reaction of the French foreign ministry, headed by Bernard Kouchner, was a "no comment," beyond questioning the Rwandan commission's independence and legitimacy (ABC news Australia, August 6, 2008).[20]

The third point, in laying the blame for the development of separatist or fundamentalist identity politics among postcolonial minorities at the door of French colonialist nationalism and ensuing historical revisionism, once again refers implicitly to the hijab issue. The outcry against this law was, fortunately, of such magnitude that the government was forced to withdraw it.

---

19. http://www.ldh-toulon.net/article.php3?id_article=555. See also Liauzu 2005.
20. http://www.abc.net.au/news/stories/2008/08/06/2325270.htm.

Prior to this law, however, and subsequent to it, have been three laws on immigration and nationality, in 2003, 2006 and 2007. The 2003 law, explicitly framed by the minister for the interior (Sarkozy) as designed to fight clandestine immigration, was the subject of much polemic in the lead-up to its adoption. Not only did it reinstate a 1945 requirement that foreigners visiting France for a period of three months or less provide a certificate of residency and that their host sign a document guaranteeing to look after their financial and other needs if necessary, but it also provided for legal action against any individual or organization helping clandestine immigrants. This would include, for example, women having arrived under family reunion legislation and having separated from their husband within the first two years of residency in France. This measure was widely condemned and a "Manifesto of Offenders in Solidarity," who declared their intention of refusing to give names of "temporary visitors" and illegals to authorities, collected several thousand signatures.[21] The "residency certificates," however, along with more family reunion restrictions, made it into law (law 2003-1119 of November 26, 2003). Law 2006-911 of July 24, 2006, was to go further. Called a "pillaging of rights" of immigrant workers by the union Confédération Nationale du Travail (National Work Confederation) and a "threat to our lives" (because of its medical restrictions) by Act-Up, it considerably upped the ante in the supposed fight against illegal immigration, severely limiting delivery and duration of work and residency permits and making regularization of *sans papiers* almost impossible.[22] This law came, predictably, in the wake of the 2005 riots. The 2007 law mandates testing in French language and in the "values of the Republic" for immigrants aged between sixteen and sixty-five, and toughens up the conditions concerning minimum income for family reunion. A controversial measure provides for DNA tests for children of immigrants entering under the family reunion regime if there is a doubt as to their identity, but only in relation to filiation from the mother.

When one also considers the government's response to the death of Pope Jean-Paul II and the creation of the French Council of the Muslim

---

21. http://petition.gisti.org/manifeste/index.html.

22. http://www.cnt-urp.org/article.php3?id_article=130; http://www.actupparis.org/article2311.html.

Faith, what had become clear, two to three years down the track from the application of the 2004 law on "conspicuous" religious insignia, was that (1) the rights of socioeconomically marginalized immigrant and racialized populations were less than low on the government's agenda, notwithstanding the latter's posturings, and (2) despite similar posturing on secularism, the government's track record on applying religious neutrality in the public sphere was patchy to say the least.

Part Three | Feminists Caught in the Contradictions

＆つ

Feminist ideas and strategies are never the object of universal consen-
sus, even in the countries where the activism occurs. Moreover, many
feminist voices are silenced—by the media, government, the male-
dominated left, and even other feminists—while others are put for-
ward as the only feminist voice in their country or on a specific issue
(Winter 2001b, 56).

I WROTE THESE WORDS IN 2001, in the context of a debate on the diversity of feminist activism and feminist positionings with relation to religion.
Nowhere are they more true than within the French debate over the hijab
and related issues, particularly in its third resurgence in 2003–6. Suddenly
everyone was claiming to be the voice of feminism. Caught in the crossfire
are members of a secular French left and feminist movement (of both European and non-European background), activists and intellectuals, who are
attempting to articulate more nuanced feminist positions or simply express
their anger and frustration at the hijacking of the debate by institutions and
organizations that fundamentally do not have the wider interests of French
racialized women at heart.

Chapter 7 will look at the politics of hijabization today: who is wearing
it, what their ethnic background is, why they are wearing it, and how these
reasons are being politically deployed or manipulated by various players,
including both the media and the girls themselves.

Chapter 8 looks at the polarization between two camps: an "integrationist" feminist camp grouped around NPNS on one hand and Une Ecole
Pour Tous-tes (A School for All, UEPT), and, particularly, Les Indigènes de

la République ("Natives" of the Republic, IDLR) on the other. Some, with reason, have accused the NPNS of being too pally with the French political class and having too narrow a focus on violence against specific groups of women by specific groups of men, which it links with the issue of secularism. It has also been rather eager to push a sanitized Westernized image of femininity that sits ill with its more feminist discourse on male violence. In particular, some of the IDLR women have accused NPNS of demonizing Arab men. On the IDLR side, there are some dodgy alliances with Islamist factions of the pro-Palestinian movement as well as French Islamists, and accusations of anti-Semitism and "Islamophobia" have flown. Most bizarrely, a "queer politics" critique of secularists and defense of Arab men against supposedly demonizing feminists has emerged. The chapter engages with feminist critiques of both sides of this polarization.

Finally, chapter 9 looks at secular feminist antiracist analyses from both Muslim and non-Muslim women that, whatever their position on the law, situate themselves outside the NPNS-IDLR polarization and suggest ways out of the maze created by it. Unfortunately, these feminists also find themselves, once again, caught between religion and state, these last two not always, unfortunately, being clearly on opposite sides, and neither necessarily, particularly at this point in time in French politics, being a good ally for women.

The Politics of Hijabization

COMMENTATORS, both headscarved and not, have advanced various reasons for wearing the hijab. Many of these reasons correspond with those I discussed in chapter 1, within the framework of the politics of reveiling in the Arabo-Muslim and Middle-Eastern Muslim world from the 1970s onward. The degree to which the argument holds that "it's not the same" in France as in the Muslim world will be investigated in subsequent chapters. In this chapter, I focus on the reasons advanced for hijab-wearing in France as well as looking at the ethnic groups concerned and offer some comments as to why these particular ethnic groups are involved. I also examine the effect of media hype, through the particular case of the Lévy sisters, and their father.

Hijab, Class, Ethnicity, and Muslimism

I have been unable to find precise data on numbers and percentages of ethnic groups involved in hijab incidents since 1989 or on the extent to which ethnicity, location within France, class, or recency of immigration are significant factors in tendencies toward hijab-wearing more generally. As I mentioned in chapter 3, one of the problems that arise in discussing this issue is the absence of finely disaggregated data, so it is unwise to advance opinions and claim them as certainties (Kaltenbach and Tribalat 2002, 55ff). That said, it is possible to tease out some information on the basis of which some generalizations may be made.

First, the evidence from the various hijab incidents over the past two decades, which, as we have seen, occurred mainly in ZEPs, indicates that class is a central element. While some young women donning the hijab are

the children of professionals or are themselves highly educated professionals, the hijab as an expression of piety and identity is largely, in France, not
a middle class or elite or intellectual phenomenon, and this is particularly
so in the case of schoolgirls. It is not even necessarily connected to upward
social mobility in the same overt way as in Egypt or elsewhere in the Muslim
world—although it may well be connected to a certain individual mobility
within tight-knit and often recent-immigrant communities. The class aspect
is more related to an experience of socioeconomic marginalization combined with a generational identity politics of the sort described by Gaspard
and Khosrokhavar (1995), Khosrokhavar (1997), Kaltenbach and Tribalat
(2002), and Djavann (2004).

Second, and even more obviously, the hijab debate in France is connected to the Maghrebian and Middle Eastern worlds. France's small, non-
postcolonial Muslim minorities from Eastern Europe and South, West, and
Southeast Asia are not involved in it to date, and its postcolonial population
from sub-Saharan Africa (Malians and Senegalese being the majority) has not
even been remotely concerned by it, notwithstanding very recent anecdotal
evidence that "Muslimism," complete with hijabization, is perhaps starting
to find a following among some sub-Saharan African–background girls.

Third, a significant number of hijab incidents involve girls who are *not*
from postcolonial populations. As we saw in part II, Turkish-background
girls are one of the two largest groups to have been involved in hijab incidents. Small numbers of Iraqi and Iranian-background girls have also been
involved. None of these populations are postcolonial, and are not all equally
racialized in France. Moreover, the history of their immigration to France is
in general more recent (although Turkish rural and working class immigration goes back to roughly the end of the Trente Glorieuses [ELELE 2006,
16]). Finally, some hijab incidents have concerned the usually very young
daughters of Western converts.

In 1996, 50 percent of France's Turkish population was under twenty
years of age and its female population was increasing, with Turks being the
second most numerous group in family reunion immigration (Petek-Salom
and Minassian, 1996). Not being postcolonial, Turkish immigrants to
France are not racialized in the same way as the Turkish-background minority in Germany, which would be more comparable, in terms of experience

of postcoloniality and associated racism, with the Maghrebian-background minority in France. Which does not, of course, mean that they are not racialized at all. Not being Arab, however, they are arguably, after converts, and, perhaps, Iranian intellectuals and professionals in exile, among France's "whitest" Muslims.

That said, Turkish immigrants have much in common with earlier generations of Algerian immigrants and current immigrants from all countries in North Africa. In a pattern common, in fact, to labor and family reunion immigration from poorer to richer countries, Turkish immigrants to France are often from poor rural backgrounds, and women arriving under family reunion are poorly educated, married young, and have little to no knowledge of French. They thus, typically for immigrant women in such situations, find themselves enclosed within an immigrant ghetto where they, and their daughters, are under much stricter social control than they may have been in Turkey. Petek and Minassian (1996) note the similarity between the situation of immigrant families to France and that of rural families having moved to the city in Turkey, which is also an argument developed by Flanquart (2003) in relation to Maghrebian-background minorities in France (see below).

Despite the significant numbers of Turkish girls involved in hijab incidents, there has so far been little systematic study of Turkish Islamic groups in France. Indeed, Franck Frégosi commented in 2001 that there had been none, a situation that has scarcely changed since. Weibel (2006) notes the existence of a "women's section" of Cojep: "New Female Perspectives," and the high level of activity of young Turkish hijabis in what she calls "Islam-action." Along with Franck Frégosi, she argues that the attraction of "Islam-action" for young Turkish-background men and women is linked to a youth-identity politics that is imbricated within French citizenship and demarcates itself from the immigrant generation of their parents (Frégosi 2001, 111; Weibel 2006). This argument does not, however, hold for the very young children of Turkish immigrants involved in many of the hijab incidents, where paternal influence—often assisted by the presence of Islamist "advisers" (not necessarily Turkish ones)—was manifest.

Paradoxically, however, Weibel notes that Turkish immigrants are far less religious than those of other backgrounds, for reasons she links to the history of secularism in Turkey. This appears to be at variance with Frégosi's claim that the Islam of reference for Turkish immigrants is the "most conservative" (Frégosi 2001, 111). In Turkey, Islamism—first radical, via the Virtue Party, then moderate, via the Justice and Development Party, in power, and much embattled, at the time of this writing—has emerged over the past three decades as opposition to an antidemocratic and somewhat idiosyncratically secularist state that has its roots among elites but has found popular expression as well (White 2002). As elsewhere, the hijab has become the symbol of this once oppositional and now ruling political movement in Turkey (Toprak 1994)—although, ironically, the party's 2007 attempt to remove the ban on hijab-wearing in public institutions (which is more extensive than the French one) was unsuccessful. Bowen argues, giving support to both Weibel's and Fregosi's arguments, that Turks in France are in fact as divided as Turks in Turkey over the issues of Islam, secularism, and public life, but notes that those Turks who support Islamicization of public life are among the most hardline (Bowen 2007, 52–53).

Fourth, among postcolonial Muslim populations, by far the largest group involved in hijab incidents is of Moroccan descent. As I noted in part I, those of Moroccan background are significantly more religious than other Maghrebian-background minorities in France, for reasons linked both to Morocco's postfeudal Islamic monarchy and to the strong and growing presence of Islamist Republican opposition there. Other Arab minorities associated with France's colonial history, such as its small Lebanese-background population (of whom some would in any case be Christian), are not involved in any hijab incidents.

Notwithstanding the frequent reference, by critics of expulsions of hijab-wearers from school and of the 2004 law, to the 1958 unveiling of women in Algiers, and notwithstanding my earlier comments comparing the situation of recent Turkish immigrants with that of earlier generations of Algerian immigrants, Algerians are, as noted earlier, the least religious of France's Muslims (Tribalat 1995; Gaspard and Khosrokhavar 1995; Silverstein 2004). Strasbourg may, however, be an exception to the rule. The ultraright albeit very marginal Parti Musulman de France is based there and, as noted in part I, appears to have recruited largely among Algerian harkis. Moreover, Strasbourg is in Alsace, which has a quite particular religious and cultural history and status.

The case of Strasbourg aside, however, the reluctance of the overwhelming majority of historically humiliated Algerians in France to embrace Islamic revivalism of any sort, let alone political Islamism, may appear curious, but in fact is unsurprising, when one considers the double-edged politics of colonization in general and French colonization of Algeria in particular. The population that France humiliated and exploited was also the population that had, unlike any other colonized population in the Franco-Arab world, been taken into the French nation: Algeria was considered part of France in a way that Tunisia, Morocco, Lebanon, and what was to become Syria never were. The consequences of this colonial policy were violent and contradictory, leaving both lasting affinities and deep scars in the French and Algerian national psyches, but it linked Algeria and Algerians to the French nation in unique ways. This is evidenced not only through the legacy of the harkis, of "worker-harvesting" in Algerian villages to provide manpower for French factories, and of the growth of an Algerian-background professional and intellectual class in France, but also through the institutionalization of a largely secularized and Algerian-linked French Islam, through the Grand Mosque of Paris.

Fifth, many if not most of the incidents have involved girls who are relatively recent immigrants or the daughters of relatively recent immigrants, often from rural backgrounds.

Finally, practically all hijab incidents over the fourteen years between 1989 and 2003 featured the influential presence of "counselors," imams and other religious advisers, who were also often representatives of Islamist groups such as the UJM, FNMF, and Rappel, close to various imported Islamist movements such as the FIS, Ennahda, and, of course, the transnational Muslim Brotherhood.

A small word on converts is perhaps warranted here. The scenarios presented by the small but significant number of hijab incidents involving converts are in many ways very similar to those involving ethnic Muslims, with one possible exception: in the case of converts, it is perhaps more likely to be the *mothers* who are the authority figures in headscarving their daughters. For example, at the beginning of January 1999, an Administrative Tribunal in the Department of Gard, in southern France, overturned an expulsion of two students, Romina and Diana (thirteen and fourteen years old, respectively), from their junior high school Léo-Larguier in La Grande Combe. There was immediate protest action against this decision, and this time it was not only teachers but parents who demonstrated against the reintegration of the girls to school. The girls, whose mother was a recent convert to Islam, were refusing to remove their hijabs for physical education and chemistry classes, resulting in their absence from those classes. The school once again expelled them on February 14, basing its decision on the precedent established by the 1996 Council of State ruling concerning requirement of appropriate clothing for certain specific activities. On July 17, this expulsion was rendered definitive.

Though not all converts are ultrapious, my own observations, and those of others, have shown that they are often more likely to be in their dress and behavior as well as their ideas, and they can even be the most right-wing of Islamists. This is the case, for example, of the co-founders of the FNMF, Abdallah Milcent and Daniel Youssef Leclerc. It is the case of some female converts in Australia who would like to see blasphemy laws introduced, which would outlaw, for example, caricatures of the Prophet such as the Danish one that created such a furor in 2006. It also appears to be the case for some female converts in France, such as those who attended a screening, in a suburb of Toulouse on April 13, 2005, of Jérôme Host's 2004 film *Un Racisme à peine voilé*, made in opposition to the expulsion of hijab-wearers from schools and to the 2004 law. I attended this screening and participated in the ensuing debate, during which the converts, who were the most conservatively dressed, framed their comments within a discourse of extreme piety. This was in contrast to many of the comments made by ethnic Maghrebian hijab-wearers, who wore more fashionable and even flashy clothes and whose comments were framed more in terms of freedom of religion, race, ethnicity, and citizenship.

A difficult issue with relation to converts, and one on which some ethnic Muslim women have commented to me, is the relationship of converts to "Muslimism" constructed as an ethnoreligious identity. Many converts have reported experiencing "Islamophobia" and even racism (Franks 2001).[1]

---

1. Similar comments have been made by converts in conversations on feminist discussion lists such as the U.S. women's studies list WMST-L and other fora.

Ethnic Muslim women argue, however—and rightly, in my opinion—that converts are not racialized in the same way and have to some extent appropriated ethnicity in ways that diminish the experience of racism by ethnic Muslims.[2]

"Appeasement" or "Empowerment"?

As concerns the reasons advanced for hijab-wearing in France, observers generally present variations on the theme of identity, piety, negotiating freedom of movement, negotiating freedom of religion within a reconfigured model of French citizenship, and in some cases, commitment to Islamist activism.

In 2004, Fadela Amara, then president of NPNS, documented three types of hijab, as Gaspard and Khosrokhavar had done almost a decade earlier in 1995. Amara added further nuance to Gaspard's and Khosrokhavar's categories and introduced one other. She sees the "identity politics" category of hijab-wearers as coupling this identity reaction with a devout religious belief. These women, writes Amara, "wear the veil like a banner" (Amara 2004, 48). Variations on the identity-plus-religion theme are also fairly systematically cited by English-language commentators on the 1989, 1994, and 2003–4 French debates (such as Killian 2003; Jones 2004; Scott 2005; Wing and Smith 2006; Bowen 2007). As Amara notes, the hijab-banner is worn within a context that has become increasingly polarized. While most women who wear the hijab regularly, in any Western country, are relatively devout, the expression of piety as a reason for donning the garment is not always clearly demarcated from this expression of identity politics.

Amara's second type of hijab is the one worn as a response to fear. Young women don the hijab as a protection from being assaulted or otherwise harassed: it becomes their "armor." Most of these girls remove the hijab-armor when they leave their local area, revealing fashionable western dress. "Those who wear the veil are never importuned by the boys . . . veiled, they become untouchable" (Amara 2004, 48). This ties in with Souad Benani's 1989 commentary: girls arrive at school veiled, drably dressed, and then emerge from the girls' toilets transformed into trendy beurettes (Assouline

---

2. Various personal communications, most recently in Australia by Muslim feminist researcher and community activist Shakira Hussein.

1989). Even in cases where the girls claim to have chosen the hijab themselves rather than conforming to a paternal imposition (parents may even be against it), curfews and other limitations to girls' freedom of movement are imposed. Donning the hijab and becoming integrated into a locally based Islamic community, even if this does not conform to the parental view or practice of religion, nonetheless provides some guarantee that daughters are safely guarding both their own and their families' honor. Their internalization of the idea of the hijab as a protection from assault or as "armor" becomes enmeshed with traditions that are a mixture of Islamic and ant-Islamic, as we saw in chapter 1 (Allami 1988). Another aspect of "appeasement" may be peer pressure, from both boys and girls, although pressure from boys is particularly marked. If acceptance by the group matters—and it usually does matter a great deal to young teenagers—and if one's school friends, especially those who take the role of group leaders, are involved with Islamic revivalist networks and acquire popularity by doing so—one is more likely to follow suit. Even if girls are not actively policing their school friends (although we saw in part II that in some cases older girls are indeed ringleaders), the pressure to belong to a peer group is persuasive. It is all the more so when the peer group in question is seen as bucking adult authority and asserting a collective youth identity.

Following Germaine Tillion's analysis of formerly rural Maghrebians who moved massively toward the city from the 1950s onward, to become disenfranchised urban fringe dwellers, Hervé Flanquart has suggested that modern hijab-wearing in France has indeed become a question of honor for Maghrebian immigrants living in France's urban ghettos (Tillion 1966; Flanquart 2003). These immigrants similarly experienced a "rural exodus" into urban ghettoization at the same time as they experienced emigration: from Maghrebian villages to work in French factories, or, increasingly to join husbands and fathers settled in France (Benguigui 1997; Belhadj 2006). Khosrokhavar (1997), among others, has adopted a similar argument, again with relation to girls of Maghrebian background, although he does mention in passing the case of Turkish immigrants as well. For him as for Flanquart, girls are under pressure to preserve family honor, particularly in situations of disenfranchisement of fathers (and brothers) due to the realities of immigration, transforming what were often formerly rural peasants with a structured community into urban fringe-dwellers. Girls are faced with two forms of radicalization as a way out. Either they put their all into adopting French norms, thus living out the "driver of integration" scenario, and cut off from their families to some extent, or they engage in a public, overdone adherence to an Islam that, while overtly pious and even rigorist, nonetheless enables their independent existence in the public sphere and as such is in many ways as far from traditionalist orthodoxy as is "integration" into French society (Khosrokhavar 1997, 116ff).

Khosokhavar's analysis nonetheless presents two major problems. First, it remains stuck in a relatively simplistic "either-or" scenario in which women opt for one of two radicalizations: ultraintegration or ultra-Islam. The reality of most French women of Maghrebian-background, however, is probably somewhere between the two—or outside them both. For example, some cut off from their families without jumping on the "integration" bandwagon: they become dropouts, street kids, highly vulnerable to male gang violence, as Samira Bellil's 2002 testimony of street-dwelling in the *banlieues* demonstrated. Alternatively, others opt for the "ultraintegration" model without cutting off from their families; indeed, in some cases, they bring their mothers forward with them. For example, Leïla (not her real name), a worker with the then fairly high profile Paris-based group Les Nanas Beurs and part-time science tutor with dropout teenagers seeking to reenter the educational system, told the story in 1992 of her mother who had finally got herself a part-time job with a cleaning company; it was the first paid work she had ever had. As Leïla put it: "in my opinion, she is exploited. But she is very happy to be able to live, to work and to have her own money." For Leïla's mother, it was a step forward. And, as Leïla added, laughing, "since then she's a bit less of a pain in the ass!"[3]

This and other stories of daughter-mother interactions point to the second problem with Khosrokhavar's analysis. It positions young Maghrebian-background women largely in relation to a father-brother dyad; the mother is a barely mentioned presence. This is no doubt because, as is demonstrated by Leïla's story as well as by research on the situation of immigrant women (see chapter 8), women who have migrated to France under family reunion

3. Interview, Billancourt, Dec. 7, 1992.

have little legal or socioeconomic power. This does not, however, mean they have no power at all and no role in the story of their daughters. Even in Bellil's case, where her mother was originally an ambiguous figure against whom Bellil rebelled, it was in the end her mother who took steps to block the continuation of a family cycle of violence and control (Bellil 2002). In my own formal and informal conversations over the past twenty years with French women of Maghrebian background who are active in feminist and/ or antiracist groups, the figure of the mother has loomed large and in many ways has been significantly more problematic than that of the father. For it is the mother who holds the delegated masculinist power to enforce son preference and load daughters with the emotional weight of responsibility for the men's aggressions and transgressions and guilt for her own, as many feminist analysts have commented (Belotti 1973; Lacoste-Dujardin 1985; Winter 1994b). Lacoste-Dujardin (1985) wrote of the "oppositional force" of mothers, in which they manipulate their designated role as agent of patriarchal power to create maneuvering room. Hoagland (1988) has even identified the development of a capacity for manipulation as a primary survival skill employed by women under male and heterosexist domination. It is with their mothers that daughters negotiate spaces, invariably by means of this survival skill and oppositional force of manipulation; it is through their mothers that they open chinks in the community armor. While it is the mother who imposes patriarchal law, it is also frequently the mother who "covers" for her daughter, often through an elaborate system of unstated understandings camouflaged in a series of small family fictions. While such arrangements between mothers and daughters, of the "what your father doesn't know, won't hurt him" type, are common in modern Western families as well, they are particularly complex, and painstakingly negotiated, in so-called traditional families, both Western and non-Western.

Unlike many and even most other young women of Muslim culture in France who seek to disengage with this obligation to preserve family and cultural honor, or, during their adolescence in particular, to "bargain" with it, to use Kandiyoti's term (Kandiyoti 1991), many and even most hijab-wearers in France willingly identify with this idea of female responsibility for men's behavior. The issue for them does not appear to be one of challenging men's behavior in male-female relations—at least, not on the level of sociocultural expressions of sexuality and virility in the public space—but of controlling and adapting their own, generally by containing or constraining themselves in some way. As Zemmour puts it, "When young girls carry virginity within them, it is the virility of male children and the virginity of other women, members of their families, that they carry" (Zemmour 2002, 65). Interestingly, the idea that problems with men's behavior are women's to solve has also, somewhat bizarrely, resurfaced in other areas of the debate around Muslim-background women, men, sex, and race in France, following the popularization of a certain "queer politics" analysis of racism, as we will see in chapter 9. It has also resurfaced, even more disturbingly, in the French courts, via the annulled marriage affair of April 2008, discussed in the introduction to this book.

Yet, the hijabis who embrace the discourse of honor and modesty are often women who have internalized concepts of sex equality in education, work, and many other aspects of economic, social, and cultural participation in public life, and as such, fit Khosrokhavar's model of antitraditionalist women. Their association of hijabization with honor and modesty becomes reconfigured as a modern, individualist, voluntarist refusal of Western decadence and objectification of women (Venel 1998; Lévy et al. 2004). These women also frequently position themselves and their hijabs within a framework of compatibility with secularism in its more "flexible" interpretation, as guaranteeing freedom of religion (Killian 2003; Wing and Smith 2006; Bouzar and Kada 2003). For them, this concept takes on the meaning of religious pluralism in the public space rather than strict neutrality, which is not dissimilar to the understanding of some Catholics. Within that understanding, however, there is a range of interpretations. Some, like the high profile Lila and Alma Lévy (see below), advocate something approaching a neoconcordatory regime (as in Grosdidier's bill mentioned in chapter 2). The two sisters see no difficulty with differential laws for people of different faiths, such as the obligation for Muslims to attend Friday prayer (Lévy et al. 2004, 97). Others suggest a less radical boundary blurring. Tariq Ramadan, for example, gives a particular interpretation to the idea that the history and sociology of religions should be taught as a secular subject in schools:

> It would be teaching of a scientific and in-depth nature, during which one
> should not hesitate, on occasion, to put students in a situation of open dia-
> logue with followers of the religions or faiths studied. (Ramadan 2004a, 255)

While Ramadan claims that this would not be "catechism," he is nonetheless advocating the (re)introduction into schools of some form of religious
teaching, not through the back door but the front, officially included in the
curriculum.

Many others, such as Saïda Kada, inscribe themselves firmly within a
Republican framework:

> I completely identify with the gains made by the French Revolution. I have no
> desire whatsoever to be determined by my religious faith. I would like to be
> perceived first as a French woman, and would like the detail of my veil to be
> perceived in the same way as my friend's cross. (Bouzar and Kada 2003, 69)

Configured as such, the hijab not only crosses over with both identity politics and a particular reconfiguration of the integrationist and indeed secularist model, but also forms part of the international discourse of "Islamic
feminism" or "Muslim feminism" that has been a subject of scholarly focus
over the last decade or so.[4] This discourse was increasingly mobilized within
the 2003–5 French debate (contrary, for the most part, to the terms of the
debate in the 1990s), as we will see in chapter 9 (Boumédiene-Thiery 2004;
Delphy 2004; Ramadan 2004b).

The "untouchability" of the headscarved woman, as Amara puts it,
along with female responsibility for sociosexual regulation through controlling their own behavior, is related to another aspect of head covering that I
identified in chapter 1. If hair is symbolic of sexuality, a headscarved woman
is both "neutralized" or asexualized, and, paradoxically, hypersexualized,
as the very fact of covering her hair draws attention to it as something that
needs to be covered. So that the hijabi becomes, on one hand, suddenly
untouchable, above reproach, a person one must respect and take care not to
offend: an image comparable, for those raised in Christian cultures, to that
of the nun. Swathed in both folds of clothing and the mystique of religion,

---

4. Afshar 1998; Karam 1998; Venel 1998; Franks 2001; Zouari 2002; Mahmood 2005.

the hijabi, like the nun, is off limits, asexual, taboo, and as the epitome of female purity and devotion, the most deserving of deference and respect. Such reactions are invariably a combination of a well-meaning desire not to be racist and a more deeply ingrained cultural response, internalized even by atheists, to religion and its female purified emblems. They are, however, ultimately as paternalistic as "saving brown women from brown men." On the other hand, the "purified" hijabi is at the same time hypersexualized, by both Muslim and Western men. Such hypersexualization is also present in relation to Western religious women: "nun" imagery abounds in Western imagery and literature of sexual deviance of various forms.

Amara's third group of hijabis are what she calls the "soldiers of green fascism," green being a color that has for centuries been associated with Islam, for various historical and largely mythicized reasons.[5] Usually well educated, these women, far from being "kids in psychological disarray, in a situation of weakness or in search of identity," are the "true activists" of fundamentalism, and "even if they are a small minority, are extremely dangerous" (Amara 2004, 48–49). This is no doubt true, but as I noted in chapter 1, distinguishing the "real" religious right from the piety-mixed-with-identity-politics is not such a straightforward question. Age is a factor, certainly, although as we saw in part II, teachers and students alike stressed that the donning of the hijab and sometimes jilbab was claimed by the girls as their own autonomous choice, many trenchantly denying that they were complying with paternal, community, or peer group prescriptions or wishes. Some girls and women would certainly fit Amara's description, and as such, they are indeed dangerous, but gauging numbers and demarcating boundaries is a less straightforward affair than it is with the Catholic extreme right, as the questions of racism and ethnicity do not come into play to cloud the issue in the latter case, although regionalism may (see chapter 2). As we will see in chapter 8, the idea of "Islamophobia" in particular has created a great

---

5. In the Qur'an (Sura 18:31), it is written that the inhabitants of paradise will wear green garments of fine silk. Green was also the color preferred by the Fatimid dynasty. There are various other explanations offered for the association of green with Islam: for example, it was said to be the Prophet's favorite color, or its symbolic association with nature and life makes it a color of choice.

deal of confusion and made it apparently very difficult for many players in the debate to sort out their right from their left.

In chapter 1 I discussed the empowerment and access to status within a group of women who embrace right-wing agendas more generally and pietist or Islamist agendas in particular. This is also the case, for some at least, in France—including, and perhaps even particularly, for converts. Wearing the hijab symbolizes access to a certain role, a certain voice, within religious communities. It has also been argued that Islamic revivalist groups have provided a space where formerly disenfranchised young people can have a voice and regain a sense of dignity and belonging (for example, Kepel 1987; Venel 1998; Khosrokhavar 1997). While this is arguably much more the case for young men than for women, women who are within networks where such young men have influence are more likely to don the hijab so as to achieve status and acceptance and acquire their own voice. They also, through doing so, express a "modern" Islam where women have access to some degree of sex equality in education, the workforce, and civil society, rather than being confined to kitchens, bedrooms, and nurseries (Venel 1998; Khosrokhavar 1997; Zouari 2002). As argued in chapter 1, however, this "sex equality" is on many levels more illusory than real, and the acquisition of empowerment and status is not in itself equivalent to a feminist project.

Ostentatious Bandanas: Media Moments

In an interview with Florence Aubenas of *Libération*, Rabat legal adviser Maria Bahnini stressed the paradoxical nature of the French hijab:

> If one refers to the spirit of the *Qur'an*, the veil's objective is that women do not attract attention, are not stared at. Young French women who wear the veil are not, however, doing so to become invisible but on the contrary to become visible; they even appear in the media with connivance. The veil does not protect them, it exposes them. There is an odd mix of rebellion, religion and Star Academy. (cited in *Libération*, December 10, 2003)[6]

6. *Star Academy* is produced by the Dutch company Endemol, the creator of the *Big Brother* reality television show. First created in Spain, it quickly spread to over fifty countries, as diverse as the United States, Lebanon, the Philippines, and India. A combination of pop singing contest and reality show, it is extremely popular among young people in France.

The timing of this interview was significant: it came as the Stasi Commission report was being handed down, as well as in the wake of the much-publicized Lévy sisters affair (see below). In her comments, Bahnini identified what had to date been little discussed in France in these particular terms: the effect of ethnic chic and the "fifteen minutes of fame" syndrome. There had, here and there, been mention of the ephemeral and deliberately provocative nature, for some, of headscarf-wearing as identity politics (Gaspard and Khosrokhavar 1995; Khosrokhavar 1997; Delphy 2003a, 2003b). Some have suggested that it is part of a transnational trend toward an identity politics that is both individualized and marketable, that concerns more than young French Muslims, and that has been developing for some time in France as in the Muslim world (Béji 1997; Sallenave 2004, ch. 1; Brouard and Tiberj 2005). Khosrokhavar has even gone as far as to characterize hijabization in France as cheerfully "consumerist": worn as a form of "ostentatious" provocation, of attention-seeking from both peer-group and school administration, almost a dare to expel them. Those who donned the headscarf as this "consumerist" form of identity were likely to remove it some months later in favor of the miniskirt, equally provocative, but located at the other cultural extreme (Khosrokhavar 1997, 131).

Today, in a so-called post 9/11 context, the hybridized hijab has become truly hip. There is a definite media-marketable "coolness" about being a modern Muslim girl in trendy jeans and a hijab: the "Star Academy" syndrome identified by Bahnini. One can be interesting, be talked about, be a hero, have one's picture in the papers. The younger sisters, nieces, daughters of the supposed "drivers of integration" from the 1980s have become the headscarved and highly media-friendly, even media-savvy, teenage martyrs of the new millennium.

The plethora of articles, television interviews, and books featuring smiling and attractive (or, alternatively, defiant) young hijab-wearers is testimony to the size of the market for such imagery and to media manipulation of the hijab debate. Some, such as Pierre Tévanian, have called the French media to account (Tévanian 2005) for engineering the rekindled debate over the hijab "problem." Whatever the political agendas of the media, however, whether at the level of owners and directors, editors or individual journalists, or documentary producers, their primary objective in a capitalist liberal society is to sell papers and magazines and score well in the television ratings. If the media beat up this affair, sections of it at least must have judged public opinion ripe for it.

It is difficult to know precisely how many articles and television interviews appeared during which period—a task rendered more difficult by the mushrooming over the past few years of independent Web-based publications, particularly in France, where they have been a little slower to develop than in the Western English-speaking world, at least in the nongovernmental organization and civil society sectors. Ezekiel (2006, 257) mentions a figure of almost one thousand articles in the French press over the 2003–4 period, and 55,000 Google hits in 2006. Wing and Smith (2006, 755) cite one thousand articles between 1989 and 1998. I would contest Ezekiel's figure of only ten articles in 1989–90, cited as a basis for comparison with the 2003–4 period: my own incomplete personal collection of mainstream press articles from 1989–90 runs to many more, as does the somewhat more comprehensive collection kept by the Marguerite Durand women's library, run under the auspices of the municipal library of the thirteenth arrondissement in Paris.

All of this said, what is certain is that since 2002 in particular, the number of books appearing on the French market with "voile" or "foulard" or some combination of words connecting "islam" and "femmes" (and often "France" as well) in their titles has increased significantly, notably those authored by women. Some of these books are research-based, some are book-length opinion pieces. As in the English-speaking world, there has been no lack of individuals or associations with something to say on the matter. If you were a hijab-wearing girl or young woman in France in the 2002–4 period, you were almost certain to be a hot topic of conversation.

Which is why the media manipulation also came, in part at least, from the girls themselves, who were often quick to "connive," to use Bahnini's word, with this media craze. After all, how seductive is it for a teenage girl to have her fifteen minutes—or days, or even weeks or months—of fame? How might one's prestige increase in local communities when one becomes a hero of cultural or religious affirmation? How might one become the object of men's respect rather than of their contempt? How might one's "rebellion" in school become a way of escaping both submission and rejection? Some of these girls, as young as fourteen, are finding that they are overnight media sensations: they have made the grade in their own personal *Star Academy*, Muslim-style. This is one aspect of the headscarves debate that has developed with alarming momentum since about 2003, and though not absent in 1989–90, 1992–94, and 1999, it did not reach anywhere near these proportions.

Imagine, then, the degree of media coverage one might expect to get if one's parents were not only secular but not even ethnically Muslim. Imagine that media coverage augmented by the association of one's father, not with Islamist movements, but with well-respected antiracist organizations, not to mention progressive European politics. Enter the Lévy sisters.

In the middle of the Stasi's Commissions round of hearings and deliberations, a new "bandana affair" hit the headlines, and was to become the new *cause célèbre* of the anti-ban camp. On September 24, 2003, Lila and Alma Lévy, 18 and 16 years old, respectively, refused a final compromise proposal put to them by the principal of the Henri-Wallon high school in the Paris inner-city immigrant suburb of Aubervilliers. The compromise involved the two students donning a less severe version of their headscarves: ones that showed their necks, ear lobes and the beginnings of their hairline. They were suspended the following day, and an October 10 hearing of the school disciplinary council confirmed their expulsion for wearing "ostentatious" religious insignia. This decision had the effect of pitting the teaching staff against the girls' classmates, most of whom supported them. The girls had worn their headscarves since the previous winter and had ignored requests to remove it; in fact, they had upped the ante by increasing its coverage. To the bandana-style hijab popularized earlier that year in Lyons, but worn in this case to carefully cover all hair and their ears, they added a turtleneck sweater over which they wore a large cardigan, as well as a tunic over their jeans. Once outside the school grounds, the pair would don full jilbabs or abayas, covering their heads, their whole bodies, and even their faces. They also wore long body-covering scarves and shawls during physical education classes and had enjoined fellow students, during various demonstrations, to headscarf-up as well, notwithstanding their later claims that they respected the choices of others (Lévy et al. 2004).

The Lévy sisters quickly became the darlings of the media, their star outshining that of Fatima, Leïla and, Samira in 1989 or Schérazade Ben

Larbi or the Goussainville girls in 1994, or the Lyons bandana girls earlier the same year.

The following year, a book was published on the sisters, titled: *Des filles comme les autres: Au-delà du foulard* (Girls like Any Others: Beyond the Headscarf) (Lévy et al. 2004). In fact, they were very far from being "like any others," and the media build-up of their case was carefully orchestrated.

Already, the day after their expulsion, *Le Monde* reported the incident with the title "Two high school girls from Aubervilliers, daughters of a MRAP lawyer, excluded from school for wearing the veil," under which the header paragraph appeared in large type: "Their father, Maître Laurent Lévy, defines himself as a 'Jew without God'; their mother is a nonpracticing Kabyle. The lawyer is concerned about the 'hysterical madness of certain ayatollahs of secularism.'" The article was authored by Xavier Ternisien, *Le Monde*'s religion reporter, who is highly sympathetic to the views of both Lévy and Tariq Ramadan (*Le Monde*, September 25, 2003).

By positioning secularists not only as fanatics but also as akin to Khomeini or Ahmadinejad, and by displaying his impeccable Jewish atheist credentials, Lévy, with the support of Ternisien, operated a couple of discursive ploys that he and others would continue to use over the following year or so. The main one of these is the assertion or implication that, as a Jewish atheist, he had nothing to do with his daughters' conversion to Islam or the hype surrounding the affair. The girls themselves are adamant that their father, with whom they lived after their parents separated, had not influenced them in their decision, that he did not like religion. At the same time, they show a decided preference for their father over their mother (Lévy et al. 2004). The second of Laurent Lévy's ploys positions secularists as hysterical and tyrannical "religious" extremists, and, in contrast, himself as reasonable and his daughters as martyrs.

Lévy did not hesitate, along with others, to capitalize further on this. Far from being the reasonable atheist quietly supporting his daughters, he showed himself to be every bit as militant and agenda-pushing as Rachid Amaoui had been in Goussainville or the UJM in Grenoble (see chapter 5). In December 2003, Lévy coauthored, with Houria Bouteldja (active with Les Indigènes de la République), Catherine Grupper, and Pierre Tévanian, an article comparing the hijab affair to the Dreyfus affair of the 1890s, in which a Jewish captain in the French army was falsely accused of espionage (Bouteldja et al. 2004).[7] Lévy signed this article as the "father of Alma and Lila Lévy, expelled from the Henri-Wallon high school in Aubervilliers for wearing the veil." In the article, which was published on January 26, 2004, on the site of Les Mots sont importants ("words are important"), set up by, among others, Pierre Tévanian, the authors made a number of shaky comparisons between the two "affairs." Though their first claim that the two affairs have divided French opinion, and notably the left, like no other in the century in between can perhaps be argued for, their second, that the Marxist left is in both cases reluctant to defend followers of religion, is ludicrous. First, it is not entirely true, and second, the Dreyfus affair was not a debate over whether Dreyfus should exhibit Jewish religious faith in the public space but whether he was guilty of espionage and whether he was being scapegoated because of his ethnicity. If the third comparison, that both affairs have racist elements, is defensible insofar as a member (or members) of a particular ethnoreligious group have been scapegoated, this is far less muddily the case with the Dreyfus affair. Apart from anything else, the latter only concerned one person, and a male adult to boot. The hijab debate concerns girls aged from eight to eighteen who are acting neither solo nor in isolation from the men around them. Moreover, if these were the only two affairs in France over the past 110 years to have been marked by racism, how different twentieth-century French history would look.

The fourth comparison made is that of consequences: the authors argue that both affairs inflamed sentiments that the populations represented were not "assimilable" in France. Again, these would not be the only cases. In particular, the authors show a remarkable amnesia concerning not only the entire history of French colonialism, but also concerning the Shoah, which, given that one of the authors is Jewish, is not a little disquieting. The final comparison concerns the question of equality before the law: a fair trial in the case of Dreyfus, equal access to schooling in the case of the hijab. Yet

7. The accusation, trial, and deportation of Dreyfus, who was later cleared following a lengthy campaign by left-wing intellectuals, among others, has gone down in history as a notorious case of state-sanctioned anti-Semitic scapegoating.

again, there are many, many examples of similarly grave debates on comparable questions over the past century: the equality of women before the law
in the Republic of *fraternité* is a case in point. As for the question of "equal
access to schooling," both supporters and opponents of expulsions or of the
2004 law would argue that their position is the most likely to guarantee this.
For Dreyfus, the legal mechanics of equality were a question of respecting
legal procedure; in the hijab debate, the question is one of how legal principles are to be interpreted and applied. Moreover, however emotively one
wishes to frame it, and however convinced one may be that the headscarved
girls are being scapegoated, they are not on trial for treason and do not risk
life deportation to a penal colony as a result.

But perhaps all of these objections are somewhat beside the point. For
the purpose of the "new Dreyfus affair" comparison was, primarily, to push
an emotional button. The point was to present the Lévy girls as martyrs.
The Dreyfus affair, and the sentiments expressed in Emile Zola's famous
text *J'accuse,* in support of Dreyfus and exposing French anti-Semitism, are
points of sensitivity, and of honor, for the French left, and in particular for
its cohort of *intellectuels engagés* (committed or public intellectuals).[8] Also,
in the context of the evolving discussion about Islamophobia, and murky
comparisons of the Jewish right with Hitler and/or those opposing Islamist
pressures as comparable to anti-Semites, colonialists, and so on, this text
appears, in retrospect, as one of the first of a variety of perverse ideological
manipulations, as we will see in chapter 8.

Lévy was also involved at the time in an alternative left group presenting a list for the European elections, called Alternative Citoyenne (Citizens'
Alternative), in which a number of feminists were involved as well. In late
2004, during planning for the autumn university of this group, it emerged
that Laurent Lévy had objected to the participation of Algerian-background
feminist Leïla Mansouri-Acherar, professor at the University of Montpellier,
as a speaker in the session called "Culture and Identity." Lévy's objection

---

8. The text of *J'accuse* was first published in the newspaper *L'Aurore* on Jan. 13, 1898,
and addressed to the then president of the Republic, Félix Faure. It is in the public domain
and freely available from numerous Web sites, such as http://perso.magic.fr/tremong/pascal/
lois/jaccuse.html.

was based on his assumption that Mansouri-Acherar would speak mainly about the hijab issue, expressing views of which he did not approve. The chair of the workshop thus decided to refuse Mansouri-Acherar's participation. This was the only feminist whose participation was refused. As one author of a series of dissident letters noted:

> Only one workshop at the Autumn University . . . has expressly refused a plural and open debate. By favoring the expression on the podium of a single point of view, that of those people who are all signatories of "Une Ecole pour tous-tes" [a group Lévy co-founded in late 2003 with Christine Delphy, among others], [the organizers] left the audience to suppose that this point of view was the "official" one of Alternative Citoyenne.[9]

Lévy subsequently presented an ultimatum to Alternative Citoyenne: either the "dissidents" left, or he did. The dissidents decided to leave.

"Agency" and Manipulation

The Lévy sisters were the first, and are to date the only, headscarved schoolgirls in France to have had an entire book written solely about them, in contrast to other studies of large or small groups. Other recent studies, like most of those published or conducted during the 1990s, have been based on a series of questionnaires and, in particular, interviews, with a number of women. Many of these, however, are with adult women who are no longer at school, and while they focus on the hijab issue, they are not exclusively with headscarved women (Killian 2003). One recent study is based on in-depth interviews with six young women, most of whom were still at high school when interviewed: it is one of the rare group studies to be mainly with high school students (Saladin 2005a, 2005b). It is likely that the paucity of studies, apart from media interviews, that feature the voices of women under eighteen is due less to a lack of interest by those doing such fieldwork than to greater difficulty of access to interviewees. Minors would need written parental consent to be interviewed and given parental opposition to veiling in some cases and tight parental, particularly paternal, control over their

---

9. Letter to *Alternative Citoyenne*, Dec. 11, 2004, communicated to me personally by the author.

daughters in others, such consent may well be difficult to obtain. These comments, however, are pure conjecture on my part.

Apart from the Lévy sisters book, the only books to date to feature solo voices have been written by adult women as personal testimony. One of them takes the form of a dialogue between two Muslim women, one headscarved, the other not, neither of whom have been involved in school controversies (Bouzar and Kada 2003). Another is a "docu-fiction" work by journalist Leïla Djitli, based on her own experience and observation of issues confronting young women and their mothers in the *banlieues*. Titled *Lettre à ma fille qui veut porter le voile* (Letter to My Daughter Who Wants to Wear the Veil), it is one of the rare works to give voice, albeit channeled through a fictional character, to the mothers of the headscarved girls (Djitli 2004).

Alma and Lila Lévy are thus unique in the world of "hijab publishing" in France, at least at the time of this writing. Had Laurent Lévy not been their father, I suspect it unlikely that they would have attracted such exclusive focus. The fact that they have, however, has given their story a symbolic and supposedly representative importance: they have become the incarnation of the modern and "typically" French young hijabi.

The book, published in February 2004, had probably been in preparation before the sisters' expulsion from school the previous October. The extent to which their father facilitated this is a subject for speculation, but given his high profile in the MRAP and elsewhere, and given his own media interventions since, it is a speculation worth entertaining. The book was published by La Découverte, an independent social sciences publishing house, originally founded as Editions Maspero by writer François Maspero in 1959. It is a publisher that has significant credentials as providing independent and progressive social critique. Apart from the introduction, the book is composed entirely of a series of interviews with the two sisters by secondary school Spanish teacher Véronique Giraud and sociologist Yves Sintomer, who had since 1998 been interviewing headscarved girls. Sintomer is an outspoken opponent of expulsions and of the law.

The two citations featured as an epigraph to the interviewers' introduction (and thus to the book) set the tone. One is by John Stuart Mill, from *On Liberty*, criticizing public intervention into personal matters, and the other is by 2003 Nobel Peace Laureate Shirin Ebadi, who declares that the prohibition of the hijab in European schools is as much an impediment to the freedom of choice of Muslim women as is its imposition in Muslim countries (Lévy et al. 2004, 3). The interviewers promise readers that we will come to "know" the girls, not just in terms of their reaction to the headscarf incident in which they were involved, but as "two personalities who may seem surprising, even disconcerting, to a number of readers" but who would be acknowledged as "endearing" by all (the French word used is *attachantes*) (Lévy et al. 2004, 4). One rather has the impression that one is about to read a book about a pair of idiosyncratic but lovable puppies. This effect is exacerbated by the now-famous photograph on the book's cover, which features the two sisters, clad in their usual bandanas, turtleneck sweaters, and big cardigans. One is dressed in mauvish pastel pink, with a hot pink bandana, and the other in pastel blue, with a pale pink bandana. The colors are reminiscent of those stereotypically associated with either baby clothes or dresses worn by little girls. The infantilizing effect, and the shadow of their father, are both further reinforced in the introduction:

> Their main specificity is that they benefit from a strong family cultural capital and that *their father's help has enabled them to confront with determination the ordeal of exclusion and mediatization*. In the end it is rather reassuring that you can't exclude just like that *the daughters of a left-wing lawyer*, and it is hardly a coincidence if their ability to react has made them into informal spokespersons for other young veiled girls. (Lévy et al. 2004, 6; my italics)

The image of these "endearing" baby-blue-and-pink-clad girls facing an "ordeal" with Daddy's help sits in odd counterpoint to that of the self-assured "spokespersons" that so easily present themselves to the public and smile prettily and unselfconsciously for the cameras. It is difficult not to sense that there is more than a soupçon of manipulation and hype sitting behind these too-demure-to-be-true media sensations.

What, then, do these not-so-typical "typical girls" have to say on behalf of those whom they apparently represent? First and foremost, they—typically—see veiling as an obligation under Islam (it is not, as we have seen). Second, they adopt the similarly typical argument concerning Western decadence and the "immodesty" of Western women, comparing the latter's garb with the "disrespectful" behavior of scantily clad girls. They even blame rape on media imagery that shows nudity and sexuality, not on men's behavior. Third, they adopt the equally familiar "different but equal" thesis: men and women must be differentiated and each keep to their place, and women's primary role is the raising of children. At times, their opinions on these matters read a little like textbook phrases learned by heart; anecdotal evidence from friends and colleagues, as well as my own experience, suggests this is a fairly widespread phenomenon among pious young female converts.

Fourth, they take a certain scholarly pride in their study of the Qur'an and classical Arabic; they go at some length into questions of translation and interpretation. They also, not unlike other converts to Islamic piety, take pride in their own "authenticity" in relation to the "ignorance" of both their less religious peers and preceding generations, notably their mother and grandmother:

> Already, when we started to wear the veil, our maternal grandmother didn't agree—she said it was Arabs and not Kabyles who did that. We replied that we saw it as an obligation for all Muslims [which is written, curiously, in the masculine]. She then said to us that she'd wear it when she came back from her pilgrimage—Inch'Allah! [God willing] Like all those of her generation, she is pretty ignorant about her own religion. She doesn't know how to read or write, in Arabic or in French. . . . We don't really talk about it with her: it's a delicate matter, it's not up to us, her granddaughters, to tell her what to do and tell her that she's been getting it wrong for the last sixty-five years! She prays five times a day, assiduously, but not in the right way. . . . But her intentions are good. And God pardons ignorance. (Alma, in Lévy et al. 2004, 54)

They have it "right," their grandmother has it "wrong." Yet their grandmother's religion is traditional, internalized from a young age and associated with her Kabyle identity. The Lévy sisters have taken on an Islamic identity during their adolescence, and performed it in *Star Academy*-style for the media. In claiming to know better, to practice a more correct or authentic Islam, and in drawing attention to the illiteracy of their grandmother, they are not only negating their grandmother's experience and "authenticity" but also putting her down as "ignorant." This assertion of superior wisdom is not, in the end, very far from the colonialist attitude toward the ignorant *indigènes* and particularly toward women; it also appears classist. Most importantly, behind it sits a story of desolidarization among generations of women. The sisters end up saying that their grandmother is "proud of them"; one does not get a sense, however, of that pride being reciprocal. The sisters' attitude to their mother is even less affectionate.

Even if the Lévy sisters' attitude toward their mother and maternal grandmother is part of their personal story, the claim to knowledge of a "true" Islam and of the greater cultural capital associated with it would definitely seem related to questions of both status and "acquired authenticity" as well as to the "Muslimism" to which I have referred in previous chapters. In the 1980s, being Kabyle would have been their best claim to high status in ethnic chic: lighter-skinned than Arabs in France, a marginalized and to some extent impoverished indigenous minority in Algeria. In the 2000s, however, Islam is the new ethnicity.

And it is one that they have freely chosen. They even state emphatically that all the girls they know who wear the hijab do so of their own free will, and many do so in the face of parental opposition, although they concede that some may do it through family obligation. These claims appear to be backed up, in relation to the women in their family at least, by comments given to the press in the weeks following the girls' expulsion. Their mother, a nonreligious teacher, who had been separated from Lévy for some ten years, was opposed to her daughters wearing the hijab, and was cited as having threatened to throw her daughters out of their home if they got themselves expelled from school over it *(Le Figaro Magazine,* October 11, 2003). Their paternal grandmother Ginette Lévy, cited in *Le Monde* the day before, said:

> It is an understatement to say that I'm sorry, saddened, despairing by what is happening to them. What happened first, and what distressed me, is their conversion to Islam. For my granddaughters, as luck would have it, they have taken refuge in the most visible religion, and this is all the more unfortunate. . . . I detest their conversion, their veil, their headscarf and their prayers to Allah, but I love them and want them to live happy. (cited in *Le Monde*, October 10, 2003)

The question of the agency of teenage girls, and their right to freedom of choice, is one of the points over which feminists who may otherwise be unanimous in their concerns about the hijab have stumbled. Opponents of the law have claimed that it is a denial of young women's agency to forbid them to dress as they please, and it is patronizing to treat all hijab-wearers as alienated and manipulated. As noted earlier, some inevitably refer to the 1958 Algerian unveiling to drive home their point (Bouteldja 2006a). Those making such claims concerning agency and colonialism are, however, conflating different attitudes and experiences. Certainly, the public unveiling in Algiers was the extreme expression of a racist and paternalistic colonial attitude toward "veiled women" and colonial France's idea of itself as a "civilizer," and criticisms of the manipulation of "emancipatory unveiling" to racist ends remain valid. That said, an incident orchestrated by rebel extreme-right generals in colonial Algeria is far from immediately comparable with the hijab debate in France today, and references to it appear to be as much of an emotive scaremongering cheap trick as French extreme-right discourse regarding "integrist" Muslim hordes that are taking over France.

This does not, of course, mean that concerns about paternalistic "emancipation" of women by governments "for their own good," and concomitant denial of their agency, are unfounded—quite the contrary. As I discussed in chapter 1 in the case of both French Third Republic nationalism and Kemalist Turkey, women's "emancipation" by governments only comes after a long feminist struggle and is invariably co-opted to nationalist ends. This is so even if such emancipatory projects contain demonstrable benefits to women, such as access to schooling or employment or the vote.

One thus does well to remain wary of justifications by any state of its legislation or policies as "emancipating" women, and the French state's discourse on the hijab and "emancipation" is, whatever one's personal views on the hijab and what it represents, certainly no exception. The problem, however, is that in this case, we are dealing (1) largely with minors, (2) with a small minority of Muslim girls and women who are making specific choices that are contrary to those made by the majority, and (3) with individuals who are subjected to a series of constraints that accompany access to schooling and that are imposed on all. I will return to the third point in chapter 9, in the context of the discussion of access to schooling and interpretation of secularism. It is the first and second points that I wish to discuss here, in relation to the argument about women's "agency."

Flora Saladin's 2005 study of six headscarved girls, mostly senior high school students, showed a variety of motivations for veiling, but also suggested that girls were encountering a variety of pressures (Saladin 2005b, 28ff). Though all but one of the girls were veiling in opposition to their parents, they were not all free from pressures in other areas. These included peer pressure: the one girl who had been forced to veil by her parents was also a friend of another of the interviewees, whose presence during some of the interviews appeared to have a censoring impact. The activity of Islamist organizations in the local area was another factor, and, to a great extent related to this, the influence of older brothers on the behavior of their sisters was considerable; most interviewees mentioned this. These young men often set themselves up as a positive role model in contrast to the stereotypical delinquent, but Saladin suggests that the at once authoritarian and protective role claimed by older brothers has simply taken on a new guise (35–36). Saladin also mentions the tradition-modernity polarization in which young women are caught up, as well as the revalorization of a "special place" reserved for women within the fundamentalist "different-but-equal" thesis (43ff). The author observed that in contrast to Alma and Lila Lévy who threw themselves into Qur'anic study, the women she interviewed had not read the Qur'an and were extremely ignorant about Islam and its different schools of thought (31–34). On that last point, however, so were Alma and Lila Lévy, who insisted on one "right" way to do things, and maintained, erroneously, that hijab-wearing was an obligation under Islam.

If an eighteen-year-old such as Lila Lévy, or most of the young women in Saladin's study, can, notwithstanding these sorts of pressures, still claim to be acting independently, and in doing so, certainly has the law on her side as she has reached the age of majority, what of a fourteen-year-old, or a ten-year-old? Or even a sixteen-year-old, who is legally old enough to have sexual relations and enter the workforce but not legally old enough to vote? Such questions concern not only women's agency but also that of the child, and the rights of the child, a complex question. Even reference to UN documents is not necessarily helpful, as they often contradict each other: children and in particular girl children have the right to be free from violence or intimidation, but core UN human rights treaties also construct the family as the fundamental unit of society, and as such, the family is invested with various forms of rights. Parents, for example, have the right to make decisions concerning their children's schooling and religion (Winter 2006b). Moreover, ages of consent and majority are at best arbitrary and often self-contradictory, particularly for women, who have in the past—within and outside the West—been marriageable while still children but legally considered to be the equivalent of minors throughout their lives. They simply moved from being the property of their fathers to being that of their husbands. It is only in very recent history that women's legal status has been different, and millennia-old customs under which women are not people but chattels, sexual objects, and child-producing machines still impact considerably on women's lives in many parts of the world, including the West.

The question of minors' "agency," then—particularly that of girls—is a complex one, particularly in the face of the enduring legal, economic, cultural, and moral weight given to parental, particularly paternal, authority. As noted by Mimouna Hadjam, of the mixed association Africa, formed in 1987 in response to racist crimes against two Maghrebian-background men and one nine-year-old boy, the hijab has played a role in France not dissimilar to the one it has played in Muslim countries. This is despite claims that "it's different here," also reiterated by the Lévy sisters. It has given girls more freedom of movement in the first instance, and has subsequently been associated with female participation in community fora set up by revivalist or Islamist groups. But the "identity headscarf quickly becomes a forced headscarf":

> On Wednesdays and Saturdays [nonschool days for primary and junior high school students], you can see in the housing-project suburbs girls, aged younger than 10, going in greater and greater numbers to religious classes, wearing their headscarves. This initiation into the [practice of wearing the] hijab is happening under the quietly determined pressure of the family and community, leading the girl to claim "her headscarf" around the age of 14, confronting her teachers and proclaiming "it's my choice." (Hadjam 2005)

"Yielding is not consenting," as Nicole-Claude Mathieu has pointed out with relation to the behavior and choices of adult women under male domination (Mathieu 1991). How much less "consensual" is it, then, when we are talking about ten-year-old girls? As we have seen, practically all the highly contentious headscarf incidents in France have occurred under pater-nal or fraternal influence and pressure, frequently along with that of reli-gious "advisers," older male "bodyguards," and so on. Even if some girls are acting in opposition to their parents by donning the hijab, and even if a small number of others, usually older girls, are demonstrably acting as active members of (usually) Islamist groups, they are not the majority. And what of the majority of schoolgirls and young women who are *not* wearing the hijab? Do they have any less "agency" than their headscarved classmates and workmates?

The question of girl children's "agency" is all the more fraught in a con-text in which wearing the hijab and exhibiting obstructive behavior in school are almost guaranteed to make a teenage girl the center of media attention. How is it possible to determine to what extent a girl is acting independently of such considerations?

And, in the end, to what extent are such considerations relevant in dis-cussions of the interpretation and application of laws? I will return to this question in chapter 9.

8

Co-optations and Instrumentalizations

IN 1989, many commentators on both sides of the fence had referred to the girls as the center of the affair as "hostages" in a social debate that was ultimately not about them. Some fourteen to fifteen years later, little had changed on this level. If anything, it had worsened.

Even if, by 2003, feminists were more vocally and visibly participating in the debate, those attempting to distance themselves from both state and Islamist co-optations were still, as in 1989, caught in the crossfire between the "pro-ban" and "anti-ban" camps, each harnessed to various nonfeminist and often antifeminist agendas. Once again, women's rights or lack thereof, and equality before the law and in the public space, became the pretext for conversations not only about Islam, race, "integration," secularism, and state, but also this time about Palestine, "Islamophobia," anti-Semitism, Islamism, male violence, prejudice against Arab men, governmental co-optation, the history and current ownership of "feminism," and, strangely, homophobia and queer politics. As a result, divisions within the left over the issue, which had been present since the 1989 affair, became exacerbated in the 2003–6 period, although at the parliamentary level at least, the Socialist Party appeared to become more united around support for the 2004 law. Yet, at the same time as the ideas of women's agency and rights were becoming instrumentalized in ever more complex ways, some of the most significant socioeconomic, political, and cultural issues for racialized women in France, and, indeed, women more generally, were far less "conspicuous" in the public debate than a couple of thousand hijabs, Arabo-Muslim men (rioting or preaching), or the carefully crafted imagery of the new millennium's answer to the 1980s beurettes.

The Mariannization of the Multicultural

In the midst of the 2003 resurgence of the hijab debate, former Socialist prime minister (1984–86) Laurent Fabius, speaking at the Socialist Party congress in Dijon on May 17, 2003, focused on what he termed *le pacte laïc* (the secular pact). He stressed that "we" (the Socialist Party) needed to be clear, "no doubt clearer than we have been." This was probably a reference to Jospin's presumably less clear stance in 1989, with which Fabius had disagreed. For Fabius, "the real question" to which his party, and an implied future Socialist government, needed to respond was the following one: "Do we or do we not wish to integrate all French people, young and less young, men and women, believers or not, whatever their background or skin color?"

He followed on from this by evoking the feminized national symbol, Marianne:

> A day will come, in Dijon as elsewhere, when the Marianne in our city halls will take on the beautiful face of a young French woman of immigrant background; Marianne cannot be veiled. That day, France will have taken a step forward in giving full life to the principles of the Left that flesh out the Republic: liberty, which is not economic liberalism; equality, which is not simply equity; fraternity, which is not charity; *laïcité*, which is not *communautarisme*. (Fabius 2003)

Two months later, for Bastille Day, non-Western-background Mariannes did indeed grace not the city halls but the façade of the Palais Bourbon, home of the National Assembly, in a photographic exhibition *Mariannes d'aujourd'hui* (Mariannes of Today), arranged by NPNS with the support of the president of the Assembly, Jean-Louis Debré (UMP). Fabius and his parliamentary colleagues would certainly have known about this planned exhibition at the time of Fabius' speech, and it is difficult not to infer, after the fact, that the lines cited above were written with the forthcoming Bastille Day exhibition in mind.

Some ten days before this exhibition was "unveiled" to the public, President Chirac announced that he was to set up what would become known as the Stasi Commission. The July 4, 2003, edition of *Libération* featured the front page headline: "Laïcité: Chirac se dévoile" (Secularism: Chirac unveils/reveals himself), complete with a graphic of the statue of feminized Republican symbol Marianne, holding out a tempering hand (palm down) toward the reader. The image was heavy with symbolism: the Republic, both amazon warrior and mother, extends, in the name of its president, her authoritative hand of leadership, liberty, justice, and *laïcité* to the newspaper's readers.

As I have noted elsewhere, in an article on the NPNS Mariannes' exhibition, women's role in relation to the values attached to modern democratic nationhood is "not to *enact* liberty or reason or justice . . . through writing, speaking, legislating or otherwise occupying positions of power or influence in their own right, but to *represent* them" (Winter forthcoming 2008). So it is with Marianne, whose role as a symbol of the Republic goes back to the Revolution. She has both official and popular versions. There have even been Marianne competitions, from paintings to postage stamp designs to, more recently, the choice of which star will the new "face of Marianne." Women considered beautiful, feminine, and unthreatening have been the usual choices: from actors and singers Brigitte Bardot, Mireille Mathieu, and Catherine Deneuve to talk-show host Evelyne Thomas and fashion model Laetitia Casta, who became the official "Marianne for the new millennium."

Enter NPNS. On July 12, 2003, Debré inaugurated *Mariannes d'aujourd'hui*. This event, which melded popular culture, becoming "multicultural" for the first time, with high political culture, made international news. On August 1, for example, the *New York Times* reported: "The face of France is changing . . . Making Marianne ethnic, working class and real is a project of Ni Putes Ni Soumises."

The fourteen Marianne photographs feature young, slim, and attractive women of a variety of ethnic backgrounds, although none are of Asian background and over a third are of Maghrebian background. All of them are artistically posed in head or head-and-shoulders shots, draped in Republican colors and imagery. Each photograph is accompanied by a caption containing a few carefully worded sentences ostensibly authored by each model about what Marianne means to her.[1] Collectively, these captions encapsulate both the ideals and values of the Republic and of a Republican idea of citizenship,

---

1. http://www.assemblee-nationale.fr/evenements/mariannes.asp.

and "an idea of modern womanhood: Marianne is tough but gentle, firm but just, combative but caring. She is France's mother, its leaders' consort and its citizens' sister" (Winter forthcoming 2008).

Marianne had certainly gone "ethnic," but how "working class and real" this "ethnic" Marianne was is very much open to debate. The idea of a multicultural Marianne may have seemed inclusive and progressive, but the major purpose of the exhibition appeared to be to harness a sanitized version of both ethnicity and feminism to the agenda of a right-wing government, in the midst of the hijab polemic on one hand and vocal opposition to tougher immigration laws on the other hand. As Debré put it, somewhat paternalistically, when he inaugurated the exhibition, "These girls have chosen to manifest their confidence in the Republic and to proclaim their adherence to its values," which were based on the principles of "tolerance, freedom, solidarity and secularism."[2] Only Samira Bellil, who unsmilingly incarnated "Marianne the rebel" in one of the photographs, appeared to convey, through her intense gaze, some idea of what it really meant to be "ethnic, working-class and real" in the French Republic in 2003.

Genealogies of Co-optation

Like SOS-Racisme twenty years earlier, NPNS managed, in late 2002 and early 2003, to mobilize thousands of young women and some men around an issue that was rightly perceived as needing the urgent attention of government. They also expressed views on the hijab and women's subordination with which the majority of French Muslim women—and certainly the majority of Muslim feminists—would probably agree. As Amara put it in her 2004 book on the NPNS movement:

> In our countries of origin [Amara's father had been an activist with the Algerian Front de Libération Nationale], the veil is not a liberating object. Women have had acid thrown at them for refusing to wear it. Algerian women and many others in Muslim countries, who fought to remove it in the name of freedom, paid a heavy price. Girls of my generation—including

2. Speech made on July 12, 2003. http://www.assemblee-nationale.fr/evenements/mariannes.asp.

practicing Muslims among whom I count myself—have combated the headscarf because it has always been synonymous with oppression and confinement of women. (Amara 2004, 49)

At the same time, the focus on Republican values, and on the violence of beur men against beur women, rather than male violence against women more generally, conveniently fed France's postcolonial and post-9/11 racism toward its Maghrebian minorities and its complacency in terms of its own treatment of its female citizens. The government, with the help of media focus on the issue of gang rapes in the ghettos, was able to instrumentalize the NPNS movement to both further essentialize and demonize Maghrebian-background men and take the focus off its own inaction on women's rights. As Christelle Hamel commented:

The same politicians who are heaping praise upon NPNS are not applying parity [the 2000 law on equal political representation for women and men], [and] have reduced (or, previously, did little to encourage) subsidies to feminist associations. They are very willing to see violence against women in the housing projects, but not elsewhere! (cited in Carrel 2005)

The *quartiers* became a semifictionalized "dark side" in which women were perceived as prey to the weight of tradition and to the constant threat, or reality, of male violence, and in as much need of rescuing from it as their foremothers had been under colonialism. Yet, as Hamel implies above—and as most feminists in France unceasingly point out, even those accused of being the most eager to demonize the men from the *quartiers*—violence against women is not a question of race or class but of male domination.

Mucchielli (2005) argues that the intense media focus on gang rapes between 2001 and 2004 occurred within the context of an electoral campaign focusing on "insecurity," and the association of gang rapes with the immigrant ghettos created an atmosphere of moral panic that the 2002–7 government was able to exploit. Indeed, it found it more convenient to focus on delinquency and on "problem" suburbs than to implement some of the measures that feminists, including NPNS, had been demanding for years to provide greater safety for women victims of violence and to facilitate their itinerary through the police and justice systems.

Unfortunately, NPNS has played right into the hands of such governmental instrumentalization of "protection of women's rights." Like SOS-Racisme, the organization has since its inception had close links with the political elite, and the cosy relationship of its leader, Fadela Amara, with the socialist party, was criticized in the media during the 2003–6 period (for example, in *Le Monde*, October 11, 2005). As early as 2003, Amara was invited to sit on several government committees, including the Observatory on Parity, the Observatory on Sensitive Urban Zones, and the National Consultative Committee on Human Rights. Loubna Méliane, another key activist with NPNS in 2003 (and, like Amara, high in the hierarchy of SOS-Racisme, where she was vice president), joined the national board of the Socialist Party at its Dijon Congress in May 2003—the same congress at which Fabius delivered his "Secular Pact" speech. In the NPNS marches, politicians of all persuasions appeared at Amara's side. A featured photograph of the post-Mariannization International Women's Day march in 2004 shows Nicole Guedj (UMP, member of the Stasi Commission, see chapter 6), Corinne LePage, founder in the mid 1990s of the centrist party Citoyenneté Action Participation pour le XXIe siècle (Citizenship, Action, Participation for the Twenty-first Century) and former environment minister with the right-wing Juppé government (1995–97), and even perennial leftist presidential candidate, Arlette Laguillier (Lutte Ouvrière, Workers' Struggle).

Since the 2007 elections, Amara has been written off as a sellout by most of the left for taking up a junior ministerial post with the right-wing government, although this should have come as no particular surprise to those who were following her words closely. In 2006, she and Mohammed Abdi published a co-written book *La Racaille de la République* (The Scum of the Republic), in an overt reference to Sarkozy's 2005 reference to rioting youths as "racaille" (scum), that needed to be hosed down with water cannon. In this book, Amara declared that when she met Sarkozy, he had "greatly impressed" her by his willingness to listen, and even went as far as saying, in relation to Sarkozy's water cannon remark, "If he wants to clean up the shit in the housing projects we live in, I for one agree" (Amara and Abdi 2006, 165–66).

Further criticism has been leveled at NPNS for instrumentalizing the women of the *quartiers* that the organization ostensibly represents. It has been suggested that this ended up being the case for Samira Bellil.[3] It is more clearly the case for the family of Sohane Benziane. In an interview with Radio Beur on March 31, 2006, at the time of the trial of her sister's murderers, Kahina Benziane spoke of NPNS's political exploitation of her younger sister Sohane's death and co-optation of her own grief to heighten the movement's media profile, even if its political combat had a "noble" aspect:

> You have to understand that we were totally distraught and alone. Without any word of support: not from our local City Hall, not from the government, not from [President] Chirac. It was me who called them [the Association *Femmes des quartiers*] to say to them: "Did you know that a young woman has been immolated on French soil?"
>
> The Association *Femmes des quartiers* contacted me via a journalist. This was an unhoped-for support. I saw *rebeus* who were like me, they wanted to pay homage to my little sister. I went for it!
>
> Fadela Amara, president of the association, gave us an appointment. But the cameras were already there. There was no private conversation. Fadela Amara didn't even present her condolences to my father, as our traditions would require. Since, then, we have no more news of *Ni Putes Ni Soumises*.[4]

"Neocolonized" *Indigènes* Versus "Multicultural" Mariannes?

In opposition, among other things, to the sanitized Republicanization of minority women, has emerged a broad and somewhat bizarre coalition opposed both to the 2004 law and to NPNS's brand of feminism and apparent demonizing of Arab men. The coalition brings together Islamists, left-wing and non-Islamist Muslims, and a range of white antiracist activists who appear to be suffering from an overdose of postcolonial guilt. While many of the key players in this coalition are well-placed within the French institutional landscape (politicians, intellectuals, prominent journalists, members of groups represented on the French Council of the Muslim Faith), they are practically all extremely eager to distance themselves from the ideology of colonization and control that many of them maintain

---

3. Nacira Guénif-Soulimas, personal communication, July 6, 2007.

4. http://www.beurfm.net/forum/showthread.php?t=10258.

underpins a number of those same institutions, or at the very least informs their current operation.

Public figures involved in or associated with this countermovement include, among many others: Alain Gresh, editor-in-chief of *Le Monde Diplo-matique* and co-founder of Islam et Laïcité; Laurent Lévy, father of Alma and Lila; Alima Boumediene-Thiéry, Greens senator, member of the European Parliament, and former president of EMAF (see chapter 4); sociologist Saïd Bouamama, who had in the 1980s been involved in organizing the SOS-Racisme-coordinated national antiracist marches, and had become an out-spoken opponent of the 2004 law; Pierre Tévanian, philosopher, director of the online magazine *Les Mots Sont Importants*; prominent Greens politician Noël Mamère, who was to hit the headlines a few months later for having, as mayor of Bègles, celebrated a marriage between two homosexual men—a marriage subsequently ruled illegal; internationally known radical feminist, and out lesbian, scholar Christine Delphy; and Nacira Guénif-Soulimas, a sociologist who has blended postcolonial and Judith Butler–inspired queer theory to develop a defense of Arab men in their face of their supposed vic-timization by feminists.

Two key activist organizations are involved. The first, Une Ecole Pour Tous-tes—Contre les lois d'exclusion (A School for All—Against Laws of Exclusion, UEPT), was formed explicitly to campaign against the 2004 law on religious insignia. The second, Les Indigènes de la République (IDLR), was formed in February 2005 by many of the same people plus a number of others, although minus some such as Françoise Gaspard, who signed the UEPT text but not the IDLR one. The IDLR was no longer specifi-cally focused on the hijab debate and the school system but more generally opposed to the racism and hypocrisy of the French state. In between the *tendance NPNS* and the *tendance Indigènes/UEPT,* a number of feminists critical of both, and desirous of finding a more nuanced position, found themselves quickly characterized by one or the other camp as being either in league with cultural relativists and antisecularist, or racist (or, if of non-European background, "Westernized").

Une Ecole pour Tous-tes was born out of a meeting of Muslim associa-tions and their supporters in the wake of the January 17, 2004, march orga-nized by the ultraright Parti Musulman de France. Picking up on some of the themes elaborated in a document published in May 2003 in *Libération* and signed by many of the same people (Aït-Mohamed et al. 2003), it called for a demonstration against the "conspicuous religious insignia" law outside the National Assembly on the day the law was to be debated and voted, and to a meeting the same evening. The call was signed by a number of antiracist groups: MRAP, the antiracist association for which Laurent Lévy worked as a lawyer; CEDETIM (Centre d'études et d'initiatives de solidarité internationale); antiracist coalition Divercité (a play on words: *diversité* and *cité*) of which some Islamist groups are members; Les Mots Sont Importants; the Collectif Féministe Pour l'Egalité (Feminist Collective for Equality), founded by Christine Delphy along with Monique Crinon of CEDETIM and a few others. It was also signed by a number of Islamist organizations, including the Ligue Française de la Femme Musulmane, Jeunes Musulmans de France, Etudiants Musulmans de France, and the Collectif des Musulmans de France. A number of individuals also added their signatures, including Françoise Gaspard, Christine Delphy, Noël Mamère, and Alima Boumediene-Thiéry.

The UEPT call, which was written in January 2004, became the basis of the organization's charter, written on July 12. The latter added a series of objectives, the main one being the repeal of the law. It was articulated around six principles:

1. The fight for equality for all before the law and opposition to laws that target Muslims in particular.

2. The right of all to public education.

3. Secularism, which, the collective argued, imposes religious neutrality on schools, staff and curricula, not the students.

4. Feminism, which implies that women's emancipation is not achieved through repression but through access to rights: women should not be forced either to don the hijab or to remove it.

5. Social justice, which implies that headscarved girls should not become the scapegoat so as to distract attention from economic liberalization and the logic of "security" and the socioeconomic and racist exclusions that are linked to them.

6. Opposition to the "logic of repression," which implies a refusal both of reactionary elements in white French society and reactionary Islamist logic, that the collective "fights without ambiguity." (Collectif UEPT 2004)

A year later, on January 18, 2005, a number of the group and individual signatories to the UEPT text added their names to another: "Nous sommes les indigènes de la République!" (We are the natives of the Republic!), in which they called for a conference on "anticolonial postcolonialism." The authors and signatories of this text (hereinafter "the Call") included most of the organizations and individuals cited above, along with individuals such as Nacira Guénif-Soulimas, Saïd Bouamama, Monique Crinon, Youssef Boussoumah (French coordinator of the International Civil Campaign for the Protection of Palestinian People), and Houria Bouteldja. Bouteldja was to become prominent in the subsequently formed IDLR organization, at the head of a women's collective called Les Blédardes (*bled* being French Arabic–derived slang for village and the suffix *-ard* being a pejorative tag denoting in this case a typical village resident; it is used ironically here). The men's group Ni Proxos Ni Machos (Neither Pimps Nor Machos, formed in opposition to NPNS), also signed. The MRAP and Gaspard, however, did not, and Gaspard appears to have distanced herself from this movement.

Among the organizational authors of the IDLR text appeared the name of the Islamist Web site called Oumma.com, of which the slogan is "Islam in all its freedom," and which claims to be the world's largest francophone Islamic Web site. On this site, one can find everything from reports on the latest UOIF congress to fashion tips and advertisements for the modern hijabi. One can also find the writings of Christine Delphy—including, bizarrely, her eulogy for Andrea Dworkin—sitting side by side with those of Tariq Ramadan, whose work is featured very prominently on the site. Delphy has not made public any personal dissociation from the systematic posting of her work on Oumma.com. It is difficult, however, to imagine that she would not be aware of these postings; I thus infer that they have happened either with her explicit consent or without her objection.

By using the colonially loaded term *indigènes,* the signatories to the Call, in a deliberately ironic statement, identified themselves as being "postcolonially colonized" *within* the Republic, even if they were its citizens. This was, in fact, the Call's central thesis: that France continued to function as a colonial power in relation to its racialized and socioeconomically marginalized postcolonial populations, who were, through this marginalization, *indigénisés*: given a subhuman status in a Republic where equality was a "myth."[5]

On the face of it, the principles on which UEPT's and IDLR's calls are based are worthy, and UEPT's charter in particular incorporates broad secular and feminist principles with which any feminist would be hard pressed to disagree. Unfortunately, however, the content of a discourse is not so easily dissociable from the politics of those pronouncing it and the context in which it is elaborated. The defense of "feminism" and "secularism" and opposition to racism and the "logic of repression" by a number of the signatories to the UEPT and IDLR texts is difficult to dissociate from the less-than-progressive politics of many of the signatories and the political manipulations of many others.

These politics are not, however, so easy to tease out at first sight. For what was singular about UEPT and IDLR is that they *were* very broad coalitions, and the presence of known feminists, homosexual rights supporters, various left-wing politicians, and venerable antiracist organizations and campaigners among and around them gave them a cachet that they may not otherwise have had. On closer inspection, however, a significant degree of manipulation by certain prominent groups and individuals becomes apparent.

From UEPT to IDLR

This manipulation, already present to some extent within UEPT, became particularly pronounced within and around the IDLR. The latter's political discourse frequently blurs right and left in a manner startlingly reminiscent of fascism, which is due in particular to the presence of Islamist movements that share many of fascism's ideological characteristics (Tazi 2004). The political manipulation has been articulated around three main interlocking axes. The first is "Islamophobia," which in one document signed by a number of IDLR people becomes the "same combat" as homophobia. The second is a "postcolonial/antiglobalization" stance, with which the defense of "Arab men" is more or less aligned, and the third axis is "feminism," around which the idea of "Muslim feminism" has developed. The arguments

5. The full text of the IDLR Call can be found at http://lmsi.net/article.php3?id_article =336. IDLR also has its own Web site: www.indigenes-republique.org.

advanced are relatively Manichaean: those who oppose Islamism and Islamist anti-Semitism in France and/or who identify the hijab as marker of both women's subordinate status and the influence of Islamism are racist, colonialist, allies of a right-wing state, "Islamophobic," and against women's right to self-determination. Accusations of *amalgames* abound (*un amalgame* being a confusion or conflation—often with dishonest or politically motivated intent—of different phenomena or ideas), but those leveling them are equally guilty of the charge.

The IDLR Call departs from the UEPT Charter in several ways. First, unlike the latter, the Call does not explicitly support secularism and feminism or oppose Islamism. Second, the UEPT Charter, which is more specifically centered on the hijab debate, explicitly objects to women being forced either to wear the hijab or to remove it. This is not the case for the IDLR text, in which the hijab and the 2004 law are relegated to a passing reference in an introductory list of grievances, and the law is deemed "sexist" without further comment.

Third, the IDLR Call and related activism are explicitly linked to Palestinian and other anticolonial causes. While this may be unproblematic and even desirable as a general statement of solidarity with the oppressed, the devil is, as they say, in the detail: all depends on which "anticolonial" movement one is defending (Allal 2005). It becomes apparent, on exploring the IDLR website, that the "anticolonial" causes it supports are those of organizations like Hezbollah and Hamas, rather than the Palestinian secular left (see, for example, Charara 2006).

Fourth, following on from this, the IDLR subsequently emerged as being formed in response not to the hijab debate and more general debate around racism associated with it—nor even in response to the 2005 riots, as these occurred almost ten months later—but to two ostensibly unrelated issues. The first of these was the "RER D" incident, as it has become known, and the second was the more Islamist-leaning anti-Semitic elements of the Palestinian cause. It appears to be for this latter reason that the Communist Party–affiliated Confédération Générale du Travail, which runs the Paris Trade Union Center (Bourse du Travail), canceled IDLR's booking of the premises for its "anticolonial postcolonialism" conference with relatively short notice.

The RER D incident occurred on July 10, 2004, when the press reported a complaint to the police, made the previous day by a young woman who claimed to have been attacked on a suburban express train (RER), in which she was traveling with her thirteen-month-old baby. She described her attackers as six teenagers, four of Maghrebian background and two of sub-Saharan African background, who stole her bag, made anti-Semitic comments, and drew swastikas on her belly. The incident gave rise to a widespread press denunciation of this "odious" and "ignoble" anti-Semitism among Arab youth. The original complaint was, however, revealed three days later to be a hoax, completely made up by the complainant, who had mental health problems. The affair was denounced by antiracist groups and a document "Marie n'est pas coupable!" (Marie is not guilty!) was posted on the UEPT Web site; the list of signatories included many of the UEPT people and many of those who were to become IDLR (Ben Hiba et al. 2004).[6] The authors named an increasing climate of racism of which Islamophobia was the main expression, manifested through such things as outlawing of the hijab; "Islamophobic intellectual output"—a likely reference to, among others, Pierre-André Taguieff's 2002 book *La Nouvelle judéophobie,* discussed below; "hysterical focus on Tariq Ramadan"—radical pro-secularist feminist Caroline Fourest's book *Frère Tariq* had been published the year before and had met with hostile reactions from the UEPT-IDLR crowd (Fourest 2004; Gérard n.d.); and "campaigns on the suburbs and immigrants as being the exclusive domains in which male domination and sexist violence occur." The authors stressed, however, that Marie, the source of the hoax, should not be a scapegoat for a wider social and political problem. The final two sentences

6. The full list of signatories is as follows: Tarek Ben Hiba (councillor with the Ile-de-France regional government, representing the group Alternative Citoyenne), Said Bouamama (sociologist), Monique Crinon (of Cedetim, identified as a feminist activist), Djamila Bechoua, Houria Bouteldja (of the feminist collective les Blédardes, subsequently associated with IDLR), Karim Azouz (Collectif des Musulmans de France), Nabile Farès (writer and psychoanalyst), Eyal Sivan (Israeli filmmaker), Pierre Tévanian (Collectif Les Mots Sont Importants), Bernard Dréano ("association leader"), Vincent Geisser (author of *La Nouvelle islamophobie*), Youssef Boussoumah, Mehdi Meftah, and Adnane Ben Youssef (members of the International Civil Campaign for the Protection of the Palestinian People), Nordine Iznasni (Mouvement de l'Immigration et des Banlieues), Christine Delphy.

of the text, which were to provide the seeds of the IDLR Call, published six months later, read:

> If there is to be a trial, it should be a trial of all racisms and of those who exploit them, of social discriminations and of public policies that aggravate them.
>
> It must be the trial of colonial history, of slavery and of their legacy.
>
> (Ben Hiba et al. 2004)

In subsequent interviews, a number of signatories to this text and to the IDLR Call spelled out that the "spark was the RER D Affair" (Youssef Boussoumah, cited in Robine 2006, 123). They also refer to the the hijab debate and to apparently unjust criticisms of Tariq Ramadan. Among the references to the hijab debate, Saïd Bouamama, echoing Tévanian and Tissot's thesis on "lepenization of minds," claimed that the "recurrent return of the debate on the headscarf is, according to us [the IDLR], an indication of the ideological victory of the National Front" (cited in Robine 2006, 134).

The fifth difference between UEPT and the IDLR is that the latter has been explicitly a movement of "children of colonization" from its inception, even though a number of signatories to the original Call, such as Christine Delphy and Laurent Lévy, do not personally fit that profile. The IDLR has nonetheless emerged as essentially an Arab movement, and its main activists are of Maghrebian background. African-background "postcolonial" participants are rare to nonexistent, and Asian-background "postcolonial" citizens are not at all involved and, indeed, have been absent from most debates in France around postcoloniality and racism. This is for many reasons that are at once structural, historical, and socioeconomic and not my brief to explore here. That said, one would have thought that the IDLR would pay Asian-background citizens and immigrants more attention, for three reasons. The first is the almost complete absence of Asian-background citizens, postcolonial or otherwise, within French political institutions. The second is the IDLR's instrumentalization of the history of Vietnamese resistance to colonization: the authors cite Dien Bien Phu as an anticolonialist model, a "victory of liberty, equality and fraternity."

The third reason is the particular marginalization of South Asian Muslims within "Islamophobic" France. Anecdotal evidence provided at the time of the 2005 riots in particular suggests that small but growing numbers of South Asian immigrants are racialized as far less "integrable" than immigrants from the Middle East or the Maghreb.

The sixth point on which the IDLR's political stance departs from that of UEPT is that it is more directly a reaction against NPNS, even if this was not made explicit within the Call itself. Many other documents associated with the IDLR subsequently made this link evident. The "feminism" behind which the supposed "agents of Bushian thought" (see below) ostensibly were hiding was the NPNS brand: the supposedly "Westernized" and co-opted Maghrebian-background women who defend Republican secularism and demonize Arab men.

The IDLR thus constitutes a radical shift from the substance of the UEPT message. Even though many of the signatories and participants are the same, IDLR has embraced a broader, more Manichaean, and more hardline stance and is visibly closer to Islamist agendas. During the 2005–7 period, it also came to claim both the moral high ground and center stage as the privileged defender of the "postcolonial" victims of French racism and "Islamophobia." Within the IDLR frame of reference, the hijab debate was frequently and opportunistically evoked as a core symbol.

"Colonized and Alienated": The Discourse of the Indigènes de la République

The IDLR's Call "to a conference of post-colonial anti-colonialism" was originally published on the site of Oumma.com and reads as a somewhat disordered grab bag of resentments of the racialized and of anti-imperialism and antiglobalization statements. Although its starting point is well-founded grievances against French racism combined with demonstrably true statements about the material operation and effects of the latter, it conflates very different positions and problems and offers no historical nuance or depth or complexity of connection between the "then" of colonialism and the "now" of so-called "postcolonialism." It also advocates an all-or-nothing approach: the Republican baby is imperfect, its values and institutions must therefore be dispensed with along with its dirty racist bathwater. Finally, despite a couple of passing, opportunistic, and token references to sexism, the experience of women is ignored and assimilated to that of men.

In the first paragraph, among the list of ills perpetrated by the Republic, is the "challenging of the *droit du sol*" (nationality rights based on being born in France). This statement is odd, as it implies that the *droit du sol* somehow existed as a given right under some unspecified international law that the Republic now wishes to remove. This is untrue. France introduced the *droit du sol* in the nineteenth century, originally for purely nationalistic and militaristic reasons, so that French soldiers born elsewhere would feel allegiance to the French nation. It is only subsequently that it became reconfigured as a more positive right. Removed in 1993 by the Pasqua laws, *le droit du sol* was partially restored by law 98-170 of March 16, 1998, and subsequent laws have not further undermined it (Lesselier 2005). The nationality provisions of the Civil Code as it currently stands are thus based on a mixture of *droit du sol* (birthplace right) and *droit du sang* (birth lineage rights)—as they always have been. In fact, while it is demonstrably true that the *droit du sol* has been periodically challenged in recent years, notably since the right wing was first reelected in 2002, the main challenges occurred in 2005 and 2006, that is, subsequent to the IDLR's Call. Many of them came from then interior minister Nicolas Sarkozy or those close to him. In particular, overseas minister François Baroin attracted considerable criticism in July 2005 by advocating restrictions to nationality laws for residents of the DOM-TOM (Calvès 2005). Some of Baroin's proposals made it into law 2006-911 of July 24, 2006, on "immigration and integration," but mainly applied to policing of coastal borders, given that all France's DOM-TOM are islands. In the post-2007-election period, up to January 2008, no new legislation that would further undermine the *droit du sol* has been introduced or mooted.

Baroin's statements, like the 2003 and 2006 legislation introduced or flagged by Sarkozy, do, however, point to another problem. There is an increasing conflation—already evident in the Pasqua laws of 1993—by right-wing governments in particular of the issues of nationality, immigration, asylum, and "integration," to fairly evident racist ends. This conflation is not, however, specifically French: it follows a trend throughout the European Union and indeed the Western world more generally. All countries—including non-Western ones—apply entry and immigration restrictions, but Western countries have become particularly, and increasingly, fortress-like. Demonizing non-Western immigrants and asylum seekers as "queue jumpers" or "economic" rather than "political" refugees has become somewhat of a popular pastime in the West, but this was the case long before 9/11, as is evidenced, for example, by the 1985 Schengen Agreement relating to border control and security in the signatory countries, which include France. A new EU directive on the detention and expulsion of foreigners approved by the European Parliament on June 18, 2008, provides, among other things, for detention of up to eighteen months (contrary to the previous French maximum of thirty-two days). Member countries will also have increased flexibility in declaring emergency situations involving, among other things, tougher detention conditions, in cases of "exceptionally large numbers" of illegal immigrants, and the directive allows for prohibition from visiting Europe of up to five years for all persons having been deported.

All of this said, France has long prided itself on being a "land of asylum" and indeed the inventor of the concept in modern political terms, so any resiling from this principle is keenly felt.

The IDLR's denunciation of unspecified challenges to the *droit du sol* comes in the midst of a litany of complaints. Among them are the lack of voting rights for residents who are not citizens, the precarious situation of tens of thousands of *sans papiers,* and the denial of freedom of movement, which "forces" a growing number of Maghrebians and sub-Saharan Africans to cross borders illegally "at risk to their lives." Once again, there is nothing unique about this. Even many of France's former colonies impose restrictions on immigration and voting rights. While the issues of political instability and economic deprivation that push people out of their countries of origin toward Europe are frequently due in great part to a colonial legacy, blanket denunciations of any border restrictions at all are unhelpful. No country in the world allows total freedom of movement across its borders, and the insistence that France should do so reads as naïve and unrealistic. It is also to some extent beside the point, as it conflates problems that are purely local, that is, the precarious situation of both legal and illegal immigrants within France, and demonstrable institutional racism, with others that are global in nature and cannot be solved by France alone.

The IDLR's breathless list of issues is compiled without historical grounding and without any clarification as to what measures exactly are being referred to or how these impact specifically on Maghrebians and Africans.

Which is more than unfortunate, as most of the measures to which the Call appears to refer implicitly do indeed impact more significantly on so-called "postcolonial" populations than they do on others, for many reasons. First, postcolonial populations are more likely, for reasons of historical association, language, and acculturation, to gravitate toward the land of the former colonizer as either a land of asylum or a land of economic promise. Second, postcolonial and other non-Western immigrants are more likely to be poor and less likely to be able to migrate to France through business or other professional or economically advantaged forms of immigration. Third, even though the text of restrictive laws may be neutral and apply to anyone in the situation described, specific restrictions impact most on non-Western and in particular postcolonial populations, simply because these are going to be the most likely to be in the situations that the laws are designed to address. This is obviously not a coincidence. All of this said, however, the important cause of antiracism is not well served by the launching of a vague and not entirely accurate blanket denunciation of anything and everything, without discrimination or historicization.

The IDLR rant on immigration and nationality is all the more problematic because the most severely affected by nationality and immigration laws are women, a fact on which the IDLR Call remains silent. Among other things, women are most affected by laws on prostitution (most women in prostitution in France are foreign born) and by restrictions introduced to family reunion (77 percent of residency permits delivered in France are either for family reunion or marriage to a French citizen) (Lesselier 2003). Women working in prostitution are often trafficked or in situations of extreme poverty or homelessness; they can in some cases obtain residency if they denounce their pimp or trafficker (assuming there is one), but fear of reprisals, or not knowing the true identity of their trafficker, keeps many women from doing this. As for family reunion, women are subjected to increasingly lengthy waiting periods for access to a work permit, residency, and nationality. A minimum period of cohabitation is imposed—this was increased by the 2003 Sarkozy law (law 2003-1119 of November 26)—and women separating from their resident spouses before expiry of this period can be deported, except if the person is primary caregiver for children born in France. Even though in recent years deportation is not allowed in cases of separation for reason of domestic violence, this violence nonetheless has to be proven, and separation for other reasons, including psychological or economic violence, for example, or simply unhappiness, could result in deportation of the spouse. Even in the case of allowable domestic violence, women with often low educational levels, minimal French language or cultural skills, and little money have an uphill battle to negotiate the French legal system. Restrictions to family reunion immigration are, in fact, among the most severely discriminatory pieces of the raft of nationality and immigration legislation adopted during the previous two decades. While the Call does refer in passing to nonrespect of equality before the law, using the application in France of Maghrebian personal status laws, this reference is not well-chosen as first, it is not specific to France, second, it is the result of bilateral agreements, and third, it is no longer imposed on Maghrebian female immigrants, who are thus not excluded from access to French law, as once was the case (Lesselier 2005).

Another ahistorical, vague gender-blind statement in the IDLR's Call is the assertion that immigrant workers are made to play the role of "deregulators" of the labor market "so as to extend to the entire paid workforce even more precarity and flexibility." Once again, this is hardly new. If anything, male immigrant workers are better protected and better paid now than they were during the Trente Glorieuses. Those men who are faring most badly are the *former* immigrant workers who lost their factory jobs during the ensuing recession and their sons, often also unemployed. These men are mainly of Algerian background and mainly French citizens. Moreover, it is, once again, immigrant *women* who are the most vulnerable to this construction of what Sabah Chaib has called the "laboratory for workforce flexibility" (Chaib 2003, 235). Eighty-five percent of part-time jobs are done by 30 percent of working women, who mostly have not chosen to work part-time, and women make up the majority of workers living in poverty. When they are of non-Western immigrant background, they suffer double discrimination: one in four or five works in a "personal service" job in either private homes or the hospitality and catering industries, as opposed to one in ten among white French women (Majnoni d'Intignano et al 1999; FASILD 2004; Maruani 2006). Chaib further notes that the experience of immigrant women in the workforce is seriously underresearched and generally assimilated to that of immigrant men (Chaib 2003, 216ff; See also Winter 1995a). Yet the Call makes no mention of these gendered aspects of economic and workforce disadvantage.

As Brigitte Allal has pointed out, "There is someone more *indigène* than the *indigène,* and that's his wife" (Allal 2005). This sentence recalls that used by feminists in August 1970 when they attempted to lay a wreath at the tomb of the Unknown Soldier under the Arc de Triomphe in Paris, bearing the slogan: "There is someone more unknown than the Unknown Soldier: his wife." It also recalls the words written in 1965 by Algerian anticolonial resistant and feminist Fadela M'Rabet: "the poorest of Algerian men has an infinitely superior condition to that of Algerian women; even dressed in rags, he is a man" (M'Rabet 1979, 23). Allal stresses that women who refuse the hijab, who do not observe Ramadan, or who resist forced marriages are as authentically "born of the colonies and of postcolonial immigration" and as authentically of Muslim culture as those who wish to don it and do so of their own free will.

But the Call dismisses pro-secularist feminists and indeed anyone on the left who disagrees with the IDLR, in the paragraph headed "The colonial gangrene is taking hold of minds." This is probably a reference to *La Gangrène,* a book denouncing torture by French military in Algeria that was banned by the French state during the Algerian war (Boumaza 1958); Lesselier (2005) also notes this subheader's biologizing overtones. The paragraph reads, in part:

> An active fringe of the French intellectual, political and media world, turning its back on the progressive combats on which it prides itself, is transforming itself into agents of Bushian "thought." Besieging the space of communication, these ideologues are recycling the theme of the "Clash of Civilizations" in the local language of the conflict between "the Republic" and "communitarianism." As in the glorious hours of colonization, there is an attempt to oppose Berbers and Arabs, Jews and "Arabo-Muslims" and Blacks. Young "immigrant-background" people are thus accused of being the vectors of a new antisemitism. Under the never-defined term of "integrism," populations of African, Maghrebian or Muslim background are henceforth identified as the Fifth Column of new Barbarians who threaten

the West and its "values." Fraudulently camouflaged under the flags of secularism, citizenship and feminism, this reactionary offensive is taking hold of minds and reconfiguring the political stage.[7]

By not identifying any particular aspect of the "active fringe" to which they refer, the authors appear to assimilate any intellectuals who promote secularism and feminism and criticize anti-Semitism among Muslims to a racist right-wing "clash of civilizations" discourse. This is as erroneous and dishonest as the French extreme-right's blanket demonization of Muslims as "integrists." It also, by setting up a simplistic and binary "bad them" and "good us" opposition, blocks any criticism of any aspect of "postcolonial" states or any members of their populations in diaspora (Lesselier 2005). Once again, this does a disservice to their cause, because there is certainly no lack within France of discourse conflating "Muslim" and *communautariste/intégriste,* and not only on the traditional right of politics. Moreover, as we have seen, there is good reason both to denounce the hypocrisy of the French state's stance on secularism and to criticize the particular brand of co-opted feminism it defends.

The authors of the Call go on to assert that "the Republic of equality is a myth" and to call for an end to its institutions that continue to reduce France's "postcolonized" minorities to a status of "sub-human." They do not clarify which institutions might be concerned by this: some of them, all of them, or whether it is political, legislative, judiciary, or administrative institutions that are concerned. Moreover, as Lesselier notes, it is reductionist to conflate the reality of race discrimination in France with the horrors of slavery and colonialism, where colonized populations had no legal citizenship, no access to the same legal rights enjoyed by white French, and certainly no access to race discrimination legislation (Lesselier 2005). None of which is the case for France's postcolonial populations today.

Certainly, structural and systemic racist discrimination is alive and kicking hard in the post 9/11 Republic, as it was in the pre-9/11 Republic. Not only does it exist in the selective application (or nonapplication) of otherwise just and egalitarian laws and principles, but as we have seen, the supposed

7. http://www.indigenes-republique.org/spip.php?article835.

"neutrality" of laws can camouflage either targeting of specific populations, as in the case of, among others, the 2004 law on "conspicuous" religious insignia, mentioned in the Call as the "anti-headscarf" law, or their disproportionate deleterious impact on specific populations, as in the case of family reunion legislation. The presumption of equality before the law does not enable real and structurally maintained socioeconomic inequalities to be addressed. This does not, however, in itself mean that the presumption of equality before the law should be dispensed with simply because it is an "institution of the Republic." It does not even mean that laws that target specific populations are *necessarily* and by definition undesirable: the 1944 granting of the vote to French women is a case in point (Allal 2005).

Most worryingly, the IDLR's Call ends up doing exactly what it is protesting *against*. Those "born of the colonies and postcolonial immigration" are locked, in simplistic and ahistorical fashion, into an identity that is constructed as being incompatible with anything to do with the French Republic (Lesselier 2005). Deniz Kandiyoti has pointed out, in relation to formerly colonized nations, that "attempting to cast postcolonial phenomena in terms of (Western) foreignness or (indigenous) authenticity" is politically unwise and ultimately futile, not the least because these are "categories that themselves emerge as dubious artifacts of the colonial gaze" (Kandiyoti 1998, 283). By extension, an attempt to cast the *indigènes* as refusers of "assimilation" and of the Republic and its values ends up, ironically, reproducing a colonialist discourse on their "unassimability" (Allal 2005).

Some of these shortcomings were also picked up by a number of those who signed the IDLR's original call, as indicated in a declaration published by a breakaway group on February 17, 2006. The authors of the breakaway text, many of whom had, as individuals, signed the original IDLR Call out of solidarity with its overall antiracist sentiment, while remaining aware of its lacunae, denounced a "sectarianism" and power-grabbing among the self-proclaimed leadership of the IDLR, largely made up of existing organizations.[8] There have also, more recently, been splits within the IDLR women's collective Les Blédardes, for similar reasons.

---

8. The dissenters' text can be found at http://www.indigenes.org/.

"Islamophobia" and Anti-Semitism

The fight against racism in France has, since 9/11, become identified by many as synonymous with a fight against "Islamophobia." This idea of "phobia" is peculiar. Phobia means fear. It is a psychological, and as such, medicalizing and individualizing concept. Even if the structures and ideologies of domination can, in their internalization and expression by individuals, become emotionally programmed and irrational and, as such, include an element of phobia, this is not *all* they are. Racism, including in its particular anti-Muslim manifestation, is a more complex phenomenon than, say, arachnophobia (fear of spiders). More worryingly, the term Islamophobia has been deployed as a smokescreen to deflect any criticism of anything a Muslim says or does and has largely tended to replace the term "racism" when used in this way, both in France and in the English-speaking world.

The term was given national prominence by Alain Gresh in an article in the November 2001 edition of *Le Monde Diplomatique*, where he criticized the Western post-9/11 panic about Islam, assimilated to extremism, terrorism, and women's oppression (Gresh 2001). He also took to task a number of authors, such as Ibn Warraq, outspoken atheist of Muslim background, and Pierre-André Tagiueff, outspoken critic of Muslim anti-Semitism.

The term "Islamophobia" was popularized by the Khomeinist regime in Iran (Djavann 2004, 39–40 and 48–49; Fourest and Venner 2003); Gresh notes, however, that it was first used in 1925. More recently, it was the title of a report prepared in England by Gordon Conway, who chaired the Commission on British Muslims and Islamophobia under the auspices of the Runnymede Trust; its 1997 report was published in book form in 2004. Tariq Ramadan referred to this study in 1998, when he wrote of "a certain Islamophobia" in France (Ramadan 1998). The same year, Soheib Bencheikh, pro-secular Mufti of the Marseilles Mosque—and candidate in the 2007 presidential election—devoted a chapter of his book *Marianne et le Prophète* to the term (Bencheikh 1998, 171–82; Gresh 2004; Richardson 2004).

In an article published on Oumma.com in February 2004, Gresh does note that "not every pamphlet hostile to Islam is necessarily Islamophobic," and raises the question of whether the term "Islamophobia" should not be done away with in favor of reverting to the term "racism" (anti-Arab, or anti-Maghrebian). He then goes on, however, to argue that, post-9/11, the mythical construction of a monolithic political Islam has superimposed itself over this racism to give it another dimension. He stresses, correctly, that Islam has schools of thought as diverse as liberation theology and Opus Dei among Catholics. Curiously, however, he then goes on to give only examples of formally constituted, conservative, and mostly Islamist organizations in France, namely, the UOIF, Collectif des Musulmans de France, and Salafists, who are not representative of the majority of French Muslims. Gresh thus implicitly confirms the thesis that he explicitly set out to refute (Gresh 2004).

The generalization of the term "Islamophobia" was further prompted by the publication in 2002 of Pierre-André Taguieff's book *La Nouvelle judéophobie* (The New Judeophobia). Taguieff argued that anti-Semitism in France was coming from new sources: an immigrant-background Muslim population, and that it was hiding behind the pro-Palestinian movement. He coined the term "Judeophobia" to distinguish this new "Jew-hatred" based, not on an idea of Aryan supremacy, but on a conflation of "Jewish," "Israeli," "Zionist," and "anti-Arab." Seen through this new "Judeophobic" prism, Sharon became assimilated to Hitler and the Israeli state became a latter-day expression of Nazism.

This view has been popularized by, among others, Franco-Camerounese comic and would-be presidential candidate Dieudonné M'bala M'bala, close to the MRAP. Dieudonné's often vulgar anti-Semitic remarks are legion, and he now rivals National Front sympathizer Brigitte Bardot in the number of times he has been fined for by French courts for incitement to racial hatred.[9] The British daily the *Independent* has characterized him as a "French Louis Farrakhan" (March 22, 2006).

Taguieff noted that in 2002, there were more anti-Semitic than anti-Arab attacks in France (Taguieff 2002; See also Conan 2003). This latter statement was confirmed by a lengthy report on "the fight against racism and

9. An exhaustive list of Dieudonné incidents from 2004 to 2006 is published on the independent media Web site www.fil-info. http://www.fil-info-france.com/actualites-monde/dieudonne.htm. Dieudonné also ran a "presidential election" Web site in 2006 and 2007, but it is now defunct.

xenophobia" published in 2004 by the National Consultative Commission on Human Rights (CNCDH), which showed an "unprecedented increase in antisemitic actions" in France since the autumn of 2000, with peaks in anti-Semitic attacks and threats in October 2000 (in the wake of the second Palestinian intifada) and in April 2002 (in the wake of the siege of Ramallah) (CNCDH 2004; Mayer 2004). Moreover, the profile of attackers had changed: prior to 2000 the attacks and threats had been almost exclusively committed by white Gentiles from the extreme-right, but the majority of attacks in subsequent years were committed by youths of Maghrebian background from ghetto areas, often with a record of delinquency, and, as Nonna Mayer puts it, "particularly reactive to the international context" (Mayer 2004; See also Winter 2002b; CNCDH 2004).

At the same time, Mayer's 2004 study shows that ambient anti-Semitism in France has remained remarkably stable since 9/11, and those most likely to be deeply anti-Semitic are still those most likely to be racist more generally: that is, members of the European right and extreme-right, men, those aged fifty or over, those with low educational qualifications, farmers, business owners, and blue-collar workers. Mayer even suggests that *opposition* to anti-Semitic remarks and acts, and to racist speech and acts more generally, has increased, particularly since the 2002 presidential runoff between Le Pen and Chirac.

There would nonetheless appear to be an increase, among high-profile right-wing Muslims, in overt expressions of anti-Semitism of the same order as the worst the white French extreme-right could dish out. In addition, they have responded to Taguieff's accusation of a "new Judeophobia," notably within both the national context of the hijab debate and the international context of the "war on terror," with what appears to be a tit-for-tat generalization of accusations of "Islamophobia."

Some of their non-Muslim supporters are even leading the charge. For example, in 2003 Vincent Geisser, a researcher with France's Centre National de la Recherche Scientifique (CNRS) published a book titled *La Nouvelle islamophobie,* a "mirror-image" title to that of Taguieff's 2002 book. Geisser made the argument, of which the IDLR text is reminiscent, that France has not left its colonial past behind, that it maintains its attitude of Enlightenment civilizer of Muslims. He even went so far as to label

"Islamophobic Muslims" those Muslims who criticized Islamic extremism and supported secularism, and accused even Algerian feminists living in exile in Paris of "facilitating" this Islamophobia. He characterizes them, and prominent French Muslim secularists and modernists, such as Soheib Bencheikh, Dalil Boubaker, Latifa Ben Mansour, and Malek Chebel, as being the token Muslims who give "ethnic" credibility to "Islamophobia." Presumably all Muslim women who are opposed to veiling, and in particular those among them who support the 2004 law, would fit Geisser's definition of "Islamophobic Muslims."

The grab-all characterization, by Geisser and others, of "Muslim Islamophobia" operates a curious piece of doublethink, on three levels. First, and most obviously, Geisser bizarrely lumps together secular and/or progressive Muslims with individuals associated with the extreme-right, such as the late Italian journalist Oriana Fallaci, known for her associations with the neofascist Northern League and for her racist attacks on Muslims, or extreme-right Frenchman Alexandre del Valle. Second, in the name of a supposed antiracism, a white male member of an intellectual and social elite set himself up as judge of what "authentic" Muslims should and should not do or say. Third, he parades what appears to be an antifeminist stance (in relation to Algerian women exiles in particular) as antiracism. In this, he is, admittedly, hardly original, but it is nonetheless worrying that women who are fighting against male violence—whatever its nature, source, or justification—are still so easily dismissed and discredited.

Rudy Reischstadt, writing on the site Observatoire du communautarisme, criticizes this reductionism and further notes that it serves to trivialize acts that are justifiably characterizable as Islamophobia, such as the desecration of graves and mosques and attacks on bookshops (Reichstadt 2004). A Collective Against Islamophobia in France, set up in 2003, compiled data on such attacks and on October 21, 2004, published a report on "Islamophobic" incidents in France.[10] The report documented 182 "Islamophobic" acts between October 2003 and August 2004, of which 118 were against individuals and the rest against institutions. Twenty-eight mosques and eleven cemeteries were vandalized, six of the mosque attacks being in

10. http://www.islamophobie.net/dev/index.php.

April 2004. Half of the attacks were in the Parisian region and in Alsace. The Collective's definition of Islamophobia appears, however, to be closer to Geisser's than to Reichstadt's.

Caroline Fourest and Fiammetta Venner, ardent defenders of secularism and outspoken critics of Islamism, also came in for numerous accusations of "Islamophobia" during 2003, notably from Xavier Ternisien, religion writer with *Le Monde,* for an issue of *Prochoix,* which Fourest and Venner edit, on the rekindling of the hijab debate. Ternisien also claimed Françoise Gaspard and Eric Fassin as allies in this accusation against the *Prochoix* editors. Not only was this not true, but the *Prochoix* issue in question actually featured a range of views, including a petition "Oui à la laïcité, non aux lois d'exception" (Yes to secularism, no to laws of exception), originally published in the press the preceding May, that defended secularism but opposed prohibition of the hijab. It even featured an article by anti-ban intellectuals Tissot and Tévanian, authors of *La Lepénisation des Esprits,* which criticized the government's public housing policy (*Prochoix* 2003a).

In response to Ternisien's accusations and claims, *Prochoix* published a double issue devoted to the idea of Islamophobia. Apart from a rebuttal by Gaspard and Fassin, it contains articles by Muslim homosexuals, a Muslim atheist, and an Iranian student exiled in France, all of whom denounce the hypocrisy of the accusation, leveled against anyone who attempts to criticize Islamism (*Prochoix* 2003b).

The issue even contains a dissenting statement from the Marseilles branch of the MRAP, which contests the position taken by the Paris head office of the organization, and in particular its general secretary, Mouloud Aounit, in a debate that was to become increasingly volatile. It led, in 2004, to the very public resignation from the organization of Albert Memmi, Tunisian-born French Sephardic Jewish author of fiction and nonfiction, the latter including well-known essays on racism and colonization, and in 2005, to the publication of a dissenting statement by a number of board and executive members of the organization (MRAP-Marseille 2003; Memmi 2004; Kurys et al. 2005).

The Marseilles branch of the MRAP distanced itself from the position taken by MRAP-Paris and in particular by Aounit against the expulsion of the Lévy sisters from their high school in Aubervilliers. In a communiqué dated October 13, 2003, and reproduced in *Prochoix,* the Marseilles branch reiterated the ideals of secularism:

> The local committee of Marseilles considers that the judgment brought down by the Disciplinary Board of the Henri-Wallon high school in Aubervilliers is not a defeat of secularism but a victory for respect for the principles of equality between men and women and against obscurantism. . . . Secularism must be a space for democratic expression and school a place that is open to all children without distinguishing, political, ethnic, or religious signs. It is the place that enables children to escape family, community, political, or religious pressures and to train their critical thinking so as to become free beings. (MRAP-Marseille 2003, 119)

The MRAP is one of France's largest and oldest antiracist organizations; positions taken by its national representatives are thus significant. In recent years, those positions have been disturbing and are typical of the general tendency that has developed within the IDLR and its supporters.

Le MRAP Dérape . . . Along with a Few Others

Le MRAP dérape (the MRAP slides off onto shaky ground) was first used in an article in *Le Figaro* in relation to anti-Semitic slogans "Down with Jews! Death to Jews!" shouted during an October 7, 2000, pro-Palestinian march in Paris, co-organized by the MRAP. Following this incident, a question was raised in Parliament on whether legal action should be taken against the organizers or other persons for incitement to racial hatred. The MRAP responded by itself taking legal action against the deputy having raised the question (*Le Figaro,* July 26, 2001). *Le MRAP dérape* has since become a slogan used by many commentators on the MRAP's increasingly anti-Semitic and pro-Islamist positions, and was used as the title of the second part of a report on MRAP's shady alliances (CCTR 2004b—see below).

The organization out of which the MRAP grew, the Mouvement National Contre le Racisme (MNCR), was formed in 1941 by French resistants wishing to fight racism as a specific part of the overall struggle to liberate France. It worked in particular, with the cooperation of some Catholic and Protestant churches, to save Jewish children from deportation, and published two clandestine publications against racism and the Vichy regime. In

1949, the Mouvement contre le Racisme, l'Antisémitisme et pour la Paix (Movement against Racism, Antisemitism and for Peace) was formed by former members of the MNCR, and its name was the source of the enduring acronym Le MRAP. It then went on to support anticolonial struggles, in particular in Algeria, and campaigned for a law against incitement to racial hatred, which became the Pleven Law of July 1, 1972. In 1977, the MRAP changed its name to the current one, Mouvement contre le Racisme et pour l'Amitié entre les Peuples (Movement against racism and for friendship among peoples).

It is thus ironic that the divisions that have come to the surface in the MRAP and largely contributed to discrediting it, and that have led to the formation of other groups such as the Collectif Contre Tous les Racismes (CCTR, Collective against All Racisms), are to do with the linked issues of anti-Semitism and "Islamophobia" (CCTR 2004a, 2004b). These issues began to emerge after the Second Palestinian Intifada in 2000 and came to a head in 2004, no doubt amplified by dissent over the hijab issue, as outlined above. Memmi was not the only one to resign from the organization: he was preceded, for example, in 2002, by longtime editor of the MRAP's magazine *Différences,* Chérifa Benabdessadok, of Algerian Muslim background. In February 2004 Benabdessadok was one of the hundreds of signatories to a manifesto titled *Retrouver la force d'une laïcité vivante* (Recovering the Strength of a Living Secularism), in support of secularism and sex equality and against homophobia and anti-Semitism. The manifesto, which was published in *Libération* and subsequently became known as the *Manifeste des Libertés* (Manifesto of Freedoms), constituted a strong counterpoint to the UEPT statement, published the previous month, although it was not written in direct response to it. It started as follows:

> Women and men of Muslim culture—believers, agnostics or atheists— we denounce, with the greatest vigor, declarations and acts of misogyny, homophobia, and antisemitism that we have witnessed over a certain period here in France and that claim to be in the spirit of Islam. We see in this a manifestation of the classic trilogy of political Islamism that has for a long time plagued our countries of origin, and against which we have fought, and are resolved to continue to fight. (Abada et al. 2004)

The Muslim anti-Semitism to which the manifesto refers came from several sources: Tariq Ramadan's article "Critique des (nouveaux) intellectuels communautaires" (2003a); anti-Semitic remarks by the comedian Dieudonné in December of the same year; and two 2003 reports by the MRAP on anti-Arab and anti-Muslim racism. In the first report, on racism via the Internet, the MRAP accused a conspiracy allying neo-Nazis and the "pro-Israel extreme-right." The majority of the sites, grouped around SOS-Racaille, were later demonstrated to be bogus, SOS-Racaille having been set up by a French con man (CCTR, 2004b). The second report similarly pointed the finger at the Jewish right; its preamble contains language remarkably similar to that used a few months later by Tariq Ramadan. In particular, it stated that "Arabophobic" racism had in recent times been "reinforced by radical 'communitarian' sectors that claim[ed] to be in the spirit of Judaism" (MRAP 2003, cited in CRIF 2004).[11]

Both *Le Monde* and *Libération* refused to publish this report, which named a number of prominent left-wing Jewish intellectuals, as did Ramadan's October 3 article. *Libération* gave as a reason for nonpublication not the fact that Ramadan criticized certain individuals but that he essentialized them, assuming a natural link between their Jewishness and the views he attributed to them and then criticized. Ramadan even included Taguieff, non-Jewish author of *La Nouvelle judéophobie,* in this essentialized Jewish population. *Le Nouvel Observateur* subsequently noted other significant errors. Ramadan claims, for example, that Bernard-Henri Lévy, who opposes the war in Iraq, supports it, and made a curious leap of logic around Lévy's book on U.S. journalist Daniel Pearl, assassinated in Pakistan by Islamist extremists (whom Lévy characterized as anti-Semitic), to portray it as some sort of Zionist set-up. Lévy, outraged by Ramadan's words, told *Le Nouvel*

11. The two MRAP reports had been withdrawn from its Web site at the time I attempted to retrieve them in 2006. It is somewhat ironic that I had to retrieve this particular citation via a right-wing Jewish organization, CRIF, whose president, Roger Cukierman, has been denounced for expressing sympathy for the views of Le Pen (Sallenave 2004). Extensive documentation on the MRAP's *dérapages* (slippery sliding) is, however, also available via CCTR (2004a, 2004b), as well as a number of other sources that are not even remotely identified with the right.

Observateur that previously, when he had been told that Ramadan was anti-Semitic, he had refused to believe it; adding "I must have been naïve" (cited in Askolovitch 2003).

Also in 2003, Hassan Iquioussen, one of the clerics associated with the UOIF, recorded a lengthy speech on Palestine that was essentially made up of an anti-Semitic and anti-Western diatribe, in which the fictitious "Jewish conspiracy" loomed large. General secretary of UOIF Fouad Alaoui publicly reaffirmed his support for Iquioussen, even though he condemned Iquioussen's anti-Semitic references, and described him as a man of "high spirituality and a speaker of great quality, showing a flawless respect for Republican values."[12] The Tawhid bookshop in Lyons, which had been selling cassettes of the speech, claimed not to have been fully aware of the content of the speech and assured the press it would be withdrawn from sale (Yamin Makri, director of Tawhid, cited in *Le Figaro,* October 28, 2003). When I checked the Tawhid Web site on December 28, 2006, it was still on sale online, although it is available for free via the Web site of another right-wing organization, the Conseil Représentatif des Institutions Juïves de France (Representative Council of Jewish Institutions of France; CRIF).[13]

On December 6, 2005, *Le Monde* published a statement titled "Démons français" by twenty-four intellectuals, mostly well-known writers, sociologists, and historians, from a range of ethnic backgrounds, including Muslim, condemning "Jewish conspiracy" anti-Semitism in general and, in particular, Dieudonné's repeated remarks on supposed Jewish control of the slave trade, banks, and the media (Amokrane et al. 2005). The list of signatories is an interesting one and represents a considerable cross-section: the name of Nacira Guénif-Soulimas, associated with the IDLR, appears beside that of

---

12. http:// www.crif.org/?page=articles_display/detail&aid=4030&returnto=dossier/ detail_doss_type&dossyd=44&artyd=5.

13. For free: http://www.crif.org/?page=articles_display/detail&aid=4030&returnt o=dossier/detail_doss_type&dossyd=44&artyd=5; or for 3.50 euros, it was available until 2007 from http://www.islam-france.com/livre.asp?onglet=4&article=587. It now appears, finally, to have been withdrawn from sale as promised some years earlier.

well-known historian and critic of Shoah denial Pierre Vidal-Naquet (Gué-nif-Soulimas and Macé 2006; Vidal-Naquet 1997).[14]

One of the most public condemnations of Dieudonné—and along with him, of aspects of the discourse of the IDLR—came in the form of an article by well-known Franco-Algerian author Leïla Sebbar, who was also one of the signatories to the 2004 *Manifeste des Libertés.* In her article, titled "Dieudonné se trompe de cible" (Dieudonné Is Aiming at the Wrong Target) and published in *Libération,* Sebbar condemned Dieudonné's "stigmatization of French Jewish intellectuals whom he designates as being the main ones responsible for his status of *Indigène* in France, 'colonized and alienated'" (Sebbar 2005). (Dieudonné had not been a signatory to the IDLR Call, published on February 22 that year, but he was quick to adopt the rhetoric.) Sebbar went on to criticize Tariq Ramadan and the signatories to the IDLR document, arguing that while they, along with Dieudonné, are right to ask why they suffer discrimination even though they are citizens of the Republic, they are mistaken in blaming the institutions of the Republic for this. According to Sebbar, discriminations are expressed in some "uncontrolled sectors of society" and mostly target the children of poorer classes, who are also the living memory of the painful colonial past. She stressed that it was possible to combat these discriminations without either incriminating the victims of the Shoah or dragging the children and grandchildren of the colonized into what she termed the "delinquent" struggle of supporters of radical and political Islam, who would like to see a separate, and discriminatory, personal status for Muslim women in France. Participation in such a struggle, wrote Sebbar, would only make these descendants of the colonized "alienated" anew (Sebbar 2005).

14. The full list of signatories to the statement is as follows: Salah Amokrane, Nicolas Bancel, Esther Benbassa, Hamida Bensadia, Pascal Blanchard, Jean-Claude Chikaya, Suzanne Citron, Maryse Condé, Catherine Coquery-Vidrovitch, Yvan Gastaut, François Gèze, Nacira Guénif-Souilamas, Didier Lapeyronnie, Sandrine Lemaire, Gilles Manceron, Carpanin Marimoutou, Achille Mbembe, Laurent Mucchielli, Pap Ndiaye, Benjamin Stora, Christiane Taubira, Françoise Vergès, Pierre Vidal-Naquet, Michel Wieviorka. The article has been reproduced on many activist Web sites, for example, the Toulon branch of the Ligue des Droits de l'Homme: http://www.ldh-toulon.net/spip.php?article1064.

Well-known radical feminist Christine Delphy immediately responded with a scathingly sarcastic attack on Sebbar and on others who had criticized the IDLR Call, notably Communist Party president Robert Hue (Delphy 2005a). Her response to Sebbar was centered on the latter's warnings against Islamism and the two sentences, in an article of about 600 words, in which she appears to let the French state off the hook (Sebbar 2005). While I share some of Delphy's concern at Sebbar's mostly uncritical support of the Republic and of the French Public Service, Delphy's caricaturing of Sebbar's denunciation of Islamism and anti-Semitism shows a scant knowledge on Delphy's part either of Sebbar's own views or her writings. Sebbar has in the past made a distinction between "moderate" Islamism, which she then appeared to use as a synonym for Islamic revivalism, and political Islamism.[15] In her fiction, she has criticized *both* Islamic fundamentalism *and* white French violence against Maghrebians, including against hijab-wearing women (Sebbar 1996, 1997). More worryingly, Delphy sarcastically trivializes Sebbar's substantive argument against Muslim anti-Semitism:

> In the end, if we listen to those around us, there are nothing but chasms opening in the path of whoever would denounce race discrimination and colonial administration: the aggravation of women's oppression, the division of the working class—united until now [this last being a response to Hue]—antisemitism, gingivopathy (I'm adding it because they didn't think of it), and this is only the beginning of a list that will, let there be no doubt, grow longer by the day. (Delphy 2005)

Delphy's misrepresentation of Sebbar's argument, and her trivialization of the anti-Semitism that Sebbar criticizes, lent a new "feminist" veneer to Islamist anti-Semitism.

The Queering of "Antiracism"

A new avenue of manipulation by the IDLR and those associated with it has emerged via the "queering" of their discourse, in particular via two documents, both first published in 2004 and both reissued in 2006. The first uses a "queer politics" analysis to argue its antifeminist opposition to NPNS and

15. Interview with the author, July 6, 1997.

defense of "Arab boys," and the second links the combat against "Judeophobia" and, particularly, "Islamophobia" with that against "homophobia."

In 2004, Nacira Guénif-Soulimas, who had previously written on young Maghrebian-background women in France (Guénif-Soulimas 2000), published, along with Eric Macé, *Les Féministes et le garçon arabe* (Feminists and the Arab Boy), in which the "feminists" in question are NPNS and their allies and sponsors. A second and slightly revised edition of this book appeared in 2006. The authors claim that prior to the creation of the high profile NPNS in 2002, there had not been a "feminist" aspect to the hijab debate. As we saw in part II, this is untrue.

Even more peculiarly, Guénif-Soulimas and Macé claim that feminism was on the wane prior to the 2002 debate because it had been not been "culturally radical" enough (whatever this means). In an argumentation that appears to be inspired by Judith Butler and French Butlerian/queer theorist Marie-Hélène Bourcier, they further claim that the existence of transgenders, transsexuals, and other "queers" addresses this failing of feminism by exposing the "symbolic order" of hierarchical and "naturalized" sex difference.[16] As Liliane Kandel points out, much of the ensuing argumentation of the book is based on the Butlerian idea of the gender-performative (Kandel 2005). Apparently the work of Simone de Beauvoir, who in the space of one thousand pages analyzed how female human beings "become" Woman, did not go far enough in identifying this "symbolic order" (Beauvoir 1949). Nor did the many scholars who have drawn inspiration from her work, such as radical lesbian theorists Monique Wittig, who argued that a lesbian is not a woman as she refuses to "become" one as defined in male supremacist heterosexuality, and Colette Guillaumin, who thoroughly critiqued the "naturalization" of sex and race difference, or indeed, radical feminist Christine Delphy, who analyzed the socioeconomic class relationship between men and women within the family (Delphy 1998, 2001; Guillaumin 1992; Wittig 2001).

In fact, almost the entire history of feminist theory and activism in France has been wiped out within Guénif-Soulimas's and Macé's representation of

16. Two of Butler's works on "performing" and "undoing" gender were published in French translation in 2006 (Butler 1999, 2004), and prior to that, Bourcier (2005) had popularized her work and queer theory in some scholarly circles.

it. More worryingly, however, the authors are instrumentalizing and diverting Butlerian-style queer/"feminist" analyses "to the benefit of an unexpected cause: the unconditional defense of 'Arab boys' (and veiled girls), *against, precisely . . . feminists*" (Kandel 2005, 41, her italics).

Guénif-Soulimas and Macé argue that feminism reappeared in France via the controversy over the hijab, with its agenda dictated by NPNS. Apart from the mobilization around the death of Sohane Benziane, the authors refer in particular to a petition calling for a law against the hijab that appeared in the women's magazine *Elle* in December 2003, at the time the Stasi Commission report was handed down (Abecassis et al. 2003). Guénif-Soulimas and Macé claim that the signatories are all activists with or supporters of NPNS, which was possibly the case at the time for most of the signatories, although I have no way of either proving or disproving this. That said, the *Elle* petition grouped a number of individuals who otherwise may not share the same political position or relationship to feminism. For example, three of the signatories, Fadela Amara, Antoinette Fouque, and Elisabeth Badinter, are all disliked within different sections of the feminist movement, but for very different reasons: the first for reasons of suspect political alliances, the second for the appropriation by her group Psychanalayse et Politique of the name "Women's Liberation Movement" and various antifeminist statements over the years (Mouvement pour les Luttes Féministes 1981), and the third for her overall hostility to the feminist movement and its ideas. Their signatures appear beside those of feminists who are not exactly pally with them and may even be hostile to one or other of them. NPNS member Samira Bellil, pioneering Algerian feminist Fadela M'Rabet, Leïla Babès (sociologist of religion and signatory of the *Manifeste des libertés*), Iranian exile Chahdortt Djavann, and Malika Mokkedem, a well-known Algerian novelist living in France, are also signatories. So are former women's rights minister Yvette Roudy, psychoanalytic theorist Julia Kristeva, who does not identify with the French feminist movement, notwithstanding certain attempts in the United States in particular to construct her as representative of French feminist theory, filmmakers Coline Serreau (popular with feminists) and Catherine Breillat (unpopular with many feminists since her 1999 film *Romance*), and a number of well-known actors, including Isabelle Adjani, Josiane Balasko, Jane Birkin, Isabelle Huppert, and Sandrine Kiberlain. Fashion stylist Ines de la Fressange, once a candidate to incarnate the national image of Marianne, and hardly a committed feminist, was also a signatory. A very disparate group, in fact.

Guénif-Soulimas and Macé make three points in relation to this petition and by extension to NPNS more generally. First, they note that the issue of secularism and the hijab have become conflated with the issue of violence against women in the *quartiers,* particularly gang rapes. This is demonstrably true, but whether the fault lies entirely at the hands of NPNS, rather than a combination of NPNS, the political class, and the media, is debatable.

Second, they note that the alliance between NPNS and certain high-profile political and cultural figures feeds a construction of co-opted "feminism" that relies on adherence to state values on the one hand and demonization of "unquestionable adversaries" on the other. Curiously, however, they identify these adversaries as "the embittered radical lesbian, the veiled girl and the Arab boy" (Guénif-Soulimas and Macé 2006, 10). They do not explain how radical lesbians enter into the frame of reference, and their allusion to them, as to queer politics, seems entirely gratuitous, a way of giving some sort of radical edge to their arguments. It is all the more gratuitous because queer politics is politically quite separate from French radical lesbianism, and often antagonistic to it, even though it has also appropriated the work of radical lesbians, notably Monique Wittig, as Fourest (2005), among others, has noted. French radical lesbians are, reciprocally, hostile to queer theory and in particular to what they see as a deforming of their work to ends for which it was not intended, as has been evidenced by many rowdy debates in France over the last decade, one of the earlier ones being during EuroPride 1997, at a controversial forum at the Centre Georges Pompidou on June 27 of that year, at which Wittig shared the podium with, among others, queer theorist Eve Sedgwick (Eribon 1998).

That French society, like practically any other society in the world (probably all of them), is heterosexist, is undeniable. That said, so, for the most part, are devout followers of conservative expressions of religion, including Islam, and including many "veiled girls," as are most heterosexual men, including "Arab boys." Moreover, the particular "Arab boys" being defended as unjustifiably demonized are not those who are active in Islamic revivalist or Islamist organizations, and are for the most part unlikely to feel concerned by the cause of the hijab. The demonized trio chosen by the authors as representative of the marginalized thus has virtually nothing in common, in terms of experience, interaction or politics, and the authors demonstrate no particular grounds for lumping them together other than in some sort of "queer alliance" of the marginalized and demonized.

Guénif-Soulimas's and Macé's third point is that what they call "feminism" locks "Arabs" into a nonassimilable, nonsecular, non-Republican, and antifeminist antimodernity. Such essentializing discourses are indeed to be combated, but whether feminism is responsible for them is debatable, and the authors' defense of Arab men is problematic, as we will see in chapter 9.

The other document published in 2004 that "queered" the *indigènes* was *Homophobie, judéophobie, islamophobie: Mêmes combats* (Same Combats). Written by members of the Blédardes (the IDLR's women's group) and Tévanian's group and online magazine *Les Mots Sont Importants,* to mark the international day of the fight against homophobia, this text claims to move beyond a "competition of victims." On the face of it, this is a worthy text. On closer examination, however, it appears, like the IDLR text, to be based on perverse and flawed logic.

It would appear that a primary motivation for the *Homophobie, judéophobie, islamophobie* (HJI) document is a reaction against the *Manifeste des libertés* (*Manifeste*), which they misrepresent and take to task at some length. The *Manifeste* explicitly denounces misogynist, homophobic, and anti-Semitic statements and acts emanating from some Muslim-background individuals and groups and justified by them in the name of "Islam," as outlined earlier in this chapter.

The authors of HJI accuse the authors of the *Manifeste* of not including denunciation of Islamophobia and indeed all forms of racism alongside their denunciation of anti-Semitism, sexism, and homophobia. This would, however, have been a little odd, as the *Manifeste* was written with the express purpose of criticizing Islamists who use both Islam and accusations of Islamphobia, as well as the pro-Palestinian struggle, as a dishonest defense against any criticism of their right-wing politics (Abada et al. 2004). The authors of HJI then extrapolate their criticism of the *Manifeste* to anyone who denounces the hijab as a symbol of male domination and religious fundamentalism and/or supports the law prohibiting religious insignia in schools. Not all the signatories of the *Manifeste,* however, support the law, and this is made explicit in the text. The authors of HJI also accuse the authors of the *Manifeste,* among others, of requiring people to choose between the fight against Islamophobia and that against homophobia, the implication being that the *Manifeste* authors are on the side of Islamophobes. Finally, the authors of HJI operate the now-familiar lumping together of secularists, many feminists, and the French state as all having the same discourse and all being on the same side.

The HJI authors then go on to invoke a "profound commonality of experience" of "stigmatization" of anyone targeted by various phobias and -isms: Arabophobia, Islamophobia, Judeophobia, negrophobia, all forms of xenophobia, sexism and homophobia. Apart from my previously mentioned reservations with regard to the individualizing and psychologizing connotations of the term "phobia," the reductionism implicit in the establishment of this indiscriminate list of "phobias" is troubling. Experiences of prejudice and rejection, such as xenophobia, are qualitatively quite different from experiences of oppression within systems of domination where one category of human beings is dehumanized and another category benefits, politically, economically, and culturally, from this dehumanization. Lumping these qualitatively different relationships into the catch-all category of "stigmatization" obscures the effect of domination and is not helpful as a way of addressing racism. As concerns Islamophobia, this technically means fear of Islam. Islam is not a person or group of people. Muslimophobia might be a more accurate expression to refer to hatred of people, although even here, my objection to the "phobia" suffix remains. Heterosexism, for example, like other systems and ideologies of domination, will not be solved simply by working on fear of homosexuals, because the fear is merely an individually and collectively internalized cultural symptom of a deeper relationship of domination, not its cause.

Following on from this listing of "stigmatizations," the authors claim that discriminated groups are locked into a "communitarian" logic by those responsible for the discriminations, and, in a manner startlingly similar to that employed by Guénif-Soulimas and Macé (2004), argue that veiled girls and homosexuals are both victims of conflations which present them as "absolute evil." To back up this argument, they note that many "Republicans" who are hostile to veiled girls in schools are also hostile to homosexuals.

They thus argue for closer interaction between various discriminated groups, which will apparently help everyone in the "stigmatized" category get past their "phobias" so that all can struggle convergently together in a renewed sentiment of commonality. Yet, it is not because one has an experience of stigmatization that one automatically has a common political project with others having had similar experiences. First, not all members of an oppressed group understand and respond to that oppression in the same way: among a range of possible responses is overt and complete collusion with the oppressor. Second, making political choices and building a political project are a much more complex matter than simply claiming some sort of collective epistemic advantage of the oppressed. Third, many marginal groups in society, from the extreme-left to the extreme-right, claim to have experienced stigmatization. Le Pen has claimed it regularly, for example, as have Islamist movements throughout the Muslim world.

The authors note that homosexuals distrust religion because religions are hostile to homosexuality, but argue that this renders dialogue all the more necessary. Certainly, there is no objective reason not to believe that if Catholics can have the Rainbow Sash movement and Protestants the Metropolitan Community Church, with equivalent movements within Judaism, that fully religious groups of Gay Muslims will emerge: there are already secular ones. This does not mean, however, that overall any of these three religions, or, indeed, any other religions, have become fundamentally more receptive to homosexuality, and religion continues to be used as justification for most although not all persecutions of homosexuals and of women more generally in the world. There are, and will continue to be, many reasons for homosexuals to distrust religion, and "dialogue" will not change this. If homosexuals are demonized by the French state as "absolute evil," the basis of this demonization comes first and foremost from the Catholic Church, as was demonstrated during the parliamentary and public debate accompanying the passage of the PaCS (Civil Solidarity Pact; see chapter 2). Veiled girls, whatever discriminations they may face, are not demonized by the state as "unnatural" or "monstrous" in the way that the institutions and ideology of both Catholicism and Islam demonize homosexuals. Even those religious conservatives who attempt to present as "moderate" and "reasonable," such as Tariq Ramadan, condemn homosexuality as "unnatural." Ramadan has unambiguously stated that homosexuality must not be made legal or socially recognized under Islam; homosexuals, who are a "dysfunctional" and "perturbing" force, should not, in his opinion, be guilt-tripped but nonetheless must be "accompanied, oriented, reformed" in order to attain spiritual, emotional and physical balance (Ramadan 2004a, 152). Whatever individuals may feel about the 2004 French law, there is no good objective reason for homosexuals—and most particularly not for lesbians—to suddenly leap to the defense of values according to which they are at best "dysfunctional" and at worst the scum of the earth, punishable by death.

The HJI document paints a humanist veneer of "acceptance of everyone" behind which it constructs a dubious and flawed defense of a recommended alliance between, essentially, homosexuals and religious pietists, along with various other "stigmatized" groups thrown in for good measure. "Judeophobia" is not, in fact, specifically discussed outside the initial shopping list of "phobias"; the word's presence in the title thus seems tokenistic and opportunistic.

There are thus significant analytical flaws in this text, and its political purpose is questionable, particularly when placed alongside other writings and actions by some of its authors, all part of the IDLR movement. They include the by now familiar names of Houria Bouteldja, Saïd Bouamama, Monique Crinon, Christine Delphy, Sadri Khiari, Noël Mamère and Pierre Tévanian. These authors are seasoned political activists and intellectuals; many, indeed most, of them have been involved in feminist, antiracist or other political movements for decades and a number earn their living in universities and research institutes. They are not naïve, they are not new to the complexities of these debates. And they most certainly are not writing in a vacuum: they have agendas and alliances, that have been clearly developed elsewhere.

9

Feminist Confusions and Confrontations

Imagine a play where the same sentence, said by a series of different characters, took completely opposing meanings. The most important thing would be not the content of the sentence but the point of view of the person having said it. For example, "I am fighting against racism" could mean "I am for the acceptance of the veil in schools," "I am for the law against religious signs that designate a community," "I am against antisemitism," "I am against the 'Jewish lobby'," "I am pro-Israeli," "I am pro-Palestinian," and so on.

It is in this type of political situation that we currently find ourselves. What characterizes this situation is that it makes exchange of views difficult, it paralyzes the exercise of thought, and favors the reign of rumor and suspicion (Allal and Allal, n.d.).

SO WROTE BRIGITTE AND TEWFIK ALLAL, co-originators of the *Manifeste des libertés* (Abada et al. 2004), and co-founders of the association of the same name founded in December 2004. With these words, they identified a fundamental problem with the hijab debate among the broader left that, already partly present in 1989, had become extreme. Among generalized expressions of outrage and claiming of moral high ground, analysis gave way to posturing, unambiguous statement of political position gave way to perverse manipulation, and argument on the basis of content gave way to mudslinging ranging from innuendo to outright accusation. In a debate where the anti-ban lobby quickly became indistinguishable from the pro-hijab one, and the pro-secular lobby became confused with a racist state, the logic of "if you're not for us, you're against us" left little place for the more nuanced logic of "the enemy of my enemy is not necessarily my friend."

Among the many instrumentalizations and discursive acrobatics operated in the IDLR and NPNS (or "cultural relativist" and laïcarde) polarization around the nest of themes connected to the hijab issue, the primary instrumentalization has been that of "feminism." It has been contorted, smoke-and-mirrored, unidimensionalized, and alternately co-opted and demonized, to within an inch of its embattled life. In fact, in the 2003–6 debate in which women, their rights, and their choices appeared, unlike 1989, to have been placed at the center, the extent to which feminist analysis and the history and practice of feminism have been ignored, dismissed, or misrepresented is staggering.

Issues that have been foregrounded within the IDLR-NPNS polarization have been where the primary responsibility for violence against women lies and what should be done about it, whether or not the hijab is in itself oppressive, whether religion and feminism are compatible, whether opposition to the hijab is a colonialist and Westernizing denial of women's freedom, agency, and cultural identity, and what antiracist feminism looks like or should look like. Feminists on both sides of the Mediterranean have been debating these and related questions for decades, even though many in the NPNS and IDLR camps have claimed, in a strange mixture of cynicism and naïveté, to be the first to have thought of them.

The renewed rehearsing of these debates during the 2003–6 chapter of the French hijab saga can thus seem depressingly déjà-vu for some, particularly those who have already been engaged in them in the English-speaking world, either nationally or transnationally. Indeed, some of the more recent French arguments have a decidedly "made in the USA" feel, particularly those concerning "Westernization," "Muslim feminism," "black feminism," and "agency" (a new word, *agentivité*, even having been coined to translate it), not to mention the queer politics dimension already discussed in chapter 8.

That feminism evolves through transnational interaction and influence is not in itself a bad thing, quite the contrary. In any case, it is inevitable. Nor is it a bad thing that young women bring to feminist debate and activism their own geographically and historically contexualized perspectives. Expressions of "feminism" within the IDLR-NPNS polarization have, however, suffered from two serious lacunae. One has been the "lost in translation" character of some of the transplanted discourse, so that supposed U.S.

"black feminism" or queer politics develops its own made-in-France perversions, via a process of decontextualizing and mythicizing that is reminiscent of the made-in-USA construction of a mythical "French feminism" from the mid-1980s to 1990s (Delphy 1995; Moses 1996; Winter 1997). The other problem is a disappearing of much of the French feminist movement and its history, as if there were no specifically French history of feminist organizing and reflection on racism, secularism, religion, violence against women, and so on. While one may forgive women who are younger or newer to the movement for such ignorance, it appears startlingly disingenuous when coming from women such as Christine Delphy or Fadela Amara, who have been around for decades.

In this chapter, I will look at some of the feminist confusions and confrontations around the issues of "Westernization," "Muslim feminism," the "new" antiracism, violence against women, *laïcardisme,* and co-optation, and in doing so, foreground the voices of some feminists in France who distance themselves from both NPNS and IDLR positions.

"Westernization" and "Agency"

While many feminists agree on the gendered meaning of the hijab, irrespective of their position on the advisability or otherwise of the 2004 law, others, notably those associated with the IDLR, claim that there is no basis for comparing the "freely chosen" French hijab to its imposition in Muslim countries or to Islamism (Delphy 2003a, 2003b). They have further argued that the hijab is a sign of reengagement with Islam that "young people" or "young women" use to affirm and valorize their French Muslim identity in the face of racism and exclusion, and as such it should be understood and supported by those who oppose racist domination and not demonized. Women who claim the hijab is a sign of alienation or oppression of women are apparently doing the latter (Delphy 2003a, 2003b, 2004). Such women are written off as Westernized, maternalistic, and colonialist, and as denying the agency of headscarved women (Boumediene-Thiéry 2004; Benzid-Basset 2005; Bouteldja 2004, 2006b). Finally, the hijab-defenders ask why the hijab should come under particular scrutiny when Western clothing practices—which, apparently, Western feminists have never criticized—are also oppressive to women (Damiens 2004).

It is undeniable that context shapes meanings: this is, indeed, one of the central theses of this book. This does not, however, mean that intelligible generalizations are impossible: this is another central thesis of this book. We have seen that the hijab in France is polysemic, and some of its meanings—and forms (such as the famous "bandana")—have developed in relation to a specifically French context, even if some of these also are manifested within, or have been exported to, other Western contexts. That said, the polysemic aspects of the hijab are not restricted to France. Conversely, the model of "imposition" in Muslim countries is not the only one.

Delphy refers to Algeria and Iran. The expressions of hijabization in these two countries are, however, not the same, and are not the same in different historical periods. Today in Iran, the chador is associated with a top-down imposition by a male-supremacist fundamentalist state. Thirty years ago, it was associated with an anti-Western revolution that was celebrated even by prominent Egyptian feminist Nawal El Saadawi, who is far from being pro-veiling (Saadawi 1980). More recently, Haleh Afshar and Valentine Moghadam have both suggested that Iranian feminist women are developing various forms of activism within the constraints of the Islamist state and are developing new forms of feminism, although they have differing views as to the degree to which working within state-imposed religion will ultimately be emancipatory (Afshar 1998; Moghadam 2001). In Algeria, notwithstanding the introduction of the shari'a-based family code in 1984, the hijab was not imposed by the state in the late 1980s and 1990s, but by an oppositional movement that terrorized women and was responsible for assassinations of thousands of feminists and other women as well as left-wing male intellectuals. Yet, in Algeria today, hijab-clad activists work alongside non-hijab-wearing feminists against both state and Islamist terrorism and oppression of women, and former champions of the autonomous secular feminist movement such as Khalida Messaoudi are now perceived as co-opted agents of the state.[1]

It is, in fact, as absurd and essentializing to lump "the Muslim world" together as it is to lump the Muslim diaspora. There is, quite simply, *no*

---

1. Personal observations and various personal communications by Algerian feminists from a number of associations, Algiers, June 2007.

such thing as a context-free hijab, and those who wear the "Islamic bandana" in France, along with Western jeans, are arguably as Westernized as those women of Muslim background who are vocally opposed to the hijab as a symbol of women's subjugation.

Many Muslim-background women in France who have raised the alarm about the hijab, irrespective of their position in relation to the 2004 law, have stressed that whatever the individual histories and personal choices of hijab-wearers in France, the hijab is being used politically by Islamist groupings to operate wedge politics. Mimouma Hadjam, for example, has argued that Islamist movements have, since the 1970s, been manipulating ground swells of resentment against racism and anti-immigrant discriminations (Hadjam 2005). Even as she distances herself from the "delirium" of those who, like then prime minister Pierre Mauroy in the early 1980s, "see integrists every-where," and denounces the injustices against Muslims when all religions con-tain their own fundamentalisms, she warns against Islamist manipulation of the effects of economic recession and social exclusion on specific immigrant populations, which has operated in the same way as National Front manipu-lation of resentment by working class and petit-bourgeois whites. She writes of increased family and community surveillance of women, which extends to constant harassment and even violence in certain areas, and exhorts the feminist community not to angelize all Muslims through misplaced colonial guilt, but to "remain in solidarity with immigrant women who are the first to suffer from this situation" (Hadjam 2005). Many other commentators from feminist to mainstream, first and foremost among them being women of Muslim background, have identified the growth of Islamist movements within France as directly related to the emergence of veiling there (for exam-ple, Abada et al. 2004; Châabane 2004; Brouard and Tiberj 2005; Saladin 2005b). These women do not all support the 2004 law, and most of them are critical of NPNS as well.

This does not, of course, instantly transform all hijab-wearers into potential Islamists, no more than every stay-at-home mother is a diehard defender of pro-natalist, "send women back to the home" positions, or every teenage so-called fashion victim an advocate of the objectification of women, or every devout Catholic woman a member of Opus Dei. This political diversity among individuals does not mean, however, that these practices should then be placed outside all feminist critique because some women enjoy them, find them fulfilling, feel duty-bound by them, or are empowered by them. In particular, the religious dimensions of reveiling and associated questions of individual faith and religious transcendence do not make these somehow a taboo subject for feminists. Indeed, given innumerable feminist critiques of religion, including from within, any gendered practice that is justified in the name of religion should particularly invite skeptical scrutiny by feminists.

Boumediene-Thiéry asks if the judgment feminists make of the hijab is not "the imprint of a Western feminism, stained with paternalism—with 'maternalism'—and even colonialism?" (Boumediene-Thiéry 2004). A number of IDLR-inspired texts pick up this theme, such as one by Houria Bouteldja (2004), writing in response to the 2003 *Elle* petition, or another by Lila Benzid-Basset, a rather confused piece posted on the IDLR Web site in 2003, in which "colonializing feminism" is associated, relatively indiscriminately, with sociologist of religion Leïla Babès, NPNS, and the Collectif National des Droits des Femmes (National Collective of Women's Rights, CNDF). The last of these, a small national coalition of various feminist groups, has in fact been very critical of the co-opted and narrow agenda of NPNS.

If the position on secularism taken by the French state in 2003–4 has been amply demonstrated to be hypocritical, and its discourse and actions in relation to its postcolonial minorities has similarly been demonstrated to be racist, the argument that secularism is an attempt to Westernize Muslims is nonetheless a peculiar one. If one follows this Westernization argument to its logical end, then the majority of women in France who identify, ethnically, culturally, and/or religiously, as Muslim, who do *not* wear the hijab, and who support secularism, are "Westernized" (and "stained with colonialism") by definition. Where is their "agency," then, if they are simply the victims of a racist and postcolonial French plot to neutralize their difference?

Moreover, as I noted in chapter 1, it is in the area of women's dress and behavior that the charge of Westernization is most consistently made. Young Muslim men who use the latest in digital technology, go about town in their jeans and T-shirts, and spend their leisure time watching or playing soccer or listening to rap music have apparently not been Westernized. Both their agency and their Muslimness are intact. They have not been neutralized, their identity has not been suppressed. But Muslim women who wear Western dress (whatever else they may happen to think or do) and consider the hijab to be an inferiorizing gender marker, are apparently all co-opted to the French imperialist project. Following the arguments of Kandiyoti (1998) and Lesselier (2005), one may well ask if the charge of Westernization laid against Muslim women who challenge ethnoreligious conservatism does not then lock them into a postcolonial Muslimist identity from which they are unable to escape.

As concerns the claim that hijab-wearing is an expression of a youth identity politics in the face of racism, most recent studies of young Maghrebian-background youth, even those focusing specifically on the hijab question, note that their identity politics are not in most cases specifically tied to an Islamic identity in a religious sense, but a Maghrebi-Muslim identity in an ethnic sense (Wallet, Nehas, and Sghiri 1996; Wihtol de Wenden 2005). This identity expresses itself more through a hybridized popular culture than through specific adherence to religion, which even today is low, including among Turkish immigrants, notwithstanding a "protest position among 18–24 year-olds" (Brouard and Tiberj 2005, 37). While it is true that the hijab is for many a question of both ethnic and religious affirmation, it is an overstatement of the case to suggest that hijabization is solely, or largely, a question of identity politics in the face of racism. The majority of racialized Muslim girls in France who do *not* wear the hijab do not suffer less from racism and are no less in need of an affirming identity.

The final Westernization argument used to deflect critique of hijabization as an argument in opposition to the 2004 law is the reference to Western objectification of women through miniskirts or G-strings and so on, and feminists have been reproached for failing to criticize this objectification at the same time and in the same terms as critiques are made of the hijab (Hamel 2006). This is a specious argument, reminiscent of those made by Islamic revivalists against Western "decadence."

In any case, the claim that those who are critical of the hijab are advocating that all women dress up like *Vogue Magazine* fashion plates or other avatars of their own sexual objectification is tantamount to the creation of a straw woman. Contrary to what is claimed by Damiens (2004), miniskirts and lipstick are not being set up as "infallible signs of women's liberation"—at least not by feminists, even if the malestream media are promoting such imagery. (Damiens was referring to media reports of Kabul beauty salons; I have also criticized such media imagery in Winter 2002c).

I share Damiens' concern about NPNS's "Fashion Solidarity" initiative, in which, with the support of *Elle* magazine, scholarships were offered to young immigrant-background women to go to fashion school (Damiens 2004). It is hardly liberating to encourage Muslim-background women desirous of distancing themselves as much as possible from Islamic conservatism to exchange one form of gender-marked restrictive clothing and its attendant oppressions for another. It is to me self-evident that if we are going to talk about clothing that is gender-marked and that in most cases limits women's freedom of movement, we need to include Western clothing in our critiques. Indeed, it is demonstrable that the hijab (as opposed to chador or jilbab or burqa) limits women's freedom of movement considerably *less* than miniskirts and high heels.

At the same time, let us not attempt to establish equivalences between things that are not equivalent. Fashion, whatever our feminist critiques of it, is not justified as a religious obligation. Western women are not being persuaded that miniskirts or G-strings are indispensable to them being good Christians, for example—although they may well be persuaded that they need to wear them to be a "real" woman. Even here, however, they are mostly not risking various forms of coercion or violence to force them into high heels.

This argument about Western clothing is all the more curious because most Western, and many non-Western, headscarved women *also* adopt Western female fashion: jewelry, jeans or Western-style long skirts, high heels, and even makeup and nail polish. It is no longer—and has not been for some time, even in Muslim countries—a question of "Muslim" versus "Western" dress, but a modern combination of the two.

In any case, it is not because many Western cultural practices are oppressive to women that this suddenly means we cannot criticize oppressive non-Western practices. This would then mean that nobody could criticize anything, as all cultures and societies have oppressive practices, particularly, in the overwhelming majority of cases, toward women. This would leave feminism in a complete impasse and leave us little hope for any improvement in the situation of the world's women.

"Muslim Feminism"?

Many in the anti-ban and pro-hijab lobbies have argued that feminism is not incompatible with religion—including Islam (Boumediene-Thiéry 2004; Delphy 2004). They have further argued that Muslim feminism is a specific expression of feminism; there is no one model for feminism and its diversity should be respected (Boumediene-Thiéry 2004; Collectif Féministes Pour l'Egalité [CFPE] 2006, 1–2). Christine Delphy, speaking for the CFPE, which she co-founded, at the February 4, 2004, meeting at which UEPT was launched, stated that many "young veiled women" were developing a feminism "not against but with Islam—and why not? We have been dialoguing for a long time with those who are Catholic and feminist, Protestant and feminist, Jewish and feminist" (Delphy 2004).

A month later, she participated at a roundtable with Tariq Ramadan and Alima Boumediene-Thiéry on the subject of "Muslim feminism" (Boumediene-Thiéry 2004; Ramadan 2004b), and other variations on the theme have appeared since, sometimes linked to elaborations of a "new" antiracist postcolonial feminism, sometimes not, but often contrasted with a "Western" or "Westernized" feminism that is portrayed as more or less aligned with NPNS, the latter being portrayed as more or less assimilated to the French state.

The question of Muslim feminism has been discussed at length in feminist activist and scholarly literature, some of which I referred to in chapter 1. There is no definitive answer to the question of whether religion and feminism are compatible that might represent some "truth" to which all feminists are bound, and it is a somewhat futile exercise to attempt to find one. I personally do not believe there is anything intrinsically feminist about religion, just as there is nothing intrinsically feminist about many other views that feminists may hold or practices in which they may engage, and I have written at length elsewhere on why I think organized religion in general and monotheistic religions in particular are not compatible with a feminist project (Winter 2001a, 2001b, 2006a, 2006b, 2006c).

The problem, as I see it, with the debate around so-called Muslim feminism is that individual and collective views and practices of some feminists have been conflated with the establishment of general principles about what feminism does or does not mean (Winter 2006d). This has resulted in attempts to code different "feminisms" according to religious beliefs, ethnicity, nationality, and other identity characteristics or particular views held by specific feminists or groups of feminists. While we may argue about what the defining characteristics of feminism might be, one thing that it is *not* is an endlessly adaptable description of various ways of being a woman. Feminism is essentially about the fight to end domination, the key element of this being male domination, and about empowering women to be able to make real choices that do not reproduce relationships of domination either of them or of others. This is the one commonality shared by feminists who are diversely located and subject to different combinations of oppressions; it does not mean that all women, or all feminists, are the same or have to be the same, or, on many matters, think or have to think the same.

We can also argue endlessly about how domination manifests and what to do to combat it, just as we have argued endlessly about women's "agency." But attempts by religious groups to define "Muslim" feminism as based in religion and incommensurable with "white" feminism or any other ethnically or religiously coded "feminism" immediately oblige women who identify as both Muslim and feminist, but not as religious, or not religious in the same way as proponents of Muslim feminism say they should be, to deny part of who they are. Women who are Muslim, lesbian, and feminist are forced into even greater compartmentalization, as the definition of Muslim feminism advanced by most is usually exclusively heterosexual and as such, heterosexist. Women who identify as Muslim in ethnic or cultural terms but as atheist in religious terms are also, by definition, excluded.

Tariq Ramadan (2001, 2004a, 2004b) explicitly situates Muslim feminism within a "different-but-equal" heterosexual family model and Qur'anic law (including polygamy and what he considers the duty of Muslim women to veil). He erroneously conflates all women's movements for equality within society and within the practice of Islam (such as space within mosques or progressive exegeses of the Qur'an), and against oppressive and erroneous applications of Islamic law within Muslim countries, and identifies the lot as "Islamic feminism" (Ramadan 2004b). Yet there is nothing specifically "Islamic" about women's struggles for equality (including within religion, if they happen to be religious), against violence, and against religious fundamentalism.

Unfortunately, Ramadan is not alone in advocating a Muslim (or Islamic) feminism that is based in conservative expressions of religion. In May 2006, the CFPE, by then presided by Cecilia Baeza and Ismahane Chouder, published in its newsletter a "feminist" defense of Hamas (CFPE 2006). Even if I agree with the authors, and with Palestinian women they cite, that the main immediate problem for Palestinian women today is the Israeli occupation, military violence and harassment, and the poverty in which Palestinians live, this does not mean that the agenda of Hamas is not dangerous for women. Articles 17 and 18 of its charter include a definition of women's role that makes them factories for producing men, managers of the household, and the means of educating their sons to follow Islam. Distraction of women from this role is, according to the charter, a Western Zionist plot. Hamas's anti-Semitism also rivals the worst Christendom has dealt out in its own anti-Semitic history. Not only is Hamas the Palestinian wing of the Muslim Brotherhood (article 2) but it is also explicitly tied to fighting all Jews, who are assimilated to both right-wing Zionism and, perversely, Nazism (articles 20 and 31), and who must be killed according to a hadith cited in article 7. Though article 31 indicates that Jews, Christians, and Muslims should be able to live in peace, this article also maintains that such peaceful cohabitation is only possible under Islamic rule. The Palestinian problem is explicitly identified as a religious one and Jihad, to which preparedness to "invade and kill," and be killed is central, is considered an individual duty of Palestinians (article 15).

Using a discourse that is common in explanations for and defenses of veiling in France, the CFPE article, like many other defenses of, or excuses for, Hamas, portrays Hamas's rise to power as a result of the occupation. Yet, as Liliane Kandel notes, this is a classic justification for the rise of extreme-right movements everywhere:

> Germany in the 20s and 30s was also vanquished, humiliated, and exploited by the Allies of the First World War, the SA were also recruited from the ranks of a population that was victim (of unemployment, of poverty, of humiliation).[2]

2. Comment made to French Women's Studies discussion list *Etudes féministes*, Jan. 14, 2007.

Most other defenses of Muslim feminism (or "feminist" defenses of Islamism—the two being sometimes synonymous, sometimes not) are more nuanced, albeit vague on occasion. Alima Boumediene-Thiéry asks, for example, if feminism is necessarily antireligion and argues for a "plural feminism" (Boumediene-Thiéry 2004). Others, more precisely, but far more rarely, particularly in French, distinguish between "Muslim feminism" and "Islamic feminism." For Valentine Moghadam, the term Islamic feminism refers to a "a distinctive, textual practice more than a form of activism," and as such is quite distinct from the feminist practices of Muslim women.[3] In her opening address at a 2006 conference on the topic at UNESCO in Paris, where she then worked as head of the Gender Equality and Development Unit (the conference was co-organized by her and Alain Gresh), she stated:

> Islamic feminism is a discourse of urban educated women (and some men)
> who have reread the Qur'an and studied the historical debates on Islam
> in order to recover their religion from violent and patriarchal interpreta-
> tions and practises, to formulate the participation and rights of women in
> religious language and to give theological legitimacy to a movement for
> women's rights in the Muslim world. (Moghadam 2006)

I personally would call this not "Islamic feminism," but "feminist exegesis of Islamic texts with a view to reforming Islamic practice," but this is perhaps a quibble within the context of this particular discussion. Unfortunately, in French this distinction between Islamic feminism and other forms of feminism practiced by Muslim women is rarely made; the French translator of Moghadam's words uses *féminisme musulman,* and that term is used indiscriminately throughout the conference, thus compounding the confusion. As we saw in chapter 1 with the term Islamism, such confusions have dogged the debate around the hijab and related issues in France (and not only in France), and no doubt many will protest at my definitions as well. Admittedly, sometimes semantic gray areas are difficult to avoid, and disagreements over terminology and meanings are probably set to continue for some time, but one must nonetheless try for clarity, otherwise I do not see how we can progress feminist debate on these issues.

3. Personal e-mail communication, Jan. 23, 2007.

Dounia Bouzar, co-author of a dialogue with Saïda Kada on veiling (Bouzar and Kada 2003), provides such clarity in her discussion of the concept of Muslim feminism, where she makes a distinction that is not exactly the same as Moghadam's but along similar lines of thought. In a 2006 interview with liberal Christian publication *Témoignage Chrétien*, she argued, in answer to the question "Do you consider yourself to be a Muslim feminist?" that it was necessary to define what one meant by Muslim feminist:

> If it means that Islam invented feminism, then no. If it means that one can be both Muslim and feminist, then yes. The method that consists of using only religious texts to claim rights seems to me to be illusory, for it evacuates the universal parameters of feminism. For me, it's never a religion that confers rights. It is always individuals who are going to understand their religion differently in function of their life experience and in function of their access to knowledge. If religion gave rights to women, then we would not have so many illiterate women in Muslim countries! (Bouzar 2006)

Bouzar (who does not veil, no more than does Boumediene-Thiéry, or than do most Muslim women participants in this debate), had in 2003 been nominated by the government to a "specialist person" position on the French Council for the Muslim Faith, but resigned in 2005. She had also been part of UEPT but had withdrawn from the group over the problem of elaborating common values with headscarved women. The latter insisted on remaining within references to the Qur'an to find the unique source of truth, which created a "separation [between them] and other human beings" who did not refer to this text. She nonetheless was of the view that dialogue with headscarved women, rather than considering them as subjugated nonsubjects, would have been the best way to bring them to explore "what underpinned their choice and to deconstruct it" (Bouzar 2006). Bouzar refers to the work of Moroccan feminist scholar Fatima Mernissi, whose work on exegesis of the Qur'an and the hadith in their sociohistorical context "showed that interpretations were male and human" (rather than divinely dictated) (Bouzar 2006). She noted, however, that because Mernissi does not veil, many practicing Muslim women do not consider her a "real" Muslim.

This is a very different argument from those advocating Muslim feminism as corresponding to particular religious practices, and who appear, like Christine Delphy, to seek an inherent "feminist" articulation with veiling.

Many other Muslim secular feminists have spoken out in a similar vein, some, such as Nadia Châabane, who identifies as a "French Muslim woman," denouncing the hypocrisy of those who would defend veiling in the name of "women's rights." Châabane commented on the many Islamist Muslim clerics, both in France and abroad, who protested to President Chirac that prohibition of the hijab was an attack on Muslim rights and freedoms in France. Châabane replied caustically that "in Islam, there is no clergy thus no supreme authority that can speak in the name of Muslims" and that those same men who are defending the rights of veiled women in France fall strangely silent when women's rights are being abused in Algeria, Sudan, or Afghanistan (Châabane 2004; See also Winter 2006c).

"New" Antiracism Made in the USA

Related to the charge of "Westernization" of secular Muslim women is the characterization of the entire French feminist movement, assimilated to NPNS, as racist, and as by definition adopting the agenda of the French state: "Feminist arguments in favor of the [2004] law have been those of the politicians"(Delphy 2006, 61). Delphy claims that the IDLR has, in an innovative way, drawn attention to the imbrication of sexism and racism, hitherto unacknowledged in France, and that the inspiration for this new analysis comes solely from the English-speaking world (Delphy 2005b, 2006).

In an article relatively characteristic of this line of argument, Elise Lemercier, writing on April 26, 2006, on the Web site Oumma.com, generalizes her critique of NPNS to the entire feminist movement. She dismisses the latter in one and a half paragraphs—and without evidence or argument—as being racist, and not up to the level of analysis of race, class, and sex of a supposed U.S. "black feminism" (she uses the English words) (Lemercier 2006). Chiara Bonfiglioli, in her interview with Houria Bouteldja of Les Blédardes, referred to comments from the United Kingdom or the United States on the 2005 riots that "France has difficulty recognizing its racism," as if the problem were acknowledged and solved in these other countries. Bouteldja commented in response that it was indeed a "new" issue in France. Later in the same interview, Bouteldja further commented that racism had been a taboo subject in France, that had not been analyzed, and Bonfiglioli responded that discussions about "race, gender and class . . . the classic triad" were everyday in the English-speaking world but not in France (Bouteldja 2006b). One does wonder where these women have been living all this time.

Fatima Ouassak, writing on the IDLR Web site, is one notable exception to this monolithic and ahistorical view. First, she distinguishes between white and nonwhite feminists—a distinction that, while somewhat simplistic, at least acknowledges diversity within the feminist movement. Second, she distinguishes between NPNS and the rest of the feminist movement, which is, once again, an acknowledgment of diversity as well as of feminist history. Third, she discusses the experiences of imbricated sexism and racism that are specific to women of immigrant background. Fourth, she acknowledges the "good intentions," "sincerity," and antiracist motivation of some white feminists, and even expresses concerns that some women focus on antiracism at the expense of focusing on sexism. Fifth, she argues for a "separatism" of immigrant-background women organizing on their own, without either men or white women (Ouassak 2006). Though none of these arguments and observations are earth-shatteringly new, they nonetheless represent a more nuanced position than is usually the case within the IDLR camp.

The defining characteristics of "black feminism," or, for some, "post-colonial feminism of the English-speaking world," are not spelled out by women who champion them, beyond the claim that sexism and racism are imbricated. Yet, even in France this is hardly a new concept. Not only does antiracist and anticolonial activism in France have a long history, but feminists have been part of that history. They have been part of it as authors and campaigners, such as Olympe de Gouges, author of the *Declaration of the Rights of Woman,* who campaigned against slavery and wrote several antislavery plays (Gouges 1986). They have been part of it as activists with clandestine networks such as the Jeanson network during the Algerian war, which, grouped around Communist Francis Jeanson, collected funds and provided fake passports to Front de Libération Nationale agents operating in France (Hamon and Rotman 1979). They have been part of it as public intellectuals, such as Simone de Beauvoir, Nathalie Sarraute, and Christiane Rochefort, who all signed a "Déclaration sur le droit à l'insoumission dans la guerre d'Algérie" (Declaration on the right to insurbordination in the Algerian War), better known as the *Manifeste des 121* (because of its 121 signatories), in support of Jacobin values of civil disobedience when members of the Jeanson network were arrested and tried for treason (Adamov et al. 1960).[4] They have risked their careers, such as Gisèle Halimi, prominent feminist lawyer who risked prison and disbarment during the Algerian war for going public on the details of the case of sexualized colonialist torture of Algerian resistant Djamila Boupacha (Halimi and Beauvoir 1961). They have risked prison by standing in solidarity with women who spoke out against racism and colonialism, as did Simone de Beauvoir, standing beside Gisèle Halimi (Halimi 2002). Yet Halimi has been vilified by "antiracists" for supporting bans on the hijab. She has also been branded "Zionist" simply because she is of Tunisian Jewish background and because she has spoken out against anti-Semitism. Such accusations are not only unjust but also demonstrate a regrettable ignorance of the history of both feminist and anticolonial and antiracist activism in France.

Such activism has continued in "postcolonial" times, through the work of both "postcolonial" feminist organizations, many of whom I have cited in this book, and solidarity initiatives such as the Réseau pour l'Autonomie des Femmes Immigrées et Réfugiées (Network for the Autonomy of Immigrant and Refugee Women, more commonly known as Rajfire). Parallel to this activism, and often informed by it, has been important theoretical and documentary work on racism and on the situation of "postcolonized" and immigrant women in France, written by both white European women such as Colette Guillaumin, Juliette Minces, Françoise Gaspard, and Claudie Lesselier, and "postcolonized" or immigrant women such as Yamina Benguigui, Chérifa Benabdessadok, Lydie Dooh-Bunya, and many, many others.

Denial of the history of French feminist activist and intellectual antiracism and anticolonialism, accompanied by a sudden fascination for an ill-defined and ahistoricized U.S. "black feminism," or "postcolonial feminism,"

---

4. The full text and signatory list of the *Manifeste des 121* can be found online in the archives of the news monthly *Le Monde Diplomatique*. http://www.monde-diplomatique.fr/2000/09/A/14199.

is peculiar in a country that has so ferociously resisted U.S. ideological and cultural imperialism on other levels. Borrowing from interesting political and intellectual developments elsewhere is one thing: it contributes to the vibrancy of our thought and action. But importing uncritically from one place a set of semidigested ideas that are then imposed imperialistically on another place, deemed not to have any ideas of its own, is spookily reminiscent of the ideology of colonialism.

One might, at a pinch, find ways to let some of these IDLR commentators off the hook for naïveté and youthful ignorance, particularly as concerns feminist antiracist activism. If one is to claim authoritative antiracist feminist voice, however, in debates of such importance as the nest of issues associated with the hijab controversy, then one really should know what one is talking about. For example, Christine Delphy, one of the most prominent feminist intellectuals in France, in proclaiming a "new" antiracist feminism, showed singular contempt for the work—both theoretical and activist—of generations of French feminists of all backgrounds, with which she is very familiar, as she has in the past worked closely with some of them. Her ahistorical claims are all the more startling in the light of her own criticism of the erasure from collective memory of the past struggles and writings of feminists in France, to the point that we are "condemned to keep repeating ourselves."[5]

This removes nothing from Delphy's past contribution to the movement or the strength of her analysis in many areas; indeed, among the writings associated with UEPT, Delphy's are among the most strongly informed by feminist analysis. Her more recent writings associated with IDLR (2005a, 2005b), however, are far less so. Above all, her current position and her association with, and apparent support of, pro-Islamist and anti-Semitic groups and individuals have been received as a great betrayal. Whatever French feminists may have thought of Delphy in the past, there was at least a broad consensus that we were, in most things, more or less on the same side. That consensus has now, for many, evaporated.

5. Plenary address at the international conference Cinquantenaire du Deuxième sexe, Paris, Feb. 1999. See also Delphy 1980.

"The Arab Boy," White Boys, and Violence Against Women

Much of the criticism and often invective launched at "Westernized" or "neocolonial" feminism by women associated with IDLR/UEPT, and the peculiar conflation of this feminism with the French state, has stemmed from opposition to NPNS's co-opted discourse on secularism and violence against women in the *banlieues*.

Some of the objections to NPNS have centered around the *Elle* petition discussed earlier, and the conflation of the hijab issue and that of sexual violence against women is certainly not desirable. That said, it is not certain that this is entirely what the *Elle* petition was doing, even though it mentions them both. Although it linked the issues of secularism, refusal of the hijab and equality for women, it related these to social justice more generally and to ending "all forms of discrimination against French people of immigrant background." In the context of this, it made reference to "the degradation of the conditions of life and the regression of the status" of women of the *quartiers* (Abecassis et al. 2003). In fact, whatever else one may think of the petition, and of NPNS more generally, they did draw attention to links between the socioeconomic conditions in the *quartiers* and ambient violence there—even if their analysis goes less far than one might wish. The petition even explicitly referred to discrimination and social degradation in the *quartiers* as it affected residents in general, although it did state that women suffered particular impacts.

Taken on its own, there is nothing especially startling or worrying about this statement. Poverty and social degradation, and the climate of tension, resentment, and violence they engender, always impact more severely on women, whatever their ethnicity or country of residence: decades of feminist research and testimony attest to this. Houria Bouteldja, however, sees in the *Elle* petition, primarily because it refuses the hijab and calls for a law against all religious signs, an expression of Western "antifeminist" racism and calls its authors "sycophants of the feministo-republicano-bourgeois order, privileged but above all ignorant of social realities" (Bouteldja 2004).

As concerns criticism of media hysteria about "gang rapes in the *quartiers*" by authors such as Guénif-Soulimas and Macé (2006): this point is well made, even though responsibility for creation of this racist "moral panic" lies more solidly in the hands of the media, government authorities, and political spokespersons than those of NPNS. If NPNS, and a certain image of feminism that they incarnate, have been so popular with the media, it is because, like the hijabis, they have served a political purpose: that of constructing "Muslim women" in particular and "Muslims" more generally in specific and polarized ways. This does not mean, however, that the French state has necessarily paid attention to NPNS's concrete demands in more than a tokenistic and image-creating fashion. Even if there was some level of government support in 2003 for NPNS emergency housing projects for women victims of violence and for promotion of respect for women's rights via a booklet distributed in schools, even NPNS noted at that time that there was a disengagement on the part of the state with regard to suburbs "in difficulty," with disastrous impacts as concerned the levels of violence (Benabdessadok 2004, 72).

Not that critics, such as Guénif-Soulimas and Macé (2006), of NPNS and the "moral panic" about violent Arab men are disputing the existence of such violence. This would, after all, be difficult to do, given the police and legal evidence and testimony by women of the same *quartiers* that it does exist. What they dispute, however, is the attribution of responsibility for such violence and what they see as demonization of "the Arab boy." They argue that if poor and racialized men bash and rape, it is the fault of racism and poverty. Demonized and socially excluded, constructed as unassimilable and violent "scum," they have no choice, poor things, but to act out violence against women, particularly if those women are feminist or in some other way transgressive of their allocated roles.

Most repugnant of all is the authors' representation of Samira Bellil—inspired, they say, by commentary by Bourcier (2006)—as "performing gender" in such a provocative and transgressive way that men, "vanquished by this harrowing incursion" into their aggressive street sexuality, are pushed into a brutal return, via rape, of girls to their feminine role and place (Guénif-Soulimas and Macé 2006, 90–91; Kandel 2005, 43–44). This aggressive and competitive interplay between men and women in the *quartiers* is, according to the authors, "much more frequent than the dominant 'victim' rhetoric enables us to see" (Guénif-Soulimas and Macé 2006, 91). This reads like a recasting of the traditional "she asked for it" justification of rape, accompanied by a postmodern pseudo-feminist critique of "victim" rhetoric, made at the same time as a feminist critique of men's "victim" justification for their own violence is, strangely, refuted.

As Kandel points out, Guénif-Soulimas and Macé, in developing their thesis of the abused and demonized "Arab boy," employ a mimetic style that recalls the language used by feminists to describe women's experience of male domination in general and male violence in particular (Kandel 2005, 42–43). Thus, the "Arab boy" is subjected to the "constraint of machism" and "condemned" to act out an "alienating virility" of which he is a "prisoner," "enclosed" within the narrowest expression of an identity that is reduced to the purely physical: sex, "physical substitute for social powerlessness" (Guénif-Soulimas and Macé 2006, 62–77). This manipulation of the rhetoric of "victim" evacuates the questions of power and individual responsibility. To suggest that women are responsible for rape via some transgressive "performance" of gender is as absurd and woman hating as the logic behind religious fundamentalist prescriptions that women must cover themselves up so as not to unleash male violence. On one hand, those who do not have the power, and who are abused, become the aggressors—and are attacked for "playing the victim card" when they speak out. On the other hand, those who do have power, and use it to abuse those less powerful than them, are justified in doing so because they have been disempowered by others, on other levels and in other circumstances, and so are the "real" victims.

Yet many of these "Arab men" defenders rightly criticize the Israeli state for doing the same thing: exploiting an experience of victimization in one context (the Shoah), to justify aggression against others in a different context. How is "I am a victim of racism within French society and enacted by the French state; therefore, I am justified in raping women, particularly those from my class and ethnic group who do not adopt prescribed gender roles" different in essence from "I, and people from my ethnic group, from my family, were victims of European Nazis and their collaborators; therefore, I am justified in persecuting Palestinians, particularly those who resist my domination of them"?

Unfortunately, this "poor, demonized Arab man" idea was picked up and repeated by many, as it was, of course, very convenient. The real injustices and racism suffered by Arab men became a useful pretext for deflecting criticism and for demonizing feminism. This, unfortunately, is not a new strategy, but Guénif-Soulimas's and Macé's book, and reactions to the 2005 riots, gave it new life.

During the three weeks of the 2005 riots (October 27–November 17), over nine thousand vehicles were burned, and extensive damage to and looting of property occurred. As we will see below, women living and working in the same *quartiers* as those where the violence was occurring denounced it as male violence even as they denounced the vicious response of the French state and the state's more general responsibility for socioeconomic degradation in their areas. Other commentators such as IDLR founding member Sadri Khiari, in a 2006 interview with Muslim news site Saphirnews, claimed that this "revolt was legitimate because these young men had no other framework in which to express themselves" within a "situation of racial and ethnic segregation" of the postcolonized. In that context, he concluded, "Burning a car was a political act" (Khiari 2006). This analysis differs little from those made of eruptions of violence by racialized and socioeconomically marginalized men the world over, and on face value it appears sound enough as an analysis of the impact of racism and poverty. The two main problems with it, however, are that (1) women, who are as disenfranchised as men—in fact, far more so, as I have already argued—were not committing this violence, and (2) it was their own areas, and property belonging to members of their own communities, that these men were mostly destroying. Even if race and class exclusion, and institutional repression, are a volatile cocktail, it requires a significant leap of logic to transform the rioters, whose acts included burning alive an elderly woman in a bus, into unchallengeable martyred heros of political resistance. Khiari, like many others grouped around IDLR, takes male experience to be the norm and male violence to be the only justified or even possible response.

Many feminists have pointed out, however, that resentment against racism cannot be an eternal excuse for refusal to take personal responsibility, and Maghrebian-background feminists in particular are starting to tire of this abdication of responsibility by their brothers. Educators and social workers with whom I spoke during the 1990s—a number of whom worked with both young men and women—were unanimous in their observation that, while Maghrebian-background boys definitely encounter often violent racism, so do Maghrebian-background girls. Racism (including acts of violence) against girls, however, is also gendered and sexualized, and its racist dimensions often escape notice within broader discussions violence against women (Winter 1995a, 1998). Girls, however, are more inclined to take responsibility for themselves and do not continually act out violence or refuse to study because of racist discrimination (Winter 1995a). Certainly, discrimination is a disincentive and the women working with school dropouts on their reinsertion within the education system all commented on the undeniable psychological barriers this creates. All the women with whom I spoke maintained, however, that such discrimination and internalized self-hatred should not constitute a pretext for abdication of personal responsibility and should definitely not be a justification for violence against others.

Feminist responses to the November 2005 riots were similar. In an interview with *Libération* in the wake of the riots, Sérénade Chafik, an employee of Family Planning in Aulnay-Sous-Bois, one of the riot-affected areas, criticized the binary logic according to which the rioting boys were either "scum" or "victims." She pointed out that the young men in the area were victims of social exclusion—"out of 450 families that I have met here I can count on the fingers of one hand those who have work"—but also that they were often brought up to be dominant and to control their sisters. The build-up of resentment that they felt was most visibily taken out on cars during the riots, but on a daily basis, whether they were rioting or not, it was taken out on young women (*Libération* online, November 14, 2005).

Ten days earlier, on November 4 (and thus roughly a week into the start of the riots), a coalition of feminist and pro-secular groups had issued an appeal: "No to violence: the call of women!" It was signed by, among others, the national office and various local branches, notably in riot-affected areas, of the Union des Familles Laïques (Union of Secular Families, UFAL), Africa, Le Manifeste des Libertés, 20 ans Barakat (20 years, that's enough, a group of Algerian feminists and their supporters formed in 2004, year of the twentieth anniversary of the introduction of the Shari'a-based family code in Algeria), and the feminist collectives SOS-Sexisme, Ruptures, and Choisir (To choose, the group co-founded by Gisèle Halimi, originally around the issue of abortion rights), and a number of individual women. The declaration began:

We are women, mothers, daughters, sisters. . . . We are nieces, aunts, cousins, friends, lovers, or neighbors. We are half the population. Half the sky. Half the world. Look carefully: on the photos of suburbs in flames . . . not one woman! (UFAL et al. 2005)

The authors went on to criticize Sarkozy, an "irresponsible and bellicose Minister" who was "insulting our loved ones" by claiming to "eliminate scum" from the suburbs, that he would clean with a "Karcher" (high-pressure cleaning hose or water cannon, so named after its German manufacturer). (They are quoting Sarkozy's own words.) They called upon the police to respect "Republican rules," and upon "givers of lessons who look down upon us and do not know us . . . who only negotiate with churches and imams"—a fairly overt reference to the CFCM—"who cut public funding and local police forces, who wave their stick at us at every turn, without ever giving us the means to live decently" (UFAL et al. 2005). They pointed out that behind the politics of these "givers of lessons" was also a contempt for women, who are fighting within the *quartiers,* with insufficient means and insufficient help, to build means to combat all forms of violence.

They also, however, called upon "our [male] children" to "come home and calm down," to stop destroying the local infrastructure and services that they need:

They make us ashamed by agreeing to resemble the insult that is directed against them. No, they are not scum. They are not garbage to be cleaned away. They are human beings who have the right to respect, equality and dignity. Like all citizens, they have rights, but also duties. (UFAL et al. 2005)

As Claudie Lesselier noted the following week, the appeal had given rise to some feminist controversy because its authors had positioned themselves primarily as mothers in relation to the rioters.[6] It nonetheless refused, as Chafik subsequently put it, the binary logic by which men justified their violence by an appeal to the status of victim of racist words and actions.

6. Message posted to Etudes-Féministes (Women's Studies) discussion list, Nov. 10, 2005.

A number of Muslim-background intellectuals in France have also developed critiques of the logic of virility within Islam and Islamic societies (Benslama and Tazi 2004). They would no doubt also be accused by many close to the IDLR of "demonizing Arab men," even though some of the leading scholars doing this work in France are themselves Arab men, which would mean that they are engaging in "Westernized" self-demonization. Among them are Fethi Benslama, who has analyzed the masculinist politics of the Qur'an from a psychoanalytic point of view and authored a "Declaration of insubordination for the use of Muslims and those who are not," of which the title recalls that of the famous *Manifeste des 121,* mentioned above, and in which he refuses to bend to oppressive practices and ideologies advanced "in the name of Islam" (Benslama 2005).

For Nadia Tazi, what she calls "virilism" characterizes a current political culture in the Muslim world that "prohibits access to democracy and modernity" (Tazi 2004, 5). While she acknowledges that Muslim societies have no patent on virilism (she refers to the Bush regime in the United States as a striking example), she argues that just as the West should look to its own backyard, so should Muslim societies, and notes that this is what prompted the *Manifeste des Libertés,* of which she is a signatory. For her, Muslim regimes at this point in time are based on theological law and do not benefit from sufficient "constraints and antidotes" to this. She also argues, referring to Chahla Chafiq's work on Islamist machism, that Islamism, like fascism, "cultivates virile values, fraternity and camaraderie, strength, vital energy, the desire for order and discipline, the sense of sacrifice and the purity of heart dear to youth, and of course, despair" (2004, 8).

Often the criticism of feminists who speak out against male violence in the *quartiers* or against Islamic "virilism" has come not from Muslims but from white French people. This was, for example, the experience of filmmaker Coline Serreau, one of the signatories to the *Elle* petition. Her 2001 film *Chaos* builds a story of solidarity between a middle-class French woman of European background and an Algerian-background woman working in prostitution, contrasted with the self-absorption and self-importance of the European-background woman's lawyer husband, who is representative of white-Western-male cowardice and indifference to the realities of the lives, not only of racialized women, but of those white women close to them. Serreau has been attacked over this film for "stereotyping" Maghrebian women and men, but as she told *Indywire* in 2003, following the U.S. release of the film:

> I've had more criticism from the French middle class and the left than from Muslims. . . . Most of the progressive Muslims and young people appreciate that the truth was told. You know, portraying a father selling his daughter is not an exaggeration. . . . For me there's no difference between a man selling his daughter and the French upper class guy treating his women the way he does. The patriarchy is causing a lot of destruction in varying forms. (Serreau 2003)

Indeed, feminists have been quick to point out that Arab men have no ethnically restricted patent on machism and woman hating. At the same time as NPNS was conducting its campaign against male violence in the *quartiers*, the results of a national study on violence against women were published. The *Enquête nationale sur les violences envers les femmes en France* (ENVEFF), the first of its kind in France, was conducted in 2000 under the auspices of the National Bureau for Women's Rights among a large sample population of 6,970 women. Published in 2003, the results of ENVEFF showed that like rape more generally, gang rapes (around 6 percent of all rapes) were not confined to immigrant ghettos, nor had they necessarily increased dramatically (Jaspard et al. 2003; Jaspard 2005). Mucchielli (2005) draws similar conclusions: Justice Department statistics show the rate of gang rape to be relatively stable between 1984 and 2002. Likewise for convictions: roughly 25 percent of individual convictions for rape are for gang rapes. The ENVEFF study further showed that of the roughly 50,000 women aged twenty to sixty-nine raped in France every year (or 0.3 percent of the total female population of that age), most were attacked in their homes or in other places where they were isolated (Jaspard et al. 2003). Correlated against Justice Department statistics, the findings show that only 5 percent of them reported the rapes to the police, with less than half of these leading to a conviction and most prison sentences not being lengthy.

With the release of the ENVEFF study and the death, on August 1, 2003, of white French actor Marie Trintignant, from blows inflicted five days earlier by her partner, well-known singer and antiglobalization and anti-extreme-right activist Bertrand Cantat, feminist focus was just as strongly on violence against women generally as it was on violence in the *quartiers*. The CNDF, in response both to the ENVEFF study and to the introduction, at the end of 2004, of a "framework law" against gender-related violence in neighboring Spain, started campaigning for a similar law in France (CNDF 2006). Even white *laïcardes* that some have associated with the "moral panic" about "Arab" violence, such as women involved with the Ligue Internationale du Droit des Femmes (LIDF), came out vocally in their denunciation of *all* male violence. When Samira Bellil died in September 2004, the LIDF wrote a short communiqué referring to her as a "resistant," beside both Sohane Benziane and Marie Trintignant, and stressed that the battles women fight are not only those of wars and terrorist attacks but also—and especially—those of the extreme violence of their day-to-day.[7]

Yet, even these broader feminist denunciations of all male violence have come under attack. Elisabeth Badinter (2003), for example, contested even the cautious ENVEFF findings on male violence against women as preposterously exaggerated, especially as concerned the deaths of women at the hands of violent men. This last assertion is bizarre, as such deaths are a matter of police record, not feminist fabulation. Similarly, legal professional Marcela Iacub claimed, in contradiction to Justice Department evidence, that "rape is more punished than murder," despite the fact that the latter has a 50 percent conviction rate (higher than rape), with significantly longer sentences (Iacub 2004; See also Le Bras and Iacub 2003). It would seem that it is not simply the demonization of "violent Arab men" that offends, but the denunciation of male violence against women more generally.

Laïcardes

If criticisms leveled by Guénif-Soulimas and others against NPNS and "feminism" more generally have been so persuasive, it is not only due to the more generalized (and often internalized) misogyny described above, but also, unfortunately, to the discourse and actions of certain *laïcardes,* and

7. http://www.ldif-fr.org/breve.php3?id_breve=17.

not only NPNS. Prominent feminists Anne Vigerie and Anne Zelensky, for example, attracted criticism from both feminists and nonfeminists when they advocated prohibition of the hijab in the streets as well as in public institutions, if violence against women who did not wear it continued (Vigerie and Zelensky 2003).

Other laïcarde positions, although less extreme, have raised similar concerns in their exaggeration of the threat of Islamism. In 2004, for example, secularist feminist Michèle Vianès wrote:

How, in France, did we pass from the "headscarves affair" of 1989, concerning three teenagers whose parents required them to go veiled to school, to the 20th annual congress of the Union des Organisations Islamiques de France (UOIF) at Le Bourget, which on April 19, 2003, assembled ten thousand people (according to the organizers). The women, all veiled, entered the hall through a special door into a segregated space. (2004, 188)

Vianès suggests in response that Islamist activism is directly linked with the generalization of the hijab phenomenon, notwithstanding various identity-politics and status-related motivations on the part of the wearers (189ff). On this, we are in perfect agreement. French Islamism opened the gates to the development of headscarves affairs. French structural and systemic racism, along with a fairly consistent refusal to pay attention to concerns raised by feminists, within a global context of "clash of civilizations" rhetoric, did the rest.

Asked as it is, however, Vianès's question implies that there is now a proliferation of hijabs all over French schools commensurate with the development and high media profile of the UOIF. This implication is patently false: all data provided via the Ministry of Education or the office of mediator Hanifa Chérifi, or any other source, indicate that the number has, despite some fluctuations and peaks, largely tended to remain in a holding pattern since the 1994 polemic.

More recently, on August 11, 2006, the laïcarde polemic was rekindled when Fanny Truchelut, owner of a bed-and-breakfast holiday property in the Vosges in eastern France, asked two female Muslim boarders to remove their headscarves in the television room and dining hall. The MRAP initiated a lawsuit against Truchelut, who on October 9, 2007, was ordered to pay a 1,000 euro fine and 7,490 euros in damages for race discrimination and given a suspended prison sentence of four months. Truchelut appealed against the decision, and a number of pro-Truchelut support groups and weblogs sprang up; her supporters ranged from extreme-right politician Philippe de Villiers and a lawyer associated with his movement, to feminist Anne Zelensky (although when I consulted the site of *laïcard* organization *Riposte Laïque,* on January 20, 2008, Zelensky's texts on the Truchelut affair had been removed).

Some prominent feminists that many have associated with the laïcarde camp, such as Caroline Fourest, spoke out against the position taken by Truchelut and Zelensky's support of her. In her critique, Fourest made a clear distinction between school as a public secular educational institution and other public or private places where "everyone of course does as he or she wishes. Otherwise, the principle of individual freedom is flouted." Truchelut, and Zelensky with her, had, according to Fourest, crossed the "fine line separating the requirement for secularism from intolerance" (Fourest 2007). That Truchelut, an ally of the extreme-right, should take such a position, is predictable. That well-known feminists such as Zelensky should support her is a matter for concern and can only comfort in their views those who would happily write off the entire feminist movement as racist.

Fourest, however, was far from the first secularist feminist to take a public position against such *derives laïcardes* (laïcard drift or slippage). In March 2004, before the first publication of Guénif-Soulimas's and Macé's book, Chérifa Benabdessadok had expressed her own concerns about possible manipulation of the revolt of women from the *quartiers* such as Samira Bellil and Kahina Benziane. She saw the media and the leadership of NPNS as operating precisely the sort of demonization, and homogenization of the *quartiers,* that was subsequently criticized by Guénif-Soulimas, Macé, and others, although she suggested that there may be some softening of that line as time went on (Benabdessadok 2004). She also noted NPNS's explicit distancing from the "historical" feminist movement, that NPNS's leadership characterized as "too bourgeois" and too far removed from the realities of women in the *quartiers,* in a criticism that was ironically prophetic of the same criticism that was to be later leveled at them by the IDLR women. It was this rejection of "historical" feminism that led Mimouna Hadjam,

co-founder of Africa, to take distance from NPNS, with whom she had originally worked:

> Feminism is important, for even if it has been carried and theorized by
> women of certain classes, it is all of us who have benefited. . . . When
> I was thirteen or fourteen, the words of Simone de Beauvoir or Gisèle
> Halimi made it through to us; I could not stand for those words not to be
> heard, for this historical perspective not to be heard. (cited in Benabdes-
> sadok 2004, 71)

Hadjam criticized NPNS for not having an analysis of the underlying
causes of male violence in the ghettos as residing in the ideology and structures of male domination, a lack of analysis that separation from the broader
feminist movement could only exacerbate.

A year after Benabdessadok's article appeared, a curious and unprecedented thing happened: two separate International Women's Day marches
took place in Paris (Winter 2006c, 293). The march was to have taken place
under the auspices of the CNDF and the Marche Mondiale des Femmes
(World March of Women). The CNDF, founded as a national organization
in 1996, has branches in several cities that group representatives of several organizations, such as Coordination des Associations pour le Droit à
l'Avortement et à la Contraception (Coordination of Associations for the
Right to Abortion and Contraception, CADAC); La Coordination Lesbi-
enne (national lesbian umbrella group); Le Planning Familial; Africa; representatives from local groups such as the Association du 3e arrondissement in
Paris, which works in particular on critiques of sexism, racism, and Islamism
(many members are signatories or supporters of the *Manifeste des libertés*);
and so on. The CNDF organizes biannual national meetings and various
campaigns, such as that for the framework law against violence against
women, referred to above, International Women's Day marches, and national
conferences every couple of years.

Ni Putes Ni Soumises split from the originally planned 2005 march
because its leaders accused the CNDF of including UEPT among the signatories to the call to the march and of being sympathetic to the UOIF's
intention of joining the march (Winter 2006c, 293). At an emergency meeting on February 24, 2005, the CNDF overwhelmingly rejected UEPT's

signature. Ni Putes Ni Soumises further claimed that its own fight for secularism and against religious integrism and obscurantism was a "new" combat, thus disappearing feminist history in an inadvertent, and ironic, inverted mirror-image of the IDLR discourse on a "new" feminist antiracism. The NPNS call to a March 6 demonstration (instead of the planned March 8 one), titled *Pour un nouveau féminisme* (For a New Feminism), was co-signed by the Planning Familial (more familiarly known as le Planning), the secularist feminist group and publication *Prochoix,* ATTAC, Femmes Contre les Intégrismes (Lyons-based antifundamentalist group), Femmes Sous Lois Musulmanes (Women Living Under Muslim Laws), the Mouvement des Maghrébins Laïques (which had, in October 2003, issued a petition calling for a law against religious insignia in schools), and SOS-Homophobie, among others. The Planning was one of the main "defectors" from CNDF, although individual members and local branches dissented from this national position, remaining allied to the CNDF. The call was also signed by prominent individuals such as Laure Adler (director of France Culture national radio and author of, among other things, a book on women in politics), Tewfik Allal of the *Manifeste des libertés,* Elisabeth Badinter, Yamina Benguigui, Liliane Kandel, Rachida Brakni (who had starred in Serreau's film *Chaos*), Bertrand Delanoë (the same openly gay Paris mayor who was later to preside the naming of Place Jean-Paul II), Socialist politicians Laurent Fabius, Jack Lang, Dominique Strauss-Kahn, Ségolène Royal, and François Hollande.

The call by NPNS reiterated feminist principles with which no one in the CNDF, nor I, would disagree, but what angered other feminists, apart from the accusation of association with UEPT (published by NPNS in a separate document), was the following:

> Through this new combat [for secularism as a core value of the combat against violence against women] we commit ourselves to the emancipation of women and men, here and elsewhere. (NPNS et al. 2005, 18)

It mattered little that in the following sentence the authors acknowledged their "historical debt toward those women who rose up so that all women could gain rights." The framing of the feminist battle for secularism as "new" contradicted that acknowledgment.

In reply, Maya Surduts and Suzy Rotjman, of the CNDF, criticized the "binary logic" of NPNS and recalled the long fight of feminists against discriminations and violence against women and against all religious fundamentalisms:

> In 1990, it was to respond to Christian integrist opponents of abortion that CADAC was created. It has to its credit, among other things, the adoption, in 1993, of a law making attempts to hinder abortion [which is legal in France] an offence. The demonstration of November 25, 1995, that grouped 40,000 people responding to the call of 140 associations, trade unions and political parties, and that led to the creation of the CNDF in 1996, contained as one of its four slogans: "Against the new rise of a moral order." . . .
>
> Let us return to more recent history. October 2003: at the opening of the European Social Forum in Paris, during the European Women's Assembly, Chahla Chafiq-Beski, Fatima Lalem of the Planning Familial and Maya Surduts of the CNDF published a protest in *Libération* against the presence of Tariq Ramadan at the ESF. (Surduts and Rotjman 2005, 21–22)

They further pointed out that in 2004, in the midst of the hijab debate, the CNDF had publicly stated that it was urgent for the whole women's movement to rally round the fight against fundamentalisms and the denunciation of the hijab as an instrument of women's oppression and not "a symbol of emancipation and revolt" (Surduts and Rotjman 2005, 22). They also stressed, however, that

> women's struggle is not limited to *mixité* and secularism, it is far broader than that.[8] It includes the fight against the patriarchy in its entirety, against liberalism, and against capitalist globalization. The antiglobalization combat is entirely legitimate, even if the problem of alliances within it gives rise to strong confrontations.

---

8. The question of *mixité* ("mixity," or working in a mixed-sex environment) in France does not mean that women-only spaces should not be respected; CNDF is not mixed, although NPNS is, and women's centers in France have never been mixed, with extremely rare exceptions. The issue of *mixité* concerns the fight against social segregation and for equal access of women to all public spaces, professions, and cultural and social endeavors.

Women's oppression and exploitation impregnate every pore of society. We combat it everywhere, without exception. (Surduts and Rotjman
2005, 23–24)

This is a key message of a secular antiracist feminism. As Surduts and
Rotjman point out, the choice should not be between a single-issue focus
and recognition of the many different arenas and priorities of women's fight
for rights. Nor should it be between fundamentalism and "fashion solidarity," or between irreducible "Muslimism" and co-optation to state agendas.
As four Maghrebian-background women, explaining why they would not
demonstrate either with the Collective of French Muslims (close to UOIF
and to UEPT), or with NPNS, wrote:

We are citizens of France, Westerners of diverse backgrounds, practicing
a religion or not, but we all share the same ideal of equality between men
and women. We have the good fortune to live in a country where those
who wish to practice their religion can do so, and those who claim their
membership of the culture of Islam while still displaying their atheism can
also do so without risking stoning or certain death in some countries. It
is in the name of this freedom that we enjoy and that we defend, that we
refuse to demonstrate with the CMF just as we have not demonstrated with
NPNS, which is attempting to minimize our demands and our aspirations.
(Akrouf et al. 2005)

Ni NPNS ni IDLR (Neither NPNS nor IDLR)

The French 2003–6 debates over who "owns" feminism, or who invented
which bits of it, and what it should be focusing on, are a fascinating reminder
of how easily feminist history is rewritten and the principles of feminism
distorted and put to the service of other ends that may not only be nonfeminist but even anathema to the longer-term protection of all women's rights.
They also, however, highlight a problem that has been central to the hijab
debate from the outset and has become particularly acute in recent years,
namely, the tension between strict religious neutrality of the public sphere
and respect for school discipline on one hand and the protection of religious and individual freedoms on the other. The difficulty that the French,
whatever their ethnic background, have had—and increasingly, others in

the West are having—is that it is a non-Western religious emblem that has introduced itself into a Western secular space. And it is a gendered and racialized one.

Which brings us back to what is ostensibly the central question: that of the fundamental right of access for all to public secular schooling. Even if this access has still been made available for hijab-wearing girls through the option of study by correspondence, it is not the same as access to a neutral *social* educative space. It also, ironically, exacerbates the isolation from others of which teachers have often complained concerning the behavior of hijab-wearing girls.

The questions around which most feminists, bar some women associated with IDLR or close to Islamist groups, have found themselves in disagreement from the outset have not been around the meaning of the hijab or the dangers of Islamism, although they have argued over the extent to which those dangers are present. They have been around the most appropriate interpretation and application of secularism:

• How does one ensure *both* access to public schooling for all girls, who demonstrably have the most to gain from its religious neutrality, *and* the rigorous protection of that neutrality?

• Is one to punish the few for the greater good of the many? And even if one is to accept this strategy, does that punishment have the desired effect?

• To whom should neutrality apply (staff, students), and to what extent should it apply?

• How does it interact with, and guarantee, freedom of speech and conscience?

• How does one protect the religious neutrality of public school without scapegoating a particular ethnic group and within that group, individuals of a particular sex?

Feminists such as Françoise Gaspard and many other signatories of the May 2003 document against "laws of exclusion," as well as of the 2004 UEPT document, argue that prohibition is not only discriminatory but that it will *not* solve the problem (Aït-Mohamed et al. 2003; UEPT 2004). On the contrary, they believe it is likely to push women into a corner and encourage them to harden their religious stance as an expression of rebellion against the state, thus "driving them into the arms of integrists," as Alima

Boumediene-Thiéry put it in 1989 (cited in Assouline 1989). (I note in passing, however, that Boumediene-Thiéry appears less concerned about such a danger today, as she reframes her arguments around the idea of Muslim feminism.) This argument does not, however, necessarily hold up. In fact, the 2004 law has been mostly well followed. Even if some young women are resenting the obligation to remove their hijabs in schools, history has demonstrated that similar sacrifices were made by Catholics in the bumpy (and as yet incomplete) ride toward secularism in France (Tribalat 2003; Winter 2006c).

The argument, made by the signatories to the 2003 petition, that if Islamist agitation is part of the problem, it needs to be addressed at its source and not through a law on insignia in schools, has greater weight. Certain aspects of that agitation could be addressed under article 35 of the 1905 law, which prohibits religious personnel from inciting resistance to the law or attacks on other groups of citizens. At the same time, there is an extent to which guarantees of religious freedom (also provided for under the 1905 law), and freedom of speech more generally, would prevent significant censorship of Islamists in France—outside obvious instances of hate speech such as anti-Semitic attacks. One can sanction force; one cannot so easily sanction manipulation. Like agency, defining manipulation is not the business of law. What one *can* do is keep religious proselytism—and related potential for manipulation—out of the public educative space.

The signatories to the May 2003 petition also note that, apart from their concerns about the impact of prohibition, the nest of socioeconomic problems out of which the hijab issue has emerged need to be dealt with in other ways, both within the school system and outside it. On this, I can but agree, but the absence of political will to address these problems is evident. If anything, the combination of state neglect of disenfranchised populations and punitive legislation aimed at those same populations has been exacerbated under the 2002–7 right-wing government and looks set to continue in this vein since the 2007 election of Sarkozy as president, notwithstanding Amara's Plan banlieues (see chapter 6). The deleterious impact of Sarkozian politics is particularly pronounced for women. Referring to the 2006 law on immigration, for example, Lesselier writes that under that law, the majority of women fall into the camp of "undesirables": "When the regularization of *sans papiers* has become almost impossible and when all foreigners are put in a situation of precarity, women are even more badly affected, for they are subjected to inequalities and to violence because they are women."[9]

Indeed, if young women from immigrant families living in ghetto suburbs and donning the hijab are marginalized, how much more so are their mothers? Perhaps a little less attention to supposedly demonized "Arab boys" or the headscarved "hostages" of a situation not of their making, and a little more attention to the extreme marginalization of their mothers, might be helpful. Perhaps in particular some attention to the voices of those mothers, such as those who responded to the 2005 riots (UFAL et al. 2005), or incarnated within Djitli's "docu-fiction" (2004), would point to other solutions than a wholesale embracing of either religion or state agendas. For it is the mothers who bear the brunt of socioeconomic exclusion and cultural denial, even by their own children, and even when those children are supposedly "re-engaging" with their culture. They also bear the collective memory of women's oppression and resistance within their patriarchal cultures of origin, as Djitli spells out to her docu-fictitious daughter: "The women who have gone before us, and before you, Nawel, have abandoned their veil. . . . Do you think they have thrown it overboard, or cut it up, without knowing what they were doing? Do you take them for idiots?" (Djitli 2004, 27). I would read these words to Alma and Lila Lévy, whose words of condescension concerning their maternal grandmother return to trouble me. Even if one could in part attribute their words to the arrogance of an adolescence bedazzled by the bright lights of the media, they remind me, yet again, that if men, and women, are both encouraged to carry on the memory of men's experience and the patriarchal order, they are actively *dis*couraged from valuing the memory of women's experience (and women's resistance to that order).

In the various championings of the causes and agency of victims and resistants in the hijab debate, the experiences and voices of mothers barely rate a mention. Surely, any serious conversation about addressing the problems of socioeccomic exclusion and legally sanctioned discrimination should start with them: not to engage in some neopatriarchal ideological valorizing

9. Comment posted to the French women's studies discussion list *Etudes féministes* on Mar. 30, 2006.

of motherhood, but to take women seriously as social and economic actors. Not only do these women merit such attention in their own right, but if more energy were put into addressing the needs of the mothers, the needs of the sons and the daughters might, to some extent at least, start looking after themselves. Unfortunately, as Vianès wrote with relation to secularism, the political will to do this is glaringly absent at this point in time.

Whether or not the hijab is an expression of agency or piety or submission or revolt against racism or ethnic chic or whatever, is a debate to be had, and it is an important one, as is the question: why does this piece of cloth matter so? At the same time, it is not a debate that can be resolved through laws and procedures dealing with secularism. Nor can it be claimed that outlawing the hijab from schools will *in itself* guarantee women's equality, as it quite obviously will not.

As Surduts and Rotjman noted, women's rights are assaulted in many areas. Moreover, many of those assaults, which are waged through the vehicle of consensual liberalism, cannot be combated by legislation, nor is it entirely desirable that they should. Should one force-feed anorexics? Should one force women who wear high heels into sensible footwear that will not shorten their Achilles tendons and deform their backs? I am one of the many to take issue with Vigerie and Zelensky's suggestion that the hijab should be prohibited even in the streets if those who do not wear it are subjected to violence. The question of male violence against women is much more complicated than this and making prescriptions about adult women's clothing and behavior in their private lives is, as Fourest argued in relation to the Truchelut case, an attack on individual freedoms. Also, what of those women who are subjected by non-Muslim men, and, unfortunately, by some non-Muslim women, to the violence and harassment of sexualized racism because they wear the hijab? If pro-IDLR Caroline Damiens and I have one point of agreement, it is that "women's bodies are not a battleground" (Damiens 2004).

Many have argued that prohibition of the hijab is schools in also an attack on individual freedoms, and scapegoats those who have the least power in the situation: teenage girls. Which brings us back to the central question of how far secularism should reach in governing the choices and behavior of individuals.

Annie Sugier and Linda Weil-Curiel, writing at the time of the 1989 debate, stressed that under no circumstances should the state, or feminists, support—even in the name of "religious freedom"—practices that "amputate another fundamental freedom, that of women" (Weil-Curiel and Sugier 1989, 46). Claudie Lesselier, writing at the same time, stated that:

> As an opponent of nationalism, I oppose first of all that which is constructed and legitimated in my name. Since I am French, the struggle, which is mine, against integrism and against the oppression of women under Muslim laws, will not make me support in any way the French state, even "secular and Republican," or "French civilization," even declared "homeland of human rights," and will never make me forget, even tactically, on what oppression that state and that civilization have long functioned. (Lesselier 1989, 43)

Yet Lesselier is also a strong defender of secularism and critical of the discourse of both the IDLR and NPNS. She, like many other French women of a range of ethnic backgrounds and religious beliefs or lack thereof, is a secular antiracist feminist caught in the middle—or pushed out of the debate altogether, as it is hijacked by other agendas.

As Coline Serreau suggested in her interview, it is almost as if the majority of secular Muslims are more problematic for everyone than the minority of fundamentalists and hijab-wearers, whether fundamentalist or not (Serreau 2003). And many of these secular Muslim women, such as Nadia Châabane, writing in January 2004, are tired of having to justify their pro-secular stance:

> Everyone's a bit tired of talking about this headscarf story, I'm also over it. I'm forever being asked to comment on it and I have ended up thinking that those of us who are unveiled pose a bigger problem than the others! We upset these communitarian divisions [clivages communautaires] that they have constructed and bring them back toward another vision of the world that bothers them.[10]

10. Personal e-mail communication, Jan. 26, 2004.

This vision that "bothers" carries the echo of the "troublesome" feminist voice to which the media turned so many deaf ears in 1989. It is a vision according to which Muslim culture and Western secular democratic values can be perfectly compatible without undermining the specificities and integrity of either. It is a vision that refuses collusion with either church or state in their manipulation of women's "agency" or "rights."

Conclusion

French Lessons for the West?

IT IS A CAUSE for deep concern that in the 2003–5 period, two or three thousand hijab-clad girls, the French Islamist "brotherhood," and a few thousand men behaving very badly indeed for three weeks in 2005 managed to hijack the French race debate, not to mention the debate on women's rights, with the main government responses being punishment on one level and courting the religious right on another. It is even more a cause for concern that this hijacking has been so successful internationally.

In 2005, I traveled to a number of countries on different continents, presenting seminars and conference papers in various fora within women's studies, French studies, and sociology. On each occasion, I suggested a range of topics to the organizers, and except for the Philippines, where post-9/11 militarism and violence captured greater interest, the topic that always appealed most was the French debate over the hijab and the 2004 law outlawing conspicuous religious insignia in schools. This interest shows no sign of waning, as I am still asked to talk about this topic, in Australia and elsewhere. Everyone seems to have an opinion about it—usually a very strong one—and at the same time, most lack sufficient information to enable that opinion to be an informed one.

At my seminars, audience members invariably expect either that I will confirm their position, providing more detailed arguments, or that I will oppose it, and have thus come prepared for battle. For example, at the University of Maryland in 2005, one French academic living in the United States, who supports the law, fully expected me, being of Western English-speaking

344

background, to strongly and unequivocally oppose it. He had thus prepared himself for a lively debate as he expressed his strong disagreement. He was somewhat taken aback, in fact even a little deflated, on discovering that in fact, I did not share what appears to be the dominant view among the English-speaking intelligentsia, feminist movement, and broader left. He did, however, on discovering that I did not express unequivocal support for the law either, come to see me at the end of my seminar saying, "But really, you must agree that the government had no choice but to adopt this law, it was a crisis situation." He was not entirely satisfied with my response: "Well, yes and no."

And so I find myself continuing: "Well, yes and no." Yes, the French state, like most of the world's states and certainly all of its Western ones (most of which are former or continuing colonial powers), is demonstrably racist. No, the law is not simply another manifestation of this: things are far more complex. Yes, prohibition of religious insignia in schools and public services is crucial to preserve the neutrality of public space. No, in theory, a new law was not essential to do this: the legal framework is technically already there through the 1905 law; what is needed is the political will to apply it (Vianès 2004, 273). Yes, in practice, given the polemic over interpretation of the 1905 law and the position established by the 1989 Council of State *avis,* the 1905 law probably needed clarification and reinforcement. No, the 2004 law does not do the job well: as Alec Hargreaves has commented, a "selective" ban on certain "conspicuous" religious insignia, rather than all of them, is "discriminatory and off-target."[1] Yes, appeals to "women's emancipation" as a justification for a law that should be dealing with something else entirely are spurious not to mention paternalistic. No, defense of the "agency" of nine to eighteen year old girls is neither a strong nor even a sensible argument in opposition to this or any other institutionalized gendered racism. "Agency" is not the business of law, and its existence or otherwise cannot be decided by law. Yes, hijab-wearing girls are being stigmatized while a range of other socioeconomic and political problems are not being addressed. No, the hijab as currently worn in France is not simply an innocuous choice of clothing, nor even simply an innocuous expression of personal cultural or

---

1. Personal e-mail communications, Sept. 17 and 18, 2006.

religious identity: whatever their personal motivations, the girls and their clothing are a banner being waved in Islamist wedge politics. Yes, the hijab is a gender marker and a marker of adherence to an extremely conservative (and, as we have seen, by many accounts erroneous) interpretation of religion and often to religious fundamentalism. No, it is not *only* about adherence— or subservience—to religious conservatism for the young women who are choosing to wear it in France: there is hijab, and then there is hijab.

These last questions, however, are part of a wider debate and cannot be addressed by a law on religious insignia in schools: even a more comprehensive one than that adopted in 2004.

Had I been education minister in France in the 2002–4 period, or in 1989 or 1994 for that matter, I truly do not know how I might have responded in the face of a range of competing voices: teachers clamoring for support and for strong directives on the hijab in difficult situations; Islamic and Islamist lobbies pushing for presence and influence; antiracist lobbies claiming persecution of headscarved girls; headscarved girls themselves claiming a right to wear it and even going on hunger strike to defend it; a highly divided nongovernmental left waging war around me and with me; and feminists aligning themselves with a range of positions, all in the name of women's rights. All I can say is, that like some feminists, my position has tended to become more "intransigent" (but definitely not *laïcarde*) over the years, as Islamist manipulation has become more multifaceted and widespread and the extent of it more obvious to me.

It is impossible, however, to legislate against manipulation per se. "Bodyguards," "advisers," or simply parents cannot be sanctioned by law simply for holding and expressing opinions, unless they start distributing religious tracts within school grounds or otherwise committing some disruptive or proselytizing act. The hijab has been targeted because it is targetable. It is visible, it is concrete, it is accompanied by behaviors and political campaigns that are clearly identifiable as disruptive and as disturbing school neutrality. That its targeting in some cases is accompanied by anti-Muslim prejudice, is an argument that I certainly do not contest. But the opposite is also true, and true as frequently, if not more so: school teachers and administrations, via the behavior of girls and the militancy of their families, "bodyguards," and "advisers," have since 1989 been held hostage every bit as much as have the girls. To claim otherwise is to deliberately close one's eyes to what has become plainer and plainer to see. To claim otherwise is to hold in contempt the lives and views of most French Muslims who do not support this behavior, and particularly Muslim girls and women.

That women believe what they wish and wear what they wish, if not harming others, is one thing. The ways in which these beliefs and appearances are coded and put to the service of other agendas is quite another. Women are neither complete automatons, socially and culturally pre- and overdetermined, nor atomized individuals, operating independently of context and choosing among an unlimited range of possibilities. Operating within a context of domination, women are always at some level and to some degree "bargaining with patriarchy" (Kandiyoti 1991). Whether this is a colonialist or postcolonialist or anticolonialist patriarchy, it is still a patriarchy.

That hijab-wearing girls are often complicit with patriarchal agendas, and manifest their "agency" through the expression of a variety of deeply felt personal reasons for donning the hijab, does not make the use of them by adults with other agendas any less suspect. The use of girls to operate Islamist wedge-politics enables the playing of a "feminist" card: any sanctioning of their behavior thus becomes not only racist and "Islamophobic," it is also sexist (as the IDLR does not hesitate to tell us). What is ignored, however, is that Islamist (or even simply "antiracist") use of the girls to fight men's battles is just as sexist and instrumentalizes them far more completely than the most intransigent secularist response.

Like many feminists in France, however, I remain caught between two positions. On one hand, I support the intransigent application of secularism accompanied by a denunciation of the dishonest discourse of "religious freedom" behind which fundamentalist agendas hide (whether Catholic, Islamic or other). On the other hand, I distrust a hypocritical and racist state that not only fails to fully apply the principles of secularism that it claims to defend, but also does not have the interests of women, and most particularly not racialized women, high on its agenda.

Which is why I agree with Nadia Tazi (2004) that if one is to address the problems of male domination, traditionalism, and religious interference in secular public space, one must begin with one's own backyard. If one is to uphold French principles of secularism, comprising both religious freedom and the strict religious neutrality of government and public institutions, one must begin with the French government's relationship with the Catholic Church. In the year marking the one hundredth anniversary of the 1905 law separating church and state, the main breach of that law came not from headscarved schoolgirls but from the government itself. In its publicly orchestrated mourning of Pope Jean-Paul II, the government clearly was breaking the 1905 law it had so ardently defended the year before, and in which it is stated that the Republic does not recognize any religious faith. The argument that the Pope is technically a head of state (the Vatican being considered a separate state with a seat at the United Nations, as we have seen), even if it may have enabled the government to circumvent a legal challenge, is an extremely lame one. (It is lame at the level of the United Nations as well but that is another story.)

Even when wresting political, economic, and institutional power from religion, the state does not automatically become women's friend. How much less of a friend is it, then, when it continues to operate shady deals with conservative religious lobbies—both Catholic and Islamic in the case of France—while claiming to champion secularism? How much less of a friend is it when it continues to abuse the rights of the racialized while claiming to favor equality of all? How much less of a friend is it when it instrumentalizes women, whatever their background, even in the name of their "emancipation," while all the time silencing their voices, and in particular feminist voices?

The subject of the French hijab debate is indeed as irritating for me as was the subject of women for Simone de Beauvoir, for many reasons. Above all, it is irritating because, once again, it is condemning those feminists who have long spoken out about the manipulation of their bodies, lives, and voices by *both* church and state, to keep repeating themselves. As one might repeat a lesson not yet learned.

Appendix

ഇ

Glossary

ഇ

References

ഇ

Index

Chronology

Date	French politics	Race/hijab debate
1981	Mitterrand elected president Socialist government Pierre Mauroy prime minister	
1983		Shooting in Les Minguettes leading to national march against racism
1984	Resignation of Mauroy following debate on funding to private schools Laurent Fabius prime minister	Second national march against racism National demonstration in support of private (Catholic) schools
1986	RPR/UDF government elected: first period of cohabitation (Socialist president, right-wing government) Jacques Chirac prime minister	Bombing in Tati Department Store, rue de Rennes (Left Bank), Paris: 7 people dead, 55 injured
1988	Mitterrand reelected president Dissolution of government Socialists reelected Michel Rocard prime minister Lionel Jospin education minister	
1989	Council of State ruling: hijab not illegal in schools unless provocation, proselytism, or propaganda or disturbing order in school	September: First headscarves affair in Creil
1990		Kherouaa affair in Montfermeil

Date	French politics	Race/hijab debate
1991	Edith Cresson prime minister	Yilmaz affair in Angers
1992	Pierre Bérégovoy prime minister Jack Lang education minister	Council of State overturns Kherouaa expulsion
1993	RPR/UDF government elected: second period of cohabitation Edouard Balladur prime minister Pasqua immigration / nationality laws François Bayrou education minister First Bayrou circular	Aoukili affair in Nantua
1994	Second Bayrou circular on "ostentatious" religious insignia Hanifa Chérifi appointed government mediator in hijab cases in schools	Second headscarves affair Goussainville expulsions Seventeen students expelled from Faidherbe high school in Lille Council of State overturns Yilmaz expulsion
1995	Jacques Chirac (RPR) elected president Alain Juppé prime minister	Council of State upholds Aoukili expulsion (disturbance to order) Bombing in St-Michel RER station: 8 dead, 117 injured
1996	François Mitterrand dies	Council of State upholds Lille expulsions but denies education minister's petition to confirm expulsions in Strasbourg Expulsion of *sans-papiers* from Paris churches
1997	Socialists reelected to government: third period of cohabitation (with President Chirac) Lionel Jospin prime minister Claude Allègre education minister	Islam et laïcité group founded
1998	Law reducing the working week from 39 to 35 hours in the public service	Unemployed people's movement places strong pressure on government
1999	PaCS law (Civil Solidarity Pact)	Council of State upholds an expulsion for inappropriate gym wear

Date	French politics	Race/hijab debate
2000	Parity law Jack Lang education minister	
2001	9/11: Security Plan Vigipirate activated	Explosion in Total's AZF plant in Toulouse: 30 dead, more than 2,500 seriously injured
2002	Chirac (now UMP) reelected presi- dent in second round runoff with Le Pen UMP/UDF government Jean-Pierre Raffarin prime minister Nicolas Sarkozy minister for the inte- rior: hardens the line on security Luc Ferry education minister	Lyons "bandana affair" Siege of Ramallah; wave of anti- Semitic attacks in France Sohane Benziane murdered Samira Bellil's book *Dans l'enfer des tournantes* Taguieff's book *La nouvelle judéophobie*
2003	Stasi Commission Sarkozy immigration law CFCM set up	Third headscarves affair Lévy sisters' expulsion in Aubervilliers National march NPNS July 14 exhibition *Les Mariannes d'aujourd'hui* Geisser's book *La nouvelle islamophobie*
2004	Law against conspicuous religious insignia in schools	UEPT Le Manifeste des libertés Fadela Amara's book *Ni putes ni soumises* Demonstrations for public school
2005	Pope dies: official mourning Dominique de Villepin prime minister CFCM elections Cité nationale de l'histoire de l'immigration Law on teaching positive effects of colonization in schools (repealed after protest)	Two women's day marches RER D hoax "anti-Semitic" attack IDLR Riots October 27–November 17 following accidental death of two young men fleeing police "Citizen's enquiry" report impli- cating French government in Rwanda genocide

Date	French politics	Race/hijab debate
2006	Second Sarkozy immigration law Ségolène Royal Socialist presidential candidate Parvis Notre-Dame renamed Place Jean-Paul II by Socialist city government of Paris	Demonstrations against youth employment contract (Contrat du premier emploi)
2007	January: Nicolas Sarkozy confirmed as UMP presidential candidate May: Sarkozy elected president June: Fillon government	October–November: wave of public sector strikes
2008	January: Fadela Amara's *Espoir banlieue* April: annulled marriage (nonvirginity of spouse) June: a "burqa"-wearing Moroccan women refused nationality June: CFCM elections	*Sans-papiers* occupy the Annex to the Paris Trade Union Center August: Rwandan commission issues report on 1994 genocide implicating French government and military

Glossary

banlieues: suburbs, often with a connotation of poverty and high proportion of immigrants

beur: French back-to-front slang for *arabe,* referred originally to those born in France of Algerian background; now generalized to refer to any French people of Maghrebian background

beurette: female *beur,* often used to patronizing or ironic effect

chador: Iranian term for long black tunic-like garment and face veil, covering all but the eyes and hands

cités: housing projects

communautarisme: communitarianism, ethnic- or religious-based insular identity politics

droit du sol: birthplace right, nationality right based on being born in France

Ennahda: renaissance, also the name of outlawed Tunisian Islamist party, formerly Mouvement pour la Tendance Islamique

fatwa: Islamic legal opinion; used as "sentences" by hardline Iranian Islamists, but this is not their usual function nor status under traditional Islamic law

foulard: light piece of material usually folded into a triangular shape and worn on the head

harki: Algerian having fought on the French side during the Algerian War of Independence

hijab: modern Islamic headscarf; original meaning: "curtain" or "separation"

indigène: term used by the French colonial state to refer to colonized peoples particularly in Algeria; it is considered racist, like saying "the natives" in English

jihad: struggle, or, for Islamists, holy war

jilbab: long tunic-like garment covering all but the face and hands

khimar: headscarf

laïcard(e): pejorative term designating an ultrasecularist, especially one in favor of banning the hijab and other religious insignia from schools

laïcisme: rigorous and intransigent attachment to French secularism

laïcité: French secularism as enshrined in political philosophy and the 1905 law on the separation of church and state

niqab: face veil

ostensible: conspicuous

ostentatoire: ostentatious in the sense of being highly conspicuous, even provocative, but not "showy"

oumma: French spelling of *umma*

pied noir: white French citizen born or having grown up in colonial Algeria

quartier: literally, "local area," usually designates working class or immigrant areas in large cities and their inner suburbs

rebeu: back-to-front slang for *beur*

rebeuse: feminine form of *rebeu*

sans-papiers: literally, "without papers," designates illegal immigrants (that is, people without residency papers)

Shoah: Holocaust

tawhid: unity, also the name of a bookshop and publishing house run by Tariq Ramadan and his brother Hani in Lyons, and the name of a supermarket chain run by the Muslim Brotherhood in Egypt

umma: community of believers, also means nation

References

Abada, Madiha, et al. 2004. "Manifeste: Retrouver la force d'une laïcité vivante" (Manifeste des libertés). *Libération,* Feb. 16. http://www.droitshumains.org/txtref/2004/france-03.htm.

Abecassis, Eliette, et al. 2003. "Notre appel à Monsieur Jacques Chirac, président de la république." *Elle,* Dec.

Abu-Lughod, Lila. 1998. "The Marriage of Feminism and Islamism in Egypt: Selective Repudiation as a Dynamic of Postcolonial Cultural Politics." In *Remaking Women: Feminism and Modernity in the Middle East,* ed. Lila Abu-Lughod, 243–69. Princeton: Princeton Univ. Press.

Adamov, Robert, et al. 1960. "Déclaration sur le droit à l'insoumission dans la guerre d'Algérie." *Vérité-Liberté,* Sept. 6.

Afshar, Haleh. 1998. *Islam and Feminisms: An Iranian Case-Study.* Basingstoke, UK: MacMillan.

Ahmed, Leila. 1992. *Women and Gender in Islam: The Historical Roots of a Modern Debate.* New Haven: Yale Univ. Press.

Aïchoune, Farid. 1989. "La Mecque du onzième." *Le Nouvel Observateur* 1300 (Oct. 5): 18–19.

———. 1994. "Intégrisme: Les soumarins de l'Islam." *Le Nouvel Observateur* 1304 (Nov. 2): 86–88.

Aït-Mohamed, Abdelkader, et al. 2003. "Oui à la laïcité, non aux lois d'exception." *Prochoix* 25: 14–18.

Al-i Ahmed, Jalal. 2002. "Westoxication." In *Modernist and Fundamentalist Debates in Islam: A Reader,* ed. Mansoor Moaddel and Kamran Talattof, 343–57. New York: Palgrave MacMillan. (Orig. pub. 1982.)

Akrouf, Sanhadja, et al. 2005. "Pourquoi nous n'avons pas défilé avec NPNS et nous ne voulons pas défiler avec le CMF." *Prochoix* 32: 25–26.

Alaoui, Fouad. 2005. "Le CFCM, réalité et conditions de réussite." *French Politics, Culture and Society* 23, no. 1: 115–17.

Allal, Brigitte. 2005. "Reponse aux 'Indigènes de la République.'" Site of Association Manifeste des Libertés. http://www.manifeste.org/article.php3?id_article=214.

Allal, Brigitte, and Tewfik Allal. n.d. "Mise au point sur le Manifeste." Site of Association Manifeste des Libertés. http://www.manifeste.org./article.php3?id_article=43.

Allami, Noria. 1988. *Voilées, dévoilées: Etre femme dans le monde arabe*. Paris: L'Harmattan.

Allègre, Claude. 1989. "La meilleure façon d'enlever le voile." *Le Nouvel Observateur* 1305 (Nov. 9): 33.

Altschull, Elizabeth. 1995. *Le voile contre l'école*. Paris: Le Seuil.

Amara, Fadela. 2004. *Ni putes ni soumises*. Paris: La Découverte.

Amara, Fadela, and Mohammed Abdi. 2006. *La racaille de la République*. Paris: Le Seuil.

Amara, Saliha, and Saïd Idir. 1991. "Le 'Mouvement beur.'" *Hommes et Migrations* 1144: 19–26.

Amin, Qasim. 2002. "The Liberation of Women." In *Modernist and Fundamentalist Debates in Islam: A Reader*, ed. Moaddel Mansoor and Kamran Talattof, 163–81. New York: Palgrave MacMillan. (Orig. pub. 1899.)

Amnesty International, International Federation for Human Rights, Human Rights Watch, Reporters Sans Frontières. 1998. *Algérie: Le livre noir*. Paris: La Découverte.

Amokrane, Salah, et al. 2005. "Démons français." *Le Monde,* Dec. 6.

Anderson, Benedict. 1991. *Imagined Communities: Reflections on the Origin and Spread of Nationalism*. Rev. ed. London: Verso.

Ardizzoni, Michela. 2004. "Unveiling the Veil: Gendered Discourses and the (In)visibility of the Female Body in France." *Women's Studies* 33: 629–49.

Askolovitch, Claude. 2003. "L'encombrant M. Ramadan." *Le Nouvel Observateur,* Oct. 10.

Assima, Feriel. 1995. *Une femme à Alger: Chronique du désastre*. Paris: Arléa.

Assouline, Florence. 1989. "Paroles de musulmanes: 'Nous savons trop ce que nous a apporté l'école laïque.'" *L'Evénement du Jeudi* 262 (Nov. 9): 22–23.

———. 1992. *Musulmanes: Une chance pour l'Islam*. Paris: Flammarion.

Audet, Eliane. 2003. "Élisabeth Badinter dénature le féminisme pour mieux le combattre," Sept. 29. Sisyphe.org. http://sisyphe.org/article.php3?id_article=598.

Augé, Hélène. 1989. "Laïcité, laïcité. . . . et l'oppression des femmes alors!" *Paris Féministe* 91–92 (Nov. 15): 35–36.

Babès, Leïla. 2004. "Féminisme, islamisme, modernité." In *Les femmes et l'islam: Entre modernité et intégrisme,* ed. Isabel Taboada-Léonetti, 235–46. Paris: L'Harmattan.

Bachelot, Roselyne. 1999. *Le PaCS entre haine et amour.* Paris: Plon.

Badinter, Elisabeth. 1986. *L'Un est l'autre: Des relations entre hommes et femmes.* Paris: Odile Jacob.

———. 1989. "Je suis fière des profs." Interview with Laurent Joffrin. *Le Nouvel Observateur* 1305 (Nov. 9): 37.

———. 1990. "La loi a perdu sa légitimité." Interview with Martine Gozlan. *L'Evénement du Jeudi* 320 (20 Dec. 1990): 56.

———. 2003. *Fausse route.* Paris: Odile Jacob.

Badinter, Elisabeth, and Robert Badinter. 1990. *Condorcet, 1743–1794.* Rev. ed. Paris: Garnier-Flammarion.

Badinter, Elisabeth, Régis Debray, Alain Finkielkraut, Elisabeth de Fontenay, and Catherine Kintzler. 1989. "Profs: Ne capitulons pas!" *Le Nouvel Observateur* 1304 (Nov. 2): 30–31.

Badran, Margot. 1994. "Gender Activism: Feminists and Islamists in Egypt." In *Identity Politics and Women: Cultural Reassertions and Feminisms in International Perspective,* ed. Valentine M. Moghadam, 202–27. Boulder: Westview Press.

———. 1995. *Feminists, Islam, and Nation: Gender and the Making of Modern Egypt.* Princeton: Princeton Univ. Press.

Balibar, Etienne. 1989. "Le symbole ou la vérité." *Libération,* Nov. 3.

Balibar, Etienne, and Immanuel Wallerstein. 1988. *Race, nation, classe: Les identités ambiguës.* Paris: La Découverte.

Barthélemy, Martine. 2001. "La logique d'ouverture de l'école publique: Une fragilisation de la laïcité française." In *La laïcité, une valeur d'aujourd'hui? Contestations et renégociations du modèle français,* ed. Jean Baudouin and Philippe Portier, 297–314. Rennes: Presses Universitaires de Rennes.

Bataille, Claire. 1989. "Trois otages pour une guerre à visage masqué." *Les Cahiers du Féminisme* 51 (Winter): 15.

Baubérot, Jean. 2000. *Histoire de la laïcité en France.* Paris: Presses Universitaires de France.

———. 2004. *Laïcité 1905–2005, entre passion et raison.* Paris: Le Seuil.

———. 2005. "Laïcité et religion dans l'Union Européenne," Mar. 6. Blog of Jean Bauberot. http://jeanbauberotlaicite.blogspirit.com/europe_et_laicite/.

Bayrou, François. 1993. *Circulaire no. 93-316 du 26 octobre 1993.* Paris: Ministère de l'Education Nationale.

———. 1994. *Circulaire du 20 septembre 1994.* Paris: Ministère de l'Education Nationale.

———. 2003. "La laïcité n'est pas faite pour mettre la religion hors la loi." Interview. *La Croix,* June 27.

Bazin, François. 1989. "La folle semaine de Lionel Jospin: Comment les fillettes de Creil ont bouleversé le PS." *Le Nouvel Observateur* 1304 (Nov. 2): 34–35.

Beauvoir, Simone de. 1949. *Le deuxième sexe.* Paris: Gallimard.

Béji, Hélé. 1982. *Désenchantement national: Essai sur la décolonisation.* Paris: François Maspero.

———. 1997. *L'Imposture culturelle.* Paris: Stock.

Belhadj, Marnia. 2006. *La conquête de l'autonomie: Histoire de Françaises descendantes de migrants algériens.* Paris: Les Editions de l'Atelier/Editions Ouvrières.

Bellil, Samira. 2002. *Dans l'enfer des tournantes.* Paris: Denoâl.

Belotti, Elena Gianni. 1973. *Dalle parte delle bambine: L'influenza dei condizionamenti sociali nella formazione del ruolo femminile nei primi anni di vita.* Milan: Feltrinelli.

Ben Hiba, Tarek, et al. 2004. "Marie n'est pas coupable!" *Les Mots Sont Importants,* July 26. http://lmsi.net/spip.php?article269.

Benabdessadok, Chérifa. 2004. "Ni Putes Ni Soumises: De la marche à l'université d'automne." *Hommes et Migrations* 1248: 64–74.

Bénabou, Roland, Francis Kramarz, and Corinne Prost. 2004. "Zones d'éducation prioritaire: Quels moyens pour quels résultats? Une évaluation sur la période 1982–1992." *INSEE: Economie et Statistique* 380: 3–34.

Bencheikh, Soheib. 1998. *Marianne et le Prophète: L'Islam dans la France laïque.* Paris: Grasset.

Benguigui, Yamina. 1996. *Femmes d'Islam.* Paris: Albin Michel.

———. 1997. *Mémoires d'immigrés: L'Héritage maghrébin.* Paris: Canal+Editions.

Benassayag, Maurice. 1989. "On ne construit pas une nation en exaltant le culte des différences." Interview with Liliane Sichler. *L'Evénement du Jeudi* 265 (Nov. 30): 14.

Benslama, Fethi. 2005. *Déclaration d'insoumission: A l'usage des musulmans et de ceux qui ne le sont pas.* Paris: Flammarion.

Benslama, Fethi, and Nadia Tazi, eds. 2004. *La virilité en Islam.* La Tour d'Aigues: Editions de l'aube. (Orig. pub. 1998.)

Benzid-Basset, Lila. 2005. "Féminisme indigène." Site of Alternative Couleur Citoyenne, Tours, Mar. 23. http://ac2.tours.free.fr/spip.php?article9.

Berque, Jacques. 1985. *L'immigration à l'école de la République: Rapport d'un groupe de réflexion.* Paris: La Documentation Française.

Bloul, Rachel A. D. 1994. "Veiled Objects of (Post)-Colonial Desire: Forbidden Women Disrupt the Republican Fraternal Space." *Australian Journal of Anthropology* 5, no. 1–2: 124–39.

Boltanski, Luc, and Eve Chiapello. 1999. *Le nouvel esprit du capitalisme.* Paris: Gallimard.

Bonnafous, Simone. 1992. "Le terme 'intégration' dans le journal *Le Monde*: sens et non-sens." *Hommes et Migrations* 1154: 24–30.

Borrel, Catherine. 2006. "Enquêtes annuelles de recensement 2004 et 2005." *INSEE Première* 1098 (Aug.).

Bouatta, Cherifa, and Doria Cherifati-Merabtine. 1994. "The Social Representation of Women in Algeria's Islamist Movement." In *Identity Politics and Women: Cultural Reassertions and Feminisms in International Perspective,* ed. Valentine M. Moghadam, 183–201. Boulder: Westview Press.

Boubeker, Ahmed, and Nicolas Beau. 1986. *Chroniques métissées.* Paris: Alain Moreau.

Boudjema, Hayette, et al. 1989. "Le Pari de l'école." *Paris Féministe,* Nov. 15, 33–34.

Boulares, Habib. 1989. "'Non à l'uniforme politique!' L'affaire du foulard, vue du Maghreb." Interview. *Le Nouvel Observateur* 1304 (Nov. 2): 36–37.

Boumaza, Bachir. 1958. *La Gangrène.* Paris: Minuit.

Boumediene-Thiéry, Alima. 2004. "Musulmanes féministes: Du paradoxe à la réalité." Web site of Islam et laïcité, Mar. 10. http://www.islamlaicite.org/IMG/ pdf/Actes_colloque_Musulmanes_feministes.doc.pdf.

Bourcier, Marie-Hélène. 2005. *Sexpolitiques: Queer zones 2.* Paris: La Fabrique.

———. 2006. *Queer zones: Politique des identités sexuelles et des savoirs.* 2nd ed. Paris: Editions Amsterdam.

Bourdieu, Pierre. 1989. *La noblesse d'Etat: Grandes écoles et esprit de corps.* Paris: Minuit.

Boussouf, Malika. 1995. *Vivre traquée.* Paris: Calmann-Lévy.

Bouteldja, Houria. 2004. "Féminisme ou maternalisme?" *Les Mots Sont Importants,* Mar. 8. http://lmsi.net/article.php3?id_article=225.

———. 2006a. "De la cérémonie du dévoilement à Alger (1958) à Ni Putes Ni Soumises: L'Instrumentalisation coloniale et néo-coloniale de la cause des femmes." Site of Les Indigènes de la République, June 18. http://www.indigenes-republique.org/spip.php?article152.

————. 2006b. "Entretien avec Houria Bouteldja, porte-parole du Mouvement des indigènes de la république." Interview with Chiara Bonfiglioli. Dec. 10. http://www.indigenes-republique.org/spip.php?article599.

Bouteldja, Houria, Catherine Grupper, Laurent Lévy, and Pierre Tévanian. 2004. "Le voile à l'école: Une nouvelle affaire Dreyfus." Les Mots Sont Importants, Jan. 25. http://lmsi.net/article.php3?id_article=214.

Bouzar, Dounia. 2006. "Les interprétations sont masculines et humaines." Témoignage Chrétien, Nov. 30.

Bouzar, Dounia, and Saïda Kada. 2003. L'une voilée, l'autre pas: Le témoignage de deux musulmanes françaises. Paris: Albin Michel.

Bowen, John R. 2007. Why the French Don't Like Headscarves: Islam, the State and Public Space. Princeton, N.J.: Princeton Univ. Press.

Brahimi, Denise. 1984. Femmes arabes et sœurs musulmanes. Paris: Tierce.

Bréchon, Pierre. 2001. "Les religions dans l'espace public: Les opinions des Français." In La laïcité, une valeur d'aujourd'hui? Contestations et renégociations du modèle français, ed. Jean Baudouin and Philippe Portier, 145–58. Rennes: Presses Universitaires de Rennes.

Brouard, Sylvain, and Vincent Tiberj. 2005. Français comme les autres? Enquête sur les citoyens d'origine maghrébine, africaine et turque. Paris: Presses de la Fondation Nationale des Sciences Politiques.

Burdeau, Georges. 1979. Le libéralisme. Paris: Le Seuil.

Butler, Judith. 1999. Gender Trouble: Feminism and the Subversion of Identity. New York: Routledge.

————. 2004. Undoing Gender. New York: Routledge.

Calvès, Gwénaâle. 2005. "Le droit du sol selon François Baroin: L'Amalgame et le mensonge." Observatoire des inégalités, Sept. 19. http://www.inegalites.fr/article.php3?id_article=387.

Carrel, François. 2005. "'Ni Putes Ni Soumises': Une arme à double tranchant." Afrik.com, Feb. 23. http://www.afrik.com/article8144.html.

Cassen, Bernard. "Altermondialisation et Islam, Bernard Cassen répond à Tariq Ramadan." Politis, July 10. http://www.politis.fr/article644.html

Caster, Sylvie. 1989. "Le Torchon ne risque pas de brûler." Le Canard Enchaîné, Oct. 25.

CCTR (Collectif contre tous les racismes). 2004a. Les liaisons dangereuses du MRAP. Self-published, Feb.

————. 2004b. Le MRAP dérape. Self-published, Nov.

CEC (Commission d'Enquête Citoyenne pour la vérité sur l'implication française dans le génocide des Tutsi). 2005. *Rwanda: 1994–2004.* http://www.enquete-citoyenne-rwanda.org.

CFPE (Collectif féministes pour l'égalité). 2006. *Inch'Allah l'Egalité!* 2, no. 4 (May): 2006.

Châabane, Nadia. 2004. "Que d'hommes dans la rue pour défendre ma liberté!" Sisyphe.org, Jan. 26. http://sisyphe.org/article.php3?id_article=902.

Chafiq, Chahla. 1991. *La femme et le retour de l'Islam: L'expérience iranienne.* Paris: Le Félin.

Chaib, Sabah. 2003. "Femmes, migration et marché du travail en France." In *Genre, travail et migrations en Europe,* ed. Madeleine Hersent and Claude Zaidman, 211–37. Paris: CEDREF/Université de Paris VII–Denis Diderot.

Charara, Walid. 2006. "Le Hezbollah ne cédera pas!" Interview with Olfa Lamloum. Web site of Les Indigènes de la République, July 17. http://www.indigenes-republique.org/spip.php?article342.

Chartier, Claire, Philippe Coste, Baya Gacemi, Valérie Gomez, Frédéric Koller, Nütke V. Ortaq, Pierre Prakash, Tangi Salaün, and Victor Simon. 2006. "Des islamistes aux évangéliques: Dieu et la politique." L'Express, Mar. 28. http://www.lexpress.fr/info/societe/dossier/religions/dossier.asp?ida=432378.

Chebel d'Appollonia, Ariane. 1987. *L'extrême-droite en France: De Maurras à Le Pen.* Brussels: Editions Complexe.

Chenière, Ernest. 1989. "Oui, la laïcité, ça se défend!" Interview. *Le Nouvel Observateur* 1301 (Oct. 12): 35–36.

Chesler, Phyllis. 2005. *The Death of Feminism: What's Next in the Struggle for Women's Freedom.* Basingstoke, Hampshire: Palgrave Macmillan.

———. 2006. "The Islamization of America." *Front Page Magazine,* Mar. 21. http://www.frontpagemag.com/Articles/ReadArticle.asp?ID=21720.

Chiennes de Garde. 2003. "'Tir ami': Réponses à Elisabeth Badinter." Web site of Chiennes de Garde, 25 May. http://chiennesdegarde.org/article.php3?id_article=243.

Chika, Elisabeth. 1990. "Chronologie." *Hommes et Migrations* 1129–30 (Feb.–Mar.): 1–11.

Chouffan, Alain. 1994. "Les deux casquettes de Rachid Amaoui." *Le Nouvel Observateur* 1561 (Oct. 6): 48.

Cissé, Madjiguène. 1997. "Une loi pour créer d'autres Saint-Bernard." *Plein Droit* 36–37.

Claire, Nadine. 1985. "Bound and Gagged by the Family Code." Interview with Sophie Laws. *Trouble and Strife* 5: 5–12.

Clermont, Jean-Arnold de. 2004. "Pour la révision de la loi de 1905." *Regards sur l'actualité* 298: 49–55.

CNCDH (Commission nationale consultative des droits de l'homme). 2004. *2003. La lutte contre le racisme et la xénophobie: Rapport d'activité.* Paris: La Documentation Française.

CNDF (Collectif national des droits des femmes). 2006. *Contre les violences faites aux femmes: Une loi-cadre!* Paris: Syllepse.

Cohen, Martine. 2001. "L'intégration de l'islam et des musulmans en France: Modèles du passé et pratiques actuelles." In *La laïcité, une valeur d'aujourd'hui? Contestations et renégociations du modèle français,* ed. Jean Baudouin and Philippe Portier, 315–30. Rennes: Presses Universitaires de Rennes.

Collectif des femmes immigrées. 1984. *Droit de vivre en famille . . . pour qui?* Paris: self-published.

Collins, Patricia Hill. 1991. *Black Feminist Thought.* New York: Routledge.

Conan, Eric. 2003. "Quatorze ans de retard." *L'Express,* Apr. 30.

Condorcet, Jean-Antoine-Nicolas de Caritat, Marquis de. 1791. *Cinq mémoires sur l'instruction publique.* Reprint, Paris: Flammarion, 1993.

Conseil d'Etat. 1989. *Avis no. 246.893—27 novembre 1989.* Paris: Conseil d'Etat.

———. 1992. *Statuant au contentieux No. 130394.* Nov. 2. Paris: Conseil d'Etat.

———. 1994. *Statuant au contentieux No. 145656I.* Mar. 14. Paris: Conseil d'Etat.

———. 1995. *Statuant au contentieux No. 159981.* Mar. 10. Paris: Conseil d'Etat.

———. 1996a. *Statuant au contentieux No. 172663, 172686.* Nov. 27. Paris: Conseil d'Etat.

———. 1996b. *Statuant au contentieux No. 172719, 172723, 172724, 172726.* Nov. 27. Paris: Conseil d'Etat.

———. 2004a. *Statuant au contentieux No. 272926.* Oct. 8. Paris: Conseil d'Etat.

———. 2004b. *Statuant au contentieux No. 269077, 269704.* Oct. 8. Paris: Conseil d'Etat.

Coran, Le. 1967. Trans. Denise Masson. Paris: Gallimard.

Correa, S. 2002. "A DAWN Genderscape on Globalization and Fundamentalism." *Development* 45, no. 2: 68–70.

Costa-Lascoux, Jacqueline. 1989. *De l'immigré au citoyen.* Paris: La Documentation Française.

Coulson, Noel J. 1964. *A History of Islamic Law.* Edinburgh: Edinburgh University Press.

Cour administrative d'Appel de Paris. 2005. *Statuant au contentieux No. 05PAO18311.* July 19. Paris: Cour administrative d'appel.

CRIF (Conseil représentatif des institutions juives de France). 2004. "Le MRAP lutte-t-il encore contre l'antisémitisme?" Oct. 22. http://www.crif.org/index .php?menu=5anddossier=41andid_doss=3721.

Crinon, Monique. 2006. "Féminisme et laïcité: Non aux amalgames."

Croutier, Alev Lyle. 1989. *Harem: The World Behind the Veil.* New York: Abbeville Press.

CSA. 2006. "Portrait des catholiques." Sondage No. 0601224. http://www.csa.eu/ dataset/data2006/opi20061025d-portrait-des-catholiques.htm.

Dabi, Frédéric, and Jean-Luc Parodi. 2004. "Les conversations des Français." Paris: IFOP.

Damiens, Caroline. 2004. "Le corps des femmes n'est pas un champ de bataille." Les Mots Sont Importants, Apr. 30. http://lmsi.net/rubrique.php3?id_rubrique=32.

Daniel, Jean. 1989a. "L'autre pari." *Le Nouvel Observateur* 1304 (Nov. 2): 32–33.

———. 1989b. "Cinq points sur les 'i.'" *Le Nouvel Observateur* 1305 (Nov. 9): 36.

Daoud, Zakya. 1996. *Féminisme et politique au Maghreb: Sept décennies de lutte.* Casablanca: Eddif.

Delphy, Christine. 1980. "Libération des femmes an dix." *Questions Féministes* 7: 3–13.

———. 1995. "The Invention of French Feminism: An Essential Move." *Yale French Studies* 87: 190–221.

———. 1998. *L'ennemi principal 1: Economie politique du patriarcat.* Paris: Syllepse.

———. 2001. *L'ennemi principal 2: Pense le genre.* Paris: Syllepse.

———. 2002. "A War for Afghan Women?" trans. Bronwyn Winter. In *September 11, 2001: Feminist Perspectives,* ed. Susan Hawthorne and Bronwyn Winter, 302–15. Melbourne: Spinifex.

———. 2003a. "L'affaire du foulard: Non à l'exclusion." Sisyhpe.org, Nov. 1. http:// www.sisyphe.org/imprimer.php3?id_article=728.

———. 2003b. "Un point de vue féministe contre l'exclusion des élèves voilées." Web site of Islam et laïcité, Nov. 17. http://www.islamlaicite.org/article113.html.

———. 2004. "La loi anti-voile: Un aveuglement collectif." Oumma.com, Feb. 4. http://www.oumma.com/spip.php?article943.

———. 2005a. "Attention à la falaise!" Oumma.com, Feb. 25. http://www.oumma. com/spip.php?article1397.

———. 2005b. "Un mouvement, mais quel mouvement? Remarques sur la construction d'un 'mouvement des Indigènes.'" Les Mots Sont Importants, June 7. http://lmsi.net/article.php3?id_article=411.

————. 2006. "Antisexisme *ou* antiracisme? Un faux dilemme." *Nouvelles Questions Féministes* 25, no. 1: 59–83.

Désir, Harlem. 1991. "Pour l'intégration: Conditions et instruments." In *Face au racisme,* ed. Pierre-André Taguieff, vol. 1, 106–19. Paris: La Découverte.

Dialogue de Femmes et al. 1990. "La presse jette le voile sur le féminisme: Lettre ouverte aux médias." *Paris Féministe* 94 (Jan. 1): 8.

Djavann, Chahdortt. 2003. *Bas les voiles!* Paris: Gallimard.

————. 2004. *Que pense Allah de l'Europe?* Paris: Gallimard.

Djebar, Assia. 1980. "Regard interdit, son coupé." In *Femmes d'Alger dans leur appartement.* Paris: Des Femmes.

Djitli, Leïla. 2004. *Lettre à ma fille qui veut porter le voile.* Paris: La Martinière.

Documentation Française, La. 2004. *Regards sur l'actualité 298: État, laïcité, religions.* Paris: La Documentation Française.

Duchen, Claire. 2000. "Crime and Punishment in Liberated France: The Case of *les Femmes Tondues.*" In *When the War Was Over: War and Peace in Europe 1940–1956,* ed. Claire Duchen and Irene Bandhauer-Schoffmann, 233–50. London: Leicester Univ. Press.

El Guindi, Fadwa. 1999. *Veil: Modesty, Privacy and Resistance.* Oxford: Berg.

El Saadawi, Nawal. 1980. *The Hidden Face of Eve: Women in the Arab World.* London: Zed Press.

ELELE. 2006. *Turcs en France: Album de familles.* Paris: Bleu Autour.

EMAF. 1989. "Communiqué de l'association 'Expressions Maghrébines au Féminin.'" *Paris Féministe* 91–92 (Nov. 15): 31–32.

Enloe, Cynthia. 1990. *Bananas, Beaches and Bases: Making Feminist Sense of International Politics.* Berkeley: Univ. of California Press.

Eribon, Didier, ed. 1998. *Les Études gay et lesbiennes: Colloque du Centre Georges Pompidou, 23 et 27 juin 1997.* Paris: Éditions du Centre Georges Pompidou.

Esposito, John L. 1995. *The Islamic Threat: Myth or Reality?* 2nd ed. Oxford: Oxford University Press.

Ezekiel, Judith. 2006. "French Dressing: Race, Gender, and the Hijab Story." *Feminist Studies* 32, no. 2: 256–78.

Fabius, Laurent. 2003. Speech to Socialist Party Congress. Dijon, May 17. http://www.laurent-fabius.net/article118.html.

FASILD (Fonds d'action et de soutien pour l'intégration et la lutte contre les discriminations). 2004. *Femmes d'origine étrangère: Travail, accès à l'emploi, discriminations de genre.* Paris: La Documentation Française.

Fatès, Feriel. 1993. "Les associations de femmes algériennes face à la menace islamiste." *Nouvelles Questions Féministes* 15, no. 2: 51–65.

Fernando, Mayanthi. 2005. "The Republic's 'second religion': Recognizing Islam in France." *Middle East Report* 235. http://www.merip.org/mer/mer235/fernando.html.

Filali-Ansary, Abdou. 1996. "The Challenge of Secularization." *Journal of Democracy* 7, no. 2: 76–80.

———. 2002. *L'Islam est-il hostile à la laïcité?* Arles: Sindbad/Actes Sud. (Orig. pub. 1999.)

Flanquart, Hervé. 2003. *Croyances et valeurs chez les jeunes Maghrébins.* Brussels: Editions Complexe.

Fohr, Anne. 1993. "Immigration: le parcours des combattantes." *Le Nouvel Observateur* 1495 (July 7): 40.

Fohr, Anne, and Alain Chouffan. 1994. "Ecole: La déchirure." *Le Nouvel Observateur* 1561 (Nov. 6): 46–48.

Forrester, Viviane. 1996. *L'Horreur économique.* Paris: Fayard.

Fourest, Caroline. 2004. *Frère Tariq: Discours, stratégie et méthode de Tariq Ramadan.* Paris: Grasset.

———. "L'Intégrisme est-il queer?" *Prochoix* 34: 63–75.

———. 2007. "Ne pas se tromper de combat." *Prochoix* 41.

Fourest, Caroline, and Fiammetta Venner. 2003. *Tirs Croisés: La laïcité à l'épreuve des intégrismes juif, chrétien et musulman.* Paris: Calmann-Lévy.

Fraikech, Abderrahmane. 2004. "Le voile est-il islamique ou non?" Sisyhpe.org. www.sisyphe.org/article.php?3id_article=1350.

Franks, Myfanwy. 2001. *Women and Revivalism in the West: Choosing 'Fundamentalism' in a Liberal Democracy.* Basingstoke, UK: Palgrave Macmillan.

Frégosi, Franck. 2001. "Jeunes musulmans turcs en France: Le milieu associatif et son rapprot à la citoyenneté et aux identités." In *L'Islam en France et en Allemagne: Identités et citoyennetés,* ed. Remy Leveau, Khadija Mohsen-Finan, and Catherine Wihtol de Wenden, 99–112. Paris: La Documentation Française.

———. 2004. "Le PMF lance une OPA sur les musulmans." Interview. *L'Humanité,* Jan. 17.

Furet, François, Jacques Julliard, and Pierre Rosanvallon. 1988. *La République du centre: La fin de l'exception française.* Paris: Calmann-Lévy.

Gaspard, Françoise. 1990. *Une petite ville en France.* Paris: Gallimard.

———. 1992. "Assimilation, insertion, intégration: les mots pour 'devenir français.'" *Hommes et Migrations* 1154: 14–23.

Gaspard, Françoise, and Farhad Khosrokhavar. 1995. *Le foulard et la République.* Paris: La Découverte.

Gaspard, Françoise, and Claude Servan Schreiber. 1984. *La fin des immigrés.* Paris: Le Seuil.

Geadah, Yolande. 1996. *Femmes voilées, intégrismes démasqués.* Montreal: VLB.

Geisser, Vincent. 2003. *La nouvelle islamophobie.* Paris: La Découverte.

Gérard, Alain. n.d. "A propos de 'Frère Tariq,' de Caroline Fourest." Islam et laïcité. http://www.islamlaicite.org/article261.html.

Godard, Jean-Marie. 2006. "Dix ans après Saint-Bernard, les sans-papiers à nouveau mobilisés." *Le Nouvel Observateur,* Aug. 25.

Gouges, Olympe de. 1986. "Déclaration des Droits de la Femme." In *Œuvres,* introduced by Benoîte Groult, 99–112. Paris: Mercure de France. (Orig. pub. 1791.)

Gresh, Alain. 2001. "Islamophobie." *Le Monde Diplomatique,* Nov., 32.

———. 2004. "A propos de l'islamophobie." Oumma.com. http://oumma.com/spip.php?article964.

Gresh, Alain, and Tariq Ramadan. 2002. *L'Islam en questions.* Rev. ed. Paris: Actes Sud/Babel.

Guénif-Soulimas, Nacira. 2000. *Des beurettes.* Paris: Grasset and Fasquelle.

Guénif-Soulimas, Nacira, and Eric Macé. 2006. *Les féministes et le garçon arabe.* 2nd ed. La Tour d'Aigues: Editions de l'Aube.

Guillaumin, Colette. 1972. *L'idéologie raciste: Genèse et langage actuel.* Paris/The Hague: Mouton.

———. 1992. *Sexe, race et pratique du pouvoir: L'idée de Nature.* Paris: côté-femmes.

Haddad, Yvonne Yazbeck. 1982. *Contemporary Islam and the Challenge of History.* Albany: State Univ. of New York Press.

———. 1984. "Islam, Women and Revolution in Twentieth-Century Arab Thought." *Muslim World* 74, no. 3–4.

Hadjam, Mimouna. 2005. "L'islamisme contre les femmes partout dans le monde." Sisyphe.org, Jan. 8. http://www.sisyphe.org/article.php3?id_article=1458.

Hafiz, Chems-eddine, and Gilles Devers. 2005. *Droit et religion musulmane.* Paris: Dalloz.

Halimi, Gisèle. 1973. *La cause des femmes.* Paris: Grasset.

———. 2002. "Simone de Beauvoir, une femme engagée: de la guerre d'Algérie au procès de Bobigny." In *Cinquantenaire du deuxième sexe,* ed. Christine Delphy and Sylvie Chaperon, 293–99. Paris: Syllepse.

Halimi, Gisèle, and Simone de Beauvoir. 1961. *Djamila Boupacha*. Paris: Gallimard.

Hamel, Christelle. 2006. "La sexualité entre sexisme et racisme: Les descendant-e-s de migrant-e-s du Maghreb et la virginité." *Nouvelles Questions Féministes* 25, no. 1: 41–58.

Hamon, Hervé, and Patrick Rotman. 1979. *Les porteurs de valises: La résistance française à la guerre d'Algérie*. Paris: Albin Michel.

Hannoun, Michel, with Pierre Todorov and Brigitte Guiboud-Ribaud. 1987. *L'homme est l'espérance de l'homme: Rapport sur les racisme les dicriminations en France au secrétaire d'Etat auprès du Premier ministre chargé des Droits de l'Homme*. Paris: La Documentation française.

Hargreaves, Alec G. 1997. *Immigration and Identity in Beur Fiction: Voices From the North African Community in France*. Oxford, UK: Berg.

Haut Conseil à l'Intégration. 2001. *L'Islam dans la République*. Paris: La Documentation Française.

Hélie-Lucas, Marie-Aimée. 1990. "Women, Nationalism and Religion in the Algerian Liberation Struggle." In *Opening the Gates: A Century of Arab Feminist Writing*, ed. Margot Badran and Miriam Cooke, 105–14. London: Virago.

Hennache, Nicole. 2007. "Carte scolaire: Plus qu'un choix d'école, un choix de société." *Perspectives Education Formation* 91 (Sept). http://www.unsen.cgt.fr/index.php?Itemid=313&id=338&option=com_content&task=view

Hessini, Leila. 1994. "Wearing the Hijab in Contemporary Morocco: Choice and Identity." In *Reconstructing Gender in the Middle East: Tradition, Identity and Power*, ed. Fatma M. Göçek and Shiva Balaghi, 40–56. New York: Columbia Univ. Press.

Hoagland, Sarah Lucia. 1988. *Lesbian Ethics: Toward New Value*. Palo Alto: Institute of Lesbian Studies.

Hobsbawm, Eric, and Terence Ranger, eds. 1983. *The Invention of Tradition*. Cambridge, UK: Cambridge Univ. Press.

Hoffman-Ladd, Valerie. 1987. "Polemics on the Modesty and Segregation of Women in Contemporary Egypt." *International Journal of Middle East Studies* 19, no. 1: 23–50.

Hourani, Albert. 1962. *Arabic Thought in the Liberal Age 1798–1939*. Cambridge, UK: Cambridge Univ. Press.

———. 1991. *A History of the Arab Peoples*. London: Faber and Faber.

Howard, Rhoda. 1995. *Human Rights and the Search for Community*. Boulder: Westview Press.

Iacub, Marcela. 2004. "De la peine et du sexe." *Libération*, Apr. 6.

Iacub, Marcela, and Hervé Le Bras. 2003. "Homo mulieri lupus?" *Les Temps Modernes* 623: 112–34.

Ignazi, Piero. 1996. "Un nouvel acteur politique." In *Le Front National à découvert,* ed. Nonna Mayer and Pascal Perrineau, 63–80. Paris: Presses de la Fondation Nationale des Sciences Politiques.

Jaspard, Maryse. 2005. *Les violences contre les femmes.* Paris: La Decouverte.

Jaspard, Maryse, et al. 2003. *Les violences envers les femmes en France.* Paris: La Documentation Française.

Jelen, Brigitte. 2005. "'Leur histoire est notre histoire': Immigrant Culture in France between Visibility and Invisibility." *French Politics, Culture and Society* 23, no. 2: 101–25.

Joffrin, Laurent. 1989. "Une petite main trop douce: Lettre à Harlem Désir." *Le Nouvel Observateur* 1304 (Nov. 2): 35.

Jones, Nicky. 2004. "Secularising the Veil: A Study of Legal and Cultural Issues Arising from the Wearing of the Islamic Headscarf in the Affaire du Foulard in France." Ph.D. thesis, Univ. of Queensland.

Jospin, Lionel. 1989. *Circulaire du 12 décembre 1989.* Paris: Ministère de l'Education Nationale.

Julliard, Jacques. 1989. "La faute à Mahomet." *Le Nouvel Observateur* 1307 (Nov. 23): 33.

Jullien, Hedda. 1989. "Navigation à voiles sans boussole." *Paris Féministe* 90 (Nov. 1): 10.

Kacem, Abdelaziz. 2004. *Le voile est-il islamique?* Montpellier: Chèvre-Feuille étoilée.

Kaltenbach, Jeanne-Hélène, and Michèle Tribalat. 2002. *La République et l'Islam: Entre crainte et aveuglement.* Paris: Gallimard.

Kandel, Liliane. 2005. "Les noces enchantées du 'post-féminisme' et de l'archéomachisme." *Prochoix* 32: 39–54.

Kandiyoti, Deniz. 1991. "Bargaining with Patriarchy." In *The Social Construction of Gender,* ed. Judith Lorber and Susan A. Farrell, 104–18. Newbury Park, Calif.: Sage.

———. 1995. "Reflections on the Politics of Gender in Muslim Societies: From Nairobi to Beijing." In *Faith And Freedom: Women's Human Rights in the Muslim World,* ed. Mahnaz Afkhami, 19–32. London: I. B. Tauris.

———. 1998. "Afterword: Some Awkward Questions on Women and Modernity in Turkey." In *Remaking Women: Feminism and Modernity in the Middle East,* ed. Lila Abu-Lughod, 270–87. Princeton: Princeton Univ. Press.

Karam, Azza. 1998. *Women, Islamisms and the State: Contemporary Feminisms in Egypt*. Basingstoke, UK: MacMillan.

Keaton, Trica Danielle. 2006. *Muslim Girls and the Other France: Race, Identity Politics and Social Exclusion*. Bloomington: Indiana University Press.

Kepel, Gilles. 1987. *Les Banlieues de l'Islam: Naissance d'une religion en France*. Paris: Le Seuil.

———. 1994. *A l'Ouest d'Allah*. Paris: Le Seuil.

———. 2003. *Jihad*. Paris: Gallimard.

Kessler, David. 1993. "Laïcité: Du combat au droit." Interview. *Le Debat* 77 (Nov.–Dec.): 95–101.

Khali, Khadidja. 1994. "Une volonté de déstabiliser." Interview with Marie-Amélie Lombard. *Le Monde*, Sept. 28.

Khellil, Mohand. 1991. *L'Intégration des Maghrébins en France*. Paris: PUF.

Khiari, Sadri. 2006. "Brûler une voiture est un acte politique." Interview, Saphirnews, Apr. 13. http://www.saphirnews.com/-Bruler-une-voiture-est-un-acte-politique-_a2427.html.

Khosrokhavar, Farhad. 1997. *L'Islam des jeunes*. Paris: Flammarion.

———. 2002. "La victoire d'Osama Bin Laden." In *11 septembre, un an après*, ed. Sylvie Kauffmann, 71–74. Paris: Le Monde/Editions de l'Aube.

Killian, Caitlin. 2003. "The Other Side of the Veil: North African Women in France Respond to the Headscarf Affair." *Gender and Society* 17, no. 4: 567–90.

Kintzler, Catherine. 1984. *Condorcet: L'instruction publique et la naissance du citoyen*. Paris: Le Sycomore.

———. 1996. *La République en questions*. Paris: Minerve.

Knibiehler, Yvonne, and Régine Goutalier. 1985. *La femme aux temps des colonies*. Paris: Stock.

Kristiansen, Wendy. 2005. "Visages féminins de l'Islam." *Le Monde Diplomatique*, Sept., 4–5.

Kurys, Nadia, et al. 2005. "Communiqué." Feb. http://www.atheisme.org/mrap-contestation.html.

Labévière, Richard. 1999. *Les dollars de la terreur: Les Etats-Unis et les islamistes*. Paris: Grasset.

Labidi, Samia. 2004. "Demain au Bourget: Pour une identité laïque de la communauté arabo-musulmane." *Prochoix* 31: 11–13.

Lacoste-Dujardin, Camille. 1985. *Des mères contre les femmes: Maternité et patriarcat au Maghreb*. Paris: La Découverte.

Lacoste-Dujardin, Camille, with Mohamed Hassini and Hayat Zirari. 1992. *Yasmina et les autres de Nanterre et d'ailleurs: Filles de parents maghrébins en France.* Paris: La Découverte.

Laïdi, Ali, and Ahmed Salam. 2002. *Le jihad en Europe: Les filières du terrorisme islamiste.* Paris: Le Seuil.

Laignel, André. 2005. "Liberté, égalité, fraternité, laïcité." http://www.andre-laignel.fr.

Lambert, Yves. 2001. "Les profils des Français selon leur opinion sur la laïcité scolaire." In *La Laïcité, une valeur d'aujourd'hui? Contestations et renégociations du modèle français,* ed. Jean Baudouin and Philippe Portier, 159–70. Rennes: Presses Universitaires de Rennes.

Lamloun, Olfa. 1998. "Les femmes dans le discours islamiste." *Confluences Méditerranée* 27: 25–32.

Lang, Jack. 2003. "Interdire tout signe religieux." Interview with Eric Conan. *L'Express,* Apr. 30.

Langlois, Bernard. 1989. "Editorial." *Politis* 77 (Oct. 26): 18–19.

Laurent, Vincent. 1998. "Les architectes du social-libéralisme." *Le Monde Diplomatique,* Sept., 1, 26–27.

Lazreg, Marnia, 1990a. "Feminism and Difference: The Perils of Writing as a Woman on Women in Algeria." In *Conflicts in Feminism,* ed. M. Hirsch and E. Fox Keller, 326–48. New York: Routledge.

———. 1990b. "Gender and Politics in Algeria: Unravelling the Religious Paradigm." *Signs: A Journal of Women in Culture and Society* 15, no. 4: 755–80.

———. 1994. *The Eloquence of Silence: Algerian Women in Question.* New York: Routledge.

Leclerc, Gérard. 1985. *La bataille de l'école: 15 siècles d'histoire, 3 ans de combat.* Paris: Denoâl.

Legrand, Claire. 1990. "Deux visages sous le voile: Le choix épineux des filles de l'Islam." *Marie-France,* July, 72–74.

Lemercier, Elise. 2006. "L'association 'Ni Putes, Ni Soumises': Une inflation politico-médiatique démystifiée par le terrain." Oumma.com, Apr. 26. http://oumma.com/spip.php?article2021.

Lesselier, Claudie. 1989. "Sexisme—racisme—nationalisme." *Paris Féministe* 91–92: 43.

———. 2003. "Femmes migrantes en France: Le genre et la loi." In *Genre, travail et migrations en Europe,* ed. Madeleine Hersent and Claude Zaidman, 45–59. Paris: CEDREF/Université de Paris VII–Denis Diderot.

————. 2005. "Une lecture critique de l'Appel 'Nous sommes les indigènes de la République.'"

Site of Manifeste des Libertés. http://www.manifeste.org/article.php3?id_article =210.

Lévy, Alma, Lila Lévy, Véronique Giraud, and Yves Sintomer. 2004. *Des filles comme les autres: Au-delà du foulard.* Paris: La Découverte.

Lévy, Bernard-Henri. 1989. "Bernard-Henri Levy réplique . . . à Finkielkraut, à Debray et . . . à l'Edj." Interview with Maurice Szafran. *L'Evénement du Jeudi* 262 (Nov. 9): 18.

Lévy, Pierre. 2005. "Laïcité et souveraineté." *Revue Républicaine*, Dec. 24. http://www.revue-republicaine.fr/spip.php?article1003.

Liauzu, Claude. 1990. "La nouvelle réalité musulmane et la société française." In *Si les immigrés m'étaient comptés,* ed. C. Liauzu et al., 65–71. Paris: Syros/Alternatives.

————. 2005. "Une loi contre l'histoire." *Le Monde Diplomatique* 613 (Apr.): 28.

Lochak, Danièle. 2008. "Les juges s'appuient sur la soumission de cette femme." Interview. *Le Monde,* June 27.

Long, Marceau. 1994. "Marceau Long s'interroge sur la validité de la Circulaire Bayrou à propos du foulard islamique." Interview. *Le Monde,* Dec. 20.

Lukács, Georg. 1971. *History and Class Consciousness: Studies in Marxist Dialectics,* trans. Rodney Livingstone. London: Merlin Press. (Orig. pub. 1922.)

Macfie, A. L. 2000. *Orientalism: A Reader.* New York: New York Univ. Press.

McLeod, Arlene Elowe. 1992. "Hegemonic Relations and Gender Resistance: The New Veiling as Accommodating Protest in Cairo." *Signs: A Journal of Women in Culture and Society* 17, no. 3: 533–57.

MacKinnon, Catharine A. 1983. "Feminism, Marxism, Method and the State: Toward Feminist Jurisprudence." *Signs: A Journal of Women in Culture and Society* 8, no. 4: 635–58.

Mahmood, Saba. 2005. *Politics of Piety: The Islamic Revival and the Feminist Subject.* Princeton: Princeton Univ. Press.

Majnoni d'Intignano, Béatrice et al. 1999. *Egaltié entre femmes et hommes: Aspects économiques: rapport du Conseil d'Analyse Economique.* Paris: La Documentation Française.

Manna, Haytham. 1989. "L'imposture du voile: Un spécialiste de l'islam accuse." Interview with Hamid Barrada. *Le Nouvel Observateur* 1304 (Nov. 2): 38–39.

Mansouri, Farouk, and Hélène Michelini-Beldjoudi. 2003. "Tariq Ramadan ou la guerre des mondes." *Prochoix* 26–27: 72–76.

Marie-Jeannes, Les, ed. 1993. *L'Extrême-droite contre les femmes: Un recueil de textes et de documents.* Paris: Les Archives Lesbiennes.

Martinet, Danièle. 1987. "Elisabeth Badinter ou les uns et les autres." *Paris Féministes* 51 (Oct. 15): 23–25.

Maruani, Margaret. 2006. *Travail et emploi des femmes.* 3rd. ed. Paris: La Décuoverte.

Mathieu, Nicole-Claude. 1991. "Quand céder n'est pas consentir." In *L'Anatomie politique: Catégorisations et idéologies du sexe.* Paris: côté-femmes.

Matine, Mahnaz (for L'Eveil). 1989. "Le voile islamique: la loi coranique." *Paris Féministe* 91–92 (Nov. 15): 25–26.

Maurer, Sophie. 2005. "Le culte musulman en France: Enjeux pratiques et réponses des acteurs publics." Working paper, International Center for Migration, Ethnicity and Citizenship (ICMEC), New School Univ., New York. http://www .newschool.edu/icmec/GMF%20FRENCH%20VERSION.doc.

Maury, Serge. 1991. "Sur la forme la plus perverse du racisme anti-Arabe." *L'Evénement du jeudi* 333 (Mar. 21): 12–13.

Mayer, Nonna. 1998. "The French National Front." In *The New Politics of the Right: Neo-Populist Parties and Movements in Established Democracies,* ed. Hans-Georg Betz and Stefan Immerfall, 11–25. New York: St. Martin's Press.

———. 2004. "Nouvelle judéophobie ou vieil antisémitisme?" *Raisons politiques* 16: 91–103.

Mayeur, Françoise. 1985. "La femme dans la société selon Jules Ferry." In *Jules Ferry: Fondateur de la République,* ed. François Furet, 79–87. Paris: Editions de l'E.H.E.S.S.

Memmi, Albert. 2004. "Communiqué." Nov. 4. http://www.upjf.org/detail .do?noArticle=9122&noCat=115&id_key=115.

Mermet, Gérard. 2002. *Francoscopie 2003: Pour comprendre les Français.* Paris: Larousse.

———. 2004. *Francoscopie 2005: Pour comprendre les Français.* Paris: Larousse.

———. 2006. *Francoscopie 2007: Pour comprendre les Français.* Paris: Larousse.

Mernissi, Fatima. 1975. *Beyond the Veil.* Cambridge, Mass.: Schenkman Publishing Company.

Minces, Juliette. 1986. *La génération suivante: Les enfants de l'immigration.* Paris: Flammarion.

Moaddel, Mansoor, and Kamran Talattof. 2002. *Modernist and Fundamentalist Debates in Islam: A Reader.* New York: Palgrave MacMillan.

Moghadam, Valentine M. 1993. *Modernizing Women: Gender and Social Change in the Middle East.* Boulder: Lynne Reiner.

————. 1994. "Introduction: Women and Identity Politics in Theoretical and Comparative Perspective." In *Identity Politics and Women: Cultural Reassertions and Feminisms in International Perspective,* ed. Valentine M. Moghadam, 3–26. Boulder: Westview Press.

————. 2001. "Feminism and Islamic Fundamentalism: A Secularist Interpretation." *Journal of Women's History* 13, no. 1: 42–45.

————. 2002. "Women, the Taliban and the Politics of Public Space in Afghanistan." In *September 11, 2001: Feminist Perspectives,* ed. Susan Hawthorne and Bronwyn Winter, 260–84. Melbourne: Spinifex.

————. 2004. "Hijab and Islam." In *History in Dispute.* Vol. 14, *The Middle East Since World War Two: Part One,* ed. D. Lesch, 121–24. Detroit: St. James Press.

————. 2006. "What Is Muslim Feminism? Promoting a Cultural Change for Gender Equality." Opening address at "What Is Muslim Feminism?" Conference at UNESCO, Sept. 18–19.

Moghissi, Haideh. 1999. *Feminism and Islamic Fundamentalism: The Limits of Postmodern Analysis.* London: Zed Books

Montesquieu. 1748. *De l'Esprit des lois.* Reprint, Paris: Garnier, 1961.

Moses, Claire. 1996. "Made in America: 'French Feminism' in United States Academic Discourse." *Australian Feminist Studies* 11, no. 23: 17–31.

Mouvement Français pour le Planning Familial. "Le Voile: Symbole de religion, d'intégrisme ou de sexisme?" *Paris Féministe* 91–92 (Nov. 15): 27.

Mouvement pour les Luttes Féministes et al. 1981. *Chroniques d'une Imposture: Du mouvement de libération des femmes à une marque commerciale.* Paris: Mouvement pour les Luttes Féministes/ Voix-off.

M'rabet, Fadéla. 1979. *La femme algérienne.* Paris: François Maspero.

MRAP-Marseille. 2003. "La base du Mrap résiste." *ProChoix* 26–27 (Autumn): 119–20.

Mucchielli, Laurent. 2005. "Recherche sur les viols collectifs: Données judiciaires et analyse sociologique." *Questions pénales* 18, no. 1. Paris: CNRS.

Myard, Jacques, ed. 2003. *La Laïcité au cœur de la République.* Paris: L'Harmattan.

Najmabadi, Afsaneh. 2006. "Gender and Secularism of Modernity: How Can a Muslim Woman Be French?" *Féminist Studies* 32, no. 2: 239–55.

Nanas Beurs, Les. 1989. "Communiqué." *Paris Féministe* 91–92 (Nov. 15): 28.

Nashat, Guity. 1999. "Women in the Middle East: 8000 B.C.E.–C.E. 1800." In *Women in the Middle East and North Africa,* ed. Guity Nashat and Judith E. Tucker, 5–72. Bloomington: Indiana Univ. Press.

Nicolet, Claude. 1982. *L'Idée républicaine en France (1789–1924): Essai d'histoire critique.* Paris: Gallimard.

———. 1992. *La République en France: Etat des Lieux.* Paris: Le Seuil.

NPNS (Ni Putes Ni Soumises) et al. 2005. "Appel du 6 mars: Pour un nouveau féminisme." *Prochoix* 32: 17–18.

Okin, Susan Moller. 1979. *Women in Western Political Thought.* Princeton: Princeton Univ. Press.

Ouassak, Fatima. 2006. "La stigmatisation du garçon arabe: Ni putes, Ni soumises," Nov. 1. http://www.indigenes-republique.org/spip.php?article524 &var_recherche=fatima%20ouassak.

Ozouf, Mona. 1963. *L'Ecole, l'Eglise et la République 1871–1914.* Paris: Armand Colin.

———, ed. 1984. *L'Ecole de la France: Essais sur la révolution, l'utopie et l'enseignement.* Paris: Gallimard.

———. 1985. "Unité nationale et unité de la pensée de Jules Ferry. "In *Jules Ferry: Fondateur de la République,* ed. F. Furet, 59–72. Paris: Editions de l'EHESS.

Ozouf, Mona, and Jacques Ozouf. 1984. "Le Thème du patriotisme dans les manuels primaires." In *L'Ecole de la France: Essais sur la révolution, l'utopie et l'enseignement,* ed. M. Ozouf, 185–213. Paris: Gallimard.

Pateman, Carole. 1988. *The Sexual Contract.* Cambridge, UK: Polity Press.

Pena-Ruiz, Henri. 2003. *Qu'est-ce que la laïcité?* Paris: Gallimard.

———. 2004. "Contre la révision de la loi de 1905." *Regards sur l'actualité* 298: 56–66.

Perrineau, Pascal. 1996. "Les étapes d'une implantation électorale (1972–1988)." In *Le Front National à découvert,* ed. N. Mayer and Pascal Perrineau, 37–62. Paris: Presses de la Fondation Nationale des Sciences Politiques.

Petek-Salom, Gaye, and Marie-Josée Minassian. 1996. Introduction to *Cahiers d'études sur la Méditerranée orientale et le monde turco-iranien* 21 (Jan.–June): 4.

Pierrard, Pierre, ed. 2000. *Anthologie de l'humanisme laïque, de Jules Michelet à Léon Blum.* Paris: Albin Michel.

Pouillon, François. 1989. "Le tchador est toujours debout." *Libération,* Oct. 26.

Prochoix. 2003a. "Voile: L'école and la laïcité sont-elles en danger?" Issue 25, Summer.

———. 2003b. "Islamophobes? . . . ou simplement laïques?" Issue 26–27, Autumn.

Prost, Antoine. 1968. *L'enseignement en France 1800–1967.* Paris: Armand Colin.

Quid. 2006. "Religions: L'Eglise en France: Statistiques en France." http://www.quid.fr/2006/Religions/Statistiques_En_France/1.

Raffarin, Jean-Pierre. 2005. "Le pèlerin exigeant de la liberté." *La Croix,* Apr. 6.

Ragache, Jean-Robert. 1990. "La laïcité, c'est la liberté absolue des consciences." Interview with Liliane Sichler. *L'Evénement du Jeudi* 297 (suppl., July 12): 28.

Ramadan, Tariq. 1998. "Immigrations, intégration et politiques de coopération: L'Islam d'Europe sort de l'isolement." *Le Monde Diplomatique,* Apr.

———. 1999a. *Etre un musulman européen.* Lyons: Tawhid.

———. 1999b. "Islam minoritaire, islam majoritaire." Interview with Robert Ristolfi. *Confluences Méditerranée* 32: 53–72.

———. 2001. *Islam: Le face à face des civilisations. Quel projet pour quelle modernité?* Lyons: Tawhid.

———. 2003a. "Les Musulmans et la mondialisation." *Pouvoirs* 104: 97–109.

———. 2003b. *Les musulmans d'occident et l'avenir d'Islam.* Arles: Sindbad/Actes Sud.

———. 2003c. "Critique des (nouveaux) intellectuels communautaires." Oumma .com, Oct. 3. http://oumma.com/spip.php?article719.

———. 2004a. *Peut-on vivre avec l'Islam? Ce que je crois, port du voile, lapidation, etc.* Interview with Jacques Neirynck. Lausanne: Favre.

———. 2004b. "Naissance d'un féminisme musulman." Islam et Laïcité, Sept. 22. http://www.islamlaicite.org/article103.html.

Rebick, Judy. 2002. "Lip Service: The Anti-globalization Movement on Gender Politics." *Herizons* 16, no. 2: 24–26.

Rechniewski, Liz. 1995. "The Vendée Myth in Contemporary French Politics: The Case of Philippe de Villiers." In *Europe: Retrospects and Prospects,* ed. John Perkins and Jurgen Tampke, 185–94. Manly, NSW: Southern Highlands Publishers.

Reichstadt, Rudy. 2004. "Vincent Geisser et la nouvelle islamophobie." Observatoire du communautarisme. http://www.communautarisme.net/Vincent-Geisser-et-la-nouvelle-islamophobie_a211.html.

Rials, Stéphane. 1988. *La déclaration des droits de l'homme et du citoyen.* Paris: Hachette.

Richardson, Robin, ed. 2004. *Islamophobia: Issues, Challenges and Action.* Stoke on Trent, UK: Trentham Books.

RIFSA (Réseau International de Solidarité avec les Femmes Algériennes). 1996. *RISFA-Infos* 5: "Spécial Droit d'Asile."

Rioux, Jean-Pierre, and Jean-François Sirinelli, eds. 1991. *La guerre d'Algérie et les intellectuels français.* Brussels: Complexe.

Robine, Jérémy. 2006. "Les 'indigènes de la République': Nation et question postcoloniale." *Hérodote* 120, no. 1: 118–48.

Rochefort, Florence. 2002. "Foulard, genre et laïcité en 1989." *Vingtième Siècle: Revue d'Histoire* 75: 145–56.

Rousseau, Jean-Jacques. 1762. *Du contrat social.* Reprint, Paris: Flammarion, 1966.

Roy, Olivier. 1992. *L'Echec de l'Islam politique.* Paris: Le Seuil.

———. 2001. *Génealogie de l'islamisme.* Rev. ed. Paris: Hachette.

———. 2002. *Les illusions du 11 septembre: Le débat stratégique face au terrorisme.* Paris: Le Seuil.

———. 2004. *L'Islam mondialisé.* Rev. ed. Paris: Le Seuil.

———. 2005. *La laïcité face à l'Islam.* Paris: Hachette.

Rozario, Santi. 2006. "The New Burqa in Bangladesh: Empowerment or Violation of Women's Rights?" *Women's Studies International Forum* 29, no. 4: 368–80.

SAFIA, La. 1992. *Les Femmes immigrées ou issues de l'immigration: Spécificité et diversité des situations, discrimination aggravée.* Lille: self-published.

Sahgal, Gita, and Nira Yuval-Davis. 2000. *Refusing Holy Orders. Women and Fundamentalism in Britain.* London: Women Living Under Muslim Laws.

Saïd, Edward. 1978. *Orientalism: Western Conceptions of the Orient.* Reprint, London: Penguin Books, 1991.

Saladin, Flora. 2005a. "Voilées." Master's thesis, Université de Paris I.

———. 2005b. "Paroles de jeunes filles voilées." *Prochoix* 34: 21–58.

Sallenave, Danièle. 2004. *dieu.com.* Paris: Gallimard.

Schnapper, Dominique. 1991. *La France de l'intégration: Sociologie de la nation en 1990.* Paris: Gallimard.

Scott, Joan Wallach. 2005. "Symptomatic Politics: The Banning of Islamic Head Scarves in French Public Schools." *French Politics, Culture and Society* 23, no. 2: 106–27.

———. 2007. *The Politics of the Veil.* Princeton, N.J.: Princeton University Press.

Sebbar, Leïla. 1990. "Beures, beurettes." In *Si les immigrés m'étaient comptés,* ed. Claude Liauzu et al., 137–38. Paris: Syros/Alternatives.

———. 1996. *La jeune fille au balcon.* Paris: Le Seuil.

———. 1997. *Le baiser.* Paris: Hachette.

———. 2005. "Dieudonné se trompe de cible." *Libération,* Feb. 24.

Sebbar, Leïla, et al. 1990. "Table ronde: L'Islam et la France profonde sont-ils compatibles?" *Arabies* 37 (Jan.): 11–21.

Serreau, Coline. 2003. "Fast-paced Feminism: Coline Serreau Talks about 'Chaos.'" Interview with Erica Abeel. Indywire, Jan. 30. http://www.indiewire.com/people/people_030130serreau.html.

Sevaistre, Vianney. 2005. "Les relations entre le Conseil français du culte musulman (CFCM) et l'État: Quelle nature?" *French Politics, Culture and Society* 23, no. 1: 66–75.

Sfeir, Antoine, ed. 2002. *Dictionnaire mondial de l'islamisme*. Paris: Plon.

Sifaoui, Mohamed. 2002. *La France malade de l'Islamisme: Menaces terroristes sur l'Hexagone*. Paris: Le Cherche-midi.

Silverstein, Paul A. 2004. *Algeria in France: Transpolitics, Race and Nation*. Bloomington: Indiana Univ. Press.

Stanley, Trevor. 2005. "Understanding the Origins of Wahhabism and Salafism." *Jamestown Foundation Terrorism Monitor* 3, no. 14.

Stasi, Bernard. 1984. *L'immigration: Une chance pour la France*. Paris: Robert Laffont.

Stasi, Bernard, et al. 2003. *Commission de Réflexion sur l'Application du principe de laïcité dans la République: Rapport au Président de la République*. Paris: La Documentation Française. http://lesrapports.ladocumentationfrancaise.fr/BRP/034000725/0000.pdf.

Stora, Benjamin. 1989. "Pourquoi la machine à intégrer s'est soudain bloquée." *Politis* 77 (Oct. 26): 29.

———. 1992. *La gangrène et l'oubli*. Paris: La Découverte.

Surduts, Maya, and Suzy Rotjman. 2005. "Femmes, la lutte est complexe." *Libération*, Mar. 8.

Taarji, Hinde. 1990. *Les Voilées de l'Islam*. Paris: Balland.

———. 1998. *30 jours en Algérie: Journal d'une Marocaine*. Casablanca: Eddif.

Taguieff, Pierre-André.2002. *La nouvelle judéophobie*. Paris: Mille et Une Nuits/Fayard.

Tavan, Chloé. 2005. "Les immigrés en France: une situation qui évolue." *INSEE Première* 1042 (Sept.).

Tazi, Nadia. 2004. "La mise à jour du politique." In *Pourquoi j'ai signé le manifeste*, 5–8. Paris: Manifeste des Libertés.

Teese, Richard. 1986. "Private Schools in France: Evolution of a System." *Comparative Education Review* 30, no. 2: 247–59.

Terrel, Hervé. 2004. "L'État et la création du Conseil français du culte musulman (CFCM)." *Cités*, 67–92.

Tévanian, Pierre. 2005. *Le voile médiatique. Un faux débat: "l'affaire du foulard islamique."* Dijon: Raisons d'Agir.

Tévanian, Pierre, and Sylvie Tissot. 1998. *Mots à maux: Dictionnaire de la lepénisation des esprits*. Paris: Dagorno.

———. 2002. *Dictionnaire de la lepénisation des esprits.* Rev. ed. Paris: L'Esprit Frappeur.

Thion, Serge. 2004. *La trouille Latrèche.* VHO Web site. http://www.vho.org/aaargh/fran/livres4/latrouille.pdf.

Tillion, Germaine. 1966. *Le harem et les cousins.* Paris: Le Seuil.

Toprak, Binnaz. 1994. "Women and Fundamentalism: The Case of Turkey." In *Identity Politics and Women: Cultural Reassertions and Feminisms in International Perspective,* ed. Valentine M. Moghadam, 293–306. Boulder: Westview Press.

Tribalat, Michèle. 1995. *Faire France: Une enquête sur les immigrés et leurs enfants.* Paris: La Découverte.

———. 2003. "Un sentiment de trahison: La question du voile." *Le Figaro,* Sept. 24.

UEPT (Collectif une école pour tous-tes). 2004. "Voile: contre les lois d'exclusion." *Politis,* Jan. 29. http://www.politis.fr/article830.html.

UFAL (Union des Familles Laïques) et al. 2005. "Non aux violences: L'appel des femmes!" Nov. 12. http://www.ufal29.infini.fr/spip.php?article393&lang=fr.

UNHCR (United Nations High Commissioner for Refugees). 1995a. "Protection Guidelines on the Treatment of Algerian Asylum-seekers." Geneva: UNHCR.

———. 1995b. "Background Paper on the Situation in Algeria." Geneva: UNHCR.

Venel, Nancy. 1998. *Musulmanes françaises: Des pratiquantes voilées à l'université.* Paris: L'Harmattan.

Venner, Fiammetta. 1989. "Contribution au débat: Le voile islamique." *Paris Féministe* 91–92 (Nov. 15): 44–45.

———. 2005. *OPA sur l'Islam de France: Les ambitions de l'UOIF.* Paris: Calmann-Lévy.

Vianès, Michèle. 2004. *Un voile sur la République.* Paris: Stock.

Vidal-Naquet, Pierre. 1997. *Les assassins de la mémoire.* Paris: Le Seuil.

Vigerie, Anne, and Anne Zelensky. 2003. "'Laïcardes,' puisque féministes." *Le Monde,* May 29.

Wallet, Jean-William, Abdeljalil Nehas, and Mahjoub Sghiri. 1996. *Les perspectives des jeunes issus de l'immigration maghrébine.* Paris: L'Harmattan.

Weibel, Nadine B. 2006. "Femmes, islam et identité religieuse dans l'immigration turque en Alsace." *Cemoti* 41, May 4. http://cemoti.revues.org/document565.html.

Weil-Curiel, Linda, and Annie Sugier. 1989. "Contre le port du voile à l'école: Une raison peut en cacher une autre." *Paris Féministe* 91–92: 46.

White, Jenny B. 2002. *Islamist Mobilization in Turkey: A Study in Vernacular Politics*. Seattle: Univ. of Washington Press.

Wieviorka, Michel. 1992. *La France raciste*. Paris: Le Seuil.

Wihtol de Wenden, Catherine. 2005. "Seconde génération: Le cas français." In *Musulmans de France et d'Europe*, ed. Remy Leveau and Khadija Mohsen-Finan, 7–19. Paris: CNRS Editions.

Wing, Adrien Katherine, and Monica Nigh Smith. 2006. "Critical Race Feminism Lifts the Veil? Muslim Women, France, and the Headscarf Ban." *UC Davis Law Review* 39, no. 3: 743–89.

Winock, Michel. 1989. "La laïcité est un combat." *L'Evénement du Jeudi* 262, Nov. 9.

Winter, Bronwyn. 1994a. "Symboles, moteurs et alibis: les femmes d'origine maghrébine dans les discours français sur l'intégration." In *Revolution, Politics and Society: Elements in the Making of Modern France*, ed. David. W. Lovell, 100–105. Canberra: Univ. of New South Wales/ADFA.

———. 1994b. "Women, the Law and Cultural Relativism in France: The Case of Excision." *Signs: A Journal of Women in Culture and Society* 19, no. 4: 939–74.

———. 1995a. "Symboles, moteurs et alibis: Critique de l'identification culturelle et nationale des femmes d'origine maghrébine en France." Ph.D. diss., Univ. of Sydney.

———. 1995b. "Learning the Hard Way: The Debate on Women, Cultural Difference and Secular Schooling in France." In *Europe: Retrospects and Prospects*, ed. John Perkins and Jurgen Tampke, 203–13. Manly, NSW: Southern Highlands Publishers.

———. 1997. "(Mis)representations: What 'French Feminism' *Isn't*." *Women's Studies International Forum* 20, no. 2: 211–24.

———. 1998. "Adherence or Appropriation? Images of Maghrebian Women and the French Ideal of Nationhood." In *Shifting Bonds, Shifting Bounds: Women, Mobility and Citizenship in Europe*, ed. Virginia Ferreira, Teresa Tavares, and Sylvia Portugal, 149–65. Oeiras, Portugal: Celta Editora.

———. 2001a. "Fundamental Misunderstandings: Issues in Feminist Approaches to Islamism." *Journal of Women's History* 13, no. 1: 9–41.

———. 2001b. "Naming the Oppressor, Not Punishing the Oppresseed: Atheism and Feminist Legitimacy." *Journal of Women's History* 13, no. 1: 53–57.

———. 2002a. "Pauline and Other Perils: Women in Australian Right-Wing Politics." In *Right-Wing Women: From Conservatives to Extremists Around the Globe*, ed. Paola Bacchetta and Margaret Power, 197–210. New York: Routledge.

———. 2002b. "Who Will Mourn on October 7?" In *September 11, 2001: Feminist Perspectives,* ed. Susan Hawthorne and Bronwyn Winter, 360–71. Melbourne: Spinifex.

———. 2002c. "If Women Really Mattered . . . " In *September 11, 2001: Feminist Perspectives,* ed. Susan Hawthorne and Bronwyn Winter, 450–80. Melbourne: Spinifex.

———. 2006a. "The Social Foundations of the Sacred: Feminists and the Politics of Religion." In *Handbook of Gender and Women's Studies,* ed. Kathy Davis, Mary Evans, and Judith Lorber, 92–108. London: Sage Publications.

———. 2006b. "Religion, Culture and Women's Human Rights: Some General Political and Theoretical Considerations." *Women's Studies International Forum* 29, no. 4: 381–93.

———. 2006c. "Secularism Aboard the Titanic: Feminists and the Debate over the Hijab in France." *Feminist Studies* 32, no. 2: 279–98.

———. 2006d. "The Great Hijab Coverup." *Off Our Backs* 36, no. 3: 38–40.

———. 2007. "Pre-Emptive Fridge Magnets and Other Weapons of Masculinist Destruction: The Rhetoric and Reality of 'Safeguarding Australia.'" *Signs: Journal of Women in Culture and Society* 33, no. 1: 25–53.

———. Forthcoming 2008. "Marianne Goes Multicultural: *Ni putes ni soumises* and the Republicanisation of Ethnic Minority Women in France." *Papers from the George Rudé Conference.*

———. Forthcoming 2009. "La 'peste occidentale': Identitarisme, antiféminisme et lesbophobie." *Sexualité, Genre et Sociétés* 1.

Wittig, Monique. 2001. "On ne naît pas femme." In *La Pensée Straight,* 51–64. Paris: Balland.

WLUML/FSLM (Women Living Under Muslim Laws/Femmes sous lois musulmanes). 1995. *Dossier d'information sur la situation en Algérie: Résistance des femmes et solidarité internationale.* No. 1. Grabels: FSLM/WLUML.

———. 1996. *Dossier d'information sur la situation en Algérie: Résistance des femmes et solidarité internationale.* No. 2. Grabels: FSLM/WLUML.

———. 2005a. "Maroc: Moudawana, an I." http://www.wluml.org/french/newsfulltxt.shtml?cmd%5B157%5D=x-157-120975.

———. 2005b. "WLUML Statement to the World Social Forum: Appeal Against Fundamentalisms." Jan. 21. http://www.wluml.org/english/newsfulltxt.shtml?cmd%5B157%5D=x-157-103376.

WLUML/FSLM (Women Living Under Muslim Laws/Femmes sous lois musulmanes) et al. 1989. "Communiqué." *Paris Féministe* 91–92 (Nov. 15): 51–52.

Woolf, Virginia. 1938. *Three Guineas.* Reprint, Harmondsworth, Middlesex: Penguin, 1977.

Yeux Ouverts, Les. 1984. *Bulletin spécial: L'immigration.* Paris: self-published.

Young, Iris Marion. 2003. "The Logic of Masculinist Protection: Reflections on the Current Security State." *Signs* 29, no. 1: 1–26.

Yuval-Davis, Nira. 1994. "Identity Politics and Women's Ethnicity." In *Identity Politics and Women: Cultural Reassertions and Feminisms in International Perspective,* ed. Valentine M. Moghadam, 408–24. Boulder: Westview Press.

———. 1997. *Gender and Nation.* London: Sage.

Yuval-Davis, Nira, and Floya Anthias. 1989. *Woman-Nation-State.* Basingstoke, UK: Palgrave MacMillan.

Zayzafoon, Lamia Ben Youssef. 2005. *The Production of the Muslim Woman: Negotiating Text, History and Ideology.* Lanham, Md.: Lexington Books.

Zéghidour, Slimane. 1990. *Le voile et la bannière.* Paris: Hachette.

Zemmour, Zine-Eddine. 2002. "Jeune Fille, famille et virginite." *Confluences Méditerranée* 41: 65–76.

Zouari, Fawzia. 2002. *Le voile islamique.* Paris: Favre.

———. 2004. *Ce voile qui déchire la France.* Paris: Ramsay.

Index